UNANIMOUS PRAISE FOR *THE BANKERS*

"Intimate knowledge of how banking works in the electronic age. Exhaustive . . . informative . . . and some very good advice."   —*L.A. Weekly*

"Mayer knows almost everything there is to know about the business of banking."   —*Washington Post*

"Mayer has cast his trained eye into all the darkest corners— electronic banking, trading, derivatives, and mergers—and has produced a clear and insightful explanation of all that has happened."   —Roy C. Smith, author of *The Global Bankers*

"Intriguing. Will have the reader engaged."   —*Business Week*

"The best book on the mystery we call money. It makes the reader feel like an insider. Terrific."   —*Seattle Weekly*

"Businessmen both small and large—not to mention anyone with an ATM card—will be interested in Mayer's predictions for the future of banks and banking."   —*Industry Week*

"Cogent . . . useful . . . carefully researched. Recommended."
                                    —*Library Journal*

"Astute . . . provocative . . . engrossing and perceptive. An informed guide."   —*Kirkus Reviews*

MARTIN MAYER has been for years the most widely recognized name in financial journalism. The author of major books on advertising, education, and the law, as well as finance, he is a frequent speaker at bankers' conventions in the United States, Europe, and recently, Brazil. A contributor to virtually every business periodical at one time or another, Martin Mayer was also for three years a front-page columnist for *American Banker*. He lives in Washington, D.C.

Also by Martin Mayer

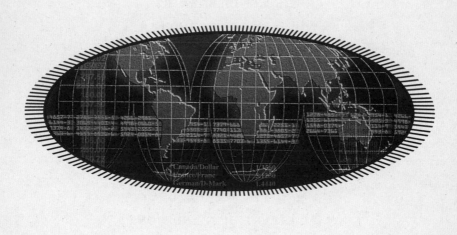

THE
BANKERS

THE NEXT GENERATION

Martin Mayer

TRUMAN TALLEY BOOKS/PLUME
NEW YORK

TRUMAN TALLEY BOOKS/PLUME
Published by the Penguin Group
Penguin Putnam Inc., 375 Hudson Street,
New York, New York 10014, U.S.A.
Penguin Books Ltd, 27 Wrights Lane,
London W8 5TZ, England
Penguin Books Australia Ltd, Ringwood,
Victoria, Australia
Penguin Books Canada Ltd, 10 Alcorn Avenue,
Toronto, Ontario, Canada M4V 3B2
Penguin Books (N.Z.) Ltd, 182–190 Wairau Road,
Auckland 10, New Zealand

Penguin Books Ltd, Registered Offices:
Harmondsworth, Middlesex, England

Published by Truman Talley Books/Plume,
an imprint of Dutton NAL,
a member of Penguin Putnam Inc.
Previously published in a Truman Talley Books/Dutton edition.

First Truman Talley Books/Plume Printing, May, 1998
10 9 8 7 6 5 4 3 2 1

The Library of Congress has catalogued the Truman Talley Books/Dutton edition as follows:
LIBRARY OF CONGRESS CATALOGING-IN-PUBLICATION DATA:
Mayer, Martin.
       The bankers : the next generation / Martin Mayer.
          p.   cm.
       Includes bibliographical references and index.
       ISBN 0-525-93865-6 (hc.)
       ISBN 0-452-27264-5 (pbk.)
       1. Banks and banking—United States.   2. Financial services
industry—United States.   I. Title.
       HG2491.M342   1997   96-34801
       332.1'0973—DC20   CIP

Printed in the United States of America

BOOKS ARE AVAILABLE AT QUANTITY DISCOUNTS WHEN USED TO PROMOTE PRODUCTS OR SERVICES. FOR INFORMATION PLEASE WRITE TO PREMIUM MARKETING DIVISION, PENGUIN PUTNAM INC., 375 HUDSON STREET, NEW YORK, NEW YORK 10014.

For six from whom
I learned
about banking

John Heimann
Charles Kindleberger
Hyman Minsky
George Moore
Scott Pardee
Tom Waage

Contents

CONTENTS

Introduction to the 1998 Plume Edition

For this Plume paperback edition, appearing eighteen months after original publication, the author has updated some substantive material, corrected errors, and added a new five thousand–word second epilogue (see page 467) to discuss two things: the few but important surprises of the year that was and the acceleration of the trends noted in the first epilogue.

Introduction

In the historic world of commerce, the bank was the city on the hill. In a Calvinist America where many things were seen to have been pre-ordained, bankers enjoyed unrivaled autonomy. Their decisions greatly influenced the lives of others. Every businessman needs money; the bank has money; the banker allocates that money to this claimant rather than that. "We decide who will live and who will die," said John Bunting, CEO of Philadelphia's First Pennsylvania, one of very few Ph.D. economists ever to run a big bank. (Not very well, by the way: he bet wrong on the direction of interest rates.) For Lenin, banks occupied what he called the "commanding heights" of the economy; the seizure of the banks was thus the key to socialist dominance. Few reformers have failed to include banks in their lists of things to be reformed.

Bankers through most of American history were very important men. They chaired the civic organizations, hospitals, community concerts, school boards, public libraries. Their opinions on the economy, often solicited but rarely offered, were taken seriously by politicians and press alike. Few were specially trained for their function; as an old-timer observed, you need a license to be a barber, but anybody can be a banker. As a group, they were drawn from a narrow cohort of the society—all male and all white, of course, and overwhelmingly Protestant and of northern European ancestry. And they were snobs. "The banker," rhymed the Catholic populist G. K. Chesterton,

> Is an expert on economy and strikes.
> He uses all your money to do anything he likes.
> And the usurer who uses it you're called upon to thank!
> I do not mind the swindle, but I do not like the swank.

What makes banking different is that the banker lends other people's money—historically and traditionally, money those other people left with the banker for convenience or safekeeping, not as an investment. The banker borrows the money on a basis which permits the depositor to call some or all of it back from him at any time. The usual IOU from the bank as borrower is evidence of a deposit which the lender can withdraw at any time by writing a check. Because it can be withdrawn "on demand," the bank deposit is unlike any other borrowing. It doesn't on either side *feel* like a borrowing, because the depositor never loses the use of his money, and the bank, honoring his check, doesn't feel that it is repaying a loan. The banker also does not think he is lending the depositor's money when his bank makes a loan by creating a new deposit for another customer. And in truth, that loan and the deposit it creates add to the total amount of money in the banking system, because this new deposit, too, can and will be drawn "on demand."

This traditional banking activity is highly charged with a public interest. In reality, as we shall see, the bank lends *the gov-*

ernment's money, because governments are the source of money. In the process of lending, the bank creates new money, which in normal times the government one way or another must recognize. This combination of broad-spectrum decision-making and quasi-governmental monetary function is what makes banks "special," to use the term E. Gerald Corrigan fought for when he was president of the Federal Reserve Bank of Minneapolis. He was the protégé and fishing companion of Paul Volcker, who was then chairman of the Federal Reserve Board. Volcker asked Corrigan to prepare a document to tell the public and the Congress why nonfinancial corporations should not be permitted to own banks and vice versa, and Corrigan wrote a pamphlet (presented as the president's annual report from the Minneapolis Fed) to prove that banks were "special." He was right, too.[1]

And in the end, bankers were expected to be public-spirited, to rise to the challenge of a crisis. The 1907 panic hit Wall Street when J. P. Morgan was in Richmond, Virginia, at an Episcopal convention (with, be it noted, one of his mistresses). He left early, saying to Bishop William Lawrence, "They are in trouble in New York. They do not know what to do, and I don't know what to do, but I am going back."[2] John McGillicuddy, recently retired as CEO of Manufacturers Hanover and then Chemical Bank, remembered the midnight meeting at Boca Raton to which Paul Volcker had summoned all the big bankers in attendance at the Reserve City Bankers annual meeting. Volcker had assembled the bankers in order to control the terrifying consequences of the Hunt brothers' failed effort to corner the silver market, which had left massive bank loans secured by clearly inadequate values of silver. "There was a real danger that the walls could come tumbling down," said McGillicuddy. "I was sitting next to Tom Clausen [CEO of Bank of America]. He said, 'We don't do that much business with the Hunts. Do you?' I said, 'Not that much.' He said, 'Then why are we here?' I said, 'Because we are perceived as having deep pockets.' "

INTRODUCTION

Bankers may have been even more important in the United States than they were elsewhere, because Americans have had a peculiar habit of using their households as financial intermediaries. Elsewhere, perhaps as an inheritance from a peasant culture America never knew, ordinary people hate the idea of being in debt. But Americans carry larger mortgages than necessary, even borrow on "home equity" loans, rather than run down their savings. Even in 1992, when credit cards were charging 19 percent and the interest rate on bank certificates of deposit was 3 percent, people kept their savings in the bank and carried a balance in their credit card account. "Do you want a sure eighteen percent on your money?" a friend of mine asked his wife, who had been complaining about how little she got on her CDs. When she assented, he said, "Pay off your credit card." But although she had the money in her savings account, she didn't.

In the cities, the executives of the banks literally looked down on their neighbors, for the bank buildings were almost invariably the tallest structures in town. In towns where there were no tall buildings, the lending officer of the bank—and in small banks, that usually meant the man who owned the place—worked on a raised platform out in common view. It was not considered good manners in the United States until quite recently to conduct banking business behind closed doors. At investment banks like Brown Brothers Harriman and Morgan Stanley, into the last quarter of the twentieth century, the partners sat in a single room, at rows of desks, illustrating that no partner had secrets from any other partner. When Bank of America built its dominating bronze monolith, fifty-three stories high from a site about a third of the way up Nob Hill, its fortieth-floor mahogany-paneled executive floor was originally planned to have bays at the windows where the top executives would sit in the open, separated from their secretaries by an expanse of carpet—but no walls. Only the conference rooms within the windowless core would be private. When the corners were walled off for the tip-top of the bank, there remained a tradition that the doors were open—until the 1970s and the leadership of chairman Tom Clausen, who didn't like to see people (a view that was reciprocated by the people), and put up a Chinese screen that guarded his office from view even when the door was open.

Bankers worked "bankers' hours"—ten in the morning to three in the afternoon. This was technologically determined in the days before computers and machine-readable checks, because the accounts of a bank must be cast every day, and it took considerable time after the teller windows were closed for the tellers to make sure they had the cash and checks and deposit slips in the till to match the paper generated by their day's work, and for the (mostly) men on high stools in green eyeshades to accumulate all the documents, debit from depositors' accounts the "on us" checks that had come in that day, and prepare the "cash letters" to other banks that would produce credits to the accounts of the depositors who had deposited checks drawn on other banks. If depositors couldn't enter the bank to do business outside bankers' hours, the doors could not be kept open for borrowers, either. "Bankers have great leisure," Walter Bagehot wrote. "If they are busy something is wrong."[3] Some bankers went out onto the golf course; more of them went calling on their customers; most got their correspondence and telephoning done. But the image of bankers' hours infected the public view.

As a man who did business with other people's money, the banker had to be intensely respectable. "Bankers as a breed are different from other men," said Gerald T. Dunne, then general counsel of the Federal Reserve Bank of St. Louis, later author of a great biography of Supreme Court justice Hugo Black. "The function of bankers is to be trusted, not to be liked." "Adventure is the life of commerce," wrote Walter Bagehot, first editor of *The Economist*, "but caution, I had almost said timidity, is the life of banking."[4] Solomon Smith of Northern Trust in Chicago carried an umbrella every workday, rain or shine. "The old ladies from

Lake Forest saw Sol Smith going to the commuter train station carrying an umbrella on a sunny day," George Moore remembered, "and they'd say, '*That's* a good safe bank.' "[5]

Bankers knew secrets, and kept them. ("The reason you went on a small-town bank board," says James Watt, once a small-town banker, later president of the Conference of State Bank Supervisors, "was that it gave you the chance to see the financial statements of everybody in town. You couldn't talk about it, but you knew.") Banking was a confidence game. When people lost confidence in a bank and came to its doors to demand their deposits, there was a "run on the bank," an infectious fevered crisis that could be overcome only by floods of cash. And it was in the nature of a bank that it could not sell assets quickly to pay back a crowd of depositors who wanted to withdraw their money; the assets were loans, there was no "market" where a bank could sell its loans, and very few borrowers can pay back what they owe immediately even if the bank has the right (which normally it doesn't) to call the loan. Banks thus incurred what academics called "term-structure risk"—they could lend only what they had borrowed, and their borrowings were for shorter periods than their loans.

Less analytical observers warned banks against "borrowing short and lending long," but there was no escape. Franklin R. Edwards of Columbia University and Frederic S. Mishnik of the Federal Reserve Bank of New York proclaim that "the traditional banking business has been to make long-term loans and fund them by issuing short-dated deposits."[6] Carried to extremes, when the savings-and-loan association funded thirty-year mortgages with deposits that could be withdrawn without notice, borrowing short and lending long was obviously an invitation to disaster. But in normal times, commercial banks—which primarily made short-term working capital loans for farmers to buy their seed or builders to patronize the lumberyard or storekeepers to stock their shelves—could count on the fact that while individual deposits might disappear at any moment, the total "on current account" in the banking system would stay pretty much the same. Unless there was a run on the banks.

The obvious way to prevent runs on the stand-alone bank was to give a government guarantee to people that the money they left with the banker would be there for them when they needed it. "Deposit insurance" began in the 1840s in New York State, but states can't print money and thus cannot give open-ended promises. The guarantee of bank deposits was not plausible in time of crisis until 1933, when Congress over Franklin Roosevelt's strong objections offered banks a federal insurance policy (compulsory for federally chartered banks and members of the Federal Reserve System) that guaranteed the repayment of every depositor's first $2,500.

Banks paid a premium for this insurance policy as for any other insurance policy, and the insurance fund (launched with money from the government's Reconstruction Finance Corporation, the earliest—Hoover era—program to boost the country out of the Depression) was supposed to be big enough to make any necessary repayments. But just in case, the newly formed Federal Deposit Insurance Corporation was given the right to borrow from the Treasury to make up any shortfall in the fund. To get the insurance guarantee, banks had to give up their right to compete with each other by offering higher interest rates for deposits: the payment of interest on transaction accounts ("demand deposits") was prohibited, and the Federal Reserve was given authority to set ceilings on what banks could pay for "time deposits" (commercial banks, as distinguished from savings banks and savings and loan associations, were not permitted to offer "savings accounts" until World War II).

Preserving banks was an important public policy. A bank was among the greatest assets any community could have: as late as the 1970s, a traveler through small-town America could tell whether or not the local bank cared about its community by noting how recently the houses and barns and storefronts had been painted. (Now dilapidation in small cities and towns is more likely to be evidence that the franchisers have devastated the luncheonettes and Sam Walton's Walmart or his imitators have damaged the retail economy beyond the capacity of the banks to mitigate.) Former bank examiner Marshall Surratt described Muenster, a town near the Red River in Texas, as it was in the early 1990s:

> Muenster had a little oil production, but not much. Milk production has traditionally been more important. . . . The new community hospital has three doctors and two dentists. . . . The Muenster State Bank serves the community. It is sound and profitable. . . . The customers are well known. . . . The community has attractive homes both in town and on the farms. When insurance companies and S&Ls would not finance new homes in the community, the Muenster bank did so. . . . The Catholic church and the Baptist church have attractive structures. The parochial school and the public school give superior instruction. The community enjoys active year-round civic projects. The annual Germanfest attracts more than 50,000 people to this town of 1,500 people. Bank president Earl Fisher has been with the bank for more than 50 years. . . . The Muenster bank has grown and prospered as it has helped the community to grow and prosper.[7]

Banks were expected to serve the needs of their communities before they looked elsewhere for business. The money the bank lent was the community's money, and local people resented its export to the big cities, to be lent for the benefit of others far away. Thus the prejudice for the *local* bank, expressed in legislation from the 1860s to the 1980s. Deposit insurance itself was and is a bulwark of the community bank, for without it locals might feel their money was safer at the brand-name institution in the big city.

Nearly half the states, including states as big as Illinois, had "unit banking" rules, which required a bank to do all its business from one location. In 1923, the Federal Reserve Board ruled that it would not in the future admit to membership any bank with branches outside "the corporate limits of [its own] city or town, or contiguous territory."[8] And when the tide turned, and it became clear that fifteen thousand scattered banks did not make an efficient system for servicing a national economy in an international money market, Congress still tried to keep the depositors' money at home through the device of a Community Reinvestment Act that denied powers of merger or acquisition to banks that were not sufficiently responsive to the loan needs of their own hometown.

In truth, all this made more sense than modern commentary would lead students to believe. In a big country with pre-modern communication and transportation systems, different regions— different towns within a region—would have different economic conditions and quite reasonably could have different interest rates. Until after World War II, with the sometimes reluctant approval of the Board of Governors in Washington, the twelve district Federal Reserve banks sometimes had different discount rates for their own loans to their member banks. Bankers making decisions for their banks quite correctly looked first to their community of depositors and borrowers rather than to national statistics, which were even worse then than they are now.

"A professional loan officer knows that he is a partner of the borrower," wrote Hyman Minsky of the Levy Institute, one of the few economists to have actively participated in the direction of a bank (Mark Twain in the St. Louis suburbs). "A loan officer is a success if his customers are successful."[9] Claire Giannini Hoffman, daughter of the founder of Bank of America, old and angry in 1986, sitting on a plush settee in her father's comfortable overstuffed Edwardian house in downtown San Mateo, where she still lived surrounded by his furniture, remembered a day fifty years earlier, when "my father and my uncle and my brother and I were in a room in the Hotel Biltmore in Los Angeles, and Walt

Disney brought these drawings [for *Snow White*, the first feature-length cartoon]. My brother said, 'We need time to think about it.' My uncle said, 'There's nothing here, forget it.' My father said, 'Mr. Disney, you have your money.' "

Bagehot in 1873 argued that "A banker who lives in the district, who has always lived there, whose whole mind is a history of the district and its changes, is easily able to lend money safely there. But a manager deputed by a single central establishment does so with difficulty. The worst people will come to him and ask for loans. His ignorance is a mark for all the shrewd and crafty people thereabouts."[10] Or as chairman Charles Rice of Florida's Barnett Banks puts it, "The Harvard Business School never graduated an MBA that can't be hornswoggled by the businessmen of the Florida panhandle." The local bank grew as the town's enterprise grew. Measuring the success of banks by their size became fuddy-duddy analysis in the 1970s, except for the purpose of demonstrating that the government was demonstrably too hard on American banks because they were losing the size competition to Japanese banks. But it was a reasonable attitude in an age when the size of banks was a direct function of the size of the business communities they served.

Until well into the 1970s, moreover, the total profits of a bank were a function of its size, or "footings," to use the old-fashioned word for a bank's total liabilities. Smaller banks tended to show better earnings per dollar of assets or equity than larger banks, but within the size categories there usually wasn't much to choose: profits rained just about equally on the wise and the unwise. In 1970, reports Lowell Bryan of the consulting firm McKinsey & Co., "among the twenty largest banks in the country, the best had a return on equity of 13.9 percent and the worst had a return on equity of 10.2 percent."[11] That, too, was in large part a consequence of deposit insurance and government limits on the interest rates a bank could pay to lure money. If all banks as manufacturers and sellers of credit got their raw material at roughly the same price, it wasn't surprising that they would in the end have roughly similar earnings with relation to their size.

Bank stock traditionally was not priced on a stock market and traded among strangers: it was closely held among a group of local people who were responsible for their bank. As late as 1960, fewer than half a dozen bank stocks were listed on any exchange. Shares in banks were different from shares in any other enterprise. Until the 1930s, bank shares typically were only half "paid-in." Stockholders were "on call" for 50 percent of the par value of their shares if the bank got in trouble and money had to be found to pay back its depositors. The transfer agent who issued new shares in a bank had to satisfy himself that the purchaser could and would meet a call if the day should come. The fact that shares in banks were closely held and not sold in the public market concealed the extent to which they were significant in investors' portfolios. In Brazil in 1889, bank stocks accounted for almost two-thirds of the capitalization of the Rio Stock Exchange,[12] and in Japan, bank stocks made up three-fifths of the capitalization of the Tokyo Stock Exchange as late as 1991. But in the United States, because so many of them were not traded, banks never accounted for as much as a fifth of the market values of listed securities.

This American plan to provide supersecurity for banks by leaving its stockholders on call still survives in one corner of the business. The twelve district Federal Reserve banks, the operating arm of the government in the execution of monetary policy, are controlled in all important respects from Washington by the Board of Governors of the Federal Reserve System, but they are "owned" by their "member banks," which buy shares in them, at a cash price of one-half the stated par value of the share, as part of their accession to membership. These shares cannot be traded, and must be cashed in at cost if a bank goes out of business or abandons its Fed membership. The district Feds taken together are the most profitable enterprise in the country because they print the nation's money, earning $15 billion to $20 billion a year because the cost of each bill is about one and a half cents and its value may be $100. More than 95 percent of these profits are returned to the Treasury (for it is the Treasury's money, after all, that the Feds print). But each share in a Federal Reserve district bank still carries to this day a commitment by the bank that owns it to put up the other 50 percent of par value if this branch of the Fed should by any chance need the money.

Except for a brief period in the 1830s and 1840s, getting into the banking business was difficult in the United States: anybody could open a store or build a factory, but to open a bank that took deposits from the public, a man needed a state or (after 1864) federal charter. (Philadelphia's Stephen Drexel did without a charter in the 1810s and 1820s, but he had very good friends in Washington.) Winning a charter usually involved buying a piece of the bonded debt of the state where the bank would be operating, or (after 1864) a quantity of U.S. Treasury bonds. Presumably the presence of salable government bonds in the portfolios of the banks served as a guarantee to depositors that the safekeeping function of the banks was alive and well, that their deposits would be refunded to them if anything happened to the bank. It was also of course very convenient for the governments to have a captive market for their paper. Lincoln was greatly helped in paying for the Civil War by the National Bank Act that chartered new banks to people who bought and held U.S. government bonds. Conceptually, there isn't much difference between issuing paper money and authorizing banks to issue their own notes backed by government bonds.

Until the 1960s, when a tide of liberalization began to rise around the financial services industry (felt in practice but not yet perceived, for these were the Kennedy-Johnson years), new charters would be issued by either a state or federal government only on a convincing showing (usually opposed by the existing banks) that this community needed another bank. Constance R. Dunham of the Federal Reserve Bank of Boston argues that when the Reagan administration brought market-knows-best philosophy to government regulation "national bank chartering policy [was] liberalized, so that new bank applications need not demonstrate a need for banking services or the impact on local banks in the community."[13] Before then, the advantages of competition were considered trivial next to the danger that banks would fail if there were more of them than the local market could support.

The damage done to a community by a bank failure is hard to exaggerate, not only because it demolishes the aura of confidence for all banks but also because a failed bank's loans—even its good loans—are virtually impossible to place in another institution. They have a stench of death about them. The local storekeeper can't get the money to stock his shelves. The local manufacturer can't upgrade his machinery. The local builder, having drawn the first two tranches of his construction loan from the bank that has now failed, finds himself with steel beams in place and heavy debts—and no way to raise the additional funding he needs to put the walls around the beams. Sometimes the final tranches of such a construction loan from a busted bank cannot be replaced even if the builder has pre-leased the property. When Franklin National on Long Island failed in 1974, a builder on the Long Island Expressway corridor called me to tell me just such a horror story; driving out the expressway, I saw *for almost ten years*, ultimately surrounded by half a dozen similar completed office buildings by other builders, the steel skeleton of the building no bank would help him complete.

Partly because the disruptions to the community are so great, getting *out* of banking was and remains even more difficult than getting in. There was—and is—no procedure for "bankruptcy" in banking, no court that can freeze the demands of creditors and authorize a management as "debtor in possession" to keep the enterprise going. Prior to 1934, when federal deposit insurance came into effect, state banking supervisors or the federal Comptroller of the Currency declared banks insolvent and closed the institutions. People whose transaction balances or savings were in these institutions suddenly found they didn't have their money anymore. Later, maybe much later, the liquidators would pay depositors as much as could be wrenched from the sale of the failed bank's assets. Then as now, this was hard and strange work. Cyril B. Upham and Edwin Lamke noted in 1934 in their Brookings Institution study of *Closed and Distressed Banks* the experience of the Guaranty Fund Commission of Nebraska, which wound up the proprietor of "a blacksmith shop, a dance hall, an opera house, a garage, a farm, a barber shop, a dental office, pool rooms and cafes."[14]

Liquidators in those days also tried to get some more money for depositors from the directors and the shareholders in the bank, who continued to be liable, up to another 50 percent of the face value of their stock, for the losses suffered by bank depositors and other creditors of banks. Even now, when capital on call is only a memory, bank directors have greater liability than directors in other kinds of companies for losses that occur on their watch. According to a pamphlet published by the Office of the Comptroller of the Currency, which charters and supervises national banks, directors "may become personally liable for losses sustained by the bank due to . . . a failure to exercise the requisite degree of care and prudence."[15]

This sort of failure still happens, too: people who had deposits in Ohio state-chartered and state-insured S&Ls in 1987, or Rhode Island state-chartered and state-insured credit unions in 1991, found themselves broke and dependent on the charity of the state when those S&Ls and credit unions had to be shut down because they didn't have the cash to meet their depositors' withdrawal demands. Some of these institutions were crooked and busted, but many more were honest and solvent, yet for a while all of them were shut down because the advertised failure of a few created a run on the bank for all, and there was no "lender of last resort" to provide the necessary floods of cash. I sat in a U.S. Senate hearing room, waiting to testify to the Senate Banking Committee about other matters, while Rhode Island senators Claiborne Pell, a Democrat, and John Chafee, a Republican, and Governor Bruce Sundlen emotionally begged the Senate to appropriate emergency loan money for their state so citizens of the state could pay their bills. And like their federal counterparts, the state authorities involved in these partial rescue operations did collect a little money from the officers and directors of the mismanaged institutions to defray a fraction of the losses.

Since 1934, failed banks with federally insured deposits—which means virtually all banks (only the state-chartered savings associations and credit unions went out in the rain without this federal umbrella)—have been turned over to the Federal Deposit Insurance Corporation. While generally under instructions to find the "least-cost resolution" of a bank failure (especially since 1991, when the Federal Deposit Insurance Corporation Improvement Act rebuked the agency for wasteful behavior in the 1980s), the FDIC can consider the impact on the community when deciding how much money the deposit insurance fund should spend to keep a bank open rather than liquidate it. The costs of paying somebody to take over such a bank almost always seem lower to the FDIC than the benefits to be gained by keeping it in business.

The pervasive and continuing attitude among government bank regulators that banks had to be saved at virtually any cost had its origins in the Great Depression, when Franklin Roosevelt announced a "bank holiday" in his inaugural address and five days later asked Congress for a "Bank Conservation Act" that would help the Comptroller reopen the banks. Congress passed the bill the day the President sent his request, *before its text was made available to the congressmen who voted to pass it.* "In the short space of five days," the President wrote, "it is impossible for us to formulate completed measures to prevent the recurrence of the evils of the past. This does not and should not, however, justify any delay in accomplishing this first step."[16]

But between 1934 and the 1980s, bank failures were

infrequent and most of them were of very small banks, destroyed by crop failures or self-dealing by the officers of the bank. (U.S. National of San Diego, for example, the largest bank failure in American history prior to 1974, went under because so many enterprises owned by C. Arnholt Smith, who also owned the bank, had defaulted on their loans. Only six years earlier, Smith had been among the relatively few friends who sat with Richard Nixon and watched the election returns that would make Nixon president of the United States.) Most banks were a lot stodgier than that. They didn't make risky loans, and the "spread" between their cost of funds and the interest rates they could charge their borrowers was relatively stable at three to four percentage points, leaving a satisfactory profit margin for the bank after the deduction of "G&A" (general and administrative) expenses and loan losses. That was, after all, the purpose of restricting entry by making charters hard to get, and limiting the interest rates banks could pay their depositors: the government wanted the banks to be stable and profitable. There was a scare in the early 1950s, when rising interest rates for Treasury bills and notes pushed down the prices of the government bonds that were the largest single portion of the average bank's portfolio in the years right after World War II. But on balance banking was a steady, routine business from the Roosevelt rescue in the Depression to the gold crisis of 1968.

Talking with me about my book *The Bankers* in 1975, most bankers said the story they had most enjoyed in it was one told originally by Kay A. Randall of United Virginia Bankshares in 1973. This story was of a man honored for fifty years of service to a Virginia bank, who was asked at the party the bank gave to celebrate him what he thought had been "the most important thing, the most important change that you have seen in banking in this half-century of service. The man paused for a few minutes, finally got up before the microphone, and said, 'Air conditioning.' "[17]

Twenty years later, this story is prehistoric. It's still funny, but it's incomprehensible. In these twenty years, banking has changed beyond recognition. Interest-rate controls are gone, and banks can exploit any and all of a variety of techniques to lure the money they need to fund their loans. Banks are no longer passive instruments allocating among borrowers the money depositors have left with them: even medium-sized banks now have the equivalent of "asset-liability committees," which decide how much money and on what terms the bank should be borrowing to buy or hold the assets it wishes to own. Both large and small loans are sold to others, in a very private market of banks and insurance companies for the big stuff, or as securities backed by the borrowers' payments on lots of loans for the little stuff.

Though the maximum covered by insurance was lifted to $100,000 in 1980, insured customer deposits, the essential link between the bank and its community, now fund only 17 percent of the assets in the American banking system. Thus the great bulk of the money a bank now has to lend is not the transaction balances of its customers but investment funds, which the individual or corporate customer has placed with the bank as his "intermediary," a role he could just as easily assign to his broker or mutual fund or insurance company. The cant line of the late 1970s and early 1980s was that the banks were being "disintermediated"— that people who wanted to make money on their money were abandoning their bank accounts (certainly their savings accounts) to put their money where the grass was not only greener but grew faster.

Meanwhile, on the other side of the intermediation front, companies that had previously borrowed from banks were shifting to other sources of loans. As late as the 1970s, a group of disgruntled borrowers sued Citizens & Southern, then the largest bank in the South, because, they complained, favored borrowers were being charged less than the bank's "prime rate," its posted rate for the best commercial customers. These businessmen argued that they had no source of inexpensive credit they could tap if the banks overcharged them. If their larger competitors could borrow cheaper from the bank than the advertised minimum rate, they would be at a disadvantage in their business. Today the "prime rate" is merely a floor on which banks build a congeries of adjustable rates for various businesses and consumers—and even for that purpose, the bank-established "prime rate" has been outmoded by market rates, the Fed Funds rate (the rate banks charge each other in the United States for overnight money the borrowers need to meet the reserve requirements of their local Federal Reserve bank); the London Interbank Offered Rate (Libor, the rate at which banks offer to borrow dollars overnight from other banks overseas, where an immense "Eurodollar" market flourishes); or the Constant Mean Treasury Rate for five years (the rate the market assesses on average for U.S. government notes and bonds that have exactly five years to run before expiration).

In late 1994, winding down his term as chairman and CEO of J.P. Morgan, Dennis Weatherstone spoke of the "major trends" in banking in his time, and said that the first of them was "The dominance of capital markets over credit markets." Banks have become takers of interest rates, not makers of interest rates, which means they can be trapped like any borrower when rates rise unexpectedly and their borrowings cost them more. Part of the resentment people felt for banks historically was that they wanted interest rates to be high, because their costs of servicing customer deposits remained the same while their income from loans went up as rates rose. Now, banks as short-term borrowers feel the added costs of higher rates long before their customers do, and their influence on banking regulators is exerted to keep rates low. Public and congressional perception has not kept pace with reality, but the markets know, and bank stocks like public utility stocks tend to go up when interest rates fall and down when they rise.

Bank stock itself is no longer traded among friends in private transactions: the "call" feature has been legislated out of existence. All but a handful of the nation's larger banks are listed on one of the stock exchanges, and those that aren't are traded almost as publicly in the NASDAQ over-the-counter market. Despite a dodgy set of special rules for bank accounting cultivated by the Federal Reserve over the constant objections of the Securities and Exchange Commission, bank profits are no longer smooth from bank to bank or from year to year. The "spread" on business loans makes up a much smaller proportion of a bank's earnings than it did, and consumer deposits are a much smaller percentage of the liabilities that fund the bank's loans.

There are no more bankers' hours. The automated teller machine in the vestibule and the telephone-access computer stand ready to do business twenty-four hours a day, and in the metropolitan banks some part of the cohort of traders is on duty to work with staff abroad in the foreign-exchange and interest-rate markets on which the sun never sets. A man named Rosenberg was until May 1996 CEO of Bank of America; a man named Shapiro is CEO of Texas Commerce; and Harvey Golub runs American Express, all of which would have been inconceivable twenty years ago. Instead of a token female officer to be trotted out at conventions, banks have begun to rely quite seriously on their women. Banking has a higher percentage of female officers than any other industry. At California's Wells Fargo bank, indeed, women constitute almost two-thirds of the officers.[18]

Everything that happens gets entered into the computer just about instantly. Almost nobody who has a job in a bank today works as his predecessors worked as recently as twenty years ago.

2

What changed banking from an institution to a business was, of course, technology. Data processing and retrieval vastly reduced the cost of information, making it possible for businesses that were not banks to compete successfully for what had been banking business. Telecommunications tied together a national money market in which all sorts of institutions and even individuals could place their bets. And these toys were at first so expensive that ordinary bankers could not afford them and thus could not compete with the megabankers' access to capital; the local banker's advantages of being on the scene and knowing the borrowers were greatly diminished. All this was beyond the control of the banking regulators, who had a steadily diminishing influence on what happened to their wards.

Bankers had always thought they were being paid for their judgment, for taking risks in lending money, but in fact most of their profits had come from exploiting a rich information advantage over people who were not bankers. They could spread over a number of loans the cost of gathering information about interest rates at various maturities, foreign-exchange rates, industry trends, and the creditworthiness of the companies in an industry. Among the services big banks performed for their "correspondents" in the lesser cities and towns was easy access to such information. Command of such information allowed banks to set prices for loans efficiently through standardized procedures. But today anyone—you or I or our children—can sit at a computer console and pull out of the air (literally, through satellite services) information as good as the bank has about all these variables.

In the late 1970s and early 1980s, restrictions on the interest rates that banks could pay threatened to denude them of lendable resources when technology made it cheap for savers to buy money market funds that paid market rates of interest much higher than the regulators allowed the banks to offer. (Banks sought to compete—in retrospect, idiotically—by offering picnic coolers or toasters or television sets as a bonus for opening an account; the banking regulators had to sit in solemn conclave to determine which merchandise premiums could be legally offered under the notorious Regulation Q to encourage public purchase of a certificate of deposit of a certain size.) On March 31, 1980, Congress legislated a policy of removing interest-rate controls, though the regulators were left to time the deregulations as they thought best. In 1982, much of that discretion was taken away.

The first of three characteristics that made banks "special," Gerald Corrigan argued in 1982, was that "banks offer transaction accounts."[19] Prior to the 1960s, that function had been, in truth, a defining element in financial services. The fellows in green eyeshades on the high stools were indispensable for check-processing and account-updating purposes, and only banks were going to hire such cadres. But in 1959, the American Bankers Association moved to adopt the MICR (magnetic ink character recognition) system that allowed a computer to sort checks by issuer. It took almost a generation for the importance of this development to be recognized by potential competitors of the banks, largely because the computer manufacturers didn't see that they would have a market here. IBM refused to work with Bank of America to design computing machinery for banks because its market research people, who had also decided at about the same time that there wouldn't be any large number of customers for the strange electrostatic process Xerox had patented, said few banks would ever be interested in doing their "DDA" (demand deposit accounting) on a computer. General Electric, which built that first B of A computer, didn't know what it was doing in this business. But the fact was that the market for this sort of thing would be enormous, and by no means restricted to banks. Once financial paper was machine-sortable, anybody with a capacious computer could adapt it for payments purposes.

By 1982, when Corrigan made his assertion about the uniqueness of banks and their relationship to the payments system, Merrill Lynch was offering a Cash Management Account through which payment could be made by check or credit card, and the savings-and-loan associations all had negotiated order of withdrawal accounts. These checks and credit card slips still went through the banking system, but in theory they could be processed elsewhere, and machinery to make the theory practical was coming onto the drawing boards. The technology had taken away from the banks their monopoly on maintaining records of individual accounts.

Among the services banks had performed for their business customers, for a fee, was the preparation of payroll, with taxes properly deducted, with records kept for later submission to the Internal Revenue Service, the Social Security Administration and all the state and local taxing authorities, and with cash or checks delivered to the workplace. But upon the arrival of the computer and the identification codes, companies like Automatic Data Processing, which by 1995 handled payrolls that paid *18 million* American employees, could do such business more efficiently, and did. Eventually, ADP would acquire a little state-chartered savings bank in Pennsylvania and move the money itself through the Federal Reserve and the automated clearinghouses without a stopover at any normal bank.

To the extent that payments were made by plastic credit cards in 1995, they were more likely to go through First Data Resources, Inc., of Omaha, which both debited the accounts of the cardholders and credited the accounts of the merchants that had made the sales, than through any bank processing center. (After its absorption of First Financial in 1995, First Data had a "market capitalization"—shares of stock outstanding times price per share—of $13.6 *billion*, larger than that of any bank except Citicorp and Bank of America.) The payments system also came under threat from telephone companies like Ameritech in Chicago and public utilities like Consolidated Edison in New York, which began suggesting to their corporate customers that in addition to their usual services they could handle other people's billing and collection through the machinery they used for their own billing and collection. These companies had something banks did not have: their wires ran into the homes of their customers, and the use that could be made of those wires was still to be explored. In 1996, bankers all over the country were in negotiations with Microsoft on the future of banking through home personal computers, and they had to face the fact that Microsoft could in the end do without them.

By then, the banks' best customers of prior years had become their competitors. In his memoirs *The Banker's Life*, George Moore, who invented Citicorp, recalls from his days as national lending officer for what was then National City Bank of New York a scheme he worked out with Sears, Roebuck in 1940 to enable the retailer to expand its sales on what was then called the installment plan. The heart of the deal was that the retailer approved the borrower but the bank ran all but the first 10 percent of the credit risk. "The customer's installment credit agreement said he was borrowing from National City Bank of New York," Moore wrote, "but his bill came from Sears, and he paid Sears. Once a month we had a settlement statement: Sears paid us interest at prime rate—during the war, about 3 percent—on the money we had advanced over the month. If the total outstandings from customers went up month to month, we added 90 percent of that increase to what they were borrowing from us; if the total went down, they paid us back 90 percent of the reduction." At one point, National City's books showed more than three million Sears customers as borrowers from the bank.

The business got too big for National City to handle by itself: "Sears began to buy the paper back from us and sell it to banks in the cities where it was generated, so that the Philadelphia stores got credits from Philadelphia banks, Detroit stores from Detroit banks, and so forth."[20] A few years after that, Sears evicted the banks, substituting its own credit arm as the purchaser of the paper. That credit arm originally funded itself with bank loans, but once technology provided potential lenders with a stream of inexpensive information about market conditions and Sears itself, the company found it could raise all the money it needed by selling commercial paper in the market. Indeed, Sears commercial paper sold at lower interest rates than the commercial paper that banks sold to raise money to lend to companies like Sears. Because it could borrow so cheaply from the market, Sears put itself into the financial services business, at one point owning a bank (Greenwood Trust), the Discover credit card, several savings-and-loan associations in California, the AllState insurance operation, and eventually the investment banking house of Dean Witter. Bill Ford, a sarcastic, very western former chief economist for Wells Fargo in San Francisco who was then president of the Federal Reserve Bank of Atlanta, suggested a slogan for Sears financial services: "If you lose your shirt, we'll sell you another."

Though Walter Wriston, Moore's successor as chairman of Citicorp, insisted in the 1970s that Sears had become a major competitor of the banks, the truth was that Sears never developed a coherent plan for its participation in the money-and-credit business. By the 1980s the retailer was in retreat. Others, however, persevered to more purpose. In the 1950s, automobile dealers were among the largest and most profitable bank customers. Banks "floor-planned" their inventory, often sending directly to the manufacturers the checks for the value of the new shipment a dealer received. And the dealer in return referred the car buyer to the bank for the financing to purchase the car. Banks employed investigators to make sure the buyer was really making his "down payment" out of his own funds (not "mouse-housing" the first payment, as the lingo had it), and really earned the money he said he earned.

Then the auto manufacturers, like Sears, learned that they did not need a banking intermediary to lend dealers or customers the money to buy their cars. They set up their own credit companies, like General Motors Acceptance Corporation, which took most of the business away from the banks. General Electric Credit, now General Electric Capital, started as a facilitator of the sales of GE's manufactures, and grew to become the largest American commercial lender and leaser, all financed without a penny of bank loans. The bankers are still atop their towers in grand offices with grand boardrooms across the hall; but GE Capital CEO Gary Wendt, who supervises the lending of more money to business than any banker, works in an unimpressive box of a room over-looking the parking lot in the company's unornamented two-story building a little ways outside Stamford, Connecticut.

Banks could reduce their risk by maintaining a diversified portfolio of loans and investments of different duration, different sensitivity to interest-rate changes. That was part of being in the banking business. Businesses that were not banks could not spread their portfolios in that way: they didn't have that much cash in their treasuries to play with. Even if they did, their instincts and competencies led them to invest in their own busi-ness or something like it. But starting in the 1970s, the growth of futures and options markets for financial instruments—the "deriv-atives" of song and story—permitted players that were not banks, and were merely taking care of their own treasuries, to hedge their financial risks at low cost.

These developments, too, permitted outsiders into the banks' businesses. Using such instruments, "government-sponsored en-terprises" like the Federal National Mortgage Association and the Federal Home Loan Mortgage Corporation (always "Fannie Mae" and "Freddie Mac," respectively) were able to give builders and realtors guarantees of mortgage interest rates while deals were being negotiated, which banks had been reluctant to do. By the 1990s, more than half the home mortgages in the United States were funded with Fannie and Freddie as the intermediaries. And the grind-it-out business of processing householders' mortgage coupons had passed into the hands of independent "mortgage bankers" and processing companies, which the banks interested in this business eventually had to purchase, at hefty prices, because the competition had become too intense.

By giving the banks competitors, technology made them infinitely more profit-conscious, on the quarterly report timescale of modern securities analysis. Bank management became much less interested in the loan officer's argument that such and such a loan was worth making because a relationship with a small manufacturer would pay off later when the company became a big manufacturer. Walter Bimson, who founded Valley National Bank in Phoenix in the 1930s and made money through the Depression, liked to say that all he was interested in was power and position—once you had those, the rest would come. By 1995, Valley National was a branch of Banc One of Columbus, Ohio, which had declared a policy of holding all its branches to strict profits targets—*annual* targets, to be verified every quarter. Power and position were things you bought from your lawyers and lobbyists, not part of your business plan.

Technology gave banks for the first time economies of scale and economies of scope. Loans to businesses have to be developed, priced, and policed one at a time; the cost of making the next loan is roughly the same at big banks and small banks. Credit cards, home mortgages, securities processing, foreign exchange and "derivatives" trading are all businesses that require elaborate and hugely expensive computer installations and telecommunications expertise, but once the installations are in place the next loan or transaction comes virtually free of charge.

In 1994, banks invested $19 billion in technology.[21] That year and the next, large regional banks purchased or merged with each other in unprecedented numbers—Keycorp of Albany and Society Bank of Cleveland (which had itself absorbed the old Ameritrust), First Chicago and National Bank of Detroit, Bank of America and Continental-Illinois, First Union of North Carolina and First Fidelity of New Jersey, Fleet Financial of Rhode Island (pur-

26

chaser only a few years earlier of the failed Bank of New England) and Shawmut of Boston. The apparent reasons for these mergers were different, even opposed: Bank of America, with a big base of depositors and a limited constituency base of industrial clients, wanted Continental-Illinois's Rust Belt borrowers; First Union, its CEO Edward Crutchfield said, wanted First Fidelity's 2.5 million depositors (and expected to keep them while closing down many of the seven hundred First Fidelity branches by providing services on an electronic chassis). But the economic logic was the desire to avoid unnecessary duplication of investment in data processing.

The banks' drive to get into businesses other than banking preceded the technological revolution, and was based on the low cost of money to the fellows who, in effect, help the Fed print it. But just as the computers have permitted non-banks to do banking business, so have they made it easier for banks to handle securities accounts, insurance brokerage and life insurance, travel bookings and much else. The Glass-Steagall Act of 1933, which decreed the separation of commercial banking and investment banking—forbidding banks to underwrite issues of securities for sale to the public—had been much relaxed through waivers authorized by the Federal Reserve System, and the law was on its last legs in the 104th Congress, though disputes between insurance agencies and the banking business kept it alive for at least one more Congress as a reason for competitors in the financial services industry to make contributions to politicians. The future of banking, by general agreement, rested with fee-earning businesses, not "net interest income," revenues from lending.

Banker's Trust very publicly got out of conventional banking in the late 1970s, selling its branches and cutting its lines of credit to nonfinancial borrowers. Morgan Guaranty while nobody was looking became a wheeler-dealer, extending the cover of its AAA rating to quite a number of trading and banking operations that could never approach such ratings on their own. In the early

1990s, the basic Morgan training program for newcomers did not include so much as a day's work on credit judgment. Like Bankers and Morgan, Citicorp and First Chicago by 1995 derived more than half their operating revenues from sources other than lending money.

Even the banks that were most devoted to lending to businessmen with top-notch credit have grown less than enthusiastic. "As we look to the future," said Bud Baker, the matter-of-fact CEO of North Carolina's First Wachovia, "the traditional ways of making money, the loans and deposits—well, that will be a much more difficult way to make money."

"There is no banking industry," Dennis Weatherstone, the Australian-born chairman of J.P. Morgan, told the Annual Symposium of the Bank and Financial Analysts Association in 1994. "Today, the label means nothing. Function means everything."

3

But the goals being set for the banking system are incompatible with each other. As the savings and loan fiasco of the 1980s demonstrated in the United States—and the even more immense real-estate finance and credit union fiascos have revealed in Japan—the guarantees of bank deposits that make people and companies feel safe from bank runs promote dishonest behavior by the proprietors of banks, especially at times when they may be asked to own up to the consequences of previous bad decisions. The insurance world knows this phenomenon as "moral hazard"—if the building is worth less than the fire insurance will pay should it burn down, somebody will be found to burn it down. A relatively few bad loans can wipe out the equity of a bank very quickly, before the examiner's next visit. If the government guarantees deposits in an institution where the owners no longer have their own money at risk, the owners will solicit money aggressively from the public, paying whatever interest rates may be necessary for that purpose, and take that cash to the gambling casino. If the little ball falls in number 17, they are rich; if it doesn't, the government pays. Deposit insurance and liberalization are incompatible: any government that guarantees a bank's repayment of its own borrowings cannot escape the need to supervise what the bank does with the money.

As proprietors of fee-earning enterprises, moreover, banks are in no way "special," and without this quality of "specialness" that gives them access to government assistance, it is by no means clear that they can compete effectively against competitors supplying similar services. Even in the mid 1990s and a time of what looks like great prosperity, banks continue to be in danger of losing their social function. And the loss of social function is death. Jim McDermott, CEO of Keefe, Bruyette & Wood, the largest bank stock specialist house, comments from his office on the one hundredth floor of the World Trade Center that "This industry is getting outdated right before our eyes."

Looking at the horror story of the S&Ls from the wrong end of the telescope, one can see quite clearly that the "thrift industry" died because it had lost its social function. Historically, savings associations had grown because they financed housing. They were an expensive way to perform that task: homeowners, who are statistically the most reliable debtors, had to pay interest charges more than a percentage point higher than the market demanded from corporate bonds issued by not very high rated corporations that were less certain to pay. The finance committee of President Reagan's National Commission on Housing (of which I was a member) spent most of its time looking for ways to induce ownership of mortgage paper by the pension funds, mutual funds and insurance companies that had become the largest repositories of savings in the country. We found the "collateralized mortgage obligation" (CMO), and developed the "real estate mortgage investment conduit" (REMIC), which Congress would later validate. This was a new kind of bond, channeling to its purchasers a predetermined share of the monthly interest and principal payments made by a large group of homeowners. This sort of investment instrument could not have been conceived, let alone traded, before computers had trivialized the cost of keeping track of so many separate payments. By the 1980s, the CMO was an instrument Wall Street could slice and dice—we shall examine the details later, under the heading "derivatives"—that would and did make it attractive for the "contract thrifts" to put their money into housing.

When the Housing Commission was created in 1981, the S&Ls were in trouble from what was earlier described as "term-structure risk." Their vaults were full of mortgages with years to run yielding them 6 to 8 percent, and every month they had to pay more for deposits that could leave them at any time as Federal Reserve chairman Paul Volcker pushed up the interest rates to fight the inflation triggered by high oil prices, the declining exchange value of the dollar, and the deficits of the Carter and Reagan years. CEOs of savings and loans came to conventions (and to meetings of the Housing Commission) with little calling cards in their breast pockets that announced the month they would go bust if existing trends continued. The solution found to their problems by the Federal Home Loan Bank Board, which chartered and supervised S&Ls, was creative accounting to conceal current losses and an opportunity to grow out of their troubles by increasing the range of investments they could make with their insured deposits. Congress later wrote these bennies into law in the Garn–St. Germain Act of 1982, signed by President Reagan with the comment, "I think we hit a home run."

In 1981, the total footings of the S&L industry were a little more than $700 billion, and the Housing Commission was conspiring with technology to make the industry obsolete. By 1988, the total footings of the S&L industry were $1.4 trillion, and its role in financing homeownership had become marginal: Fannie and Freddie and the CMOs were the names of the game. Wall Street had made tens of billions of dollars trading slices of collateralized mortgage obligations with bewildered S&L executives throughout the nation's hinterlands. The taxpayers got off cheap with a loss of about $150 billion. But the essence of the matter was that the United States government had encouraged an industry to grow after it had lost its social function.[22]

In 1990, there was a real danger that the banking system would be led by the government down the path broken for the S&Ls. Many larger banks were solvent only by grace of regulatory rulings that allowed them to carry assets—especially real estate assets—at prices far in excess of their market values. The pressure on both the regulators and Congress was to help the banks enter new businesses and "grow out of their problems." With increasing competition from others for business that had traditionally been banking business—especially, one notes, from Drexel Burnham and its imitators, who had made the issuance of junk bonds cheaper than borrowing from banks and had mastered the art of turning consumer receivables into securities—it was not entirely clear that the social and commercial functions of the banks could be safeguarded for them any more than they had been retained for the S&Ls.

Fortunately, Drexel and its colleagues had overreached, and had exposed the information weakness inherent when there is no bank lending officer to monitor and discipline a commercial borrower's business. And Congress (more than the banking regulators) was still obsessed by the losses its foolish legislation of the 1980s had invited in the S&L industry. Its contribution to the banking crisis was a long list of requirements for bank lending and restrictions on possible forbearance by the regulators when dealing with troubled banks. This Federal Deposit Insurance Corporation Improvement Act of 1991 was described by former FDIC chairman L. William Seidman as "the Credit Crunch

Enhancement Act of 1991 . . . the most oppressive piece of bank legislation that I have ever witnessed."[23] The most important factor in preserving the banking system from the fate of the S&Ls, however, was the fear of law firms and accounting firms that if they participated in hiding the true condition of troubled banks, they could themselves be liable for the consequences.

On January 2, 1991, A. A. Sommer, Jr., chairman of the Public Oversight Board of the SEC Practice Section of the American Institute of Certified Public Accountants, sent a letter to "Selected AICPA Officers" and "Other firms that are members of the SECPS Executive Committee." "We have observed with considerable concern," this astonishing document reads,

> the attacks on the accounting profession resulting from the savings and loan debacle and the ensuing litigation which in the estimation of many threatens the profession's very existence.
>
> Concern about the banking system and its components and other financial institutions is rapidly replacing the savings and loan crisis in the headlines. In the next few months your firm and those of your colleagues will be performing audits of virtually all major banks in the system. These could well be the most important audits ever conducted by members of the accounting profession in this country. If, as happened with respect to many savings and loan audits, these audits are followed quickly by bank failures or disclosures of previously undisclosed writeoffs which imperil the viability of the institutions, we may expect a new wave of litigation against auditing firms and renewed public criticism of the profession.
>
> Because of our concern with these matters we have conferred with a number of government officials. All of them have expressed concern with our banking system, the troubles it and its components are experiencing, and the dangers these problems pose for auditors. . . .
>
> We fully realize the restraints imposed upon auditors by generally accepted accounting principles and the difficulties of

urging upon clients disclosures that may not be technically required, but which do contribute to an understanding of the financial affairs of the client.

In ordinary times auditor responsiveness to these concerns and protestations would be understandable. But these are not ordinary times. These are times in which the future of your profession as you have practiced it may be in peril. . . . The burden more than ever before is upon the individual auditor to exercise his professional judgment to assure that the embarrassments that have attended the savings and loan debacle are not repeated in the context of banks and other financial institutions."[24]

This letter, never before published, has the quality of a bronzed antique today, not least because the Republican Congress elected in 1994 was so eager to insulate accountants from lawsuits. Banking regulators who kept fingering worry beads about a "credit crunch" in 1991–92 were not conscious of the extent to which the bankers were under threat from their auditors to value their assets more conservatively. Bankers and bank directors were deeply troubled by the loss of their sovereign prerogative to decide (with only an occasional look over the shoulder at what was usually a friendly bank examiner) when to take the hit on a bad loan or a misguided investment. There was a case to be made that most of the nation's retailers would also go bust if they were forced to value honestly the stock in the back room. (Of course, 1991 was also a year when a lot of the retailers were going bust, which was not helping the banks.)

The decision to hold the banks down rather than prop them up—plus the replacement of William Seidman by Albert Casey at the Resolution Trust Corporation disposing of the S&Ls, which sped up the sell-off of bad assets at market prices—established a base from which the economy could grow and the banks could help rather than hinder. But the questions about their social—and economic—functions persist. Through much of this book, we shall be concerned with the practical question of how banks are to make a living in an information-soaked economy where none of their franchises can be considered stable. In the end we shall have to return to the larger question of whether in the future we will need banks, and what we might need them for. After all, no less an authority than Citicorp CEO John Reed has said, at a meeting in Washington sponsored by the Treasury Department in September 1996, that he expects banking to become "a little bit of application code in a smart network."

PART

I

UNDERSTANDING MONEY

1 / The Nature of Money

Whatever man can measure, calculate, and systematize, ultimately becomes the object of measurement, calculation, and system. Wherever fixed relations can replace indeterminate, the substitution finally takes place. It is thus that the sciences and all human institutions are organized. The use of coin, which has been handed down to us from remote antiquity, has powerfully aided the progress of commercial organization, as the art of making glass helped many discoveries in astronomy and physics; but commercial organization is not essentially bound to the use of the monetary metals. All means are good which tend to facilitate exchange, to fix value in exchange; and there is reason to believe that in the further development of this organization the monetary metals will play a part of gradually diminishing importance.

—AUGUSTIN COURNOT, 1838[1]

There have been a lot of definitions of money, one of the most ancient and most useful of human inventions, but the old definitions remain the best. By those definitions money is a medium of exchange, a unit of account, and a store of value.

A MEDIUM OF EXCHANGE

Money is a common currency that permits people to trade the fruits of their labors for goods and services that are the fruits of the labors of others. Without money, the division of labor on a large scale would have been impossible, and thus the modern economy that brings so many goods and associated evils would have been impossible. Money is the first requisite for freedom in a society, because in the absence of money every economy would

37

become a command economy as the leaders of the tribe dictated what everyone did. The sharecropper is much worse trapped than the farmer who sells his crops for cash, even if the rent is high. This fact gets confused with the ideological insistence that freedom requires a market unfettered by government, while the truth is that neither markets nor money are likely to exist except within a legal order created and maintained by a government.

The nineteenth-century English economist William Stanley Jevons told a story of Mademoiselle Zelie of the Théâtre Lyrique in Paris giving a concert in the Society Islands. "In exchange for an air from *Norma* and a few other songs," Jevons reported, recounting information from a letter the prima donna sent home, "she was to receive a third part of the receipts. [That's roughly what Pavarotti gets from his stadium concerts 150 years later; the world changes less than you think.] When counted, her share was found to consist of three pigs, twenty-three turkeys, forty-four chickens, five thousand cocoa nuts, besides considerable quantities of bananas, lemons and oranges. At the Halle in Paris . . . this amount of livestock and vegetables might have brought four thousand francs, which would have been good remuneration for five songs. In the Society Islands, however, pieces of money were very scarce; and as Mademoiselle could not consume any considerable portion of the receipts herself, it became necessary in the meantime to feed the pigs and poultry with the fruit." Jevons drew the conclusion: "Modern society could not exist in its present complex form without the means which money constitutes of valuing, distributing and contracting for commodities of various kinds."[2]

But there remains an element of mystery. John Maynard Keynes in the 1920s conducted a voluminous correspondence with a French financial journalist named Marcel Labordere, who traveled only in taxicabs and claimed to live five months a year on bread and water so he could indulge in taxicabs. "It is self-evident," Labordere wrote in a letter to Keynes, "that man will never be able to know what money is no more than he will be able to know what God is, or the spiritual world. Money is not the infinite but it is the indefinite, an astounding complex of all sorts of psychological as well as material reactions."[3]

The creation of money is a political act, and the Roman emperors' portraits are on the Roman coins for reasons beyond the vanity of the gentlemen involved. The enforcement of official money as a medium of exchange is one of the key attributes of sovereignty. "Everyone can create money," the economist Hyman Minsky wrote in 1986; "the problem is to get it accepted."[4] When Wright Patman was chairman of the House Banking Committee in the 1960s and 1970s, he liked to define legal tender by saying that if you take dollars out of your pocket in America and offer them to a man to pay what you owe him, and he refuses to accept the dollars, you can put your money back in your pocket and declare your bill paid, and the courts will be on your side. Abraham Lincoln argued while president that "Money is the creature of law, and the creation of the original issue of money should be maintained as an exclusive monopoly of the National Government."[5]

Tom Paine, it should be noted, had been on the other side. He thought paper money an excellent idea, but would permit only banks—not governments—to issue it. Banknotes would be accepted in the marketplace only if they were backed by a bank's credible promise to redeem them in "specie"—gold or silver. They were, in Paine's nice phrase, "hostages to be exchanged for hard money." Legal tender that could not be converted to coin Paine considered counterfeiting by the state; he wrote that the punishment of a legislator who would "move for such a law ought to be *death*."[6] More measured analyses spoke of the "fiduciary" nature of government money backed by nothing except the government's credit, and stressed that in most countries paper money was *not* fiduciary, but really was backed by the gold in the government's possession.

South African economist Robert A. Lehfeldt wrote in 1926 that U.S. Treasury "notes are simple certificates of deposit of gold (or silver), and the metal is kept ready to pay out again on demand. The United States Treasury issues such certificates, in denominations of ten dollars and multiples of that amount; they are extensively used as money in the United States, because people find them more convenient than gold coins."[7] British paper currency (issued, of course, by what was then a privately owned Bank of England and not by the government) was strictly convertible to gold from 1821 to 1914.

A government can decide to make anything legal tender. In late 1994, Viacom, proprietor of the Star Trek trademarks, announced that Liberia will accept as legal tender coins made for Viacom at a British mint, some in nickel, some in silver, some in gold. The coins have the Liberian coat of arms on the reverse, and on the obverse portraits of Captain James T. Kirk and Captain Jean-Luc Picard of the starship *Enterprise*. John Knox, who licenses Star Trek properties in Britain for Viacom, told a reporter that "There aren't too many other products you could do this with—it's highly unlikely that you could create a Mickey Mouse coin and have it be legal tender."[8] But he can't know that for sure: nobody has tried.

Powers of legal tender, of course, do not cross borders. Efforts to spend Ghanaian cedis outside Ghana will be unavailing, and anybody who tries to offer French francs or Italian lira in a coffeeshop in Terre Haute, Indiana, will find himself more or less politely asked to find some dollars. (Indeed, despite the European Union, an Italian who offered lira in a Paris cafe would probably be told to get to a bank and change it himself.) Dollars have been useful just about everywhere in the twentieth century—shopkeepers who tried to refuse zaire (it's not easy to refuse the national currency when offered by a man with an Uzi) would have been delighted to take dollars—but you can't be really sure, not always and everywhere.

In 1979, when I tried to pay for my dinner in dollar-denominated traveler's checks in the dining car of a TEE train between Brussels and Paris, I was asked if I didn't have anything else to use as payment. The dollar's writ in that year of deep distrust of U.S. policy did not run automatically in Europe. People who accepted dollars in payment had to fear that before they could get to the bank to change them to their own currency, the dollars would lose some of their exchange value. Eventually, the TEE waiter took my dollars—but he had made the point that he didn't have to. The taste was especially sweet for Europeans who remembered how much they had wanted dollars in the first twenty years after World War II.

Moreover, the ability of government to insist on the use of its money within its own borders is in effect limited to final sales, when a consumer acquires a finished product. On an intermediate basis, when it's a manufacturer buying from a supplier, the means of payment may be specified in the contract between the parties, which led R. S. Sayers, the historian of the Bank of England, to assert that "The money-quality of assets is something imposed by the business habits of people; it is attached in varying degrees to various assets; and the attachment can be and is varied over time in a completely unpredictable manner."9 As Robert Mundell of Columbia University stressed, smaller countries in the absence of legislated prohibition may wind up using the currencies of larger neighbors even for everyday retail purchases and sales.

The essence of sovereignty, then, may be less in the power to declare legal tender than in the power to outlaw within the jurisdiction moneys that are not controlled by government. The strongest effort to compel people to use the government's paper and no other was that of the Convention in the early days of the French Revolution in support of its issuance of *assignats*, a paper currency presumably secured by the lands seized from the Catholic church and the aristocracy. In 1793, it was made a crime to make any difference between payment in gold coins and payment in assignats, and anyone who refused to accept assignats at face value was to be fined three thousand francs for a first offense, and six thousand francs plus *twenty years* in irons for a second offense. In September of that year, the penalty was raised to death, plus confiscation of the criminal's property, with a reward to be paid to anyone who informed the authorities of the crime.[10] This was not necessarily a failure: the Harvard economist Seymour Harris argued that the assignats kept fourteen armies in the field. Fidel Castro for thirty years got away with forbidding Cubans to use anything but his peso when buying or selling what little they were permitted to buy or sell.

In 1933, Franklin Roosevelt became convinced that the path out of the Depression was to depreciate the currency. If foreigners could buy more dollars for their own currency, the price of American goods in those currencies would fall, and foreigners would buy more of them. Moreover, inflation at home would make the debts of businessmen and farmers easier to carry. Roosevelt's free-trade policies—most favored nation and the like—were designed to give the United States the full value of the depreciated dollar Roosevelt planned. Gold had been priced at $20.74 an ounce. Roosevelt announced that from that date on, the United States government would buy gold at $35 an ounce. That was a huge windfall gain for people who held or mined gold, and it brought a lot of gold into the United States. To the extent that other nations still maintained the price of gold in their own currencies, dollars became cheap.

Roosevelt explained the devaluation to the American people in a fireside chat. Our exports were down, he said, "not because our own prices in terms of dollars had risen, nor because our products were of inferior quality, not because we did not have sufficient products to export. But because, in terms of foreign currencies, our products had become so much more expensive, we were not able to maintain our fair share of the world's trade. It was, therefore, necessary to take measures which would result in bringing the dollar back to the position where a fair amount of foreign currency could again buy our products."[11]

Among the measures Roosevelt took was squelching the gold standard once and for all. The Gold Exchange Act of 1934 forbade Americans to own gold and specifically outlawed all contracts between Americans that called for payment in anything but U.S. dollars. (What made the New Deal different from the French Revolution was that the French Convention did not want inflation, and Roosevelt did; the penalties for breaking the law were rather different, too.) Now, in the 1990s, the European Commission has moved to ban the use of "money" ("e-cash") generated on the Internet by private parties, and the Federal Reserve has considered a rule requiring that companies that issue "stored-value cards" (a category that would include the transit authorities in New York, Washington and San Francisco if they could persuade shopkeepers to honor fare cards) must register their activities with the Fed and keep reserves at the Fed against the value on the cards.

The new electronic money, which we shall look at in Chapter 5 (though of course one can't actually *see* it), is offered purely as a medium of exchange. David Chaum, founder of DigiCash, a company based in Amsterdam in the Netherlands but really resident on the Internet, is a Ph.D. in computer sciences. His crusade has been to keep electronic money as anonymous as cash, so that nobody can trace where you got it—but an individual can tag it to prove where he spent it.

Chaum got the ball rolling for his "money" (useful pro tem solely as a way to buy products from merchants offering their wares on the Internet and willing to take payments in this medium of exchange) by giving the first thousand users who applied five hundred dollars of Digibucks. The merchants of software who sold their products for these Digibucks could set whatever price they pleased. Because Digibucks were useful to them entirely as credits to be spent on the Internet, they typically charged three times as much in Digibucks as they did in the alternative means of payment, which was U.S. dollars to be paid through credit cards. Chaum didn't see that there might be problems with his money system if prices were different in Digibucks and dollars—and vendors selling their product in Digibucks had to convert them to dollars to shop for anything, like meat or electricity or booze, that can't be delivered electronically. Since fall 1995, Mark Twain Bancshares in Missouri, which had previously offered depositors accounts denominated in marks, francs and pounds, has been carrying open accounts denominated in Chaum's Digibucks.

A UNIT OF ACCOUNT

Money measures the comparative values of what people want to buy or sell. Because different goods and services command different quantities of the same money, markets can provide price information that directs human efforts toward the goals that offer the greatest rewards.

As David Chaum contends, money does not have to be the unit of account to be a medium of exchange. Arguably, money's role as a unit of account is more important than its role as a medium of exchange. "In Milan in the eighteenth century," the MIT economist and historian Charles Kindleberger writes, "as many as fifty different coins were in circulation which could be handled only by equating them to an abstract, even imaginary unit, the livre or lira."[12] But for unit-of-account purposes there cannot be more than one money. Sixty years ago, Lionel Edie of Yale pointed out that the elimination of gold coins did not mean that gold could not be used as a means of exchange. But "under these conditions, it is farfetched to argue that the wheat producer or the cotton producer is able to make any fine calculation as to the amount of his product he is willing to exchange for gold."[13]

After some months of passionate exploration of historical and archaeological records in the 1920s, John Maynard Keynes came to believe that in fact money was used as a unit of account before it came into widespread use as a medium of exchange. Augustin

Cournot, the first mathematical economist, had almost a hundred years earlier reached the conclusion that it was the stability of the unit of account that made possible the commercial phenomenon of the contract of sale: "What characterizes a contract of sale, and distinguishes it essentially from a contract of exchange, is the invariability of the absolute value of the monetary metals, at least for the lapse of time covered by an ordinary business transaction. In a country where the absolute value of the monetary tokens is perceptibly variable, there are, properly speaking, no contracts of sale."[14] Among the oddities of American history is the fact that all Revolutionary War–era businesses that kept books at all kept them in pounds, shillings and pence, though the Continental Congress that financed the war had proclaimed in 1775 that the bills it was issuing would be paid off in Spanish pieces of eight, otherwise known as dollars.

Economic life does become very complicated when the medium of exchange and the unit of account are different. At the height of the Brazilian inflation in spring 1994, prices were sometimes quoted in Brazilian Treasury bills, which were adjusted in value every night—or in dollars, with the number of cruzeiros to be paid to be decided according to the exchange rate on the day payment was made. For several months before the introduction of the new "real" as the nation's currency, prices were quoted in reals, and the officially calculated price of the real in cruzeiros was published every day, which allowed people to pay with cruzeiros. In late 1995, a *Wall Street Journal* reporter led a front-page story about Brazil with the suggestion that the central bank had printed lots of reals when the switch came because it expected a huge inflation. In fact, the Brazilian inflation had meant that there were very few cruzeiros in circulation—I saw a man write a check to buy his children ice cream cones in the park—because the money lost value so fast. The central bank printed a lot of reals in the hope, which was realized, that the currency would *not* lose its value and people would be willing to use it.

There are enormous advantages for trade across borders when the same money can serve as both a unit of account and a medium of exchange in different countries. Roman coins are found everywhere around the borders of the old Roman Empire, and could be used to buy peace from barbarian chiefs. The startling economic growth of Europe in the nineteenth century had many causes, but not the least of them was the easy transferability of money from one country to another. The Belgian-American monetary economist Robert Triffin estimated that prior to World War I, 70 to 80 percent of the money in circulation in Europe was in the form of gold and silver coins of known metallic weights, which could in fact be spent in any country on the Continent: you didn't have to change your money when you crossed the border.[15] In 1867, at a Paris Monetary Conference with delegates from nineteen countries, Samuel Ruggles speaking for U.S. Secretary of State William H. Seward proposed unification of the world's coinage, establishing a uniform gold content for the British sovereign, the U.S. five-dollar half-eagle and a twenty-five-franc coin the French agreed to mint for that purpose. The motion garnered seventeen votes, but a British veto killed the idea.[16]

Under the terms of the Maastricht Treaty negotiated in 1990, the nations of the European Union (*fifteen* of them, at this writing) are to join in establishing a European Monetary Union, which would issue a currency ultimately named the Euro, to be the circulating medium in all the member countries that can bring their national economic policies sufficiently in line with one another to qualify for the honor. The EMU was to come into existence in 1997 if a majority of the members of the Union had reached the Nirvana of stable currencies, low deficits and reasonably low interest rates. In June 1995 this official date was dropped, seeing that no more than three or four of the countries in the European Union had a chance to meet the specified targets for deficit and inflation reduction. But the plan remained (for now) to bring a common currency into existence in 1999 for any members that qualified and wished to proceed. In 1997, a surprising number of countries approached the criteria, and the southern countries got rich rewards in terms of lower interest rates. The Euro will happen: an enormous weight of inertia and bureaucratic rule-making has built up behind it.

Several advantages were foreseen for the creation of the Euro. As noted, and as clearly true in the United States, trade benefits when a continent uses one currency. Nations that have had to pay very high interest rates on their national debt in their own currency could pay much lower rates in a tightly supervised Euro (and nobody doubts that the German Bundesbank will be tightly supervising). The driving force behind this revolution, however, was the desire of the Europeans to escape the distortions created in their economies when the U.S. dollar strengthened or weakened precipitously in the international currency markets. People fleeing the dollar because they thought its value would decline did not buy Italian lira or Spanish pesetas or even French francs; they bought German marks. Thus the value of German marks in terms of lira or pesetas or francs rose, regardless of the state of trade or investment or tourism or economic progress between Germany and its neighbors. German exports became more expensive in France, Spanish exports became cheaper in Germany, for no reason other than concerns about the dollar.

It is an instructive example of the importance of money *qua* money in economic relations. Not everyone recognizes that importance. Toward the end of their great *Monetary History of the United States*, Milton Friedman and Anna Jacobson Schwartz approvingly quote John Stuart Mill: "There cannot, in short, be intrinsically a more insignificant thing, in the economy of society, than money; except in the character of a contrivance for sparing time and labour. It is a machine for doing quickly and commodiously what would be done, though less quickly and commodiously, without it; and like many other kinds of machinery, it only exerts a distinct and independent influence of its own when it gets out of order."[17] That case can be made domestically, though I wouldn't accept it. But Friedman and Mill are even arguably right only when the money they write about is restricted in circulation to a single sovereignty.[18]

Adoption of the Euro would remove some of the worldwide demand for dollars for purposes that have nothing to do with the American economy. The dollar is the "vehicle" currency for foreign exchange—that is, someone wishing to buy large quantities of marks and pay in lira will probably use his lira to buy dollars, and the dollars to buy marks. The "cross rate" of the mark against the lira is an arithmetic product of the rate of each against the dollar. Roughly *$900 billion* of settlements related to foreign-exchange transactions pass through the computerized international Clearing House Interbank Payments System (CHIPS) in New York every day, and another $400 billion to $600 billion are settled in other ways. The Euro would greatly reduce the volume of foreign-exchange trading, by eliminating some of the currencies now traded. The six months after the signing of the Maastricht Treaty was the only such period since CHIPS came into being in the 1960s that the average daily volume in its computers declined. Then the daily maelstrom of settlements resumed its steady escalation. For now, the dollar continues to be the unit of account not only for goods and services produced in the United States, but also for the money of foreign countries. One of the things the Euro will change for sure is the vehicle through which European currencies will be exchanged for each other in 1999–2002.

A STORE OF VALUE

Money enables people to save for the future. These savings become capital that can be invested in the means of future production. Money tends to lose this function in times of inflation, when people look to gain from holding objects that will rise in price rather than from the earnings of the companies in which they can invest. "I know I should buy grand pianos," R. S. Sayers said at the height of the British inflation in 1975, acknowledging that things keep their value as money buys less, "but where would I keep them?" Historically the great advantage of gold and silver coinage was its durability. "Although gold and silver are not by nature money," Karl Marx wrote, "money is by nature gold and silver."[19] One of the reasons to use paper currency was that gold and silver in vaults did not deteriorate, while some of their substance would "sweat" off if people kept handling the coins.

It should be noted that Marx accepted both gold and silver as "natural" money. "Bimetallism" was indeed the norm in most countries prior to the eruption of paper money. Sir Isaac Newton, while Master of the Mint, proclaimed that a gold coin of the same weight should be worth fifteen times as much as a silver coin, and Alexander Hamilton (citing Newton) adopted the same ratio for the new United States when as secretary of the treasury he issued the first orders for the U.S. Mint. This undervalued gold, with the result that Hamilton's silver dollar disappeared from circulation. In 1834, Congress found the wrong remedy, declaring that gold should be worth sixteen times as much as the same weight of silver. As most of the silver coins circulating in America were of foreign origin, the effect was to raise the price of gold. The discovery of gold in California a few years later guaranteed that silver dollars would not be made, and Congress in 1853 got silver back into use as money by authorizing coinages in the value of half a dollar or less.

When there are two different moneys in circulation in a community it is likely that only one of them will be used as a store of value. Thus Gresham's Law, named for Sir Thomas Gresham, treasurer for Queen Elizabeth I, who founded the Royal Exchange in London in the sixteenth century, but did not in fact think up his law, which Kindelberger has traced back to Nicholas Oresme, bishop of Lisieuz, in 1360.[20] The law says that "bad money drives out good"—in other words, that when there are two different moneys available, the one less respected will be used for transactions, while the one more highly regarded will disappear into people's mattresses. The law survives as a slogan because it sounds wrong—people usually think that good products vanquish bad—and like many surviving slogans it gets to be used by people who don't understand what it means.

For some years in the mid nineteenth century in the United States, people were free to start their own banks without much supervision by political authority, and each bank printed its own banknotes. In theory, as Tom Paine approvingly wrote, the notes were backed by "specie," coins minted from precious metals, which would be delivered to the holder of the paper note if he presented it at the window. Bad banks that issued rapidly depreciating notes tended to be far away from where they put the notes out for circulation. The worst of them were called "wildcat" banks, because to find them, noteholders had to go into the wilderness, "out among the wildcats." Robert E. Litan, disapproving of the "chaotic explosion of state banks" in the 1840s and 1850s, notes the "remarkable fact that until Congress authorized the Treasury to issue paper currency in 1862, the United States had no national paper currency, but instead 7,000 different kinds of notes issued by 1,600 state banks. Many of these notes were almost worthless."[21]

Until the latter part of the twentieth century, paper money from any source was considered no more than a surrogate for coins, and worthless if the gold and silver wasn't there to back it. But coins themselves must be worth more than the metal in them, or (by Gresham's Law) they would not circulate. (This happened to Mexico in 1935, when Franklin Roosevelt's silver-buying policies made the metal in the peso worth more than its purchasing power as money.) Thus the power to issue money, either in precious-metals form or in paper, is inevitably a source of revenue. The term of art in the business is "seignorage," the economic equivalent of the *droit du seigneur* by which the lord of the manor had first crack at the virgins on the estate before their marriages were consummated.

Archaeologists can measure the strength and quality of an ancient government by weighing the quantity of precious metals in its coinage: strong governments maintained the gold content of their coins, weak governments "clipped" the coinage, putting less gold or silver into coins of the same face value. Similarly, weak governments today run deficits and print money to pay their bills, inflating the currency and indirectly taxing not only their citizens' store of wealth but also their workers' salaries, which buy less every week. Thomas Mann blamed the German inflation of the 1920s for the eruption of Hitlerism: "Having been robbed," he wrote, "the Germans became a nation of robbers."

Lincoln's $300 million of greenbacks, to pay some of the cost of the Civil War, came under challenge as unconstitutional in 1869 by litigants emphasizing that the Constitution gave Congress the power to "coin money," implying a metal currency. In February 1870, the Supreme Court (with Chief Justice Salmon P. Chase writing the opinion) declared the Legal Tender Acts unconstitutional if they compelled people whose contracts had been written before their passage to accept greenbacks in payment. This was especially interesting because Chase, whose name would be perpetuated in a New York bank, had been the secretary of the treasury who authorized the issuance of the notes—and signed them.

The next case in this area involved a contract written *after* the passage of the Legal Tender Acts, and it quickly appeared that this case, too, would be decided against the government. Chase told President Ulysses S. Grant what was going to happen to the greenbacks, and agreed to let the matter pend till the next session of the Court, where there were two vacancies. Grant got Congress to pack the Court, securing a 5–4 vote for the constitutionality of the greenback, Chief Justice Chase now in the minority.

Through the nineteenth century, the call of the populist left in America was for "bimetallism"—coinage of both gold and silver. In 1873, the authorization to coin silver dollars in the United States was withdrawn, a very peculiar exercise of congressional power, because the coin wasn't being made anyway. This "Crime of '73," to take the political slogan that lasted the rest of the century, was followed in 1879 by the restoration of convertibility to the paper dollar, which had traded as low as 79 cents of face value of the gold coins that had survived the closure of the mint in the Civil War. Through the world, the scarcity of gold created deflationary pressures, relieved in part in the United States by the compromise under which the Treasury bought silver and issued paper "silver certificates," which were the basic dollar bills until the 1960s. ("Payable to the bearer in silver on demand" it said on the face of the bill.)

Accepting the Democratic nomination for president in 1896, William Jennings Bryan ("silver tongue," the novelist John Dos Passos wrote scornfully, "in the big mouth") told the Republicans that they must not "crucify mankind upon a cross of gold." But argument was about to be destroyed by technology: a cyanide process for refining gold would make possible the profitable exploitation of the South African mines. The economist and economic historian Roy Harrod in his Oxford lectures in 1953 argued that if South African gold had not come on stream, Bryan "would have become President of the United States in 1900. And then the fun would have begun."[22]

The American compromise was that coins worth a dollar or less were silver; coins of five dollars or more were gold. But the lure of gold never entirely faded, even when populist, not to say socialist, sentiment was at its strongest. In 1934, writing the Gold Exchange Act that killed the gold coins and fixed the price of gold at $35 an ounce, Congress continued to insist that each of the twelve Federal Reserve banks, which would now supply all the country's currency except the one-dollar bills, keep in their vaults gold to a value of one-quarter of each bank's share of the total national note issue.

When the finance ministers and central bankers of the triumphant Allies met at Bretton Woods in New Hampshire in 1944 to build the foundations for the future world economy, they set up a system in which the dollar would be the measure of value for all the world's other currencies—and American policy would keep the dollar itself valued at one thirty-fifth of an ounce of gold. If the managers of the dollar permitted inflation, this couldn't work. Milton Gilbert, the cynical American economist who became the chief adviser to the Bank for International Settlements in Basel in the 1960s and 1970s, liked to say that the United States government couldn't have bought a Chevrolet or a bushel of corn for the same price in 1978 that it would have paid in 1934, and should not have been surprised that it couldn't buy gold at that same price, either.

The gold crisis of early 1968 never got much play in the press but so frightened the American government that Lyndon Johnson proposed and the Congress adopted new taxes large enough to give the United States in fiscal 1969 its first and only balanced budget since the 1920s. Congress had to hustle to reduce the gold coverage of the dollar, and went whole hog. The Federal Reserve banks were released from the obligation to back their notes with gold, and the Treasury Department was put out of the business of printing its one-dollar "silver certificates." Under the terms of the Bretton Woods treaties, however, the United States was still bound to purchase gold at $35 an ounce or sell it at $35 an ounce. President Lyndon Johnson and Federal Reserve Board chairman William McChesney Martin finessed this requirement by announcing that it applied only to gold that was already in the official reserves of governments and central banks, and that the United States would no longer sell to or buy from the private gold market in London or elsewhere.

Though more attention was paid to the imposition of price

controls and a 10 percent tariff on all imported goods, the most surprising of the shocks that emanated from President Richard Nixon's Camp David weekend of the economists in July 1971 was his closure of the gold window, denying to all the countries that had been holding their national reserves in dollars the right to switch into gold at $35 an ounce. In December of that year, at a conference in the Smithsonian Institution in Washington, in what Nixon called "the greatest economic agreement in the history of the world," he and his treasury secretary, John Connally, signed on to a restoration of the Bretton Woods rules, with the dollar valued at one thirty-eighth of an ounce of gold—to be sold, however, only to other governments or central banks for their official reserves.

The Smithsonian, however, wasn't even the second greatest economic agreement in the history of the world, and within eighteen months the world's major currencies were all "floating" against each other. Gold was out of the picture as a monetary factor (though there remains no shortage of analysts who will find evidence for theories in the fluctuations of the free-market price of gold). Trading in an informal interbank market determined every day what quantity of other currencies each currency would buy. These prices for currencies in theory should equalize the "purchasing power" of each currency in its home market, but in fact the foreign-exchange market operates with a dynamic all its own, mixing current purchasing power, trade surpluses or deficits, capital flows tracing to confidence in the course of each country's economy, and yields in the home country bond market (the higher the interest rate, presumably, the more attractive the currency as a place to park some money and the more expensive a trading strategy that bets against it). Perhaps even more important than these examples of economic analysis is raw, undisciplined fashion. As more and more countries became actively participant in world trade, more and more currencies are bounced up and down by traders.

By the 1970s, all the discussion of a "gold standard" had become entirely theoretical from the point of view of people who actually *used* money: there were people, especially in Europe, who had hoards of gold in their houses or their safe deposit boxes, but nobody anywhere actually used gold coins in economic transactions. Arab sheikhs bought breeding camels with shrink-wrapped $10,000 bundles of hundred-dollar bills, not gold. The importance of "specie" as backing for paper money had been permanently hammered into the ground by John Maynard Keynes's insistence that gold was a "barbarous relic."

Still, even Keynes had found himself worried about what would happen once metallic constraints were removed from the creation of money. Money was, Keynes noted, "the one commodity to the rapid manufacture of which there was no serious impediment."[23] Or as Alan Greenspan, later to be chairman of the Federal Reserve Board, argued rather more tendentiously in 1966, "In the absence of the gold standard, there is no way to protect savings from confiscation through inflation."[24] Maintaining paper money as an acceptable store of value is in truth a conundrum to which there will never be a single acceptable answer, though the activity itself is entirely plausible, and Alan Greenspan himself has been among the more successful players of that game in the 1990s.

Jack Bennett, who as corporate treasurer of Exxon managed a $5 *billion* book of currencies and made money every year on his decisions to buy one and sell another—and who served as under-secretary of the treasury for monetary affairs in the Nixon administration—remembered that "my father administered the German currency reform after the war, for Allied Military Government. I was at the press conference where he announced the new German mark. A reporter said, 'What's the backing for this new currency? Where's the gold?' My father said, 'There isn't any gold backing. The value of this currency depends on the willingness of the German people to show self-restraint, because they want their money to keep its worth.' The reporter shook his head and said, 'Never work.' But that's the only backing any currency ever has."[25]

Even in an economy where prices never change, money as a store of value has the great disadvantage that it is inert: what's in the mattress earns no interest. And there is a further problem with money as a store of value, which is that the growth of the economy requires that the money *circulate*. One of George Abbott's few failures as a Broadway producer was *Tenderloin*, a musical about low life and high living in New York in the earliest years of the twentieth century. The first act finale was set in a fancy brothel, where the girls explained and acclaimed the virtues of the circulation of money: the johns pay the girls who pay the madam who pays the cops who pay the grocer, who pays the aldermen, who pay the mayor "and the mayor spends it here—and everything is grand, just so long as the money changes hands."

Gold bugs are antisocial: believing with Karl Marx that money is gold and gold is money, they would withdraw from general use the money commodity that underlies the production of all other commodities. Misers are hated not because they are rich but because they take money out of circulation. In his *General Theory of Employment, Interest and Money*, Keynes argued that one root of great depressions is the "liquidity preference" that leads people to hoard their money. "Our desire to hold money as a store of wealth," Keynes wrote, "is a barometer of the degree of our distrust of our own calculations and conventions concerning the future. . . . The possession of actual money lulls our disquietude."[26] Robert Skidelsky in the second volume of his great biography of Keynes says that to Keynes money "is first and foremost a store of value, an alternative to consumption and investment, a 'subtle device' through which the fear of the future takes its revenge on the hopes of the present."[27] But Keynes also offers a more general and more enlightening statement of money's function as a store of value: "The importance of money essentially flows from it being a link between the present and the future."[28]

The great invention of capitalism is the creation of *titles* to money—bank accounts, bonds and stocks that can be cashed in with varying degrees of ease and that make money available to enterprise. These titles to money supplant money as the store of value, as long as they can easily be cashed. When it no longer seems that such monetary instruments can be easily sold at a fair price, the money goes into the mattress, and a whirlpool of economic decline can result. It happened in Japan in the '90s. Money does matter.

2

Keynes's analysis of the damage done by strong liquidity preferences in hard times lay behind the development of both "fiscal policy" and "monetary policy" as stabilizers for capitalist economies. When private parties were withdrawing money from circulation, the government could restore it by running a deficit. The issuance of government bonds to pay these deficits sucked money out of the mattresses: people who were holding cash had every reason to prefer government bonds. Paper money is nothing but a claim on a government: "the part of the national debt," Britain's parliamentary Radcliffe Commission noted in 1960, "on which no interest is paid."[29] (It is an interesting fact, which very few Americans realize, that by taking and holding $40 billion of our currency to keep in their mattresses or use for domestic purchases, the Russians have made a $40 billion loan to the United States.) A government bond represents a similar claim which yields an income. If a public hoarding cash would not buy government bonds, however, money could be inserted into the economy by selling the bonds to the central bank, which would buy them with new money printed for the purpose.

That an increase in the supply of money could stimulate economic activity was a truth recognized as early as the mid eighteenth century, by the great Scottish philosopher David Hume. Hume had studied John Law's inflation of the French currency in 1718, creating paper money to be backed by the profits of the American colonies, hence the "Mississippi bubble." And he had lived through the comparable "South Sea bubble" in England a few years later. He drew his central example, however, not from the recent expansion of paper money but from the flood of gold and silver that had come to Spain more than a century earlier from its exploitation of its conquests in Mexico and Peru. "[I]n every kingdom into which money begins to flow in greater abundance than formerly," Hume wrote, "everything takes on a new face; labour and industry gain life; the merchant becomes more enterprising, and even the farmer follows the plough with greater alacrity and attention."

Hume had an explanation. "Some time is required before the money circulates through the whole state. . . . By degrees the price rises, first of one commodity, then of another; till the whole at last reaches a just proportion with the new quantity of specie which is in the kingdom. In my opinion it is only in this interval or intermediate situation, between the acquisition of money and the rise in prices, that the increasing quantity of gold and silver is favorable to industry."[30] Thus an increase in the quantity of money available in a society creates a "money illusion"—people feel richer, and more willing to spend. But unless the increased demand can in fact generate increased supply, the end result is simply higher prices.

Sir John Hicks, Keynes's first biographer, provided the definitive explanation in 1967, two hundred years after Hume: "Inflation does give a stimulus, but the stimulus is greatest when the inflation starts—when it starts from a condition that has been noninflationary. If the inflation continues, people get adjusted to it. But when people get adjusted to it, when they *expect* rising prices, the mere occurrence of what has been expected is no longer stimulating."[31] The *Wall Street Journal* and *The Economist* both reported in 1995 that Robert G. Lucas of the University of Chicago had won a Nobel Prize in economics for discovering these things for himself. In fact, it's worse than what Hume and Hicks and Lucas said. The good that rising prices do, making inventories more valuable and increasing profits, gets destroyed by rising interest rates as expectation catches up to reality. And the destruction turns to overkill, because the rates must be high enough not only to keep up with inflation, but also to dissuade borrowers drawn by the fact that declines in the value of money make debts easier to repay.

Still, price movements are a one-way ratchet: the trend cannot safely be reversed. If prices actually fall, enterprise will come to a halt unless wages can be reduced to a comparable degree. Interest rates can never fall below zero, because it can never pay anybody with money to sign a contract that leaves him with less money on its conclusion than he has now. (Actually, some of the fancy "derivatives" we shall examine in Chapter 10 have produced that result, to the great embarrassment of the International Swap Dealers Association.[32]) Once it is anticipated that what is manufactured now will have to be sold later for less than the costs of making it, nobody will invest. Keynes's liquidity preference becomes the liquidity trap.

In the modern world, then, inflationary expectations, dangerous as they are, can perform a service. Karl Marx drew his "iron law of capitalism" from the pressure for wage reduction in a time of deflation that poisoned economic life in the 1870s. Much the same phenomenon made the Great Depression so intractable in 1930 and thereafter. During the 1970s, we worried about a condition called "stagflation," when prices rose without stimulating employment. But it was the pressure of that continuing inflation that created the conditions for the restoration of economic growth. In the 1970s, everybody knew that money would be worth less tomorrow than it was today, so people had reason to borrow it and spend it, the "automatic stabilizers" of the federal budget set a floor under declining consumption, and eventually productive facilities were fully employed again. As Hyman Minsky points out, government deficits increase private profits.

Thus, money matters in its own right even within a closed society. Irving Fisher in the 1920s wrote the tautological equation:

$$mv \equiv pt$$

which says that the quantity of money times its average velocity (how often the mayor spends it here) must equal the number of transactions times their average price. This doesn't in fact tell you anything except that a change in the quantity of money must make *some* other change—perhaps only a change as trivial as a change in velocity.

But one can assume that the velocity of money is simply the result of people's demand for money to have in their pockets. Assume further that this "demand for money function" is stable (or changes only in response to changes in interest rates—higher rates make people less willing to keep cash). This is the central assumption—"the basic premise," as Warren D. McClam of the Bank for International Settlements put it[33]—of the Milton Friedman school of monetary economics. Then an increase in the money supply from whatever source must change either the price level or the number of transactions (presumably the output of the economy). Assuming once again, as Friedman does, that an economy will tend to produce to its capacity if government leaves it alone, the role of the monetary authorities is to maintain a steady growth in the money supply to permit an increase in transactions without an increase in prices. His great predecessor Henry Simons puts the case in 1936 in terms very recognizable sixty years later: he wanted the elected representatives of the people to set rules to prevent "discretionary (dictatorial, arbitrary) action by an independent monetary authority."[34]

But even if the quantity theory of money explained what happened inside a closed economy, where people traded only with others who use the same money (though in fact it doesn't), it would still be confounded by the modern world, in which foreign trade makes up a significant fraction of every country's income. Once any substantial part of a country's economic life involves foreign trade, the exchange value of that country's money in the units of account of another country can be crucial. A very tight monetary policy that drives up interest rates domestically may give the country that chooses this approach an inflow of foreign capital (come to seek higher returns) and thus a rise in the exchange rate of its currency. An example that made a lot of trouble recently is Mexico in 1994. Such a policy enables its citizens, especially its rich citizens, to buy foreign goods at lower prices, which reduces inflationary pressures at home at the cost of making local industry less profitable and depriving local workers of jobs. Inflation taxes wealth and money income; an overvalued exchange rate taxes jobs and investment. The strength of the currency became in the United States in the 1980s and 1990s a fault line almost as visible as bimetallism in dividing political opinion: a right wing led by the *Wall Street Journal* wanted a strong dollar so the BMWs and trips abroad would be cheap; a left wing wanted a depreciated dollar to protect industrial jobs.

In the 1970s and into the early 1990s countries with an intractable inflation and no political will to beat it down domestically were able to use an overvalued exchange rate to dampen price increases. Martín de Hoz in Argentina, Paul Volcker in the United States, Margaret Thatcher in Britain, François Mitterrand after his disastrous first two years as president of France and Carlos Salinas de Gortari in Mexico all followed policies that reduced the prices of foreign-made goods at the cost of piling up a large foreign debt and losing both employment and investment at home. This was also the policy Britain had followed in the middle 1920s, when it was advertised as a plan to return to the gold standard, and Keynes denounced it in a famous article entitled "The Economic Consequences of Mr. Churchill."

For all its cruelty, the policy of keeping interest rates and foreign-exchange value high can be defended as a way to force domestic industry to restructure itself and become much more efficient—as the Japanese have done throughout the postwar period, and the American Rust Belt did in the 1980s. "Tight money" forces attention to its allocation. But there may be countries—France seems to be one of them, and the reunified Germany another—where the industrial component cannot improve its efficiency because necessary capital investment has been crowded out by consumer spending and government spending or because work rules, governmental or union-based, have kept costs high. In the end, though it takes a while and the efficiency of the process may be poor, money will be the servant, not the master, of the real economy.

2 / What Money Does

"Papa, what's money?"

The abrupt question had such immediate reference to the subject of Mr. Dombey's thoughts, that Mr. Dombey was quite disconcerted.

"What is money, Paul?" he answered. "Money?"

"Yes," said the child, laying his hands on the elbows of his little chair, and turning the old face up toward Mr. Dombey's. "What is money?"

Mr. Dombey was in a difficulty. He would have liked to give him some explanation involving the terms circulating-medium, currency, depreciation of currency, paper, bullion, rates of exchange, value of precious metals in the market, and so forth, but looking down at the little chair, and seeing what a long way down it was, he answered: "Gold, and silver, and copper. Guineas, shillings, half-pence. You know what they are?"

"Oh, yes, I know what they are," said Paul. "I don't mean that, Papa. I mean what's money after all . . . I mean, what can it do?"

—CHARLES DICKENS, *Dombey and Son*

Lord Kelvin was the Milton Friedman of physics, always shaving reality to simplicity. The scale of absolute temperature is named for him. His most famous aphorism was that if you can give something a number, you can understand it; if you can't, you're still guessing. When we consider money, we're guessing. And soon we may not even be able to guess, just evaluate after it's all happened.

When the emperors minted coins, the amount of money in circulation was the total that had been turned out by the mint, less some losses for sweating. Nobody knew how much was in circulation, because there were misers who hoarded it, and got a deservedly bad name for doing so, because a shortage of money by making money more valuable leads to lower prices for everything else and thus, as noted, economic distress. Some of what the misers took out was made up by the product of counterfeiters; people bit coins to make sure they were hardened gold rather than some base metal.

From the fifteenth century on, and with rapid acceleration in the nineteenth century, the money in circulation was likely to be something that had been created by banks, a situation we shall explore in Part II. Banks issued their money against deposits of value—gold coins or government bonds—and created money in a lending process, by issuing letters of credit or bankers' acceptances that could be used for purchases. Various devices were employed to control the issuance of banknotes, most notably the organization of a single government-approved or government-owned entity—such as the Bank of England or the Banque de France—that would have a monopoly on such business. This could not be done in the United States, where the states themselves retained (and continue to retain) sovereignty in the chartering of banks. Licenses to operate banks could be got from an honest state government by purchasing the state's bonds, from a crooked state government by greasing a few palms in governors' offices and legislative chambers.

More conservatively operated banks were not without defenses against such behavior. They could accept the notes of other banks only at a discount, which was good business if the issuing bank actually had the specie to back its notes and the bank that discounted them had the resources to go and collect the coin. "Note brokerage" was an important part of the banking business, and the Bank of the United States, the one nationally chartered bank with offices in most states, profited heavily by it. In 1803, three Boston banks united to split the cost of redeeming at the issuers' home offices the notes issued by up-country banks in Massachusetts, and a year later a Boston Exchange Office was set up to specialize in such work.

Bray Hammond, the great historian of American banking,

tells a tale of the New England Bank, chartered in 1813, which accepted out-of-town banknotes and charged depositors only the cost of collection. In 1814, the bank sent its man to New York to redeem $140,000 of notes, which was paid in silver coin, and started off to Boston in three wagons. "The wagons had not gone far," Hammond wrote, "when they were halted by order of the federal Collector of Customs for New York; and the money was carried back by force and placed in the vaults of the Bank of the Manhattan Company, of which the Collector was a director. The action was protested by the New England Bank's agent, but the Collector declined to alter his purpose, alleging a suspicion that the coin was on its way to Canada, with which, since it was British, the States were then at war.... The Massachusetts authorities laid the matter before the President of the United States, James Madison.... Their effort 'so far succeeded as to have the money restored.' "[1]

A year earlier, Stephen Girard had made arrangements with banks from South Carolina to Boston, and country banks in Pennsylvania, to accept their notes at par in his new bank in Philadelphia, provided that they kept sufficient deposits with him to cover their likely liabilities. The deposits did not have to be in specie— they could be the notes of Girard's other correspondents, or the better banks in Philadelphia. Girard also had international correspondents, with an unsecured line of credit for £50,000 from Baring Brothers in London. Girard's was a private bank, not chartered by the state of Pennsylvania, and thus always in some danger, and he policed his country correspondents, informing the Bank of Delaware that he had too many of their notes and would take no more until they straightened their accounts, and suggesting that the Farmers Bank of Lancaster remit banknotes from other Philadelphia banks to exchange for their notes that were piling up in Girard's bank. On average during the twenty years of the bank's existence, its deposits from other banks were double the amount of the deposits it kept in other banks, thereby increasing the funds Girard could lend or invest.[2] When the War of 1812 made specie tight, the Philadelphia banks agreed to pay interest on the notes their fellows accepted, which was from their point of view (but not their customers' point of view) a discount.

In 1819, the Suffolk Bank of Boston entered into competition with the New England Bank with a more formal and extensive system for the crediting of the notes issued by country banks, finally enforced by the Boston banks acting as a group to require all banks in the northeastern states to become depositors at the Suffolk Bank or risk having their banknotes returned to them to be redeemed in specie. (In Vermont, state law required state-chartered banks to be members of "the Suffolk System" or pay a tax of 1 percent of capital each year.) The cashier of the Suffolk Bank, William Grubb, personally indemnified the bank against losses on its acceptance of "foreign" banknotes. Grubb kept a record of depositors who had presented counterfeits, which was a great help to the country banks in tracking the bad guys. He also monitored the portfolios of the banks that sent him currency, stressing the need for short-term credit only. "Too large a portion of your loan is in accommodation paper [i.e., term loans]," he wrote to the president of the Bank of Woodstock, "which cannot be relied upon at maturity to meet your liabilities."[3]

After 1825, the Suffolk Bank honored the notes of all participants in the system at par, and the endorsement was so highly regarded that New York City banks charged a discount of only one-eighth of 1 percent on paper from New England (as against a discount of one-quarter of 1 percent on banknotes from upstate New York, which was the maximum allowed under state law for intrastate redemption). In their paper on the Suffolk system, Charles W. Calomiris and Charles M. Kahn of the University of Illinois at Champaign-Urbana claim that whether or not they felt the profits to the Suffolk Bank for these services were excessive, historians agreed "that the system was effective in creating a uniform currency area throughout New England and in promoting stable banking due to the disciplinary role of the Boston banks. As the 1878 Report of the Comptroller of the Currency observed: 'The country banks kept their circulation as extended as possible for their own profit. Their overdrafts on the Suffolk enabled them to do so, but at the same time put them completely into its power.' " Calomiris and Kahn, studying the price of stock in Boston banks as against the price of stock in New York banks, come down on the side of supporters of the Suffolk system, arguing that the country banks gained more by their seignorage on a larger note issue than they lost by the requirement that they keep permanent deposits interest-free at the Suffolk Bank.[4]

When a borrower from a bank walked away with a fistful of the bank's newly minted banknotes, the fact that banks created money was obvious—and so was the case for the desirability of a large number of local, specialized banks that would know their borrowers and what they would do with the money. Money would be called into existence when it was needed, because throughout the system borrowers would need it to grease the wheels of production and consumption: the textile manufacturer would borrow to buy cotton, and pay back the loan when the dressmaker bought the cloth with the money she had borrowed for the purpose, and if there was a retail establishment involved it would borrow from the bank to stock its inventory, paying the dressmaker so she could pay her bank.

Harold van B. Cleveland and Thomas Huertas in their history of Citibank explain how the system worked from a bank's point of view: "Traditionally, corporations had borrowed from banks to finance inventories and goods in process or in transit. Such short-term borrowings were normally seasonal, and loans were fully repaid at least once a year. At times when it had no loan outstanding, the customer maintained balances at the bank, which entitled the firm to credit, as a matter of custom if not of legal right, when its borrowing season came round again. Since seasonal patterns of inventory build-up, production and shipment differed among industries and trades, a well-managed bank had sufficient deposits to cover loan demand in all seasons. As a group, a bank's business customers funded themselves."[5]

This "real bills" theory, arguing that in the absence of conspiracy or government misbehavior an economy would *automatically* generate as much money as it needed, was generally believed well into this century. In the splendid formulation of Britain's Radcliffe Commission in 1959 (why can't we write these things the way the British do?), "All businesses and a large proportion of persons find it essential to hold deposits. . . . [T]his has the advantages from the point of view of the banks that they can always rely on the maintenance of a very large total of balances related, in a broad way, to the money value of the national income. Individual balances go up and down, depositors come and depositors go, but the total on current account goes on forever."[6]

Indeed, such doctrine underlies the original Federal Reserve Act and the early New Deal legislation on financial matters. It is also not entirely untrue: there are many of us of widely varying political persuasion who believe that in a better world the linkage between the abstractions of money and the realities of getting and spending would make production rather than speculation the dominant force. The problem is that a system which permits the money supply to grow when businessmen are euphoric may invite inflation, while it risks depression by permitting the money supply to shrink when recession comes. Milton Friedman was perhaps the doughtiest warrior against real bills, but his monetarism is essentially the reverse of the coin of the real bills doctrine, holding that if the government follows a rule of gradual increase in the money supply, the economy will gradually increase the production and consumption of real goods and services.

When the bank instead of issuing banknotes gives the borrower a deposit he can withdraw at will by writing checks against it, the fact that the bank has created money is not quite so obvious—and, indeed, sober bankers will solemnly deny that they "create money" when they lend, because they can't lend anybody more than depositors have left with them, or than they can borrow in the market. But the essence of a demand deposit is that it can be withdrawn by the depositor at will, so the original depositor has not in any sense lost the use of his money. Because the borrower now has the use of that same money through the deposit created in his name, the bank has in fact created new money. The banking *system* then creates money because each borrower in spending the proceeds of his loan deposits the money in another bank, for which it becomes the source of another loan. Each bank must continue to hold as a reserve some fraction of its deposits, to pay back those depositors who want their money. So the system is a "fractional reserve" system, a black box into which a central bank can drop some cash with reasonable confidence that the box will produce a multiple of that cash in consumer deposits. The lower the reserve ratio, the higher the multiplier.

The money that people use for transactions is known to central bankers and economists as M-1—currency in circulation and checking accounts at the banks. In the 1960s, people who drew charts found it was possible to predict the level of economic activity six months in the future in the United States by measuring the quantity of transaction balances. "On the average," Milton Friedman wrote rather grandly, "a change in the rate of monetary growth produces a change in the rate of growth of nominal income about six or nine months later. . . . On the average, the effect on prices comes about six to nine months after the effect on income and output, so the total delay between a change in monetary growth and a change in the rate of inflation averages something like 12–18 months."[7] Friedman found many followers for his doctrine that the Federal Reserve System should concentrate its efforts on ways to generate a slow and steady increase in M-1.

Improvements in technology and rising interest rates changed the meaning of M-1. The Glass-Steagall Act of 1933 had prohibited banks from paying interest on "demand deposits"—checking account balances. At the large corporations, "cash management" departments grew up to find ways to earn interest on funds that would otherwise lie idle in the banks. Since they couldn't beat this tactic, the banks—starting with Morgan Guaranty in New York—decided to join it. They began to offer such customers a "sweep" service that invested their balances in Treasury bills overnight, with the money restored to them at the opening of business the next morning. M-1 was a measurement of balances the banks found when they closed their books at the close of day, there being no sensible way to determine how much money was in circulation while the maelstrom of payments was happening. So the tight control of balances by corporations affected the measurement of money, though not the real quantity of money available for trade.

Meanwhile, the gurus of "cash management" (and no small number of ordinary householders) learned to profit by the "float" inevitably generated when payment is made by giving the person being paid a claim on the assets of the person making the payment. Payment by check means that the payee receives credit from his bank—perhaps only a provisional credit, but from the point of view of those tracking M-1 it's money like any other—before the payor's debit is deducted from his bank account. In 1982, Greenwich Research Associates did a study of the *Fortune* 500 and found that 59 percent of them maintained "controlled disbursement" accounts in banks remote from their headquarters. Some even used computer-controlled check-printers that chose the company's bank furthest away from the payee to whom the check would be sent.[8] In 1995, United Airlines still paid its Los Angeles employees with checks drawn on a bank in Chicago, and its Chicago employees with checks drawn on a bank in Los Angeles, to give the company an extra day or two to earn interest on the money.

Elliott McEntee, who runs the National Automated Clearing

House Association that promotes and executes direct deposit of payroll into employees' bank accounts, says that the airlines have been the most reluctant of all employers to offer that service. But it isn't just airlines. A few years ago, I gave a lecture at the business school of the University of Southern California, in which I ridiculed this abuse of the checking system, which facilitates kiting checks and other crimes. USC being a respectable employer of lecturers gave me my check as I completed my talk. The check was drawn on a bank in Durham, North Carolina. People who write op-ed pieces for the *New York Times* find that their (trivial) payment comes in the form of a check on a bank in Syracuse, New York.

When interest rates rose, corporations were more eager to sweep their balances into overnight-earning assets, and case managers labored earnestly to expand the float. Neither of these activities had much to do with the course of business, and the relationship between M-1 and economic growth deteriorated. Meanwhile, money was leaving the banks' interest-bearing savings accounts because the Fed had set a low ceiling on the maximum interest rates banks and savings associations were permitted to pay for such accounts. To keep money from bleeding out of the banks and the savings and loan associations, the Fed had to raise the ceilings. By the 1970s interest-rate controls were obviously an anachronism: forbidden to pay market rates of interest, the banks were making gifts of everything from toasters to television sets as a reward to people who bought their certificates of deposit, and the seven august governors of the Fed had to waste time at their meetings deciding which gifts were and which gifts were not suitable.

The matter was not in fact quite that simple, and the really dangerous aspect of the situation in the 1970s was not interest-rate controls but deposit insurance. A few years later, the ceilings were finally removed and the S&Ls promptly raised their rates beyond what could legitimately be earned on the money. Rushing to get higher rates that were certain to be paid because these accounts carried the same government guarantee as lower-rate deposits, millions of Americans put their money in incompetent and dishonest S&Ls, which eventually lost hundreds of billions of dollars. The government had to buy the bad assets of these busted S&Ls at something close to the price that had been paid for them to provide enough money to pay the insured deposits.

Meanwhile, Ron Haseltine, newly installed CEO of the Five Cents (later Citizens) Savings Bank of Worcester, Massachusetts, an ingenious former Citibanker with the aggressive attitudes of his training, had found a loophole in the law prohibiting the payment of interest on demand deposits. That law had been part of the deposit insurance act, and the Massachusetts savings banks had their own state deposit insurance fund, which was in fact better funded than the Federal Deposit Insurance Corporation. Haseltine offered his depositors what he called a NOW account, for negotiable order of withdrawal, which was just a fancy name for a checking account, but paid interest on deposits. Consumers could use that account to pay any bills they wished, just as they could use checks on a commercial bank.

The Massachusetts banking regulators took Haseltine to court, and lost. Other Massachusetts and New Hampshire savings banks, which were similarly free of the legal restraint, copied Haseltine's idea, and the Federal Reserve decided to permit banks in just those two states to offer interest-bearing checking accounts. Elsewhere in the country, banks with Fed approval began to offer automatic sweep accounts, by which consumers with balances over a certain amount could get the equivalent of the deal the banks had been offering the big corporations for years—overnight movement of their surplus checking-account balances to interest-bearing accounts.

What was systemically significant about Haseltine's venture was the fact that his S&L was able to issue to its depositors checks that would be processed like normal bank checks in the normal bank clearinghouses and Federal Reserve processing centers. What made it possible for Haseltine to follow through on such an offer was that State Street Bank in Boston in effect sold him great quantities of its checks, imprinted with the State Street routing number, for him to make available to his depositors. State Street regarded all the checks drawn on the Five Cents Savings Bank as one account, and debited all of them against the account, which Haseltine replenished every day from his depositors' funds. This created a horrendous back office problem at Haseltine's savings bank, which kept its customers' checks in shoe boxes, and had to sort them by hand to debit them properly against the account on which they had been written. When the business got big enough, of course, Haseltine and his imitators could buy machines just like the banks' machines, and get the money out of the depositors' accounts more rapidly.

With savings accounts not only payable to the saver whenever he wanted the money but available for third-party payments, more people chose to keep their cash in interest-bearing accounts. M-1 lost its magic as a predictor. "I don't think there's any way we can create an M-1 today that corresponds to M-1 in 1975," Frank Morris, president of the Federal Reserve Bank of Boston, said in 1983. "But there's an unbelievable reluctance to give up the concept." At a meeting in Washington in spring 1995, former Federal Reserve chairman Paul Volcker, who had used all the Fed's tools to control the "monetary aggregates" in the late 1970s and early 1980s, asked current chairman Alan Greenspan, "Whatever became of M-1?" Greenspan nodded thoughtfully and said, "It was once the name of a pretty good rifle."

We proceed, then, to M-2, which is M-1 plus savings accounts of all sorts except retirement plans, plus money-market funds. (In 1969, Friedman as guru ruled that M-2 should not include bank certificates of deposit, because these were written with a penalty on "premature withdrawal," and were therefore expensive to use for transactions. Nevertheless, the Fed began to include them.) At best, changes in M-2 never had the tight fit with future economic activity that were once attributed to M-1, and the time lag between movements of M-2 and developments in the real economy had to be adjusted frequently—sometimes M-2 took nine months to work its magic, sometimes eighteen months, sometimes two years. Academics drew complicated graphs showing what happened with differing lag times, and Robert Weintraub explained them to Congress—an oddity of the 1970s was that the economic adviser to the House Banking Committee in its Democratic heyday was a devoted Friedmanite.

The grand efflorescence of M-2 came in the late 1970s and early 1980s, when in fact the relationships were breaking down. The Thatcher government in Britain was thoroughly monetarist and Paul Volcker as chairman of the Fed gave Friedman a whirl. I know he really did, because when he first announced that he was going to tighten the supply of money I wrote a piece saying that he was hiding behind monetarist philosophy to justify actions intended to choke down economic activity by raising interest rates. I saw him a few weeks later, and he said I'd got it wrong, he really was trying to control the monetary aggregates, though he admitted in his rough, honest way that he wasn't entirely sure what they were.

So we try M-3, which includes various institutional accounts and Eurodollar deposits of Americans in foreign branches of American banks. None of these aggregates (not even M-1) seems to respond to the Fed's efforts as the Fed would wish, and the measurements are fairly seriously imprecise, relying on seasonal adjustments that can be large and wrong. Different measures of money can actually move in different *directions* from one week to another.

The truth is that relations among monetary aggregates just collapsed in the 1970s, when there were oil shocks, serious recessions, spectacular growth in the quantity and use of dollars abroad, and major inflationary pressures. But the targeting of *some* "monetary aggregate" became the normal policy process in the United States, Britain and Germany in the second half of that decade and the first half of the 1980s. The Fed published the monetary aggregates each week on Thursday afternoon after the markets had closed. "Fed watchers" were paid fortunes by Wall Street houses to guess what the numbers would be the day before they were issued—and to interpret what they would mean in terms of changes in Fed policy immediately after they were available.

Increasingly, they didn't mean anything. In Britain, a Bank of England more committed than the Fed to a monetarist analysis switched from M-1 to M-2 to M-4 (currency, demand deposits, savings accounts at banks, wholesale deposits at banks and "building society"—S&L—shares and deposits), then to M-0, the amount of currency in circulation. Hardworking academics developed "Divisia" measures that weighted the numbers for degrees of "moneyness" to improve their forecasting accuracy six or twelve or eighteen months down the pike, or wherever the curve-fitters could fit the curve. Charles Goodhart, professor at the London School of Economics, partner in a brokerage house and adviser to the Bank of England, an aristocratic fellow and dedicated teacher, proposed Goodhart's Law, which I have condensed to read "Any monetary aggregate watched by a central bank loses significance."

2

In the United States, calculating what money is and how much of it we have is hugely complicated by the use of the dollar abroad, as a domestic money and as a denominator for trade between countries neither of which need be the United States. In the 1990s, *cash* moved abroad in great quantities—roughly $200 billion in five years—to be part of the payments systems of foreign countries. This had long been legal in Panama and Liberia, where for years there was no local paper money. In Argentina, a one-to-one equivalence of the dollar and the peso was the device by which the Menem-Cavallo government of the early 1990s put a stop to the country's runaway inflation. Increasingly in Latin America and elsewhere—in eastern Europe and the former Soviet Union especially—distrust of the local currency led to the use of dollars first as a store of value, and ultimately as a medium of exchange. It should be noted again that countries where U.S. currency piles up have in effect made interest-free loans to the United States.

Finally, there is a large demand for U.S. dollars from the criminal community worldwide. Efforts have been made to limit this use of dollars by requiring banks to report deposits or withdrawals of cash of more than $10,000 (Treasury wanted $3,000), but mules can easily be hired to take out one dollar less than the reporting total and spirit the money out to, say, St. Martin in the Caribbean, where there is a casino that uses and thus can launder a lot of cash. One of the indicia of criminal use of cash is the balance of cash transactions in the various branches of the Federal Reserve bank. Beat-up currency gets returned to these branches, which issue new currency for old. Most bills circulate for a little more than a year, and then have to be replaced. Most branches have a negative balance—that is, they print more new bills than they accept old ones, because currency gets lost or destroyed. Until the late 1980s, the branch that had a big surplus, that took in more cash than it printed, was the Fed office in Miami. In the 1990s, the Fed branch where the currency floods in has been Los Angeles, which has been so befuddled that its reports on its cash holdings have had to be corrected by tens of millions of dollars every month. The middlemen of the drug trade are no longer the Panamanians but the Mexicans.

Pumping up the American economy in 1991, the Federal Reserve increased M-1 by almost 13 percent, the fastest rate of growth in American history—but almost half the increase was in the form of cash, and the cash was leaving the country. By the end of that year, real green-and-gray dollars in circulation would have been sufficient to put $1,200 in the pockets of every man, woman and child in America. And in addition to the currency the Fed had authorized, there were uncounted sums in counterfeit U.S. dollars all over the world, especially hundred-dollar bills. By the mid-'90s, it was a pretty good idea for an American to do the modern equivalent of biting the coin—looking for tiny colored threads in the paper—before accepting a hundred-dollar bill.

In 1996, the Fed began issuing a new and more elaborately printed hundred-dollar bill and destroying old bills as they came into the hands of the district Federal Reserve banks. A very high fraction of the first millions of the new hundred-dollar bills were shipped immediately to Russia, many of them no doubt to banks controlled by the Russian criminal syndicates (but the Fed, which makes $99.96 profit for the Treasury on each $100 bill it prints, was very resistant to any efforts by the FBI to track who really got the money and how[9]). For the time being, counterfeiting is mostly other people's problem, but if the Russians develop a viable payments system based on bank deposits and checks (or bank deposits and electronic transfer)—and come to feel that they can really trust the ruble—there could be a roller-coaster ride in our monetary future as these bales of paper return. All the attention to the hundred-dollar bill obscures the fact that most Americans never see such a thing, and that of the 260 billion cash payments made in the United States in 1995, about 210 billion were under two dollars.

The invisible money, of course, makes a much bigger total and a much bigger worry, for now we move into the realm of financial *systems*. Since World War II and the decline of the British pound as a store of value, most of the world's trade has been denominated in dollars, which means that people abroad need dollars to buy the necessities of life. Commodities from oil to copper to wheat are priced in dollars and sold for dollars. Other currencies are traded through dollars as a vehicle—that is, if you have Danish kroner and you need Thai baht, you will sell your kroner for dollars and use the dollars to buy baht. Currencies also are a commodity, after all, and swapping one minor currency for another would be like bartering eggs for an easy chair.

The basic reason for the use of the dollar overseas was the strength of the American economy at the end of the Great War. More than two-fifths of the economic product of the world was created in this one country in the first years of peace. But the use of the dollar as a vehicle currency was also promoted by political factors in the period after World War II. Much of the aid the United States had given Britain and the Soviet Union in the war was on a "Lend-Lease" chassis, leaving the British and the Russians with the equivalent of war debt. We excused the British, but given the incivility of relations we were not going to excuse the Soviets. The Soviets needed dollars to buy imports, but feared that if they kept their dollar earnings in American banks, the U.S. government could seize the money. This fear was heightened when the United States froze the American assets of the British, the French, the Israelis and the Egyptians in the 1956 war over the Suez. So the Soviets kept their dollars at their own bank in Paris—and found they could generate substantial earnings on those dollars by lending them to European borrowers.

What with foreign aid, military assistance and trade deficits, the dollars piled up in Europe. Under the terms of the Bretton Woods accords of 1944, the United States was obliged to sell gold at $35 an ounce to any foreigner who came to the door with some dollars and asked for gold. In 1963, concerned about the leakage of gold from the American stockpile because the United States was running a current-account deficit with the rest of the world, the Kennedy administration decided to discourage the lending of dollars abroad. The president imposed an "interest equalization tax," designed to make foreign borrowers pay more to borrow dollars than domestic borrowers paid. The tax created a bonus for people who could get dollars overseas and lend them in Europe rather than in the United States. As there was a payments-deficit—America was buying more and investing more abroad than could be paid for by its exports and incoming investments—lots of dollars were going overseas. Soon there was a large and busy "Eurodollar" market where lenders and borrowers did business at interest rates higher than those where the dollar made its home.

By 1969, the Eurodollar market was so large (all of $15 billion!) that American banks were able to bring back enough dollars from London to evade the Fed's efforts to restrict the American money supply. Soon after becoming chairman of the Fed in 1969, Arthur Burns warned the European central banks that by putting dollars back into market instead of repatriating them for investment in the United States, they were making it more difficult not only to limit the world supply of dollars but also, because these dollars were convertible to every other currency, the supply of their own money. By the 1980s, a great deal of financial business in the United States was priced at "Libor"—the London Interbank Offered Rate—rather than at the traditional American "prime" rate set by domestic banks. In 1994, the "Eurodollar" contract, giving its purchaser the obligation to borrow (its seller an obligation to lend) a million dollars in London in three months' time, was the most heavily traded financial instrument in the world, with 105 million contracts (a notional value of $105 *quadrillion*) changing hands over the course of the year.[10]

The use of the dollar internationally created a need for a secure international information system by which banks could send and receive instructions for payments far away, and a clearing and settlement system by which transactions could be closed. The information system was set up in Brussels as the Society for Worldwide Interbank Financial Telecommunications, universally known by its acronym, SWIFT. The clearing and settlement system was established by the New York Clearing

House, which had been netting the obligations of its member banks to each other since 1853. Originally, international transactions had simply fed into the exchange of checks at the daily settlements, when each bank delivered to every other bank all the checks drawn on that bank its customers had deposited to their accounts that day. For each bank, the total of its claims on the others would be compared with their claims on it, and a net settlement—so much owed to or from the clearinghouse—would be calculated for each participant.

At the very beginning in the 1850s, each bank paid out or took home a measured sack of gold at the end of the process, but soon the banks found it more convenient to leave gold on deposit at the clearinghouse and simply adjust its ownership each day through exchanges of clearinghouse gold certificates. After 1914, the net settlement was accomplished, as it is today, by a transfer of money on the books of the Federal Reserve Bank of New York. For the domestic clearing, until the end of 1995, messengers still dragged sacks of checks through a loading dock into a pit in the low, anvil-shaped clearinghouse building on Broad Street a couple of blocks from the stock exchange, and delivered them at ten in the morning, every business day, to messengers representing the banks on which they were written. After January 1, 1996, clearing was done electronically: each bank presented to the others for calculation purposes an electronic file representing checks from their depositors. But the *settlement*, which became continuous during the day, was still in the form of the paper checks themselves, which still had to be available for return to the person who signed them. For some reason, lugging these sacks of checks has always been a job for rather eccentric people. In 1995, the favorite messenger of the clearinghouse staff was a jazz nightclub musician who every once in a while showed up wearing a yellow tux.

The separation of paper settlements and electronic settlements was begun as a convenience in 1970, when the New York

Clearing House purchased a Burroughs B3500 computer that would receive and keep track of all payments related to dollar-denominated foreign business by New York banks and their correspondent banks around the world. (For the clearinghouse, any bank with an office within 250 miles of the Empire State Building can qualify as a New York bank.) The computer was installed in the basement of the New York Clearing House, a neat little green thing with a tape-drive memory and a printer. The computer printout became part of the overall settlement at ten the next morning. The system was called CHIPS, for Clearing House Interbank Payments System.

This tail was destined to become a lot bigger than the dog. In 1973 the system moved to a pair of B6700 computers, one backing up the other; in 1974, the operating hours of the computer center were expanded to seven a.m. to midnight. That was the year Bank Herstatt, a big foreign-exchange trader, failed in Germany, and the German authorities carelessly closed it down at the close of the German banking day—which was the beginning of the banking day in New York. A number of banks had made payments out to Herstatt, or were anticipating payments in from Herstatt. Chase had $50 million of Herstatt's money, and decided to keep it. This was July, when staffs tend to be thin. On Friday night, July 28, CHIPS was unable to settle, and the system was kept open over a fearfully nervous weekend. In all countries, the language of finance was enriched by the term "Herstatt risk," which is the risk that a payment you were counting on won't be coming in because the payor is in a different time zone and is open while you are closed, closed while you are open. Once people begin to be concerned that the "cover" for the payment they have agreed to put into the machine may not arrive to make them whole, they become very reluctant to follow through on their own contracts. Before the Herstatt episode could end, the New York Fed had to send senior vice president Tom Waage to the daily morning show at the New York Clearing House to assure the member banks that if worst came to worst, the Fed would see to it that the money moved.

In 1981, a new site was acquired for the electronic operation (which, after all, did not have to be near Wall Street), the computers were upgraded again, and the CHIPS system acquired its own settlement at the end of the day, quite independent of the paper-based morning settlement that closed out *yesterday's* transactions. Same-day settlement meant the money would move a lot faster, and thus by Irving Fisher's tautology that there would be more of it.

By 1995, there were 142 domestic and foreign banks that had taken a membership in CHIPS to reap the benefits of same-day settlement, though all of them wind up settling through one of the eighteen local members. CHIPS had moved from the New York Clearing House building and was based in its own quarters in midtown Manhattan, with an identical backup plant running full-time across the Hudson River in New Jersey—a total of four full-sized Unisys A-19 systems. They were registering, clearing and arranging settlement for 200,000 transactions involving no less than $1.3 *trillion* every day. About two-thirds of this is foreign-exchange trading, another fifth is government-bond and interest-rate derivatives trading, and the rest really does relate to world trade in goods and services. By comparison, about $20 billion a day moves through the exchanges of paper checks in the old auditorium of the New York Clearing House. The average transaction on CHIPS is about $6 million; the cost is 18 cents to the payor and 18 cents to the payee, with volume discounts that can bring it as low as 13 cents each.

With the possible exception of manning the machine that lowers the graphite rods into the nuclear reactor, running the New York Clearing House is the scariest job in the world. The person who holds it is Jill Considine, a serious blonde in a tailored suit who has retained her Irish apple cheeks. Considine was working in the international operations division at Chase when these institutions were a-borning. Indeed, she was engaged in designing a proprietary international payments operation that would tie large corporate customers forever to the apron strings of the bank that shepherded them past the dragons of delay in receiving and haste in paying. "SWIFT," she recalls, "we regarded as a threat to our ChaseNet." Governor Mario Cuomo made her New York State superintendent of banking, a very big job (J.P. Morgan, Bankers Trust, and Chase are state-chartered), and on the retirement of John Lee, the gracious but outspoken westerner who had built the CHIPS operation, the big New York banks chose Considine as his most credible successor.

The way the system works is that one of the 142 CHIPS member banks (often their large corporate customers or correspondent banks, through a communications node supplied by the bank) sends a message to CHIPS to pay another bank on the system. The code on the message will enable the receiving bank to identify the account to which the money should be paid, but a parallel SWIFT message will convey additional security. The payments message is stored in the CHIPS computer for execution at the settlement that evening, and can be accessed while waiting by the bank to which the payment is to be made. Each bank sets a limit on the total size of the payments it is prepared to receive in this way from each of the other banks in the system, and this limit can be changed at any time. The total of all the limits applied to this bank by all other participants is the total of net payments this bank will be allowed to have in the system at any given time. Each bank gets a message every morning on the size of its debit cap for that day. All messages must be authenticated with a security key supplied for that day by CHIPS. When connections are broken between a bank and CHIPS, the bank makes a telephone call to CHIPS and CHIPS reactivates the line—nobody on the outside has authorization to enter the system.

During the course of the day, each participant can look into the computer and see the status of the accounts for each participating bank. If a bank seems to be getting in trouble, others in the system can cut back on its limits. In 1994, the big Spanish bank Banesto, crippled by stupid investments and loans to insiders, looked endangered, and CHIPS members began cutting back on what they would agree to receive at a clearing still some hours away. Then the Bank of Spain stepped up to the plate and announced that it would stand behind Banesto's debits, and the door was reopened. This process of cutting back on the extent to which any bank can endanger the system is known in the trade as "graceful degradation."

At four-thirty in the afternoon, CHIPS closes to new entries and the computers tally how much each participant has promised to pay and how much other banks have promised to pay it. If the figure is positive, a message goes to the bank asking whether it will receive a certain sum in settlement. If the figure is negative, the message tells the bank how much it is to wire to the clearing-house. Each of the eighteen clearing members has a number of correspondents who pay CHIPS and receive from CHIPS through its facilities. Within five minutes, the system has received confirmations that the deficit banks will pay and the surplus banks will receive according to the numbers supplied. At five o'clock, CHIPS opens a "settlement account" in its own name at the Federal Reserve Bank of New York, and instructs the member banks to wire the money to pay their debts to this CHIPS account at the Fed. When the Fed confirms that the payments have been received, CHIPS instructs the Fed to make payments from this balance to the banks that are to receive money, and orders the account closed with its zero balance.

In many clearinghouses, there are arrangements by which participants that haven't delivered the cash or the securities can borrow to allow the settlement to take place—indeed, J.P. Morgan for years made its largest single slice of profits as the lender to the Euroclear system in Brussels, which it owned and operated. At CHIPS, it's got to be cash on the barrelhead, though the eighteen clearing banks may make loans to their correspondents if they wish. "The Fed demands that we be self-contained," says executive vice president John R. Mohr, who was at Irving Trust setting up systems that would permit all banks on the SWIFT system to work through Irving when Considine was fighting for the Chase brand. "We're not going to demand credit from them so we can close."

Failure of any participant to pay what the computer says it owes will trigger a dozen telephone calls, one to the bank that represents this participant at the clearing, one to the Fed to ask that the account remain open a while longer, and ten to the other banks to explain the source of the delay. The defaulting bank has one hour to make the payment. Failure to pay would trigger the opposite of graceful degradation, which is called "big bang." There have been several threatened big bangs—Herstatt in 1974; the failure of Banco do Brasil to make a CHIPS payment in December 1982, which kept the system open till Chemical and Citibank agreed to lend the Brazilians money late at night; October 20, 1987, when FedWire collapsed in Chicago for two hours and banks that weren't receiving the cash payments they had expected stopped making their CHIPS entries; the invasion of Kuwait; and the World Trade Center bombing, because ten members had their offices there (staff came and worked out of the CHIPS office, using CHIPS's own telecommunications).

In fact, however, the system never has failed. Technically, its record of zero downtime for the entire year 1993 is unique in the history of large computers. But the possible failure of the system is never far from Considine's mind. When she took over, she instituted the practice of running a disaster scenario on a Saturday morning once every three months. All around the world, the operations people of the big banks come to work to play a simulation game with the New York Clearing House and test the fail-safe systems against power failures, the emergence of a hacker into the computerized communications, the need to reconstitute files, the failure of a big bank, or a revolution that closes the banks in a major country.

In New York, there is a complete backup system running in the main office, with two complete systems running in New Jersey. Everybody who has a job in New York also has a desk in New Jersey, in case he might have to move for a while: doesn't take much; a few dozen people do all the work. Everything is written at least three times to the memory disks. NYNEX and New Jersey Bell have special protocols by which CHIPS can switch messages from New York. Everything is fiber-optic. Both sites have battery power to keep the machines going for some hours if necessary, and New Jersey has a diesel generator with a loading dock for receiving fuel shipments. Before the Bank for International Settlements in Basel proclaimed its "Lamfalussy Rules" about how to make clearing operations safe, CHIPS already exceeded all of them.

The most dicey day CHIPS ever had was the Tuesday after Martin Luther King Day in 1994, with orders stacked high from a CHIPS holiday when the rest of the world had kept doing business in dollars. It had been the coldest winter in decades. On the floor above the CHIPS New York installation, the water pipes had frozen during the weekend and then burst as the heat came on, cascading water onto the computers. The Halon gas protection was triggered at once, preserving the machines, and the staff switched the telecommunications net to New Jersey, a process that took about five minutes. Because of the enormous electricity demands in the freezing weather, the power companies were providing erratic voltage, and CHIPS was plugged into the diesel generators. But the generators had only a few hours' supply of oil, and the loading dock where fuel could be received was frozen in. CHIPS made it with half an hour to spare.

"Three hundred and fourteen thousand transactions and 1.8 trillion dollars processed without a hitch at a backup site," says Jill Considine wonderingly. These numbers give pause in another respect, too. Overseas transactions in dollars built up to such an extent on a day when the American banking system was shut that they created a processing volume building up to 30 percent of America's annual gross domestic product. When the Federal Reserve is really trying to move interest rates and influence what banks do, it may buy or sell as much as $3 billion of Treasury paper in the open market. King Day led to a day when mostly foreign-based banks traded *hundreds of times* as many dollars as the Fed was likely to employ for domestic monetary intervention. Any big bank inconvenienced by the Fed's actions could dip into this immense golden stream and meet its reserve requirements by repatriating a tiny spoonful of it. How do you measure money supply in the United States?

"There is a risk," Federal Reserve governor Henry C. Wallich said in congressional testimony in 1979, "that, over time, as the Euro-currency market expands relative to domestic markets, control over the aggregate volume of money may increasingly slip from the hands of the central banks."[11]

3

But the real challenge to the Fed's control of the money supply would come domestically—from the brokerage house of Merrill Lynch. Donald Regan, who was Merrill's CEO, had come to the firm from the Marine Corps, and his first important job at Merrill had been the redirection of an over-the-counter department that had been seriously tainted by scandal. He believed in management control (as Nancy Reagan would find to her considerable irritation when he became chief of staff to her husband), and he did not like the idea that his business was dependent on a few hundred individuals who could take their customers out the door and down the elevator and into another brokerage house whenever they wished. Merrill became a corporation in 1971, the year Regan became its chief, and he began a long quest for some *product* the firm might offer, which would tie the customer to Merrill rather than to his "customer's man."

One way to tie the customer more closely would be to expand the services—offer real estate and insurance brokerage and financial management, with the customer's man as merely a coordinator for the others at the firm. The idea of the "financial supermarket" comes from Don Regan. But the competition in all these areas was going to be stiff. Regan hired Stanford Research Institute to do him some studies on products Merrill could offer. And SRI, at the inspiration of *its* consultant Andrew Kahr, came up with the idea of a brokerage account that would act like a bank account, with checks that could be drawn against an interest-bearing money market fund, which could in turn be replenished by borrowing on margin from the customer's securities holdings.

This would not be the first mutual fund against which checks could be written. The pioneers of the money market funds had very brilliantly structured their invention so that the shareholder's earnings were automatically reinvested and expressed not by an increase in the *value* of each share, which would remain pegged forever at one dollar, but in the *number* of shares held. Thus there was no problem extinguishing a number of shares matching the number of dollars for which a check was written. Fidelity Fund in Boston, using the services of the same bank that had helped Ron Haseltine give checks to the customers of his S&L, had stepped in ahead of Merrill. But Fidelity did not want the expense of processing a lot of checks, and had limited withdrawals to $1,000 or more.

Customers of brokerage houses often have cash in their brokerage accounts, because dividends have been paid on stocks held in the firm's name, or a stock has been sold and the receipts have not yet been reinvested. Prior to Merrill's launch of its "Cash Management Account," that money, which was not a "deposit" (the same Glass-Steagall Act that forbade banks to deal in securities forbade brokers to take "deposits"), came under the heading of "free customer balance." Operationally, that meant a broker was free to use his customers' money for his own purposes without paying anything for it. Hurd Baruch, a former SEC general counsel, reported in his book *Wall Street: Security Risk* that on July 31, 1970, Merrill had enjoyed the free use of $338 million of customer balances, which was $48 million more than the book value of the partnership—plus another $83 million which customers had paid for stock not yet delivered. The total capital of all Wall Street firms was $3.8 billion, and the Wall Street firms as a group had the free use of $5.3 billion of customers' money. "Wall Street," Baruch wrote, "runs on Main Street's money."[12]

The decision that took courage on Regan's part was to abandon the income on Main Street's money, which may have been as much as 40 percent of his profits in the bad year 1974, and start a money market mutual fund into which the customer's free balances would be swept, automatically. The public posture of the brokerage firms had always been that they would like to pay interest on that money, but, gee, the Glass-Steagall Act forbade the payment of interest on deposits, and these balances were like deposits. Now they wouldn't be deposits anymore; they would be money market mutual fund shares.

But customers could participate in this new system only if they signed up for a "margin account" that allowed them to borrow against the value of the stock they already owned. The margin account had been used almost exclusively as a source of loans to customers to purchase other securities. Now it would provide cash to cover any check that overdrew the customer's money market fund. Margin accounts were much more profitable to the firm than ordinary brokerage accounts. A customer who is "on margin" must keep his stock in "street name," and gives his broker the free use of all the shares in his account—and the broker lends that stock, for a fee, to short-sellers who need it to complete their transactions. The income from fees for lending stock would be greater than the income from the free use of customer balances.

All this was going to be extremely difficult to do, and costly. Paul Stein, the Merrill Lynch sales manager who had to run it when the planners had gone home, said he spent a good deal of his time begging suppliers "to invent something new in computers." Traditionally, brokerage houses opened their clients' accounts only on days when the client did business. Now Merrill's systems people would have to produce machines and programs that would run through *all* customer accounts daily to keep the accounting straight on everybody who was writing checks or using credit cards with the company's traditional bull on them. The cost for programmers, Stein reported, was a hundred man-years of time between Regan's enthusiastic decision to go ahead with CMA and the launch in 1979.

Merrill's checks would have to be cleared through the usual banking process. Even more important than the checking account would be a credit card, which could serve as a debit card generating a reduction in the customer's money market fund to pay the immediate bill or a customary credit card that would generate debt—but debt to be carried at the interest rate on margin accounts, *much* lower than the interest rate the banks charged on credit card balances. The firm was big enough to start its own credit card processing company, but it made much more sense to use the credit cards owned by proprietors who had already signed up the merchants to accept their card. The three finalists for the contract were Valley National Bank in Arizona (a MasterCard processor), the American Express subsidiary First Data Resources (with which Merrill could offer an American Express card) and Banc One (then still City National Bank and Trust, a Visa processor) in Columbus, Ohio.

Tom Chrystie, Regan's vice president for planning, later said that Banc One won the contest partly because Visa was about to spend $10 million on its brand name. He liked the idea of hitchhiking on their publicity. Anyway, he said, he and Bob Potts, the bank's chairman, had done an Outward Bound white-water rafting trip together on the Green River, and "I thought it would be fun to see him again." Banc One president John B. McCoy was then notable in large part as the son of Banc One chairman emeritus John G. McCoy, but in reality he was at the beginning of a process that would see him take his bank from a local Columbus, Ohio, operation to the seventh largest in the country. He said he thought his people had won the Merrill contract because they proposed important modifications in the Merrill program: "Merrill had a certain naivete about what banking was. I think we really won it by changing some of their concepts."

Among the things Banc One contributed was the idea that the entire CMA account had to be processed through the Visa system rather than the bank. Only Merrill, not the customers, would have an account at the bank. The checks the customer received would carry Banc One's magnetic ink character recognition code at the bottom of the check. Those numbers told other banks and the Fed to debit these checks from Banc One's clearing account. Then there were two additional numbers in the MICR line, which told the Banc One computer to spit them out to the Visa department when they showed up in the check-sorting machines. Every morning at six-thirty, the Merrill computer updated for the Banc One computer the outstanding balances in the individual CMA accounts, calculating margin values based on the market close the night before. With this information, Banc One would approve or reject Visa queries, accept or bounce CMA checks.

The Merrill account at Banc One started and ended each day with a zero balance. By one o'clock in the afternoon, the Banc One Visa department had a number for the total debit to the Banc One clearing and Visa accounts over the past twenty-four hours, and a telephone call went off to New York. Merrill then wired off a payment that cleared its account. Merrill paid Banc One 9 cents a Visa item and 11 cents a check in the early days, diminishing on a sliding scale as the volume grew. The price to customers was $28 a year.

Merrill rolled out CMA in three markets—Columbus, Atlanta and Denver—in autumn 1977, and it didn't do much except outrage the Colorado State Banking Board, which brought suit to force Merrill to apply for a charter if it wanted to stay "in the banking business." The Oregon superintendent of banks, John Olin, publicly announced that so far as he was concerned CMA looked like a duck, walked like a duck, and quacked like a duck. He was empowered to regulate ducks, and he was going to make rules for this one. Not seeking a fight, Merrill moved Oregon to late in its list. In Utah, the local bankers' association backed legislation to prevent the introduction of any brokerage account with checking privileges, but Merrill's friends in the legislature blocked them with a ruse.

For the first couple of years, in any event, CMA did little business, mostly because the customers' men hated it. The reasons given were that placing customer money in money market mutual funds paid them no commissions; the real reason was that the new account tied the customer much more closely to the firm rather than to the customer's "account executive." The reps were placated in part by the discovery that some of their customers really had much larger holdings than they had realized—and were now doing all their business through Merrill because their dividends were quickly put to work in the money market funds and because they liked the idea of having value in margin accounts they could draw on at will. Customers' men also found that the availability of this original service brought new customers walking in the door—some to open the first brokerage account they'd ever had.

Jack Armstrong, a mountainous former football coach who ran the Merrill Lynch office in Morristown, New Jersey, noted that "There's an old saw in the brokerage business, that there is no new money in the stock market, just old money that moves from one broker to another. This account gave us the first time we'd seen new money in quantity. In this business, the rule is that you never have anything nobody else has. Now it's not true anymore."

At the beginning, people didn't use CMA as a substitute for a bank account. The most frequently written check was one to American Express, exploiting the fact that the Amex card did not charge interest and thus could be delayed longest without penalty. Some of the uses to which the CMA credit facilities were put were pretty spectacular. An antiques dealer at a show in Atlanta caused a considerable stir when he drew $50,000 on a Visa card, after an officer of the Trust Company of Georgia got personal assurances from Banc One president McCoy in Columbus that there was indeed that much and more backing for this card. The first major national publicity CMA received was an article I wrote in *Fortune* in October 1980, when the account was still available in less than two-thirds of the firm's 391 offices.[13]

I wandered around Washington to see what the banking regulators had to say about this remarkable intrusion on the banks' turf. In summer 1977, the Fed, still chaired by Arthur Burns, had given Merrill a letter to the effect that no existing regulation blocked the house from what it wished to do, but there were no promises about the future. Two months later, a letter arrived from the Fed asking Merrill how the launch had gone, and Merrill sent the information—and never heard from the Fed again.

Consulted in mid 1980, chairman Paul Volcker growled that "this is one of those things where when it's new everybody says it's experimental and too small to make any difference, and then when it becomes a problem it's so big you don't dare interfere with it." At the Office of the Comptroller of the Currency, who was then John Heimann, people were positively enthusiastic. Asked whether the program as I outlined it had raised any questions in his mind, one deputy said, "Yes. Can I open a CMA in Washington?" Chuck Muckenfuss, Heimann's general counsel, said cleverly, "After a generation of the government monetizing its debts, the private sector has learned to monetize its assets."

By 1982, most of the larger brokerage houses had copied Merrill, and there were the first accounts that permitted people to write checks against their equity in their home—a kind of borrowing that Congress would greatly encourage in the 1991 tax act that took tax deductibility away from interest on all consumer credit except home mortgages. Suddenly there were hundreds of billions of dollars of purchasing power available to consumers on signature.

CMA and its imitators are in many ways a parallel banking system. Dividend payments go to money market mutual fund shares instead of into the banks, and their recipients write checks against them that do not draw down their bank account balances. At some point, today, all payments do go through the banking system—but we measure the money only in the middle of the night. And it is by no means clear that in the twenty-first century the payments *will* go through the banks. In 1995, says Merrill vice-chairman George Kenny, more people wrote checks on Bank of America accounts than on any other bank's accounts, Citibank came in second—and Merrill Lynch CMA customers came third. The relationship with Banc One is long gone, and these checks now process through an S&L Merrill owns, mostly through the Federal Reserve processing system. But if somebody else could do it cheaper, Merrill would be interested.

3 / Paying Bills

*This is an industry in its electronic form where there are
clearly returns to scale . . . and the definition of the marketplace is totally altered by electronics.*

—John Reed, chairman of Citicorp, 1996

Twenty-plus years ago, I tracked a check of mine for $27.33
from Piccozzi's gas station, on Shelter Island at the eastern
end of New York's Long Island, to my branch of what was then
the Manufacturers Hanover Trust Company, in a famous Skid-
more Owings & Merrill three-story glass-walled building on
Forty-third Street and Fifth Avenue in Manhattan.

Jake Piccozzi made a package of my check and a score of
others, to create, as his adding machine tape showed, a total
deposit of $396.30. His assistant Gene Tybaert, first marshal of
the American Legion's Memorial Day parade, took the check to
the center of the island and the office of Valley Bank.

At the bank, Mrs. Harriet Case looked at the checks and saw
that they were properly endorsed, gave Tybaert one of the dupli-
cate deposit slips, and stored the Piccozzi deposit with the other
deposits to await the arrival of—

Pete Pearson, a retired state parks guard, who came at three-thirty and picked up all the Shelter Island deposits in his own battered Plymouth and carried them over the ferry to the bank's East Hampton branch, which did all the processing for Valley's branches at the end of Long Island.

Here, in a basement room in a mock Colonial building on Main Street, Carol Salisbury ran the checks and the deposit slips through a National Cash Register "proof" machine the size of an upright piano, with a keyboard she punched to print onto the check, in the lower right-hand corner, in machine-readable magnetic ink, the amount for which it was written. The check was already encoded in its lower left-hand corner with an MICR (magnetic ink character recognition) number that gave the code numbers for the city, the bank and the branch of that bank where I had my account, plus my account number. Salisbury also ran the deposit slip itself through the proof machine, registering the amount deposited prefaced by the numbers 01 to tell the machines to treat this item as a plus rather than a minus in the depositor's account. The checks and slips ran through Salisbury's machine at the rate of about fifty a minute, which is very fast (the average proof operator does less than two thousand an hour). The fingers of her left hand danced on the keys. This MICR system, which today seems to have been handed down by Moses from Pisgah, was less than twenty years old in 1973; people still remembered the handwork it had displaced.

At five-thirty in the afternoon, Walter Denbeck, a moonlighting A&P manager, picked up the gunny sacks of checks and slips and tossed them into his station wagon. He picked up another bunch of sacks at Valley's East Islip branch and delivered them all to yet another courier, Hank Schaffer, a post office clerk driving his family's four-door sedan, who took the lot to Valley's processing center in the then-new Green Acres shopping mall in Valley Stream, halfway to New York, where Valley Bank had an operations center in the basement.

The checks arrived in Green Acres at 7:55, and presently made the first of what would be many passes through reader-sorter machines about the size of a subcompact car, moving checks on conveyor belts past magnetic heads at a rate of about ten thousand an hour. (In 1996, some reader-sorters can process *eighty thousand* an hour.) The machines took the information off the MICR lines and sent it to be preserved both on magnetic tape and on paper manifolds that ran at freight-train speed through laser printers, meanwhile conveying the check itself to one of thirteen slots that would determine its next destination.

Some checks were "on us" items that the bank would charge against its own customers' accounts; they would stay in the processing room. Separating out and retaining the "on us" items remains the most profitable activity of the operations department, especially if the computer system has been programmed to integrate the wholesale and retail sides of the bank. Bank of America is believed to keep within the bank, flowing through B of A's computers and nowhere else, 80 percent of all payments to public utilities in the state of California, which means that the bank's operation expenses are lower and it can offer the utility companies faster access to their revenues. "Shareholder value," says Mark Burns, who was manager of Chase Bank's joint ventures with Microsoft, "lies in the elimination of these horrendous back offices."

Other checks in my packet were drawn on other Long Island banks, and these would go to the Federal Reserve's regional check-processing center beside the Long Island Expressway in Jericho. Others, like mine, bundled and rubber-banded together with the adding machine tape that totaled them as a "cash letter" for credit to Valley National, were stacked on their edge in boxes about five inches high and three feet long. These were picked up at nine o'clock that night and carried in the backseat of a moonlighting postman's Mustang to an assembly point in Syosset, where all Long Island banks dropped their boxes of checks into the same Purolator truck, for delivery to the main office of the Federal Reserve Bank of New York in its Florentine palazzo near Wall Street.

Here in the processing center that occupied the whole of the fourth floor (one end glassed off to maintain the temperature and humidity conditions demanded by the reader-sorters and tape machines), the cash letters were verified and the banks given their credit, and the checks were run through the reader-sorters yet again, and again, to separate them out according to the bank on which they were drawn. A little before ten o'clock the next morning, all the boxes and all the checks and all the cash letters were trucked the half mile from the Fed to the little clearinghouse building on Broad Street, where they joined similarly boxed checks and cash letters from the then-twelve New York Clearing House member banks that "settled" with each other (for themselves and on behalf of their correspondents) through this institution. Citibank messengers, I noted, wore uniforms; Morgan delivered and picked up checks in a splendid steamer trunk; most of the rest dressed like construction laborers, and stacked their boxes in canvas bins that hung from frames on wheels.

On December 6, 1973, the day after the night when I tracked my check for $27.33, the total amount of the cash letters banks presented to each other with the checks at the clearinghouse was $8.645 billion. Each bank compared the amount the other banks' cash letters declared it owed on its depositors' checks with the amount owed to it by those other banks for its cash letters on them. Subtracting the one from the other, the bank declared that it owed (or was owed) so much in total *to or by the clearinghouse*. A process of "multilateral netting" vastly simplified and reduced the actual task of moving money from one bank to another.

Barbara Gomez, whom clearinghouse officers considered the quickest and most accurate adder in New York, quickly totaled the pledges and claims, which "proofed"—that is, the numbers were right. It should be noted that in 1973, in a world already heavily computerized, this final, crucial activity remained hand-work. The clearinghouse proof sheet then went to the New York Fed, which credited the gainers among the clearinghouse banks for the net their depositors had collected through these checks, and debited the losers for the bills their depositors had paid with checks on them. Any checks in the bundle that were rubber would bounce back to the clearinghouse that afternoon, triggering credits to the bank that bounced them and debits to the banks that now had to reverse the process I had observed the night before. Then and now, something approaching nine-tenths of one percent of the checks processed in the United States are returned "dishonored," most frequently for "insufficient funds." Fees for bounced checks can run as high as $25 in American banks. At most banks, the fees for bounced checks are in proportion to cost the most profitable single activity in the business. The customer doesn't complain because he feels guilty about bouncing the check. This business, incidentally, has a lot of geographical variation. Paul Bauer of the Federal Reserve Bank of Cleveland reports that in Los Angeles one of every 34 items is returned; in Montana, it's only one in every 192 items.

Meanwhile, my 1973 check went to the Manny Hanny processing center in the enormous tower of 55 Water Street, a couple of blocks from the clearinghouse, where it passed through several more reader-sorter machines to debit my account in the bank, and then to find a slot in the pocket devoted entirely to checks written on my branch, and then again to sort it in a pre-established order of accounts in that branch. Half a dozen additional people handled it here, before it was trucked up to Forty-third Street and Fifth Avenue, and carried on the elevator to the third floor, where a young lady with a computer-generated list of checks on which payment has been stopped and accounts that have insufficient funds to pay out the arriving checks segregated out these rejects to make sure the checks were not stamped "PAID" in the one last machine, a microfilm recorder through which all the other checks ran.

My check, found good, was photographed for the bank's records and then placed back in the box with the others, sorted to come to the front of the stack in a sequence that matched the order of the little file drawers in the great row of dark green metal cabinets that ran the length of the wall in the big bullpen. There one of several file clerks who divided the work picked it up and dropped it into the long, low, narrow drawer, a "till" for checks to be returned to me at the end of the month. My signature was on the lid of the till, so she could compare it with the signature on the check, but in fact she didn't bother.

Among the footnotes to this narrative which are most interesting today, more than twenty years later, is the identity of the three vice presidents for operations whose views I quoted then. Bob Lipp of Chemical commented that "The operations division had been considered the ass-end of the bank. When you brought in professional management, the benefits were tremendous—big dollars." Lipp himself would be stolen from Chemical by Sanford Weill, to become the number two man in Weill's giant financial conglomerate, which combined Travelers Insurance; the brokerage house Smith Barney; and Commercial Credit Corporation. The other two were John Reed, who would become chairman of Citicorp, and Barry Sullivan of Chase Manhattan, who would become chairman of First Chicago.

2

"For all this work," I noted after I described the lady putting my check to bed in its till, "neither I nor Jake Piccozzi had been charged a penny." This was a little misleading. Others less well established than ourselves would have had to pay cash, for by 1973 most banks had begun to impose a monthly charge for "account maintenance" and a fee per check unless you kept the right size "minimum balance" in your account to qualify for "free checking." And of course there was no free anything; by keeping that balance in a checking account, Jake and I incurred what economists call an opportunity cost: we could have had the money out there working for us, but instead the bank had it out there working for the bank. In 1973, however, it was still illegal for banks to pay interest on "demand deposits."

Banks did not cost out very precisely what they made on the demand deposit money, and the services probably cost more than the bank earned by lending that money. The theory, by no means wrong, was that people were more likely to finance their car or their home with the bank where they did their checking, buy their traveler's checks at their bank when they went on trips, and so forth. And the Fed didn't charge for its work as a check-processor: that was bundled into the group of services it offered to members, who had to put 3 percent of their capital into stock in their district Federal Reserve Bank, and keep 10 to 15 percent of their deposit liabilities sterile as a liquidity reserve of cash in their vaults or on interest-free deposits at the Fed itself. Even the collection of checks from the other end of the country was free to Fed members, though it put the Fed to great expense, chartering aircraft to fly these pieces of paper from one city to another.

Only members of the Fed had to keep reserves there. Nationally chartered banks had to be Fed members; state-chartered banks, subject to (usually lower) reserve requirements set in state laws, did not. Most of the money was in nationally chartered banks, but most of the banks were and are still state-chartered. Big state-chartered banks like J.P. Morgan and Bankers Trust were of course members of the Fed, but smaller ones were not.

The way the game played was that nonmember banks left their reserves with their correspondent banks in the cities, which were Fed members. The correspondents handled the clearance of the checks the nonmembers' depositors wrote or received, either through the 130-odd nongovernmental big-city clearinghouses or through the free services of the Fed. And they got the use of the smaller banks' reserves—plus, of course, first grab at any Fed Funds the smaller banks had available for sale. They gave the smaller banks' important customers the keys to their cities when the CEOs visited, took participations in the loans too big for the smaller banks to handle by themselves and helped with securities trading. The calculation of benefits from the use of the reserves against costs of services performed was something the big-city banks did on an ad hoc basis. As rates rose in the 1970s, the smaller banks wanted interest on their reserves, and mostly the big banks paid them. The fact that the smaller banks thought they got bargains from the bigger banks was illustrated by the gradual, continuing withdrawal of banks from Fed membership, at a rate of about one-half of one percent of the total deposits in the system, every year.

Under Arthur Burns, a Republican but a strong centralizer, the Fed tried to get Congress to require *all* banks to keep reserves at the Fed, whether they were members or not. The big-city banks objected to the loss of corespondent business. Burns was disliked in the Congress because he lectured people (he had been a college professor), but when Paul Volcker took over in 1979, the Fed's needs began to receive more serious attention. Henry Reuss, chairman of the House Banking Committee, was about to retire from Congress, and was building his monument in the form of the Depository Institutions Deregulation and Monetary Control Act. A serious-minded Democrat and a former banker who looked as though he should be wearing a celluloid collar, Reuss really and truly understood everything said on both sides of the issue, and he brokered a deal by which everyone would have to keep reserves at the Fed—but the Fed would have to make its payments services available to all banks and S&Ls, and charge at least its real costs, permitting private banks to compete for the check-processing, clearing and settlement business.

Compelled to compete for business, the district Feds developed marketing strategies and elaborate, beautifully printed brochures, most of which suggested that after all you were a lot safer doing business with the Fed. I made fun of this in a chapter of a book called *The Money Bazaars*. Paul Volcker, then chairman of the Fed, generously found time in 1983 to read proofs on some of the book, and complained to me that I was maligning his district Feds—they were *not* marketing their services in a Madison Avenue way. I sent him some of the material I had collected, and he called. "They told me they weren't going to do this," he said rather plaintively.

Volcker assigned his sidekick and fishing companion Gerry Corrigan, already president of the Federal Reserve Bank of Minneapolis, to make a study of whether the district Feds had played fair and square in their competition for check-processing business—especially, whether they had abused their essentially zero cost for their machinery and their exemption from federal income tax. Corrigan said there were no problems. A General Accounting Office study at about the same time said there were few problems. The big banks, especially PNC of Pittsburgh, which had gone after this business pretty hard, said the Fed had pushed them around.

All of us—Fed, banks, GAO, myself—missed the long-range significance of what the 1980 act had mandated. *Banks* were going to find it hard to compete with the Fed, because the Fed kept its hand on their throats and was quite prepared to squeeze to preserve its own full-time-equivalent employees at the district banks. But the invitation to compete with the Fed for payments system business was not limited to banks. "Non-banks," from Visa and MasterCard to FiServ in Wisconsin, First Data Resources in Omaha, ADP (Automatic Data Processing) in New Jersey, EDS (Electronic Data Systems) in Dallas, could offer aspects of payments services to banks that found the Fed expensive or unresponsive. FiServ, FDR and EDS among them now handle about half as many checks as the Fed, every day.

Eventually, these services would take over much of the payments-processing business—initially just credit card payments, then direct deposit of payroll through the Automated Clearing House (ACH—mostly an unloved and ill-managed subsidiary of the Fed, but in some places an independent operation), then automated teller machine (ATM operations and networks), then, starting in 1995, chunks of the checking business, which firms like Toys "R" Us learned to convert checks to ACH entries at the cash register. K Mart has purchased twenty thousand cash registers that can read MIRC codes.

Finally, in the mid 1990s, the big banks found their own way around the Fed. A National Clearing House Association launched by Huntington Banks in Columbus, Ohio, developed a system by which member banks can make an electronic presentment of a cash letter—the total of checks on this "receiving" bank deposited to the accounts of depositors in that "sending" bank—directly to other member banks anywhere in the country, through NCHA. By eleven o'clock in the morning Eastern time, all the claims are filed in the NCHA computer. By twelve-forty-five, the "receiving banks" confirm their receipt of the real cash letters, and NCHA informs each member of its net position in the settlement. By one-thirty, those whose depositors wrote checks for more money than they collected will pay what their depositors owe to an account at the Federal Reserve Bank of Cleveland, which on instruction from NCHA will send the requisite payments to the banks whose depositors collected more than they paid. By mid 1996, NCHA was processing transactions at a rate of 4 million a day for 160 banks—including most of the big guys east of the Rockies: Chase, Citibank, NationsBank, Bank One, First Union, Crestar, Boatmen's, CoreStates, Fleet, and Barnett.

The NCHA system rests on the efficiency of an air courier operation, U.S. Check, a company created by Gerald Mercer, a compact, handsome forty-plus former stunt pilot gone commercial. U.S. Check operates two dozen Learjets and more than fifty propeller aircraft out of and into forty airports every night from a major hub in Columbus, Ohio, with lesser hubs in seven other cities. All the banks send their checks in heavy plastic bags tagged with preprinted Tevlar airbills, each with its own barcoded tracking number. A crowd of a dozen strong kids—most of them Ohio State college students—push large bins, orange bags on a steel frame, out on the tarmac as the planes wheel off the runway, and load them with the incoming bags. They run the sacks into a hangar that is used as a maintenance shop during the day, plane-repair stuff on shelves along the walls, and throw them onto a conveyor belt about eighty feet long.

Another fifty of the strong kids stand on either side of the conveyor belt, grab the bags destined for the cities they service, and hurl them into transparent plastic containers already tagged for destination. The first lot of bags arrives from nine-fifteen to nine-fifty, and everything is sorted, weighed, back on the planes and out of Columbus by ten o'clock. Another bunch of planes comes in starting around eleven-thirty, and a final (largest) group, most of them on their second run to Columbus this night, shows up at four-thirty to get its parcels sorted by destination and out by five-thirty. With a five-thirty departure from Columbus on a Learjet, U.S. Check can guarantee delivery anywhere on the West Coast (given decent weather) by eight Pacific time—which allows the receiving bank to put the cash letter through the machine and confirm to NCHA that it has received for payment checks in the amount the sending bank has claimed.

The Fed is doing the same sort of thing through its Interdistrict Transportation System for "transit items" that move from one of its forty check-processing territories to another, renting forty-seven aircraft every night—and, says U.S. Check, subsidizing its suppliers by about $8 million a year. The Democratic staff of the House Banking Committee found a speech by a Fed first vice president complaining that thanks to U.S. Check, "the ITS operates under more public scrutiny than is fair or reasonable. . . .

Concerns over our management of ITS have to date stymied any consideration of pricing options that might legitimately promote expanded use of ITS by large volume check shippers."[1]

With all respect to all involved, this entire procedure is nonsense. A cash management guru for McDonnell Douglas in St. Louis may decide that he can get an extra day's use of the money by paying his employees with checks drawn on a bank in Lewiston, Maine. The St. Louis bank that receives the check from the McDonnell Douglas vice president who deposits it turns it over to the U.S. Check truckdriver who hustles it to the airport so it can get to Columbus in time to make the flight to Lewiston that will get the bank credit on it by tomorrow at two. This Bugs Bunny-and-Doc game would be silly if it were free, but it costs money.

In fact, the question of who processes checks and how they are processed ought not to be asked at all, because the checking system—all 65 billion checks a year, and counting—should be a dodo in an age of data processing. Europeans for years have paid their domestic bills through a "giro" run either by the post office or a private consortium of banks. The mortgage holder, the plumber, the doctor, the telephone company—all send bills that include the sender's bank account number. The householder adds up the total of the bills, writes a check for that amount, and tosses it all over the counter at the post office or in the private giro, which subtracts that one check from the payor's account and parcels out the money to the payees. In Switzerland in 1992, 81 percent of all bill payment was by such "credit transfer"; in Sweden, 77 percent; in the Netherlands, 61 percent; in Germany, 50 percent; and in the United States, 1.8 percent.[2]

Jill Considine of the New York Clearing House likes to tell the story of the American banker who was seconded for a two-year tour of duty in Belgium, opened a bank account at a local bank, and asked for a two-year supply of checks. A week later he received a call that his checks were ready, went in for them, and was handed a book of forty checks—"because we thought you should have some extras."

American Express had plans in 1995 to introduce the equivalent of a giro in the form of a plan called "One Check," which would involve the power company, the telephone company, the mortgage holder, the gas company, the TV cable company, the city for water and sewer service—all the people who send repetitive monthly bills. "It was hard to get started," said Richard Pickering, a young systems designer who was in charge of the project, "because there are eighty-three gas and electric companies, each with its own billing protocol." Under the plan, the companies would transmit their bills electronically to Amex, which would print them in a standard format and send them all in a single envelope to the householder, who would send Amex a single check for the total. At the end of the year, Amex would send a record of all the bills paid, for tax or other purposes. The cost would be $1 a month, saving a customer with five such accounts $1.60 in postage (Amex would provide a postage-paid envelope) and an average of $1.00 in check fees. The billers would save their postage, too, communicating the bills to Amex electronically, and they would save processing costs by receiving the payments electronically, by direct deposit to their bank accounts.

This project was exhaustively researched for four years. The survey results said that a tenth of American households would buy the service early, and more later. (Some people would never be interested: "There's a retired population," Pickering said, "that goes to a storefront office to pay the utility bills, it's a social interaction, a highlight of the month." In most states, public utilities are required by law to maintain storefront offices or arrangements with banks so people can pay in person. The banks want out; they estimate that the teller time in processing such payments costs them $1 to $1.50 each.) Amex invested more than $25 million in this one, with television commercials prepared and ready to run in the fall 1995 football schedules, when some of the power companies pulled out and Amex scratched the venture. The reason the companies gave was that they would lose the publicity they gained from the stuffers they sent with the bills. And they would not be moved by Amex's consumer research showing that more than 98 percent of the recipients of these bills tossed the stuffers in the wastebasket without looking at them. "Well," said Pickering, very stiff upper lip, "it took twenty years to get the ATM accepted."

Note now for subsequent retrieval that the giro or one-check system for bill-paying represents a difference in *kind* from the multicheck system. In the multicheck system, what moves is a claim on the payor. Thus the system shows a positive balance from credit for that claim through the period between the deposit of the check and its deduction from the payor's account. This "float" is an inevitable by-product of a debit-transfer system. In the giro system, the first action is the deduction of the total amount of the payor's bills from his account, and what moves through the system are the credits generated at that moment.

The legal differences are extreme, and interesting. "In a credit transfer," the "official comment" on the Uniform Commercial Code states, "the instruction to pay is given by the person making payment. In a debit transfer, the instruction to pay is given by the person receiving payment."[3] Sometimes the debit-transfer system generates windfalls: George White, formerly in charge of electronic payments for Chase and for many years the leading theoretician of the Automated Clearing House, estimated that the blizzard of January 1996 gave payors several days' use of an additional $30 to $40 billion.[4] A credit-transfer system, on the other hand, may in practice require the extension of credit to the payor, like the daylight overdrafts the Federal Reserve gives the large banks when they settle their accounts in the morning over Fed-Wire. The Swiss National Bank and the Bank of Japan have been over that hurdle, requiring that their banks have the money on deposit at the central bank if they want to make wire payments through the facilities of the central bank; but the Fed doesn't have that kind of courage.

Israel Sendrovic, senior vice president for operations at the Federal Reserve Bank of New York, has been consulting with the Chinese government about payments systems. Private parties don't have checking accounts in China; only companies. Sendrovic thought that was probably a good idea. "I told them, 'We have checks by accident. You avoid it.' They probably won't." But maybe they will: in China today, most companies don't write checks. They pay their bills with a corporate MasterCard, the information goes up to the satellite and down to Shanghai and Singapore, where MasterCard International keeps track of what they owe and what they are owed. The World Bank is involved in this project, but the Fed is not. The Chinese want a payments system much more up-to-date than anything the Federal Reserve in the United States has ever contemplated.

3

If I had tracked a similar check from Piccozzi's to a New York City account in early 1996, I would have had a different experience. Jake died in 1995, having worked in the office behind his gas pumps into his eighties, asking me on every visit when I was going to write another good book like *The Bankers* of 1975. Valley had been acquired by Bank of New York, which would have shorted out the stops in Valley Stream and at the Federal Reserve Bank of New York—my check would have gone directly from the East Hampton branch to the Bank of New York processing center in Manhattan. A more capacious reader-sorter with twenty-five instead of thirteen slots for targeting the checks to their bank of issue would have eliminated some passes through the machine. And instead of physically moving to the floor of the New York Clearing House the next morning, my check would have provoked an electronic message that night, through a clearinghouse computer to the computer at my bank (now Citibank), as part of a project called CHECCS, for Clearing House Electronic Check Clearing System. If for any reason my bank did not wish to honor my checks—checks had been stolen, or I had closed the account, or I was out of funds—my bank's computer would block payment on my checks before Jake or anyone else seeking to deposit them received credit. "The bank sends an electronic file at eight p.m.," says Hank Farrar of the clearinghouse, "and we can tell them at eight-oh-five that there are bad items on there."

This system of "electronic check presentment" was made mandatory for members of the New York Clearing House as of January 2, 1996. Its use was opened to nonmembers, and a number of them joined the system, including the many branches of Providence-based Fleet Bank and Cleveland-based Key Banks, New Jersey's First Fidelity, First Tennessee Bank, and Texas Commerce, a subsidiary of New York's Chase Bank. Acceptance of paper checks at the ten o'clock clearing was permitted only for deliveries by the Federal Reserve Bank of New York, which was not ready to participate in an electronic check-clearing system.

The odd part of this story is that if I *had* followed my check from Piccozzi's in early 1996, I would have been on a path rather like the one I had traced twenty-three years before. In the interim, I had moved from New York to Washington, where my account was at Citibank, inheritor of an S&L license rather than a commercial-banking license in Washington, and therefore by law a separate processing entity. Bank of New York would therefore have had to send my check to the Federal Reserve Bank of New York as part of a very small cash letter on Citibank FSB (for Federal Savings Bank) in Washington, and the Federal Reserve Bank of New York would have flown it in the early morning to the

Richmond, Virginia, headquarters of the Federal Reserve district that includes Washington. (Washington does not have so much as a regional check processing center; to swap old dollars for new, the Washington banks must go to Baltimore; to borrow at the Fed's discount window, they must go to Richmond. "I asked Henry Reuss to okay a Fed branch in D.C.," says Bob Auerbach, Democratic counsel to the banking committee, "and he said, 'How many congressmen from D.C. do you see around here?' ") After passing through a gaggle of reader-sorters in Richmond to become a credit to Citibank FSB, my check would drop into a pocket from which it would be trucked, oddly enough, to a file of tills in Newark, New Jersey (where Citibank does not have a banking office), and finally home to me in Washington.

Except in New York, for the New York Clearing House banks, the checking system remains one of embarrassing and expensive redundancy. There is no good reason today why any check has to pass through a reader-sorter more than once. Today, the first reading could but does not take from the check all the information that is there—it does not, for example, identify the account to be debited for the payment, because the bank where the check is first deposited cares only about the routing number of the bank on which the check is drawn. But that first reading can quite easily record information about the payor's account number, too. Then the check can be "truncated"—that is, the check itself can remain with the bank where it is first deposited, and all the information on it can be communicated electronically to everyone who needs it. For Bank of America and the larger interstate banks, which process many "on us" items—payments from one depositor to another—it would be more efficient to take account numbers off a check on its first pass through the reader-sorter even under current circumstances, but so far they don't do it, largely because adding another "field" to the information taken off the check can increase error rates.

Even more can be done in this first pass through the

machinery. The check comes as part of a deposit, which is signified by a deposit slip (still, in the case of anybody who makes multiple deposits, rubber-banded around the checks). The information on the deposit slip is put on the computer at the payee's bank in sequence with the registration of the checks that slip represents. There is, again, no good reason why the account number of the payee cannot be made part of an electronic message that identifies the payor's bank, the payor's account at that bank, and the amount paid. The monthly statement to everyone who writes checks could then include—like the credit card statement—the name of the recipient of each payment. Except in extraordinary circumstances, a bank statement proclaiming that a bill was paid by such-and-such a check deposited on such-and-such a date should serve as evidence of payment quite as well as a canceled check. All that is needed is some minor modifications of the Federal Reserve's Regulation E and the Uniform Commercial Code.

"Well," said Dan Fisher, senior vice president and cashier of Victoria Bank and Trust in Victoria, Texas, and chairman of the American Bankers Association committee on electronic commerce, "we have a saying that it takes five years to get a change in Reg E, and seven years to get a change in the UCC."

The impatient Republicans of the 104th Congress introduced a bill to exempt most of the forms of electronic payment that are on the drawing board from the stranglehold of Reg E. "The industry," vice-chairman Alan Blinder told a subcommittee of the House Banking Committee, "seems worried that, without such an exemption, the Federal Reserve will apply Regulation E in a heavy-handed manner. On behalf of the Board, I would like to assure industry participants and this Committee that we have no such intention."[5]

The Fed has nothing ambitious in its own plans. In 1997, New York will join an intrasystem mainframe consolidation program that ships data from the reader-sorters at the district banks and the regional check-processing centers to computers at the East

Rutherford Center in New Jersey or a computer building at the Richmond Fed. The paper will still move along the same paths; just the information will be processed centrally. (The name for the New Jersey installation is "Eroc." Israel Sendrovic, who runs the operations end of the New York Fed and speaks with a considerable New York accent, had a Polish assistant who got it wrong and was shocked to learn that the Federal Reserve did its account processing in Iraq.) Otherwise, the Fed has no plans.

"History cautions," chairman Alan Greenspan told a conference at the Board on December 7, 1995,

> that changes in large-scale economic infrastructures, such as a decisive shift toward fully electronic payments, take time, even when these changes are likely to produce significant gains in efficiency.... Increases in payment system efficiency imply additional costs, particularly costs resulting from increased capital investments in computer and communications technologies. Like all capital investments, the return must exceed the cost of capital, if efficiency is in any meaningful sense to be improved.... [W]hen evaluating the many ideas currently being discussed for electronic payments, we should think in terms of an environment of different technologies in a competitive market that offers consumers and businesses many choices.... This type of dynamic setting is the one that has most consistently produced gains in economic efficiency.[6]

But so long as the Fed requires the return of paper items, there is no chance for technological change to give returns that exceed the cost of capital. John Major's government in Britain has finally, at long last, agreed to changes in section 45 of the Bills of Exchange Act of 1882 to permit British banks to truncate checks. Part of the argument was that such a change in British law would "bring the UK into line with most other European Union countries."[7] That's not a matter of great interest at the Fed.

The Fed spends its money on enhancing the paper system,

which is where its employees work. The one form of check truncation that has met its approval involves imaging, a high-speed digitized process that asks the computer to read the handwritten numbers on a check. Where the machine cannot read the handwriting, it throws a blown-up picture of the check onto a screen before the keyboard operators who used to read these numbers themselves, and they key in the numbers as they always have. To date, this operation has not been entirely satisfactory, and the error rate in those banks that have adopted imaging is up 25 percent. In 1996 the Fed centralized its own clearing work in three huge processing and imaging plants (total cost, approaching *$500 million*), in East Rutherford, New Jersey, in Dallas, and in Richmond, Virginia.

But these plans involve *the Fed*, not the banks, taking the account numbers off the checks and passing all the information electronically. The Fed has indeed set up a system for variably pricing its work on check bundles. Lower prices are charged to banks that "fine sort" their work before sending it to the Fed, relieving the Fed of the responsibility for separating out checks for each receiving bank. Smaller banks have turned to larger banks and service companies to do this work for them. This has increased the presence of private clearinghouses where the larger banks of a metropolitan area can settle the payments credits and liabilities of smaller banks, cutting out the Fed. Coupled with the merger and acquisition drive in the banking industry, which has converted many "foreign" checks to "on us" items, the competition for work from smaller banks has reduced the Fed's share of check processing. If the Fed required banks to clear by electronic check presentment, keeping images themselves, there would be no need for these Fed imaging plants. If prices were set to reward electronic check presentment to the Fed, the imaging would be done by the correspondent banks and the Fed would lose still more of its business, and the Fed does not plan to lose more of its business.

In fact, the truncation made possible by the expensive imaging plants will be only for the first pass through the system, to determine whether items are on the paying bank's reject list. Chase Bank, which is spending $50 million for IBM's ImagePlus High Performance Transaction System, hopes to reduce the number of passes an average check makes through its own back-office reader-sorters from twelve to two, which will probably pay for the equipment, but does not advance the system. As the Fed is structuring payments-system reform, paper checks will still be sent on for storage at the payor's bank and return to him; the savings that are to pay for the plants, an operations analyst at the Fed explained to a staffer of the House Banking Committee, will be gained by the substitution of inexpensive trucks for the costly airplanes the Fed now rents as the means of delivering the paper checks.

The truth of the matter is that imaging is roughly 90 percent nonsense. American Express for some years presented its bills with "images" of the slips its cardholders had signed. This was enormously expensive, and duplicative in all but one respect, because the information in the image had to be stored electronically anyway if it was to be retrievable. Eventually, Amex switched to its current all-electronic format, which is different in appearance but not in reality from the format used by Visa and MasterCard. The other 10 percent of imaging, which is not nonsense, is the fear of forgery. Banks don't in fact examine signatures on most checks today—the cutoff below which nobody looks ranges from $5,000 to $50,000, and of course is not publicized—but if the banks accept a forged check, it's their loss. If the payor's bank doesn't see a signature, it's going to be somebody else's loss.

The problem looks larger than it is. High-value checks have become an anomaly in commerce, where wire transfer of funds is the norm. It would not be difficult to impose a maximum on the size of checks not previously approved by the payor's bank.

Fifteen years ago, Peter Henderson, who reworked the FedWire system, noted that "we shouldn't be writing checks for more than ten thousand dollars." Even easier would be a program that kicked out of the stream, as "exception items," checks of more than a certain sum. For those checks the signature could be digitized for comparison by telecommunication with the signature on file at the bank where the check is to be paid. Most of today's check fraud involves checks cashed at convenience stores and the like, where the bank ultimately bounces the check on the poor devil who cashed it because the value was changed or the blank check was stolen or the check is a photocopy with an unreadable code because the ink is not the magnetic ink imprinted on a real check.

Scientists like to speak of the importance of the existence theorem—the proof that something for which they can express the equations actually exists in the real world. The great strength of the advocates of check truncation and electronic check presentment is the credit card system called electronic draft capture. This came about largely by accident. In the early 1970s, some of the banks that had issued credit cards went to their local Feds to see if the Fed would be willing to process credit card drafts with checks. "The Fed, fortunately," Donald R. Hollis of the First National Bank of Chicago told a meeting on payments systems twenty years later, "declined to do so for two reasons: it was not sure this action was appropriate . . . and the Fed was busy opening regional check processing centers. In turn, the card-issuing banks installed truncation at the initial merchant-processing bank and leap-frogged the check system in efficiency. . . . Thank our lucky stars for the free enterprise system!"[8]

From the mid 1970s, the credit card system left the merchant's copy of the slip at the merchant's bank and electronically forwarded that bank's claim on the bank that had issued the customer his card. Visa and MasterCard ran electronic clearinghouses, crediting and debiting the banks for their merchant-customer's sales and their cardholder-customer's purchases. Today the slip is truncated at the merchant's cash register: the slip the merchant keeps remains with him, and the bank learns of the transaction electronically—and immediately.

For the credit card industry, speed was of the essence. A bank check in process of collection was an asset to the bank that had put it in the system but not yet a liability for the bank that would eventually pay it: it generated float, extra money in the system. But a credit card slip generated a credit to the merchant (which meant a debit to the bank) from the moment of its presentation, which was to be as soon as possible after the moment of the sale to speed the discovery of fraudulent cards. And it did not become a loan on the books of the bank that paid it (usually interest-bearing, because most people don't pay their credit card bills on time) until the claim arrived from The Interchange, the electronic clearinghouse operated by the credit card company. Thus the normal banking system push to *delay* the completion of a transaction was transformed in the credit card environment to a push for fast payment. In that atmosphere, electronics blossomed.

Citicorp Credit Services, Inc., takes care of the accounts of *20 million* cardholders all over the United States, and among them they owe Citibank about $35 *billion*. The work is done in three identical two-story sprawling brick buildings, in Hagerstown, Maryland; Fargo, North Dakota; and Reno, Nevada. The wiring is below the floor, all walls are temporary. The three sites are linked by fiber optics, replacing their original linkage through Citicorp's private satellite (too slow). Fargo works alone from midnight to six in the morning, Eastern time; otherwise all three are on-line always. For most of the day, there are about seven hundred operators on duty, sitting in cubicles with walls about five feet high, open at one end, watching screens, talking and pushing buttons.

On the February morning when I was in Hagerstown, the multicolored screens in the control center were predicting 8,018 calls for that half hour, and reporting that the average waiting time for a caller was five seconds and the average length of a call (the

"handle time") was 139 seconds. The calls can come from anywhere: if everyone in Hagerstown is busy, an automatic call dis-
tributor switches the customer to an open operator at one of the
two other centers. Among them, the operators will field about
200,000 calls a day. Most but by no means all of the operators are
women. At each center, Citi runs a day-care center for 250 to 300
children of the operators. In the small, square lobby of the
building hangs a painting of a farmhouse on a farm, and a banner:
"SATISFACTION. It lies in the Joy of Achievement, in the Thrill
of Creative Effort." Inside, the atmosphere is more human. For
birthdays, people get a display card reading, "Ask me how old I
am." At Halloween, the floor is "a ghost castle." A sign beside a
computer reads, "I Can Handle Anything. I Have Children."

Citicorp has utilized imaging of the customer's bill since
1984. The operator brings to the screen the customer's most
recent bill, the record of charges and credits to his account since
that bill was sent, plus—on the right half of a split screen—the
customer's letter and any other documentation related to his
reason for calling. Customers have sixty days to protest a charge
against their account. As a matter of policy, Citicorp gives a
complaining customer immediate temporary credit (advertised,
not unreasonably, as consumer "advocacy"), and automatically
sends an electronic message to Visa or MasterCard, asking for
confirmation from the merchant, who now has a use for that
white slip of paper you signed. There are wide variations in the
ability of the merchants to retrieve that paper. At one point when
Macy's was heading into bankruptcy—and Citi was Macy's merchant bank, responsible for refunding the money to the customer's bank if the sale could not be documented—something
like 40 percent of customer challenges had to be allowed because
Macy's couldn't find the slip. Some of the calls are initiated by
the operators from instructions on an otherwise blank screen, to
remind customers that they have bills still unpaid—or with reference to very recent charges, to ask the customer whether he really

bought something with that card in Boston and San Francisco on the same day.

All this, mind you, is for the *exception* items. Normal transactions flow untouched by keyboard or human hand from the merchant's register to the merchant bank (now, most often, a third-party service provider: the banks have decided that it's just too risky to accept money for airlines and furniture stores and mail-order companies that may go bust before delivering what was bought); from the merchant bank to the Interchange (when Citicorp still had a merchant business, "on us" payments from Citicorp cardholders to Citicorp merchants were separated out by the computer and handled internally); and then cleared and settled, money moving either through correspondent banks or FedWire, every two hours. Citicorp processes through Hagerstown, Fargo and Reno. Visa clears the Interchange through processing centers in Basingstoke, England; Singapore; and McLean, Virginia—each system being set up to handle the entire international volume of Visa payments by itself on any given day. The computer installation in McLean occupies sixty thousand square feet of office space; and two million miles of copper wire, used for credit card transactions alone, feed into the building. First Data Resources, Inc., a service provider for the multitude of banks that don't do their own processing, handles even more business than Citicorp from a computer array in Omaha, Nebraska. (Headquarters are in Hackensack, New Jersey, but there are only thirteen employees at headquarters.)

The paper in Hagerstown is the bill preparation and bill collection, and the applications for cards, which go out at a rate of roughly a million a month. Nearly the whole of the first floor of the building is devoted to the issuance of cards, and the most tedious work in the place is editing the returned applications to make them ready for "scoring" by the "judgment court." Thirty elements of "behavior" are considered, and the effort is "to book as many accounts as possible within the risk parameters."

Statements are printed on the laser printer in zip-code order to maximize the discount the post office gives for pre-sorting, and stuffed into envelopes with inserts, carefully weighed to make sure no envelope will be more than one ounce, in a machine that holds the flaps of the envelopes open like the beaks of baby birds and then glues them closed. This outgoing operation runs from two in the morning to two in the afternoon, when the post office trucks carry the work away. (Citicorp Hagerstown has an in-house post office; most of the trucks go only to the local airport, where a post office plane picks up Citi's paperwork and flies it to a hub.) The envelopes for the arriving checks are slitted on three sides by one machine, the contents oriented for processing in another machine, and the checks themselves are imprinted with the required MICR numbers through an imaging machine that marks the numbers and feeds directly to a twenty-five-pocket reader-sorter. The name of the game is then to get credit for the checks as fast as possible. From Reno, they go straight to the San Francisco Fed; from Hagerstown, which is inconvenient to Richmond and a dependency of Citi's minor-league Maryland subsidiary, they go through CoreStates in nearby Pennsylvania, with a guarantee of speedy credit through the Philadelphia Fed.

Citicorp is far ahead of the field in credit cards largely because John Reed, who came out of the operations end of the bank, was fascinated by payments questions and put up the money for a subsidiary company called Transactions Technology, Inc., which was initially established across the street from MIT in Cambridge, Massachusetts. Among its early employees was James Bailey, a pure mathematician, product of the Cournot Institute. ("I was born in Sante Fe," he says, "my father was an MP at Los Alamos, drove trucks from Los Alamos to White Sands, never knew what was in them, died of neural palsy.") Reed turned TTI over to a Californian who took it off to Santa Monica, but he wanted to keep Bailey and moved him to credit cards, where he arrived in

1980, to do what David Phillips, one of Citibank's earliest imports from the world of marketing, described as "consultative selling"— persuading the owners of the big department stores that their future lay with the acceptance of bank credit cards. That was the year Volcker pushed the cost of money far beyond anything the bank could earn on credit cards, and the division lost $100 million. "How do you get that back?" Bailey asked rhetorically. "You lend it to countries that don't go bust."

In addition to Citicorp's technological strength, Bailey argues, it benefits from efficacies (not just economies) of scale. "If I want to spend a hundred million dollars on advertising," he says, "that's five dollars a card. The guy with five million cards, it's twenty dollars a card. Let's say the profits are fifty dollars a card: the cost is ten percent for me, forty percent for him. I tell my people, we fly 747s around here. The fact of the matter is, though my people tell me it's impossible, that credit cards are a business that earns more than its cost of capital."

The man who operates the Citicorp credit card business is J. R. "Jim" Stojak, a steelworker's son whose own working life started off in the factories of Gary, Indiana, in the early 1960s. He rose from a job on the loading dock for Continental-Illinois in Chicago in 1969 to executive ranks in that bank's technology and international operations divisions, leaving shortly before the stuff from Penn Square Bank hit the fan in Chicago to join Wells Fargo in San Francisco. Here, working with Lew Coleman (who would later become vice-chairman of Bank of America), he became one of CEO Carl Reichardt's raiders in submerging Crocker Bank within the ocean of Wells Fargo, which had just acquired it. "Carl," he said reminiscently, "is a unique character. The velocity of deposits in that market is very slow, and what he had acquired that he wanted in Crocker was a bunch of deposits when money was expensive. Then he sold the real estate—Crocker Center—at a time when the California market was still high. He had a very

Spartan office, and he kept a Spartan discipline, took no prisoners. The people who came out of his subs were all small businessmen when they left."

What was on Stojak's mind in 1994 ran the gamut from practical cleverness to Buck Rogers invention. For example, Stojak is "trying to take the check out of the system. Sixty percent of the people pay either all the bill or the minimum. The machine can compare the check with the bill, which helps it mark the check, but about ten percent of the people can't check a box on the bill and write a check for the same amount—it's amazing. We can read about 53 percent of the other checks, unaided. So now we're beginning to ask people if they would like a service which pays ten percent (or some other percentage) more than the minimum they owe, every month, by direct transfer from their bank account. We've had surprising success with it—two hundred and fifty thousand people in California accepted the offer." Looking at the people editing the application forms, he said, "We need better technology to verify: we hope to replace all these key entries with voice commands."

Among the ventures in which Stojak placed his greatest hopes was a photo-trace system to reduce credit card fraud. The most common source of losses has been "white-card fraud," in which the crook opens a store in a tourist center and gets an arrangement as a merchant with a local bank. He then copies the information from the cards used in his store, normally from a wide variety of locations so there is no concentration of protested charges to alert the banks. His accomplices then make cards with the name and number and mag-stripe information on his customers' cards, and those new cards are used to make purchases of easily resold high-ticket items. The center of such activity for many years was the Cuban community in Miami, but more recently Hong Kong has become their preferred hub. Some card issuers, including Citibank, have begun offering free photos to be laminated onto the cards. This is a throwback: Chemical Bank in the early 1970s staged a demonstration of the uselessness of this device, sending out employees with pictures of Stalin and Hitler on their cards, and nobody turned them down. (This was the same year that John Reed commissioned a contest with a $5,000 prize for the best way to counterfeit a magnetic stripe; it was won by two students at the California Institute of Technology, using a steam iron.) Not everyone was enamored of credit cards in their early years.

What Stojak wanted was something subtler: an assembly of bytes on the mag stripe in the back of the card that would trace out on the sales slip to be signed a recognizable likeness of the cardholder. The clerk at the register does not normally look at the card, but he does look at the slip, to make sure the purchaser has signed it. And the fraudster presumably would be much more worried about using a card that printed out a picture of someone other than himself. Eastman Kodak, intrigued, had given Stojak access to the technology used in the spy satellites that photograph the Earth, sending a handful of bytes to the computer on the ground to reconstruct the picture.

Also in Stojak's plans was a digitally communicated signature that could be verified with the rest of the information on the card. (He would like information about what was purchased with the card, too, but the stores won't give that, fearing—quite correctly—that Citicorp would make a salable product from such data.) John Scully showed Stojak the prototype of Apple's Newton scratchpad, and Stojak asked him to capture signatures, which the Newton in the end wouldn't do. Then Stojak made a deal with National Cash Register for a device that looks like a child's Etch-A-Sketch. "We produce the credit card receipt on the computer," he says enthusiastically, "and you sign the pad, which prints a receipt for you—and all the information is transmitted to me, including the signature." Stojak has explored a similar device with Moore Business Forms of Canada, which makes the handheld remote pad United Parcel Service deliverers present to the recipient of a package for his signature. "That has to be very *sturdy*," Stojak adds. "Part of the testing is that it must be under water for one hour and still work." Prototypes of the NCR system were made at $500 each, to be produced for much less in volume. All these things are pending, and some of them unquestionably will happen. The aim is to get *all* the paper out of the system. "Individuals," Stojak says acceptingly, "will always be more comfortable with a printed receipt. Otherwise there will be no paper."

Lawrence Summers, deputy secretary of the Treasury, echoed the theme unknowingly when he gave the introductory talk at an awards ceremony for "pioneers of electronic funds transfer" at the Mellon Auditorium in November 1995. "It costs forty-three cents for the federal government to send a check," he said, "and two cents to make a payment electronically. Our goal is that every transaction of the federal government will be conducted electronically within ten years." Shirley Cates of the Social Security Administration, accepting an award on behalf of her employer, noted that Social Security payments were made by direct deposit not only to some 80 percent of domestic beneficiaries, but to beneficiaries in nineteen foreign countries. The SSA's target was 80 million recipients of direct deposits in the year 2015.

4

A year after Stojak sketched out his visions for a paperless payments system on a credit card chassis, some months before Summers and Cates expressed their hopes at a Treasury Department award ceremony, a committee of Federal Reserve System staffers prepared a "Summary of Discussions" by the staff and "representatives of ten depository institutions" on the subject of electronic check presentment. "Our discussions indicated," the summary reported, "that there is not one definition of ECP."

Speaking to a conference at the Federal Reserve Board in December 1995, I translated that sentence for the benefit of the group of Fed staffers and academics gathered in the auditorium of the Martin Building. It means, I said, "Nothing is going to happen." The Fed's summary continued, "In general, participants cited more obstacles to ECP than potential benefits." I translated that statement, too: "It means, We're not even going to try." Further: "ECP competes with limited resources and is a lower priority than other issues such as interstate banking." No need to translate that one. And yet the summary also noted that "Banks want to truncate checks as early in the process as possible," and that "In general, there was strong interest in the Federal Reserve's providing leadership in bringing the industry together to develop and implement a broad-based, strategic approach to ECP."[9]

"Banks," said Elliott McEntee, who runs the National Automated Clearing House Association, "still look at payments as a group of activities, not as a line of business."

"Banks," said Fed vice-chairman Manuel Johnson in 1988, explaining the persistence of a hugely expensive checking system, "typically do not price their services to encourage the use of the most efficient payment method."[10]

"The banks are defending their niche," says Ed Furash, who operates a consulting company that did a large-scale study of payments arrangements for The Bankers Roundtable. "But the nonbanks are the system providers."

"Don't worry," says John Backus of U.S. Order, a company making specialized transaction-technology telephones. "Visa will save the banks from themselves."

We have, after all, been here before. The efficiency of direct deposit of payroll was a function of universal access: only if S&Ls and credit unions could be members of the Automated Clearing House could an employer be sure that all his workers could receive direct deposit of their payroll. But the Fed refused to permit access by S&Ls and credit unions to the ACHs under its control until the Justice Department sued the Rocky Mountain ACH on anti-trust grounds and forced open the doors.

The Fed's system for ACH processing was as like to checks as it could be made: entries were accepted *only* on reels of tape to be physically carried to the door, and electronic messages were not accepted for the first decade the Fed ran the system. Finally, the New York ACH, privately operated by the New York Clearing House, not only accepted but required members to make their ACH submissions electronically. The Fed then agreed to accept wire entries to its ACHs as an alternative to reels of tape for those banks that wished to operate in the modern world. In 1988, Manuel Johnson suggested that with PCs capable of handling wire transfer costing something like $5,000, the Fed might join the New York Clearing House: "Perhaps the time has come to establish a sunset date for institutions to convert to ACH electronic access."[11] The Fed got there in 1993, but it didn't push the banks. In 1996, Ted Shaw of EDS reports, *every one* of the sixty-four centers from which his company services its banking customers still needed a tape drive to convert tapes for data delivery to ACHs.

Of course, the Fed defends itself. The Federal Reserve Bank of San Francisco helped set up the first ACH. For years, the Fed charged less than cost for ACH services, subsidizing the system from its other revenues. In the mid 1980s, the Fed did begin to accept electronic access to its ACHs, and even adjusted its fee schedule to charge more for tapes than for direct entry as an encouragement. But the truth is that when General Electric tried to get into the ACH business in California, the San Francisco Fed set presentment schedules that made it impractical for California banks to use any ACH but its own, and the Fed's technical staff refused to cooperate in setting standards for the electronic data interchange fields (what is this payment for?) that would have made the system infinitely more useful in corporate payments. The same attitudes suffuse today's approach toward electronic payments: in the ACH world, for example, the rules require that the three privately owned systems—New York, Phoenix, and Visa—pay the Fed for each message transported through a Fed ACH, but carry Fed ACH messages to their customers without charge. But the world moves faster now, and there are many more players in the game; and they don't all need the Fed.

It would be interesting to know what the Fed plans to do with the building after the last train has left the station.

4 / The Computer Age, Part I: Credit Card and ATMs

It was necessary to reconceive in the most fundamental sense, the nature of bank, money, and credit card; even beyond that to the essential elements of each and how they might change in a microelectronics environment. Several conclusions emerged: First: Money had become nothing but guaranteed, alphanumeric data recorded in valueless paper and metal. It would eventually become guaranteed data in the form of arranged electrons and photons which would move around the world at the speed of light.

—DEE HOCK, former CEO of Visa, writing of the
theoretical framework he developed in 1968[1]

Visitors to Kyoto are taken to Ryoanji, the most famous of Zen temples, where the square garden is flanked on two sides by an unornamented high fence and on the other two by a railed, roofed wood platform attached to the temple. The garden itself presents a flat space rough-surfaced with curved lines of raked white pebbles broken by fifteen black stones of uneven size. There is no discernible pattern in the placement of the stones, and there is no place on the platform from which all fifteen can be seen. My host on this day's travels was a city planner from Osaka, who stood beside me as I contemplated. I am not much for mysticism, but as my consciousness somewhat reluctantly submerged in the panorama of the stones, I recognized beyond doubt that there is something here. I leaned against the railing and relaxed, unable to decide how important, if important, that something might be. I wasn't sure whether it was proper to ask the question. My companion said nothing.

Suddenly there burst onto the platform a regiment of school-children, with all the extraneous energy of pre-pubescent young-sters released from class. A loud rather harsh voice came over the loudspeaker built into the eaves of the roof where the two plat-forms met. Shocked from contemplation, hating the intrusion, I turned away from the stones to my companion and complained: "*What* is that loudspeaker saying?"

"Oh," he said, "it is explaining to the children what the stones mean."

Everyone has to start somewhere. Let us look at electronic money within the frame of the Zen stones. There is, unquestion-ably, something here. How important that something may be, nobody knows. For most of us, what is here is so far unknowable with any precision. But we have an obligation to explain, and I am turning on the loudspeaker.

2

Joseph Nocera credits the arrival of electronic banking to Dee Hock, a mostly self-educated, domineering mountain man from Utah who became CEO of the Visa credit card operation. Nocera starts by quoting a former associate of Hock: " 'He used to say that money had evolved from shells to green paper to the artful arrangement of binary digits.' . . . Dee Hock wanted Visa to con-trol the binary digits. . . . Once he persuaded Visa's international board to pass a resolution that began, 'Resolved: That the Visa system should become the premier worldwide system for the exchange of value.' "[2] All the wonders of Citicorp in Hagerstown trace back to the vision of Dee Hock.

Stores had long offered credit facilities to their better customers, and banks had been involved in consumer credit as lenders to finance companies that made personal loans and to the stores, which normally, however, had to put up more security than just their consumer receivables to be entitled to the credit. As noted above, in the introduction, George Moore in 1940, as a national lending officer, put National City Bank of New York into more direct contact with Sears customers. Among the noteworthy aspects of this story was the fact that Sears, not the customer who signed the note to Citibank, paid the interest to the bank; it was Sears's decision whether to carry that interest payment as part of its costs, pass the cost on to the customer, or charge the customer a lot more than prime to make the credit arrangement a profit center for the store. Eventually, of course, the Sears credit company became a major profit center for the retailer, which led eventually to the emergence of Sears itself as a financial intermediary. In 1983, Clayton Banzhaf, Sears's CEO, told me that 58 percent of all Sears sales were on credit—but that he still needed accounts in 3,700 banks to deposit his cash and checks every night.

Most of the larger department stores issued their own "charge cards" in the 1930s and 1940s, after greater or less investigation of the bona fides of the customers. B. Altman in New York was considered the most rigorous: customers who could display a B. Altman card could get a credit card from just about any store in town. (Nieman Marcus served the same function in Dallas.) In some cases the card was entirely a convenience, part of the store's marketing strategy—the customer was expected to pay the entire monthly statement when it arrived, and there was no interest charged. In other cases, the card represented a "revolving credit." In all such cases, the resulting "receivables" were financed by the banks, with the store itself as the intermediary, guaranteeing repayment.

On the larger scene, the card with the greatest clout was the Air Travel Card, issued by the airlines to businesses that made a

$425 deposit, which was a lot of money in the 1950s. Gasoline companies issued credit cards usable only at gas stations, and the station owner would use the credits to pay the company for his next delivery. The J.C. Penney catalog operation offered credit to mail-order customers.

Social commentators from J. K. Galbraith (who approves of puritanism, at least for others) to Joseph Nocera (who doesn't) like to say that Americans distrust debt. In fact, borrowing has always come easier in North America than anywhere else in the world, as demonstrated by the rank growth of banks throughout the national history—and by the relative leniency of the bankruptcy code. Henry Wallich liked to observe when he was a Federal Reserve governor that in the United States, unlike Europe or Asia, households themselves have long been financial intermediaries—that is, people will have mutual fund holdings or own savings bonds or deposits while carrying a heavy mortgage on their homes, and may even keep balances on their credit card when they have excess cash in the bank that issued the credit card.

Moreover, the American consumer has been an excellent credit risk: in the worst years of the Great Depression, Household Finance never saw credit losses greater than its interest income, and as the economy recovered, people came through the door to pay their old debts. George Moore approvingly quotes Roger Steffan, who started Citibank in the consumer lending business: "The clerk is a better risk than the boss, and the boss is a better risk than the company he works for."[3] Bank of New York had a "co-branded" credit card with the AFL-CIO, available only to union members, and in June 1996 the total credit outstanding on these cards was $3.4 billion. "Best credit in the bank," said its CEO John Bacot. "Fewest charge-offs." When the contract with AFL-CIO came up for renewal in 1996, Household Finance outbid Bank of New York for the business. Estimates of the price range up to $375 million, of which the unions would get $94 million, financing their role in the 1996 election and then some.

Congress had to forbid the distribution of unsolicited credit cards to potential customers not because the banks were losing money to people who didn't pay their bills but because thieves were getting their hands on the cards and making trouble for the credit ratings of their intended recipients. Even today, despite much public hand-wringing about delinquencies and years of unscrupulous credit peddlers (some of them banks) sending out psychologically tested switch-to-us offers that include a check for cash, credit card write-offs at all but the most aggressive banks are 4 percent of volume. This is a *safe* business, for credit providers. The normal means of financing credit card receivables has become securitization—the bank packages a large volume of outstandings on its customers' accounts and sells notes for a little less than their face value (to allow for some shrinkage) on the money market. An outside insurer writes the bank an inexpensive policy to guarantee the purchaser of the paper that he will be repaid, rocket scientists generate derivatives dividing the paper into separate tranches that pay on different schedules, and everything runs like clockwork.

Credit cards to be used in a number of establishments start with the Diners' Club, a charge card for restaurants, launched in 1949 by a New York businessman and his lawyer, neither with any experience in credit or banking. (The publicized story is that the businessman thought up a credit card when he found himself short of cash to pay the check in a restaurant; insiders say that the card grew out of the discovery that people would pay for the privilege of buying airplane tickets on someone else's Air Travel Card.) Diners were recruited originally from a list of five thousand sales managers, who liked the idea of a record of their entertainment expenses. The costs of the club were to be covered entirely by the restaurants, which would pay a commission of 5 to 10 percent, and what they got for it was guaranteed payment perhaps a month later, after the club member had paid his bill. Only a minority of sophisticated restaurateurs recognized at the beginning that membership in this sort of "club" would be an effective marketing tool, and that the costs were less than they seemed, because increased sales in a restaurant come at low marginal costs. But in New York and Los Angeles, where Diners joined with a similarly amateur venture called Dine and Sign, that minority was large enough.

The problem the restaurants had in the early days before data-processing machinery was that Diners Club, as it is now known (it is now a subsidiary of Citicorp, marketed abroad as an upscale card), could not keep up with the paperwork. Payments were late, and only the fear that customers who had grown accustomed to using the card would stop coming kept the restaurants participating. Diners Club did not begin to make money until 1954, when a $5 membership fee was assessed against cardholders.[4] American Express, fearful that credit cards would erode its travelers check franchise (as of course it will—half a century later!), issued its own first travel-and-entertainment (T&E) cards in 1958, charging a six-dollar fee to prove it was a little upscale of Diners Club.

Franklin National Bank in Franklin Square, Long Island, two dozen miles from the New York City border, was the first to attempt a multistore bank charge card—a "universal card"—that could be used in as many Long Island stores as would sign up for it. Arthur Roth, Franklin's rambunctious and imaginative founder, sold it as a promotion device in 1951 for local stores fighting the eruption of the shopping centers. Bank of America and Chase-Manhattan picked up the idea in the mid 1950s and tried it out on a larger scale. The argument was that such a card would appeal to merchants relieved of their bookkeeping and billing duties and to customers who would no longer have to carry either cash or wads of individual cards.

As pioneered in a Fresno test in 1958, a few days before American Express entered the lists, BankAmericard would have three sources of profit: a fee to the merchant (originally 6 percent discount on the amount of the sale), a 1½ percent monthly charge on the balances in an account not paid off within a few weeks of its presentation, and eventually an annual fee. There was a lot of credit business here: the merchants in effect got cash in advance for 94 percent of their accounts receivable, a very stiff price for what might be only a one- or two-month acceleration of payment, and the cardholder got the use of the merchandise before he had to pay for it.

By October 1959, Bank of America had put two million cards in circulation in California, mostly by mailing them to the bank's existing list of depositors, and had signed up twenty thousand merchants. It had become apparent quite early that if you sent people an invitation to apply for a card, nobody applied—but if you sent someone a card, he used it. Quite a lot of money was lost, because costs dramatically outran revenues (and would for another two years), and quite a lot of ill-will was generated, because people whose cards had been lost or stolen (often before they received them, the post office being what the post office was) were billed for thieves' purchases. "In isolated cases," a System Task Force Group from the Federal Reserve reported glumly in 1968, "participating merchants cooperated with improper card-holders to bill large quantities of merchandise until the card appeared on the 'hot card list' and then turned in the card and split the 'hot card' reward with the improper holder."[5] Congress had to pass a law limiting the cardholder's liability to the first $50 charged on a lost or stolen card; then the banks became more responsible about card issuance.

The bank coded each card with a purchase limit; below that limit the merchant could simply honor the card and the bank would pay whether or not the customer paid, but above the limit the merchant before honoring the card had to call the bank and make sure the transaction was okay. That took a lot of time at both ends. And, of course, the card could be used only at stores and restaurants, hotels, airlines and gas stations that had accounts at

Bank of America, which in effect meant California. The Chase card was in even worse shape, being restricted by New York State law to branches in the five boroughs of New York City, and in 1962 Chase gave up on it.

For eight years, BankAmericard was the only bank card in California, and the only significant bank card anywhere. Clearly, however, this was a business others were going to enter. At Christmastime 1966, the four big Chicago banks blanketed northern Illinois with credit cards and arranged with each other that every merchant signed by one would honor the cards issued by any. Buffalo's Marine Midland formed a consortium of banks in Richmond, Milwaukee, Phoenix, Seattle and Louisville to create a national identity for their own regional shopping cards, and Bank of America's four largest California rivals launched their own "Mastercharge" card. These groups were going to get together someday. If rival California banks could offer a card useful outside California because they had made a deal with banks in other states, BankAmericard was going to suffer.

Beginning in 1967, Bank of America began to offer banks elsewhere in the country the chance to franchise its name and system, for only $25,000 a pop. Among the takers was Chase in New York. Now the authorization for a purchase over the coded maximum on the card involved long-distance calls from the merchant's bank to the customer's bank, and the flimsy slips of paper with their carbon insets, which were the paper record of the transaction, had to travel from bank to bank. The merchant's bank was out of pocket to the merchant until the cardholder's bank remitted. Ed Hogan, who was the third person hired by MasterCard in New York, remembers the first days of that operation: "We had 25,000 merchants and 500,000 cardholders. We had a pigeonhole frame for slotting the slips. At the end of day one we were ninety days behind; we *had* to make the banks settle with each other."

Given the state of the mails—for all this was done through the mails—it was hard to establish rules on how quickly banks had to pay money to each other. The quality of the "merchants" available in each city was a function of how hard the local bank worked, how good its contacts were, and how greedy it was in setting merchant fees. No national chain of stores accepted a bank credit card until the late 1970s, and American Express through its dealings with the American Hotel Association for some years blocked the bank cards' access to that part of the travel business. The banks for the first time found themselves second-class citizens: their cards were for lesser fry.

By 1968, BankAmericard had a hundred franchisers, and none of them was happy. At a meeting of angry bankers in Columbus, Ohio, Dee Hock, present as the delegate from National Bank of Commerce (later Rainier Bank, which would be absorbed by Security Pacific and then by Bank of America itself), suggested the appointment of an "executive committee" that would help Bank of America get a grip on its own creation. Tom Clausen, a dour, conservative lending officer who had risen through the corporate office to be Bank of America's new CEO, wanted others to drink from this cup, and told his people to cut Hock some slack. Hock convinced Kenneth Larkin, who ran the bank's personal loan division and thus supervised the credit cards, that a wholly separate co-op of banks would have to be formed to clean up the BankAmericard mess, establish firm fee and presentment schedules among the banks, and move the concept forward.

In 1970, Hock at age forty-one became president and CEO of a newly formed National BankAmericard, Inc., a separate company to which Bank of America sold its trademark. He designed a board of directors that could not be dominated by any category of bank—big, small, eastern, western—which meant that he could manipulate it. And he insisted that the board members be CEOs of their banks, which meant that decisions taken by the board would be executed without fuss. He held his board meetings in exotic and pleasant places which small-town bankers had read about but never seen—Hawaii, Rio, Monte Carlo. He expected his board to agree with him, and he could throw temper trantrums when there were indications that it might not. A man who was at some of the meetings reports: "He'd say, 'All in favor say Aye; anyone opposed can leave the room.' "

Among Hock's first thought, no doubt, was to get rid of the Bank of America name, which made him B of A's servant; that would take six years, until his board (and B of A) accepted the name Visa for both the card and the company. Among his first actions was to budget $3 million for a computerized switch that would first replace telephone calls as the mechanism for authorizing the transaction, and then in later refinements would eliminate paper in clearing the transfer of money. Today there is no paper at all in the clearing and settlement system; the slip off the merchant's cash register that the customer signs produces one copy for the merchant and one copy for him, but nobody else ever sees it unless the transaction is protested and has to be verified. Everything to do with acceptance and payment is electronic. Costs are a very minor fraction of what they used to be; merchants are paid much more quickly and charged a much smaller percentage of the amount charged—indeed, the margins are so small that the banks have dropped out of the merchant service business, contenting themselves with the interchange fee the merchant's bank pays the cardholder's bank for supplying the funds.

The immense efficiency of this system and its MasterCard companion have set huge obstacles before would-be competitors: Sears started its Discover card in the mid 1980s and applied to use the Visa processing system in 1989, and was denied; AT&T came in 1990 and General Motors in 1992, and the bank-card consortia drove them away. All three survive—and benefit consumers by offering a no-fee card, which most banks have felt impelled to match—but none has become a major factor, largely because they can't pay merchants as fast and efficiently as the bank cards. Discover is substantial, with 6 percent of the business, but a lot of its credits are Sears-related. In spring 1996, American Express announced that it was going to try to persuade banks to offer its card even if that meant sacrificing their Visa franchise. As American Express was already in some difficulty because it paid its merchants *much* later than the bank card companies—one of the longest-running and most successful negative television advertising campaigns is the one in which Visa announces triumphantly at the curtain that "they *don't* take American Express"—not many observers gave the company much of a chance.

From early on, Hock also insisted that the Visa systems be designed to operate internationally. "Without Hock," says Jim Bailey of Citicorp, which has *eight million* cardholders outside the United States, "we couldn't be where we are." The need for a name that made sense outside the United States was also one of Hock's reasons for dropping the brand BankAmericard and calling both the company and the service "Visa," a step he took in 1977. In 1984, as the on-line communications systems associated with credit cards became ubiquitous, he began gearing Visa to push into the debit card business, allowing people to access their bank accounts rather than just their credit at the cash register. This was going to be an expensive promotion. His board didn't think it would work, and was terminally tired of being pushed around, so when he threatened to resign they took him up on it.

I spent two days visiting Visa's technical and planning offices in the hills behind Palo Alto in 1982, while Hock was still running the show. They had a strong grip on the future. By 1985, they said (actually, it took a little longer), 85 percent of all American merchants would be verifying cards by swiping them through a reader, and by the end of the decade the Visa switch would deliver rolling settlements every few hours, making the interbank payments on Visa quicker than the checking system. But the only time I ever met Hock, unquestionably the progenitor of these arrangements, was after his retirement, when I was doing an article for the *New York Times* on the problems besetting Bank of

America. Having had one interview with Hock puts me above the average for reporters who have written about him: he always avoided publicity. I found him at his working ranch in the dry coastal hills between the avocado farms and the Monterey Peninsula—a landscape not unlike that of his native Utah. He was wearing jeans, cowboy boots and a leather jacket. He walked to the rail fence and looked at his spread stretching up into the brush-laden hills. He was willing to talk about what was happening at the bank, an old adversary, but not about the credit card business: he wasn't interested in visions that weren't his own. In the '90s, he totally disappeared from view.

One of the things that got him fired was the extravagance of the executive offices for Visa that he installed at 101 California Street, a new San Francisco skyscraper across from the Bank of America tower. There was a fortieth-floor sauna, and marble floors beneath the oriental rugs, but what really got to the bankers was the elaborateness of the bookcase installation in his anteroom, where he kept the custom-bound testimony of the great minds whose guidance, all alone, he had sought. He was never a techie; his genius was to give the rocket scientists their target. And you can still learn more about targets from the great books than from computer programs.

The Merrill Lynch Cash Management Account had blurred the line between securities portfolios and money. Hock's Visa system with its rolling settlement of credit card charges, quickly imitated and perhaps surpassed by MasterCard's clearing systems, in effect erased the line between credit and money. From a banker's point of view, the only difference between a deposited check and an item reflecting a credit card purchase is that the credit card purchase item was collected faster. But the truth is that the banks have become agents and fee-takers rather than principals, movers or shakers in the credit card world. Today, non-banks like First Data and GE Capital stand behind more credit cards than banks, and those two and First USA, FiServ, NaBanco,

Litle and EDS process more credit card transactions than any bank except Citicorp. Credit cards are sold by mail-order (the cost of acquiring a new customer is variously estimated anywhere from $60 to $160), and few people know who issued the one they use. The Visa or MasterCard logo on the card is infinitely more important than the name of the bank, and the bank's name has shrunk even further with the boom in "affinity" cards (the most popular, believe it or not, are not the frequent-flier cards but the cards with the logos of the professional football teams).

At the end of 1995, Visa members had issued almost 350 million cards, half of them outside the United States, and signed more than 11 million merchants. MasterCard is even more widespread. The ubiquity of the credit card is astonishing. "There is no business where product portability is so important," says Joe Tripodi of MasterCard. "The card is not a bottle of beer, and it's not a deodorant. People take it with them—and expect it to work perfectly in thirteen million places." Credit card debt outstanding in the United States alone totaled more than $340 billion in mid 1996. No doubt there remains a line between credit and money, but it's gotten pretty blurred.

Perhaps the most remarkable extension of credit cards is to China, where MasterCard has created a payments system for Chinese industry. In Russia, state-owned companies ignore their bills, and nothing can be done about it; eventually, the central bank issues credits to the suppliers whose bills haven't been paid. In China, the bills are paid with the MasterCard, the message goes out on the cellular phone to the dish farm, and is sent up to the satellite with the MasterCard transducer, which sends the message to both the substation in Shanghai and the great big super-computer in Singapore. Beijing knows in real time what the state enterprises owe, and informed decisions can be made. The system is used so intensively that China has become the second-largest generator of MasterCard debits in the world, trailing only the United States.

3

In the 1970s, technology was advertised to bring us not a checkless society but a cashless society. Cash after all is the least desirable payments mechanism. It gets dirty. Handling it is labor-intensive and expensive. It's subject to forgery—in the age of color photocopying, easy and good forgery. It has to be protected from theft, and usually can't be traced after it's stolen. From the consumer's point of view, the use of cash generates negative float—that is, there are opportunity costs involved in taking your money out of the bank, where it can be earning interest, and carrying it with you to make payments.[6] The anonymity of cash makes it the preferred medium of exchange in criminal transactions of all kinds.

For office workers over the age of forty (factory workers were paid with cash envelopes, offering opportunities for stickups of armored cars), payday is inextricably associated with the nuisance of taking your check to the bank on Friday (or on the 1st and 15th of the month) and waiting in line to get cash from a teller. If you were working on deadline and three o'clock passed, the bank was likely to be closed and you had to hope that some neighborhood storekeeper knew you well enough to cash your check—supermarkets in the cities wouldn't do it.

What has kept cash alive as the payments system of choice—300 billion transactions a year in the United States, most of them under $2—is another of our technological miracles, the automated teller machine. From the consumer's point of view, the ATM minimizes negative float, because it means cash can be drawn as needed. From the bank's point of view it greatly reduces the cost of the basic consumer interface, quickly earning back its investment, which may be as little as $10,000, in teller salaries alone. By 1996, there were roughly 120,000 ATMs installed in the United States, and cardholders were making *nine billion* withdrawals a year.

Banks initially handled the introduction of these devices very foolishly, insisting that each machine was proprietary to its owner, a selling tool for a single bank, that accepted cards issued by that bank and no other. This also permitted the larger banks to brutalize smaller banks, which couldn't offer ATMs convenient to their depositors' workplace. The first switch among ATMs was in Colorado; part of the background of Hock's dismissal from Visa was his effort to make Visa the ATM as well as the credit card switch for all his members, and the fierce counterattack by a Colorado banker who wanted to make his own deals. Many banks, shortsightedly, saw the ATM as primarily a profit center that could generate fees, and reduced the use of the machines by charging for each transaction. Indeed, they may do so again; in 1996, consumers found a rash of new fees associated with ATM usage.

Gradually, the banks came to the realization that the reason for the ATM was to reduce the expense of offices. Their interest lay in widening the number of machines to which their depositors had access on a reciprocal basis, and promoting the most frequent use of the machine by everybody. This again, it should be noted, required system: encrypted communication links from the machine to the bank that owned it (stand-alone machines were vulnerable to unauthorized use and possible jackpotting; among the data transmitted from the machine after each use is the weight of bills removed, which can be matched against the valid payments orders registered), and then the movement of validations, debits and credits through the switch. Some operators of the switches were consortia of banks, like NYCE, Pulse, Honor, MAC, Most, TYME, Money Station, Cash Station, Money Network—at one time there were two hundred of them. Some were outside service providers, like Automatic Data Processing (ADP), First Data and Electronic Data Systems (EDS), which made it possible for relatively small banks to participate in the linked chain of ATM proprietors.

The 1990s saw a swift consolidation of ATM switch networks, and shows of concern from the Federal Trade Commission, the anti-trust division of the Department of Justice, and the attorneys general of various states. The first major case against a switch involved a challenge to the MAC network, then owned by Banc One, CoreStates, PNC and Society Bank (later bought by Keycorp). In 1995, MAC (for "Money Access Center") handled transactions at the rate of 92 million a month for 27 million depositors at more than 13,000 ATMs. Unlike most ATM networks, MAC for many years was exclusive—if you belonged to MAC, you couldn't also belong to another switch. "These exclusivity rules," David A. Balto, an adviser to the Federal Trade Commission, wrote in the *Review* of the Federal Reserve Bank of St. Louis, "created an almost impervious barrier to competitive entry because if a bank wanted to join a competing network it would have to withdraw all of its ATMs from MAC. Faced with that all-or-nothing decision, few banks chose to align with competing networks."[7]

That rule was dropped in 1992, in response to a private lawsuit, but MAC retained rules that restricted participation in other networks and denied members the right to use third-party processing services. This would require smaller banks that used EDS or FiServ for their normal demand deposit processing to pay extra for MAC processing, and in effect froze out competitors who might charge less for processing. MAC eventually signed a consent decree requiring the company to "permit its participants to use third-party providers of ATM processing, to display multiple network trademarks on all their ATMs, and to permit multiple branding of ATM cards issued by MAC members. . . . MAC is also required to sell its network services 'at prices that will not vary with the process selected.' "[8]

The Federal Reserve has approved every merger that has come to its attention. While noting the need for equal access to the switch to prevent the imposition of monopoly rents, the Fed has let others take whatever actions might be necessary to level the playing field as between owners of and guests on the network. Then the argument is that there's nothing for the Fed to do. "The Board's understanding of the purpose of consent decrees appears mistaken," Balto noted dryly, referring to the Fed's approval of National City Bank as one of the owners of the MAC network after the operators of MAC had agreed to suspend for ten years certain uncompetitive practices in their history. "The purpose of the decree is to remedy the competitive problem at the time the decree is entered, not during the pendency of the decree."[9]

From early on, the switch and the bank that owned the machine charged a fee for each use, usually 50 cents, to "foreign" banks that issued cards honored in this switch. Machines owned by supermarket chains like Publix in Florida typically charged the card-issuing banks more than 50 cents per transaction. For years, the banks had charged the supermarkets a fee when they deposited the huge bundles of their customers' checks. Now the supermarkets were getting even. Charles Zwick, the irascible former CEO of the former Southeast Bank in Miami (previously director of the budget bureau for Lyndon Johnson), once vented his fury in my direction when he complained that Publix was charging him 59 cents when he couldn't, or thought he couldn't, charge his depositors more than 50 cents for the service. He didn't count what he saved in teller time when transactions were done at the supermarket ATM rather than in his lobbies.

Citibank in the early 1990s (and then First Chicago in the mid 1990s) tried to wean people away from live tellers to the cash machine by charging for every teller visit, which produced horrendous customer relations. (Jay Leno on the *Tonight* show suggested that the fee for a transaction at the teller window would be raised to $3.95 for people who wanted to talk dirty to the teller.) Bank of Montreal, having thought the thing through more intelligently, added 25 cents to every deposit made at the ATM rather than at a teller's window. Citibank also decided, eventually, to use carrots rather than sticks, making all usage of the bank's own machines free to all depositors. Republic Bank in New York went a step further, absorbing the charges of the switch and other banks to give its cardholders unlimited free use of any bank's machines.

The importance of the ATM switch as a payments mechanism has not been widely recognized, partly because the number of switches has been so great and the pattern of their interconnection was so confusing. In some ways, the transaction most like the check I followed in 1974 is a tourist's ATM withdrawal from a bank in a corner of the country served by a local switch. "There's a huge series of hubs and spokes," says MasterCard's Henry Mundt, in charge of the Maestro debit card program, a hugely enthusiastic young man who comes to work every day in Master-Card's new I. M. Pei building in a park in a New York suburb, hoping that this is the day he will get a chance to invent an entirely new system. "If you used your Most card in Beaumont, you would go through the GulfStates switch, to the Pulse switch, to our Cirrus switch, to your Most switch, to your bank."

Consolidation is creating simplification—and opportunity for an independent management of a switch owned by a consortium of banks that don't understand what switches can do. The NYCE (New York Cash Exchange) network, having absorbed New England's Yankee 24 and become a preferred member of Cirrus, has made a deal with Microsoft to take effect when Visa closes *its* deal with Microsoft. NYCE will then have its own PC diskette for customers to do home banking—"a light product," its chief operating officer Dennis Lynch says modestly, "just for account information and bill-paying." Specially configured, ATM machines themselves could be used to pay third-party bills, but such machines would have to be separate from the cash withdrawal and deposit machines or risk the fury of customers waiting in long lines (like the old lines at the banks on payday when somebody was getting payroll envelopes filled) while people do interminable business ahead of them. Many German ATM machines are geared to pay out exactly 400 marks each time, because, Kleindienst's Rainer von der Dunk explains, Germans get mad if there are more than four people in line to use the machine.

The expectation of the switch owners was that the ATM card would be widely used as a debit card in a POS (point of sale) system, where storekeepers could take payment on the card for overnight credit to their accounts (and same-day debit to the customers' accounts)—and would make change, which ATM machines don't. The debit card caught on slowly, perhaps because people can use their credit card and believe they'll pay it off before they have to pay interest. "The challenge," says MasterCard's Mundt, "is to get the dog to eat the food. Maybe it's like the ATMs. When they were new, we said there was a ten percent ceiling. Then there was the $33^1/_3$ percent wall. Now it's twice that—almost two-thirds of cash withdrawals are at ATMs." In 1997, heavily promoted (and surcharged), the debit card began to move.

Visa and Master purchased and created nationwide (indeed worldwide) ATM switch services—Plus and Cirrus, respectively—and linked them into virtually all the regional switches, which benefited by giving their card-issuing banks access to machines everywhere. But the credit card companies do not now offer any service other than cash withdrawal—deposits cannot be made and information usually cannot be retrieved—and they charge more for what they do. In its "Competitive Impact Statement" on this subject, the Department of Justice argued that "National ATM networks exist, but these are by design networks of last resort"—a comment that especially infuriated MasterCard CEO Gene Lockhart, who sees the ATM switches and the associated POS networks as the great field for his company's expansion. Competition between Plus and Cirrus has been guaranteed by forbidding "duality"—machines may offer both services, but any individual card can offer only one or the other. Thus Visa and MasterCard must compete for the business of the card-issuers.

In the POS area, Visa and Master in the mid 1980s made a

deal to collaborate in the creation of an Entree card that would be a nationwide debit card. Neither the Fed nor the Department of Justice said boo, but a group of state attorneys general brought suit to force the big card companies to compete in the POS market, and also to divest themselves of the nationwide ATM switching services. In 1990, the card companies backed off the joint POS venture, and the states backed off their effort to force divestiture of Plus and Cirrus. The competition between the two competing POS systems, Visa's Interlink and Master's Maestro, has demonstrably lowered the fees the cardholder's bank has had to pay the merchant's bank for accepting the card.[10]

Bank regulation grew up in an atmosphere of protecting the banks. For years, people seeking a charter for a new bank had to prove that there was enough business for two banks in such-and-such a neighborhood and certainly could not argue that the existing franchise was badly managed and/or greedily gobbling up monopoly rents from its customers. Inherited attitudes, then, especially at the Fed, leave little room for understanding the values of competition. Anyway, if there is to be a monopoly, who in the end should wind up the proprietor of the franchise? The Fed itself, of course.

5 / The Computer Age, Part II: Smart Cards and the Internet

Q. What makes a system insecure?
A. Switching it on!

The only system which is truly secure is one which is switched off and unplugged, locked in a titanium lined safe, buried in a concrete bunker, and is surrounded by nerve gas and very highly paid armed guards. Even then, I wouldn't stake my life on it. (The original version of this is attributed to Gene Spafford.)

—America Online White Paper on Security, generated
07/27/95 at 6:01 P.M. (This document is of course secret.)

In Belgium, a driver who parks his car on a meter can pay his hundred francs for an hour by inserting into a slot in the meter a bank card with an integrated circuit silicon chip embedded in its plastic. If the driver stays longer, the meter, having noted the ID on his card, will simply add to the charges against it. The same card buys telephone calls, transit rides, newspapers, groceries and Big Macs. Two years after these cards were introduced by BankSys, a co-op of all Belgian banks, they were in the wallets of a majority of adult Belgians and virtually all adult Dutch.

These "Proton" cards are also in use in Switzerland, Sweden, Australia and Brazil; they are advertised as "the card for the little things in life." They follow on seventeen years of Belgian experience with electronic funds transfer in a giro payments system. Every Belgian bank account comes with a debit card, and bills can be paid through ATM machines. The Belgian authorization system, called STEPS, has been sold to eleven countries in Europe. In summer 1996, the seven thousand banks associated with Europay (the European affiliate of MasterCard) began issuing a "clip" card which can be reloaded with cash either at an ATM or from a home computer.

In Germany, where 88 million smart cards have been issued to help manage the record-keeping associated with national health service benefits, a patient being admitted to the hospital need no longer fill out pages of forms. The card contains his name, his address, the names of certain relatives, his age, his occupation, his medical history, his blood type, his allergies, the name and phone number of his internist, and baseline data of various kinds. For various reasons, including the timing of the introduction, money matters are not on the medical card, and as of mid 1996 there were 16 million other chip cards for payments and security use plus an experimental "EC" (European Community) card originally just for buses and rail and plane tickets. But there is no inherent reason why a single card can't perform both functions.

In Finland, where the central bank itself issues the health and social security card, an "e-purse" is already superimposed on the identification elements. More capacious cards cost more, but all prices are coming down. Tiny chips embedded in cards the thickness of the normal mag stripe credit card can now carry 8 kilobytes of memory plus a processor, and 64K is within reach. Cathy Allen, formerly Citibank's chip card director, likes to point out that the original IBM PCs had only 64K of internal memory.

In Italy, the corporation of the Autostrade, which owns and operates all the toll roads in Italy, developed a chip card to be inserted in an inexpensive radio-frequency oscillator that can be attached to the back of the rearview mirror of an automobile. As the car approaches the tollgate, a signal generator in the gate sends a message to the oscillator, which sends a message identifying the chip card and registering the appropriate deduction from the card.

The card is purchased from and loaded with value by the Autostrade, and can also be used to purchase gas, snacks and tchotchkes from the roadside stores. In 1995, the card could be used to pay bus fares in Florence and pay-per-view charges on cable video.

In Japan in 1997, Nissan cars will come with a smart card that will record all repairs and retrieve the data.

In 1995, Florida State University arranged to have students' financial aid distributed through an FSU ID card with a mag stripe. "During the first weekend distribution for the fall term," said Bill Norwood, who bears the title of executive director of the FSU Card Application Technology Center, "nearly $10 million in federal financial aid money entered the FSUCards system. About 40 percent of that money was transferred to the university as tuition payments, leaving almost $6 million in disposable student income. Merchants who had previously avoided accepting the card as a payment method lined up to take advantage of this huge influx of dollars. For the academic year 1995–96 more than $60 million have flowed through the card."[1] In fall 1996, this program and many others "migrated" to an FSU smart card, which offered, among other things, secured Internet access; an "electronic checkbook"; special campus payphones for collecting salaries or other money transfers through stored accounts on the card; access to library, computer, and sports facilities; access to copying and vending machines; and meals. As of June 1996, American Express claimed an on-line stored value system in operation at two hundred "university, hospital and business campuses." At year's end, Citicorp had 177,000 cards circulating at campuses of the State University of New York.

In September 1996, the first of 19 million benefit payment cards were issued by the Central Computer and Telecommunications Agency of the British government. By the spring of 1997, a "Southern Alliance" of states—North Carolina, Missouri, Alabama,

Arkansas, Florida, Georgia, Kentucky and Tennessee—will be running pilot programs with Citibank, Deluxe Data Systems, Lockheed Martin and First Union to pay out *all* social cash benefits, from Aid for Dependent Children and food stamps to Social Security SSI, through chip cards.

Anyone who doesn't hear distant thunder hasn't been listening.

2

The stored-value card is the natural substitute for cash. Originally a piece of cardboard with a laminated magnetic stripe that could be pre-loaded with money, the stored-value card was pioneered in the United States by the Bay Area Rapid Transit (BART) System in San Francisco as a way to achieve a pay-by-distance fare on a subway. Money was deducted from the mag stripe with each use, and when all the stored value was gone, the card would be discarded. This sort of special-purpose money has been widely used over the years, the most obvious example being the chips the cashier at the gambling casino sells and redeems. Tokens that had no other purpose had long been used for pay telephones in Europe. Entertainment parks of various kinds sold tickets that could be used on the rides, which did not accept cash. On a less jovial level, mining companies had paid their workers in scrip that could be used for purchases at the company store. In all these cases, the people who issue the value get it back by delivering services for it. These are "closed" systems.

The planners of BART had a larger goal. They hoped that the money on the BART card could be used not only for subway fares but also for purchases. Neither the merchants nor the banks were interested, and the idea died on the vine. The same hope surfaced again in New York in 1996, when the Metropolitan Area Transit

Authority announced a deal with Chase Bank to set up a profit-making joint venture that would receive a small (probably three-quarters of one cent) commission on each use of a pre-loaded Metro Card. Chase would supply merchants with readers through which the card could be swiped (or modify a storekeeper's existing Verifone for credit card purchases). The announced goal was $50 million a year for the transit system.[2] Alas, the deal was premature, and in the end all MTA was invited to do was participate in a pilot program permitting the use of a Visa-MasterCard card issued by Citibank and Chemical as a way to pay for subway and bus rides—with a *cost* to the MTA as just another merchant.

When one moves to "open systems," to stored value that can be spent for products or services other than those made by the issuer of the value, one needs a redemption process. The value taken off the card by the seller of the goods and services bought with the card must be useful to him, ideally as useful as money itself. We return to Hy Minsky's truism that anybody can issue money; the problem is getting other people to accept it. Just as the promoters of credit cards needed a switch where the merchants could enforce their claims against the card issuers, promoters of stored-value cards for general use need an arrangement with a bank that will transfer that value to those who have accepted it. If the only bank that will give money for stored value is the bank that issued the card, then the card will be useful only with vendors that have accounts at that bank.

But just as the giro system is easier to run than a checking system, a stored-value system is easier to run than a credit card system. The fact that the payment rather than the debit moves means that the complex of problems surrounding the bounced item never arises. The cardholder has already paid for his card: the money is in the system, at a central depository (at the beginning, the agent bank that sells the card; later, a pot shared by the consortium). The bank accepting payment in stored value receives reimbursement from the system instantaneously. An interesting illustration of the advantages banks get from stored-value cards rather than credit cards is that the bank pays for an "affinity" label—a ball club or union logo or a frequent-flier benefit—to put on the credit card, but can sell the face of the stored-value card to advertisers. The manufacturers of the Danish "Danmont" card, which is the source of the Visa Cash technology in the United States, say that half the cost of making disposable cards is paid by advertisers. Stores use the reloadable memories on the cards for their "loyalty" programs.

The pioneers of this sort of system are the French, who from the beginning used not a mag stripe that can only diminish in value but a "smart card," a silicon wafer with an integrated circuit on it. This could be a "read only" card with a memory chip, to be discarded when the value on it was used up. But it also could be a "programmable" card with a microprocessor that could be reloaded, and used for some time (two years is the anticipated normal duration). IBM had got patents on a kind of chip card as early as 1970. "Mag stripe," said Jerry Svigals, who was at one time in charge of growth planning at IBM, "is World War II technology." Indeed, mag stripes are inherently insecure, a fact that has been concealed by the congressional decision to limit the losses of cardholders to $50, which made the card issuers very vigilant in defense of the system. Banks are protected from check fraud losses by the holder in due course doctrine of the Uniform Commercial Code, and pay only about $800 million of the annual $12 billion losses from check fraud, so they don't care much. But credit card fraud they really hate.

The first marketable chip card—a *"carte à mémoire"*—was developed and sold in France in 1974 by Roland C. Moreno, then twenty-nine, a journalist and self-taught tinkerer. He thought of it as strictly a substitute for the mag stripe, but more secure, because the password registered on the chip couldn't be copied. Coupled with an electronic cash register to capture the data about the customer and the transaction—and with a communications device to report the transaction to a bank at the end of the day—the *carte à mémoire* would substitute for checks at the point of sale. This was important for France, where checks were costly to process and increasingly popular in the 1970s; indeed, the French still write more checks per account per year (86 in 1993) than any people other than the Americas (234).[3]

Moreno persuaded a handful of smaller French banks that a microchip card would enable them to offer retail services comparable to those of the bigger banks, with much smaller up-front costs and greater flexibility. But the sale he made that mattered most was to the state-owned PTT (the postal and telecommunications authority). PTT was up to its eyeballs in videotex technology and projecting, accurately, a future in which every home would have a French-made Minitel terminal with screen and keyboard that would allow the household to tap various data bases to be transmitted by PTT, starting with the telephone directory. (The French were having terrible telephone directory troubles. On a visit to Paris in the late 1970s, I couldn't find the phone number of someone I was to see. When I finally did, through a friend, I complained to my target that he wasn't in the phone book, the Bouttin. "Of course we're in the Bouttin," he replied. "We're a business." Then he went and looked himself up in the book and came back to say, "*C'est bizarre*. We're there, but we're not in the right alphabetical order.")

With Moreno's smart card as a secure device for granting customers access to the system and as a personal record-keeping tool, the PTT could proceed more rapidly to program the Minitel to offer mail-order purchasing, home banking, airline ticketing, electronic mail, and other services. (In 1996, while the European Union Payments Systems Working Group was proclaiming that only banks should be allowed to offer stored-value cards, the PTT issued more than 300 million read-only disposable smart cards.) With PTT on board, it was easy for Moreno to interest what was then CII-Honeywell-Bull (now, once again, just Bull, the

American affiliations having collapsed). In 1976, Bull licensed the Moreno patents—and, most importantly, gained patents of its own to add a microprocessor to the memory chip, to create what it called "a portable computer for the Eighties."

When I wrote my first article about smart cards, in *Fortune*, in 1983,[4] there were three French experiments using smart cards as debit cards to replace checks in shops and shopping centers in Lyons, Blois and Caen (the customers got a three-day float). Smart cards were already in use at gas stations in Phoenix in a General Electric pilot program; at a Defense Department installation at Fort Lee, Virginia, as a basic ID; and in an experiment by J.C. Penney and First Bank Systems in Minneapolis as a device to convince two hundred farmers that their home banking program on Minitel terminals was really secure. The future was almost here. "In five years," said Paul Finch, vice president for systems research and development at Valley National Bank in Phoenix, taking a prototype card out of his wallet and throwing it on his desk, "everybody's going to be carrying one of these." George Hubbard, who came on board at Bull's American subsidiary in 1987, remembers that he was then one of seventy people in the operation. In 1996, there were only five. The smart card is now the portable computer for the third millennium.

But it will come. There are now about 50 million rechargeable smart cards in consumers' hands, 30 million of them in France, where all bank cards now have a programmable chip. The French card is still an off-line instrument, with the transaction lifted electronically from the merchant's cash register each night by his bank, credited to him that night and debited against his customer's account three days later, to preserve the consumer's float. In most places, the smart card has shaken down as a stored-value card, not as an especially secure and capacious credit card. The Norwegian banks have issued more than a million Bull cards (the equivalent market penetration in the United States would be 60 million). Denmark is the home of the chip card with the highest levels of consumer use, called Danmont; Visa has licensed the rights for the United States.

Club Med, which gave guests a necklace of beads that were the chain's private wampum, has switched most of its resorts from beads to chip cards. In addition to Florida State University, chip cards have taken over record-keeping, access and payments function at Duquesne, Michigan University, and Washington University at St. Louis. Parents give their college-age children spending money on stored-value cards that can be used in ATM machines. The 1996 Olympics used a stored-value Visa card—"Visa Cash"—which was also accepted by the subway system and at vending machines and hotels and restaurants and presumably at shops all over tourist Atlanta. Three banks—First Wachovia, NationsBank, and First Union—actually issued the cards. Only First Union, however, offered rechargeable cards good for a year; NationsBank cards expired in October. Though 4,500 terminals were installed, the experiment flopped pretty badly. At a meeting in September, Gaylon How of Visa confessed that only a million dollars had been stored on smart cards in Atlanta, and only $250,000 of that had been used in the three weeks—the rest had disappeared to dealers in "collectibles." Edgar Brown of First Union Bank told the annual conference of the Smart Card Forum in San Francisco that there had been much storekeeper resistance to Visa's insistence on charging the usual 2¢ per transaction "interchange" fee for credit authorization when there was no credit to be authorized. You bet.

Locked out of Atlanta, MasterCard ran television commercials during the Super Bowl and 1996 basketball championships to say how much the Aussies loved the large-scale introductory program Master had launched in Australia. The people who were supposed to be first off the mark were Electronic Payments Services, owners of the MAC ATM switch, with Banc One carrying the largest piece of the development load. But, not for the first time, Banc One found itself with a system that wasn't workable. Citicorp, a skeptic about smart cards in the 1980s, has won an auction to supply the state of Ohio with a chip card–based Electronic Benefits Transfer program to handle that state's food stamp distribution.

At about the time this book is published, Chase, Citicorp, Master and Visa—all four—will have equipped some five hundred merchants all over the Upper West Side of Manhattan in New York City to accept payments on chip cards, and will have issued some tens of thousands of cards to local residents. The Visa cards issued at the Atlanta Olympics will work in the New York readers. "By choosing to issue cards in both the MasterCard and Visa electronic cash programs," Saul Hansell of the *New York Times* reported, reflecting the industry's angst about the Fed's failure to help standardize formats for stored-value cards, "the two New York banks are helping to establish standards for card-reading equipment that will help speed the deployment of compatible cards in other regions."[5] By the time the pilot was launched, eight months late, MasterCard and Chase had gone to the Mondex system (see next page), and the two cards in circulation were not at all "interoperable."

Meanwhile, the uses keep expanding. Utah planned and still hopes to issue its driver's licenses in the form of a smart card. A "Multi-Technology Automated Reader Card" issued to 18,000 Army personnel in Hawaii in 1995 includes a mag stripe and a bar code as well as a chip, and takes care of all identification and medical, food-service and library records. At the University of Rome, students gain access to the computer, the library and their own records and exam results—and faculty verify that the right person is taking the exam—through a smart card; 300,000 have been issued for this purpose. At Expo '92 in Barcelona, smart cards that recorded the cardholder's fingerprints were used for identification by both staff and visitors, and they were used as a security screening device in Atlanta, too. Phil Verdi of MasterCard says that well before the end of the decade there will be a fingerprint identification system, measuring points and distances on one finger, that takes up only 60 bytes. The U.S. Department of Agriculture has issued 160,000 smart cards to peanut farmers—and a thousand terminals to peanut purchasers—to monitor and control their sales, which are strictly regulated in what is perhaps the most lunatic of all the American agricultural price-support programs.

A card-reader small enough to be carried on a keychain will allow the cardholder to determine the balance on the card and to recall the ten most recent transactions. People who don't carry readers will be able to access the data through ATMs, through "card phones" in the home supplementing the usual telephone features with a screen, or through personal computers—Bull already has a system for playing a smart card onto a floppy disk to make it readable by any PC. Readers for stores, incorporating both a magstripe swipe slot and a chip card slot (and a little adding-machine printer, if so desired), cost perhaps $70 more than the usual Verifone terminals. Because the microprocessor is actually in the card, readers and writers can be very simple.

A British smart card system, Mondex, uses a handheld reader-writer about the size of a passport case, that can transfer value—in any of five different currencies!—from one person to another as well as from a consumer to a merchant. This is not a fly-by-night techie dream, either—even before MasterCard took over, it had the backing of National Westminster Bank (the largest in Britain), British Telecom, AT&T, and Hitachi. The Hong Kong and Shanghai Bank, owners of Britain's Midland Bank, is also on board, as are the Royal Bank of Canada and the Canadian Imperial Bank of Commerce, the two largest in that country. Wells Fargo has run a lengthy pilot involving 800 of its own employees at its own cafeteria and nearby shops. Verifone, of necessity in New York, has added a Mondex reader to its Visa Cash slots in the United States.

The initial Mondex tryout was in Swindon, a city of about 120,000 people about 170 miles from London, and the announcement in the fall of 1995 was that by spring 1996 there would be 40,000 Mondex cards. The actual figure of 10,000 was greeted enthusiastically, however, by Mondex's promoter and CEO, Tim

Jones. Jones is a tall, forty-one-year-old Cambridge University graduate with blow-dried reddish-blond hair who came to banking from two years as a soft-rock guitarist and could sell raccoon coats to Amazon Indians. What makes Mondex different from the other chip cards is that it is "unaccountable"—that is, once the bank issues the value on the card, it loses touch with the money, just as it does when it gives currency across the counter or through the ATM. The card can be used not only at stores equipped to read it, but also between any two people with Mondex reader-writers, which will be made by Hitachi and Panasonic—and NCR and Unisys, among others.

Visa Cash is a short loop: it goes from the bank to a consumer to a merchant and back to the bank, because only the merchants have the readers that give them value when they accept the card. Mondex credits simply go out into the world. The security is in an encryption process, which permits only those with a Mondex-generated key to decode the numbers. Each card has an "active" and a "dormant" code; as cards are used or recharged at banks or terminals in stores, a signal from headquarters can phase in the dormant code and phase out the old active code. Mondex cards are the path to Bill Gates's "wallet," an infinitely capacious smart card that can put anybody in the world in touch with anybody else in the world through infrared signals.

The possibility of holding different currencies on a chip card greatly excited Giles Keating, research director of CS First Boston in London, who suggested that in the absence of a single European currency, "e-money" could become the dominant medium of exchange in Europe. "With private-sector transactions voluntarily taking place in strong foreign currencies," Keating argues, turning Gresham's Law on its head, "weaker currencies would progressively be reduced to being used for a residual lump of 'legal tender' transactions, such as tax payments." Keating assumes not a single e-cash with its own purchasing power, but electronic money denominated in different national currencies, which people would hold "in non-interest-bearing accounts, kept for making electronic transactions."[6]

Mondex would indeed facilitate such a future, but the more common and plausible worries about Mondex relate to its anonymity: "[C]ard systems that would allow person-to-person transfer of value and transfers over specially equipped phone lines . . . would allow holders of prepaid card value to move funds rapidly to remote locations where they could make several smaller, undetected deposits. Under these circumstances, electronic purses could facilitate money laundering."[7] George Hubbard of Bull points out that card-to-card transfer would be "an unaudited transaction. You could create value, and spoof the system: put it on my card, and not take it off yours." A written submission by Mondex to a committee of the U.S. House of Representatives in June 1996 noted that "the architecture of Mondex is designed to allow for high value as well as low value transfer." Eric Clemmons of the Wharton School says wonderingly and dubiously, "Mondex means I can buy all the money I want, across borders." Central bankers worry, too, about the loss of information to the monetary authorities: cash mostly goes back into and then out of the banks, but Mondex credits might circulate, unregistered and unaccounted, from card to card for quite a long time. Different classes of purses will have different value limits, and high-value purses will be able to transfer the ownership of value only through banks. Maybe.

Some of this concern bleeds over into the effects of *any* chip card as a substitute for cash. When a depositor draws cash from his account, a bank reduces both its assets (the cash) and its liabilities (the deposit). But cash in the vaults is a special kind of asset that can be counted as part of the reserves the Fed requires banks to keep. Thus a cash withdrawal triggers either a purchase of Fed Funds or a shrinkage of the bank's footings. Demand for cash is among the control levers the central bank can grasp. If the depositor takes a credit on his chip card, the bank merely swaps one kind of liability for another, with no change in its reserve position. Thus the Fed would have less control over the banking system if stored-value cards replaced any considerable part of the cash in circulation.

Getting the money from a bank account to any stored-value programmable chip card is no problem at all. Though modifying older ATM machines is an irritatingly difficult and expensive process, most of them can be adjusted to charge a card in addition to giving cash. And—most importantly—the thing can be done in a matter of seconds *at home*. In 1994, U.S. Order, a company linked to Visa (and through common venture investors to Verifone, which makes the swipe card readers in stores), began manufacturing a telephone with a slot for the introduction of chip cards and an alphanumeric pad hidden under the usual panel of dialing buttons. By dialing the bank and supplying a personal identification number (plus additional authentication that can be encrypted onto the smart card), the cardholder will be able to head out into the world on his daily round with however much "cash" he thinks he may need that day. Citibank has commissioned the production of its own card-reading and card-writing Minitel-like telephone. Robert Haddock, who organized the development phase of the Citibank phone, has produced a screen phone which can be used for payments and also gives access to the Internet in black and white.

The record-keeping functions of the multipurpose chip card raise other concerns. Who will have access to the medical records on the card? Transaction records involving, say, the rental of obscene videos? Religious contributions? Union dues? Social security numbers will be on the cards. Steven A. Bercu of the law firm of Foley, Hoag and Eliot, representing the Smart Card Forum, warns of "a basic reaction against a technology that 'compels' an individual to carry around at all times the seeds, as it were, of her own self-incrimination. . . . If the government uses Smart-Card records to run computer 'matching' programs in efforts to surface benefits or tax cheaters, a range of due process issues may come into play."[8] The question of what happens when a card is lost is easy in the value sphere—it's cash; finders keepers, losers weepers; the Fed has now promulgated a rule that says so. But it's less easy when the card contains its holder's life history. Where are the duplicates?

And there remains a question of who can issue value on smart cards, both practically and legally. Asked who should issue stored-value cards in a public opinion poll commissioned by Citibank, a plurality of respondents said, "the telephone company." Telephone companies, transit authorities, Club Med clearly can use stored-value cards to pay for delivery of their own services. Merchants would probably be willing to accept payment through stored-value cards from any financially solid operation, provided a system for transferring the payment to a useful account or another asset was in place—and, as we know from the Merrill Lynch experience with Banc One, banks are often ready to cooperate in such matters.

In May 1994, the Working Group on European Payments Systems of the European Union proposed that only banks should be allowed to issue stored-value cards. "The report cautions," John Wenninger and David Laster of the New York Fed write, "that cards issued by nonbanks would not be subject to the banking regulations, supervision, and deposit insurance schemes that have traditionally protected consumers. The absence of such safeguards is important because the failure of an electronic purse scheme could undermine public confidence in other electronic purse schemes, possibly causing a run on them."[9] One can see that a bank might not be happy about setting up a program by which a man can use his telephone company stored-value card to give a haberdasher authority to order a bank to increase his account. On the other hand, companies like Microsoft and GE and MCI have better credit ratings than banks, and if they wish to set up in the value-issuance business, it's hard to see any market forces that would stop them.

Devil's Advocate asks, "What do you do if the bank fails?" A bank that had issued stored-value smart cards did fail in Estonia in 1995, and until early 1996 nobody knew whether the people who thought they had money on their card would ever see it. They did; the government stepped in. I have suggested that this would be an ideal venue for experimenting with private deposit insurance. The banks that issue stored-value cards could set up a fund to reimburse holders of cards issued by failed banks. The sums involved in the early years will be small enough to make such a scheme plausible, and by restricting access to the scheme to depository institutions, the banks could give themselves a strong marketing edge against others attempting to tread on their turf.

In the United States there is always the Fed, philosopher kings sitting in Washington, as unconscious as George Bush of the realities in the supermarkets around them. In March 1996, the Fed put out for comment proposed amendments to Regulation E that would exempt stored-value cards with less than $100 on them from the requirement of receipts for transactions and monthly statements to cardholders. The issuers would have to tell people that the card had an expiration date (if it did), and that if they lost it, *tant pis*. It should be noted that the decision to exempt lesser-denomination stored-value cards from receipt requirements was to some degree forced on the Fed by the spread of stored-value cards as means of access to telephones and transportation systems: if the Fed required the printing of a receipt for each use of a bank-issued smart card, bank cards would be excluded from such uses. But the Fed also permitted banks to promote the system by sending people free cards loaded with some initial value (sending credit cards without a request for them has long been forbidden) and—interestingly—exempted from any Regulation E coverage all Mondex-like systems, which do not keep records on the use of the money though the cards can be loaded with any amount. David Boyles of American Express has objected bitterly, and intelligently, that

> The Federal Reserve's proposal to distinguish between on-line and off-line technology is not rationally related to protecting consumers' interests. . . . On-line stored value . . . is the most secure and affords the consumer the greatest protection because every transaction is authorized and recorded. That means that stolen cards can be "turned off" and that users can track all of their spending. In contrast, the off-line cards have gaps in their capabilities and lost or stolen cards often cannot be refunded or replaced. Moreover, emerging technologies make it possible to blend both on-line and off-line capabilities on the same card. In such cases, different levels of regulation for different kinds of technology will be confusing to customers, difficult for regulators to apply, and nearly impossible for the judiciary to interpret. . . . [S]ome specific requirements simply make no sense. For example, the proposed rules require that receipts be issued for all on-line transactions, but not off-line transactions even though they involve an identical activity. . . . [E]ach can of soda would require a separate paper receipt. [10]

The industry should be under no illusions that the Fed is favorably inclined to this innovation in the payments system. Testifying before Congress in October 1995, Vice-Chairman Alan Blinder started his comments with

> a potential revenue issue that will arise if the stored-value industry grows large. The Federal Government currently earns substantial revenue from seignorage on its currency issue. . . . Discussing that point raises the question of whether the Federal Government should issue its own electronic currency. Government-issued electronic currency would probably stem seignorage losses and provide a riskless electronic payment product for consumers. In addition, should the industry turn out to be a natural

monopoly, ... government provision might be an appropriate policy response.[11]

Outside Washington, it would be considered a twisted notion that Congress should be legislatively influenced because improvements in the payments system which yield large benefits to the public might impose minor revenue losses on the government. Inside Washington, it seems a reasonable point to make.

3

What really makes chip cards such a likely bet for the next decade is their convenience as a guarantee of security and privacy in purchasing through the Internet and bill paying at home through the telephone or the PC. For the smart card through its capacity to generate encryptions—not to mention the possibility of authorization by digitized fingerprint or signature—can guarantee that the user's bank account or credit card number is safe from wiretapping snoopers. The "triple DES" version of the Data Encryption Standard published by the National Security Administration in 1975, which is what the banks still use, is in fact much more secure than the telephone lines over which people order from mail-order catalogs or cable TV shopping programs. "There's a protocol in the handshake," says Daniel Schutzer of Citicorp, "and it says that you're authenticating that you're a good processor and I'm authenticating that I'm a good processor. It must be independent of the verification."

Even better encryption is available, not very expensively. RSA, a sort of co-op of Ph.D. mathematicians, has developed a program charmingly described in the trade as "Pretty Good Privacy," coupling a public key generally advertised to give access with a secret key known only to the intended recipient. The system probably provides security good enough for anybody but a drug dealer.[12] (Note the word "security," a weasel compromise between "privacy," which is good, and "secrecy," which is bad.) In spring 1996, RSA sold the remaining five years of its patent and its business for $200 million. Nevertheless, everybody worries.

The loss of a bank account number is a much more serious matter than the loss of a credit card number, because the credit card companies are geared to catch fraud and the banks are not. Fear that bad guys will learn a bank account number has greatly slowed the growth of bill-paying services from the home. The elimination of that fear will be a necessary, though not a sufficient, condition for moving the country toward a more efficient payments system. And the smart card can diminish fears.

The first payments services were pay-by-phone, an idea that sprang full-grown from the brow of Howard Phillips, a debonair Boeing aerospace systems designer, who decided in 1971 that there was money to be made by bringing computer services to the home through the telephone. "Computer gear was expensive then," Phillips recalled. "We offered six services to the Seattle market—bill payment, income tax preparation, home budgeting, a calendar of events, records retention (you'd call in the purchases when you bought something, for insurance purposes), and the telephone as a calculator—a popular service. Those were the days when a handheld calculator cost $150. We called it 'In Touch,' and Seafirst purchased an interest in us in April 1972. We brought up the service in June 1973, and it fell on its face in six months. We had gone at it the way aerotech engineers would go at a problem, with no consideration of marketing, with a brochure in aerospace black and white, and a manual an inch thick. Seafirst said, 'We're ten years too soon,' and after an ugly shouting match, I became the sole owner of the company again."

Phillips's TCS (Telephone Computing Service) looked like a viable enterprise because the S&Ls wanted to get into the transactions business. AT&T's new 800-number service made a nationwide service practicable. Phillips designed a turnkey package, "hardware and software, systems and procedures," by which an S&L or a bank could offer telephone bill-paying. In 1978, he dropped the other features and concentrated on the banking business. The flow was that the payor called TCS in Seattle, and an operator punched in the payor's personal identification number, producing his and his bank's names and routing numbers, his account number, and a list of the payments he had made in the past. The operator registered the payments the payor wished to make with this telephone call (recording every word spoken by both parties), then notified the bank or S&L to pay this money *to* TCS, which then paid the billers, benefiting from the float. Phillips's largest competitor did even better on float, being located in Lewiston, Maine.

ADP bought the business (and Phillips), and some large banks subscribed, including Citibank, which supplied Phillips with bundles of blank Citibank checks, so Citibank depositors wouldn't realize somebody else was providing the service. Between 85 and 90 percent of all payments made through Phillips's phone bank in Seattle involved somebody at ADP writing an actual paper check to be put into the Fed's usual clearance and settlement system. ADP started an ACH in Chicago to control electronic payments and encourage companies to accept them, but it was too hard a sell. Only a handful of public utilities and insurance companies got organized to accept payments directly to their bank accounts, matching the lists of payors and the bills that had been sent out. ADP finally gave up; Phillips got the business back again, and sold it again, this time to EDS, which has built $1.5 billion a year of revenues on demand deposit accounting and payments processing, but only a very minor fraction of that on telephone payments. Some banks do telephone payments themselves, using software from PegaSystems in Boston.

In the 1990s, hoping to keep customers while closing

branches, banks have increased their efforts in "telephone banking." Nearly all offer account inquiries by phone, and of course those that have stock brokerage services make them accessible by phone, as brokers do. With the right password, customers can shift money from one account in the bank to another. Most larger banks take loan applications by phone. But according to an Ernst & Young/American Bankers Association survey, only 35 percent were offering "third-party payments" by phone in 1996.[13] With the development of the screen phone, which will give people a chance to *see* what they are doing without the fuss of computers, "telephone banking" could come alive, though like computer-based "home banking" it will make sense only after the payees have geared up to receive electronic payments.

4

In 1981, Chemical Bank in New York began work on a videotex service that would bring to people with television sets or personal computers, through TV cable or telephone, words and pictures—information about the stock market, airline schedules, the state of the world, the availability of tickets to shows, restaurant menus, the history of Bosnia—and banking services. One hundred and thirty people worked on the project, which was called Pronto, but when Chemical finally took it public, in fall 1983, it offered only home banking—and in home banking, only the power to pay about four hundred payees that had agreed to receive the payments through an ACH. Anybody else, you wrote your check, as usual. For $12 a month. One early customer told the *New York Times* that the only bill Pronto had let him pay was one from American Express.[14] Citibank did a little better with its parallel Home Base project for home computers only, offering part of the Dow-Jones "broad tape" news report on business, and payment to anyone the customer wished to pay. If the customer you wished to pay did not have the capacity to receive electronic payments, Citibank wrote the check for you. This one was dropped in fairly short order; the techies said it was because the program gummed up after the first five hundred users.

Meanwhile, the newspapers and AT&T had got into the videotex act: the *Miami Herald* (for the Knight-Ridder chain), the *Los Angeles Times* and the *Chicago Tribune* all developed information-cum-shopping-cum-entertainment services to be delivered to television sets on telephone lines. Viewtron, as Knight-Ridder called its services, offered national and international news via the Associated Press and local Little League scores from the Dade County Recreation Department; any page from a Grolier encyclopedia; the Scott Foresman reading series for the tykes and a cram course on the Scholastic Aptitude Test for teenagers; the Official Airlines Guide; shopping at a hundred Miami stores that would have what are now called home pages; road maps; and nautical maps showing where the fish were biting—all in living color, twenty-four hours a day. This cornucopia could be accessed through an attachment with a keyboard of little chiclets designed and sold by AT&T for *$600*. In 1983.

All this was to be supported by a $12-a-month charge to the subscriber, plus advertising and commissions on merchandise and services sold through the system. Home banking would be a feature. Banc One of Columbus, Ohio, led a consortium of four banks which would provide these services through an Orlando-based company they called Video Financial Services. (The other banks were Wachovia in North Carolina, Southeast in Florida and Security Pacific in California; the two latter are no longer with us.) In this case, nobody had to worry about whether or not payments could be made electronically, or whether the bank where they had an account was participating in the venture, because the program didn't work.

Videotex flopped, too. The false assumption (quite widespread and durable, a true Lazarus of commercial ideas) was that people wanted to interact with their television set, and they didn't. People who want to be active don't watch television, they go to their computer. The videotex menu item with the largest amount of use in Miami was the six o'clock summary of the day's developments in the soap operas; "If we didn't get that up by six o'clock," says a veteran of the experience, "the switchboard lit with complaints." By contrast, when Dow-Jones made its information retrieval service available to computer users, the menu item with the largest amount of use was something prospective: the movie reviews.

What revived home banking almost a decade later was the growth of check-writing, bookkeeping and financial programs for home computers, especially Quicken from Intuit and Microsoft Money from the folks who brought you the Microsoft Disk Operating System and the C\>: prompt. They in turn brought payments services like CheckFree and National Payments Clearinghouse (NPCI). The big banks have mostly made alliances with Intuit or Microsoft to ease the interface between home computers and their electronic-payments projects (Citibank, typically, has gone it alone; NationsBank and Bank of America have bought a small software company for the rights to its home banking program).

Microsoft's pilot project involved four banks that have become three—U.S. Bank in Portland, Oregon; Chase; and First Chicago and Michigan National, now merged. On the other hand, Microsoft made its own deals with computer manufacturers Tandem and Stratus, whose "no-fault" parallel-processing machines dominate the electronic payments field. Microsoft also has a separate venture with Visa, and the two of them have published an eighty-one-page standard for Secure Transaction Technology, which a vice president of the software firm Netscape says will put Microsoft in a position "to exact a toll for every payment on the Internet." (In early 1996, Visa and MasterCard agreed to proceed for now with a simpler encryption process.) Visa was rebuked by its board when it first suggested ventures in home banking, but then the less-than-giant banks that dominate the board reversed course and urged Visa to get in the fray and help them.

But all the bank plans still must write paper checks (legally, "drafts") for 70 percent of all the "electronic" payments people make from their computers. For most of the bank plans, the checks are written by CheckFree or NPCI, which also make a lot of money in the check-printing business. CheckFree is the largest customer for the post office in Columbus, Ohio, larger than the state government or Ohio State University. NPCI was bought in 1994 by Intuit. That was one of the reasons Microsoft wanted to buy Intuit in 1994 and one of the reasons the Justice Department suggested the purchase might be a bad idea, killing the deal. The result is that every one of the home banking plans involving Microsoft Money requires in effect that Bill Gates pay a per-use fee to Scott Cook, the owner of Intuit. Reliable sources report that it just kills him.

The demand that the industry find something better, and soon, comes from the Treasury Department, which is under pressure from—of all places—Congress. Among the quaint folkways of Congress in recent years has been a demand that when additional expenses are to be incurred by the government or revenues are to be lost, cost must be cut elsewhere or substitute revenues found. The North American Free Trade Agreement (NAFTA) involved the loss of some customs duties, and the planners scrambled and scrambled to find replacements. One of the things they found, worth about $140 million, was ordering corporations to pay their payroll and profits taxes electronically. Then, in spring 1996, a Congress desperate to end a budget impasse decided to save hundreds of millions of dollars by transferring to an electronic chassis all payments *by* the government (except tax refunds). All new federal contracts with private vendors now specify electronic funds transfer, and all new individual recipients must agree to direct deposit unless they can prove hardship. First Chicago won the contract for the Western states, and NationsBank for the eastern states, and First Data made a deal with Chicago to do the work involved in converting old-fashioned tax returns to machine-readable entries.

People who are concerned about (rather than just talking about) international competitiveness may also apply public pressure. In the words of Markus Reithwiesner, product manager for Intuit in Germany, "There is no home banking in the United States. Germany already has it." There are already a million people in Germany paying their bills through Telekom On-Line, which allows customers to transfer money directly from their bank account to the bank account of the company that sent them the bill, and Japan is making a rapid transition from a cash society to an electronic-payments society, largely skipping the checking stage. A survey by Booz Allen & Hamilton reported in summer 1996 that by 1997 56 percent of European banks would offer "fully fledged banking service." Integrating these services with existing "dinosaur" systems will be an experience, an author of the study reported. "Moreover, it will be easier for customers to pick and choose, and harder for banks to differentiate their Web sites from their competitors—including non-banks which can bundle financial services together on the Internet."[15]

5

What revived videotex in the United States was of course the Internet, which is a hyper-videotex with e-mail for all and millions of retrievable pages placed there by whomever and all his friends, worldwide. Its enormous ganglia twist through telephone wires (but can run much faster and more effectively through fiber-optic or coaxial cable or frequency spectrum) through the millions of computers that pass their messages through modems to the outside world. In September 1995, the Financial Services Technology Consortium, a group of big banks, organized the first establishment purchase (a teddy bear from a gift shop) through the Internet. A senior vice president of Chemical bought it for Vice President Albert Gore as a gesture of thanks, using a credit card in a slot built into a PC, generating an electronic check sent by e-mail to the merchant, which passed it on for deposit to its account at Bank of Boston, which converted it into an ACH item on Chemical. Dan Schutzer of Citicorp, president of the consortium, hailed the purchase of the teddy bear as "the first collaborative effort by major banks . . . to develop from inception a new financial standard.[16]

Like Knight-Ridder promoting Viewtron and Chemical selling Pronto, but on a much larger scale, the protagonists of the Internet expect profits from commissions on sales made through the medium. This expectation can be realized only to the extent that there are means of payment. Meanwhile, to take advantage of the convenience of Internet access, and to save the cost of dedicated lines, the banks want to be able to set up shop on the Internet. Some people have jumped the gun.

Lee Stein is just about what you would expect a pioneer of Internet banking to look like—mature hippie (forty-two), a long, pale face, thinning hair tied back into a bun, staring eyes. An enthusiast. His background, he explains cheerfully, is not banking but law and Hollywood and the management of rock concerts. His first idea for making money on the Internet was a daily joke people would find in their e-mail when they turned on their computer. If they liked the joke, they would pay Stein a penny; if they didn't, they wouldn't. This was not very practical, and Stein turned to banking.[17] His slogan reads, "The Future Is Here with First Virtual." You ask him where his office is and he replies, "I live in San Diego, but my office is the 800 number." His card says, however, that "media relations" are conducted from a 619 area code, which is San Diego.

First Virtual is a way for customers to buy software and information—or, indeed, mail-order merchandise—without leaving the Internet. Anyone selling on the Internet can for $10 set up an account with First Virtual, which will process the orders he receives, verify the purchaser's Visa, MasterCard or Discover card in the usual way (the buyer pays $2 the first time he uses First Virtual to make a purchase, otherwise nothing; and the merchant never learns the customer's credit card number). The payment from the card is credited to the "merchant's" account at First Virtual, minus a fee to First Virtual of $0.29 plus 2 percent of the transaction plus a $1 "settlement charge" for each "deposit." If the seller doesn't want to be troubled filling orders for his services by locating the buyer and downloading onto his computer, First Virtual runs an InfoHaus which "handles storage, distribution and billing functions" for an additional 8 percent of the selling price plus an information storage charge of $1.50 per megabyte per month. In June 1996, Stein's newly acquired operations vice president, John J. Donegan, claimed that in its first two years First Virtual had "settled over 184,000 transactions. These have been almost all software, documents, or other intellectual property that can be delivered electronically. Today, First Virtual has grown to over 145,000 customers and over 1,800 merchants in *more than 140 countries*."

EDS moves the money and handles the bookkeeping, and First USA acquires the merchants. Indeed, First USA, the largest issuer of credit cards in America, bought a piece of First Virtual in late 1995. We are told by Stein that First USA will issue a "Virtual PIN" (personal identification number) to the 14 million holders of its credit cards to enable them to do business more quickly with Stein. By 1997, Stein claimed, there would be 100 million "Virtual PINs" out there to build his market. The Virtual PIN will be an e-mail address for the customer, and Stein will sell advertisers information on which e-mail address is likely to be a profitable recipient of messages about what the advertiser wants to sell.

The trick is that the "merchants" Stein has served did not have the credit ratings or the volume of traffic to qualify as recognized

Visa or MasterCard or Discover merchants, and without that status they really couldn't at this point sell their products to those who "hit" their page. These are not customers who are going to write checks and address envelopes, and even if they would, the sellers of information would have to download their software or data before receiving payment, inviting what the retail world calls slippage. The danger would be especially great on the Internet, where quite a lot can be downloaded free of charge, and many users have politico-economic biases that lead them to believe that what they see on their screens *should* be free.

"Superimpose financial services on the wild and woolly Internet," says Michael Slade of CheckFree, "and you've got a consumer problem." Howard Strauss, who runs the computer end of Princeton University, says, "If you put a copyright bug on your page, I have a program that will take it off. What do I know from legal or copyright? I'm a techie." (On the other hand, once somebody has established an Internet address, nobody else can use it. Toiletpaper.com and underarmodor.com were registered by Procter & Gamble to make sure nobody else could do so.) Stein is not concerned, at least so far as the information and software sellers are concerned: "When you're selling a piece of software on the Internet, you don't have production costs, you're not out anything if you don't get paid."

First Virtual gets more from these tenants on its merchant's franchise than just the account and transaction fees, however. The rules the Federal Reserve sets for credit card companies permit purchasers to protest their purchases for sixty days, and Stein can argue that, especially in the Internet world, buyers are likely to complain that what they bought was no good. So First Virtual keeps the use of the merchant's money for sixty days. "We move the risk of collection onto the merchant," Stein says. This means a substantial additional fee for the merchant, who borrows his working capital at a rate much over prime. The total of these fees considerably exceeds what First Virtual has to pay the credit card company for the transactions forwarded to it. And the size of First Virtual's cut guarantees that as soon as a First Virtual merchant achieves enough volume to qualify as a direct Visa merchant, he will fly the coop.

There is also a little problem that Visa and MasterCard merchants are not allowed to franchise the use of their license; "We watch how much business First Virtual is doing," says a MasterCard executive, "and if it gets to be a lot, we'll cut him off." But so long as the credit card companies are tolerant, and the increase in the numbers of businesses wishing to sell on the Internet exceeds the numbers of those businesses graduating to membership in the credit card merchants club, Stein should have a very good business. "The merchant," he says, "has two choices—not being in business or waiting until the Reg Z period [the Federal Reserve's sixty-day rule] has passed."

Except that there will be competition, and the competition will be able to avoid credit card charges entirely by using a virtual medium of exchange. The first of these—patented—is e-cash, the product of a company called DigiCash, the creation of David Chaum, a burly, ponytailed, bushy-bearded American mathematician resident in Amsterdam, The Netherlands. This is a doubly encrypted credit which can be spent with those who will receive it; the recipient doesn't know whose money it is unless the customer wishes to tell him, but the customer has proof of payment if needed. This privacy feature is a crusade for Chaum, who feels that any payments system which permits people to trace who bought what opens the door to fascism: "Do you want to build a system that basically undoes the kind of freedoms that are the basis for our society? There have been a number of think tank reports that come out of Washington that suggest that the best way to turn this into a police state would be to use identification-based payments and outlaw currency, banknotes and coins. There are studies to that effect."[18] He really did say it, and he really did mean it.

The DigiCash pilot involved the free distribution of $500 in

"Digibucks" to each of a thousand applicants, who then could spend it with whoever would accept it. What those accepting it would do with their DigiCash credit was unclear. The pilot did not produce many transactions. The first commercial use of DigiCash was in November 1995, when Mark Twain Bancshares in Missouri began advertising an Internet account ("The Mint") that would issue Digibucks. Anyone with a real account at Mark Twain could transfer dollars from that account to a DigiCash account in an Internet site. Buying from a merchant on the Internet, he could offer to pay in e-cash. If the merchant also had an account at Mark Twain, the transaction could be completed (payment against delivery, too, when what was purchased was a computer program to be downloaded or an extension of service on the Internet) without the use of either conventional money or credit. The merchants got next-day credit in dollars at their Mark Twain bank account—this is not a wire transfer of funds, because for banking purposes Mark Twain Banks is not on-line with its web site(!). And, of course, only companies with an account at Mark Twain can participate. Meanwhile, the Mark Twain web site offers chat rooms for an investors' forum where people can exchange comments on the markets.

The Mark Twain operation was not like the Security First Network Bank, "the world's first Internet bank," a "Federal Savings Bank" (chartered by the Office of Thrift Supervision rather than by the Comptroller of the Currency, but in fact approved by the Comptroller) offering "banking so private, you can do it from just about anywhere you can take your computer." Security First's address is http://www.sfnb.com. In 1997, Citicorp bought into the consortium, to benefit from the experience. But it is really just an ordinary bank in Pineville, Kentucky, owned originally by Cardinal Bancshares of Lexington, Kentucky, but spun off in early 1996 to the Cardinal shareholders and three banks—Wachovia, Huntington and Area, which wanted the technology. SFNB deals in the U.S. government's own dollars, subject to all the rules the regulators make a bank follow. And, indeed, its web page shows how ordinary it is: the pictures on the screen are of a Greek Revival bank building, and then of a banking floor and a teller window—nothing to be frightened of at all. Its advantage is that it jumps the gun on interstate banking. In fact, SFNB reports that in its first eight weeks in fall 1995 it acquired 1,100 accounts in forty-two states.[19]

At present, Mark Twain's Internet presence is a triviality. Its e-cash is used entirely as a vehicle for people spending and receiving dollars. (DigiCash has spread a rumor that Deutsche Bank is about to adopt its e-cash for payments in deutsche marks.) Nobody is going to accumulate an account in Mark Twain Digibucks, which pay no interest, and the merchants who maintain an account to collect payments from their customers are going to transfer those Digibucks payments rapidly into dollars, which they can use with their suppliers, landlords, employees, and so forth. But as the use of the Internet for commerce expands, one can imagine a closed loop like Mondex, within which people pay various bills in e-cash rather than dollars—especially if the costs of operation are low enough, in comparison to brick-and-mortar dollar banking, that Mark Twain can afford to hang bells and whistles on the accounts.

Moreover, even more in this context than in the stored-value context, there is the possibility that the issuer of e-money will not be a bank. Visa and MasterCard have enormous files of merchants and professionals to whom they direct payments, and card processors like FiServ and First Data and EDS, with tens of billions of dollars in capitalization, would surely be acceptable issuers. First Data does the processing for *92 million* credit cards in the United States alone, both bank cards and its own cards—so long as the Visa or MasterCard logo is on the card, people don't care who actually issued it. The company has thirty-six thousand employees, most of them in Omaha, and a headquarters staff of thirteen in Hackensack, New Jersey.

Visa and MasterCard are presumably owned by syndicates of banks, though in fact they operate as independent companies, and First Data and EDS are examined by the members of the Federal Financial Institutions Examination Council, just like banks. Their issuance of a new money might not entirely escape bank regulators' supervision. But Microsoft, partner now with a number of banks in home banking, could also offer accounts denominated in whatever currency Bill Gates might wish to create, and there would be takers. "Intuit," said Stephen Hirsch of Chase, speaking of Gates's rival, "is a product-sales company. Banks are lower on the food chain, and have no leverage on Quicken [Intuit's product]." One can indeed envision a world where the backing for e-money would be so strong, and the Federal Reserve's regulation so obtuse, that a dual payments system would develop through the Internet.

One thing is certain: the future, whether money moves through the banks or through service providers, will belong to the man who owns the file of payees. The economies of electronic payment require that the money move directly from the payor through the computers to the switch to the credit of the seller and then to the payor's account with the seller. These economies are the big bucks, with perhaps as much as $40 billion a year of cost savings available to the country if the payments system operated at maximum efficiency, with universal participation. For individual providers who might hope to process as much as three billion transactions a year, a 20-cent-per-item saving of which they kept half would yield revenues of $300 million a year. A few tens of millions of dollars' cost for computer installation and programs—and security precautions, because these files can be abused—doesn't look like much on that scale.

Corporate payments through what is called EDI/ETF (electronic data interchange/electronic funds transfer) have been growing, though much less rapidly than the potential cost reductions would lead an observer to expect. It's easy to blame the banks: as of 1995, only 750 of the 11,000 U.S. banks were capable of accepting and passing on EDI messages.[20] Kevin O'Brien of Texas Commerce notes the dead hand of sunk cost: "Direct debit of households through ACH would be more efficient, costs for banks would be less, but net income, short term, would decline because of the check capture infrastructure that already exists." But David Kvederis of Wells Fargo blames corporate inertia and "treasury anorexia—we've been shrinking these departments so over the years that they don't have the personnel to do anything but the big things."

Mark Burns, then of Chase and Microsoft, at this writing with Charles Schwab, thinks the problem is the relative efficiency of the paper-based system the big bill collectors have now—"They have these five hundred people in Secaucus [New Jersey], and everything runs smoothly. You tell them you can save them money, but it's going to cost money now—nobody in management today can afford to take that attitude. Meanwhile, the home banking payments are exception items for them, because they come in without the associated bill. You call one of these companies and ask to talk to the person who supervises exception items, and nobody knows where to find him." Which is serious: Michael Slade of CheckFree reports that "If you don't know it has to get to John's desk on the second floor of Commonwealth Edison, the chances are it isn't going to get posted on time."

George White, who operates a consulting service for users of electronic payments and runs conferences for which people pay fees in advance, says that when participants pay him electronically, "Our bank—United Jersey—usually loses the addendum record. The payments come in fine, the doctors and the hospitals get their money, they just don't know who it's from." People in the operations end of the banks note scornfully that the mortgage-servicing sections of their own banks are not ready to receive electronic payments.

Part of the problem is that FedWire and the ACH operations, having been designed as substitutes for checks, have not been geared to carry and distribute much information. "ACH and Corporate Trade Payments," says Ed Hogan of MasterCard, "are like you have a tank of gas and you're wondering why there isn't a car to take you somewhere." For large payments, information about the transaction the payment completes is likely to come in separate messages, most frequently (about 500 million messages a year) over SWIFT, the Society for Worldwide Interbank Financial Telecommunications. For ACH items (about 3 billion a year), there is a charge for each "segment" (nine-tenths of a cent), and recipients must be equipped to receive information as well as money. To save real money by making consumer payments electronic will require building the list of payees, and the payor's account numbers at the payees. And, says Mark Burns, "building a file is not a cool thing to work on—hey, it's just a billing program. It's much less exciting than virtual reality."

But there are enough players now, with enough surplus capacity on their machinery, that someone is going to reach for the gold. Pricing to modify behavior is easily available here. As William Moroney said in 1983 when he was running the National Automated Clearing House Association, "Once the banks start charging the doctor a dollar to deposit a check, you won't have any trouble finding out his bank account number to make a direct payment: he'll print it on his card with his phone number." But the banks didn't do that, so the doctors didn't do it, either.

Visa and MasterCard already have files of millions of "merchants," including plumbers and hospitals and grocers as well as airlines and hotels and department stores—and some doctors. CheckFree in Columbus, Ohio, raised $108 million with a public offering in 1995, and there was $67 million of it left for the business after the underwriters and the selling shareholders took their cut—and much of that has been made available for the tedious work of asking everybody to whom the company now writes a check to organize for what would be the faster receipt of electronic payments. "That's the only way you can build a file," says Michael

Slade. "One name at a time." Verifone, already a $180-million-a-year business with its swipe boxes on the counters of more than five million merchants, launched an electronic wallet in late 1996. Its purpose, general manager Denis A. Calvert told a subcommittee of the House Banking Committee in June 1996, was "to pursue strategies that enable 'physical' merchants to methodically upgrade their terminals . . . to accept new Internet-based payment schemes, as well as enable 'virtual merchants' to accept payments."

ADP and EDS have webs of relationships with payors and payees. Microsoft has a deal with Visa; MasterCard has an alliance with Netscape, the largest of the programs for finding things on the Internet. In early 1996, Netscape and Verifone, the manufacturer of the swipe card readers (which in summer 1995 had purchased Enterprise Integration Technologies, a software house specializing in security products), announced a joint venture for secure payments on the Internet, including a smart card and a Mondex-like "wallet."[21] The service providers, ADP and EDS for sure, are looking hard at how their existing product mix and machinery might be integrated into the Internet. An EDS deal with Microsoft, not etched in stone as of this writing, would permit a bank to buy Microsoft Money for eight or nine dollars, and offer it to its depositors in a form that permits them to use *only* this bank for electronic payments.

Telephone companies like Chicago's Ameritech and public utilities like New York's Consolidated Edison with large bill-collecting capacity are beginning to rent it out to other businesses. (This may be the real reason why the utilities stiffed the American Express One Check venture.) The intrepid explorer in these ghostly grottoes can scarcely turn around without finding a mysterious light in yet another chamber—for example, in the cavern occupied by our ubiquitous hedge funds, where the Ph.D. mathematicians of D.E. Shaw & Co. talk of expanding their creation of algorithms to the reduction of payments messages. These people are problem-solvers. Bankers have a lot to worry about.

PART
II

UNDERSTANDING
BANKING

6 / The Way We Were

*Banking is a distribution system that has become archaic.
Banks will feel a desperate need to change. Some will know
how to do it—like Morgan. Others will just be desperate.*

—GEORGE KENNY, vice-chairman,
Merrill Lynch, 1995

*I still think there is money to be made in the banking busi-
ness, and the more people that drop out of the banking
business, the more money there is to be made.*

—RICHARD ROSENBERG, chairman
of Bank of America, 1994

There is no good old definition of banking, and the word itself
is now going out of fashion. Nobody except an S&L wants
to be a bank these days; everybody wants to be a Financial Services Institution. The first person to worry about what this shift of
nomenclature might portend was Paul Volcker, who had been
named chairman of the Federal Reserve Board by President
Jimmy Carter in 1979 because the American dollar was going
through the floor on the world's exchanges. Volcker, then president of the Federal Reserve Bank of New York, formerly under
secretary for monetary affairs to Treasury Secretary John Con-
nally in the Nixon administration, was the only man with the size
(six foot eight) and substance to convince the world that
American monetary affairs were in the hands of somebody who
knew what he was doing.

For reasons we shall look at in Chapter 14, the chairman of

the Federal Reserve Board gets paid only about half what the president of the Federal Reserve Bank of New York gets paid, and Volcker was a New Yorker with no great love for Washington. (He maintained his home in New York through the eight years he was chairman of the Fed, and went back there for weekends and during the week whenever he could. On his coffee table in the chairman's office at the Fed he had a big pewter ashtray for his cigars, and around the edge was engraved the legend "If you've left New York, you ain't gone nowhere.") As it happens, I spoke with him a few days after Carter had announced his appointment, and he said he'd been summoned to Washington for an eight a.m. meeting with the President, who had asked him what he would need to be persuaded to take the job. He'd made a list of about twenty requirements, which Carter noted on a sheet of lawyer's yellow lined paper. The last of them was that there would *never* be any sniping at him, never be a word of criticism of Fed policy, from "the kids" who surrounded the President in the White House. When he came home, he reported, he said to his wife that he'd scotched that job, but the next morning the President was on the phone to tell him his name was on the way to the Congress.

Among Volcker's great strengths was his knowledge that there were things in the changing world he did not in fact understand, and should study. He deferred in matters of monetary philosophy to fellow governor Henry Wallich, Austrian refugee, Yale-trained economist, open-minded large-minded conservative, author of a splendid book called *The Cost of Freedom*. And he deferred in matters of bank administration and operations to Vice-Chairman George Mitchell, a nitty-gritty man with a growly voice and gray cropped hair, former banking professor from the University of Illinois who knew why bankers did what they did, and was kept on as a consultant at the Fed when his fourteen-year term as a governor ended. But when it came to defining banks and banking, Volcker turned to a protégé from the New York Fed, a beefy, red-faced Irish-American Fordham-trained economist, E. Gerald Corrigan, with whom Volcker liked to go trout fishing. He arranged Corrigan's appointment to the presidency of the Federal Reserve Bank of Minneapolis, and from that perch Corrigan wrote a pamphlet, his annual report, about why "banks are special." Banks have functions financial service institutions don't have. The quality of a capitalist economy will depend in large part on how well the banks perform those functions.

The two functions, which have been joined at the hip, are (1) the creation of the money supply through (2) lending for the use of its borrowing customers the money left at the bank by its depositing customers. Indeed, the 1970 amendments to the bank holding company act define a bank for purposes of law as an institution that offers checking accounts and makes commercial-and-industrial loans. Within the memory of living men, this symbiosis was physically illustrated by the presence of the lending officers at desks on a raised platform in the center or at the rear of the banking floor, where the customers came, *faute de mieux*, there being no automated teller machines, to deposit and cash their checks. There was no way of escaping the relationship between payments and loans. Every time a loan was made, as noted above, the nation's money supply grew, because there were two deposits where there had been one.

There can be two different views of the fundamental process that produces the bank loan. Thomas Jacobsen, a Chicago banker transported to Jacksonville for Barnett Banks, who kept wistful pictures of snow scenes on his walls, said that "We're not selling loans; we're trying to find uses for our liquidity." Economist Hyman Minsky argues that the provision of the money is a secondary aspect of banking: "The fundamental banking activity is accepting, that is, guaranteeing that some party is creditworthy. A bank, by accepting a debt instrument, agrees to make specified payments if the debtor will not or cannot. Such an accepted or endorsed note can then be sold in the open market. *A bank loan is equivalent to a bank's buying a note that it has accepted.*"[1]

For the New Deal economist Lauchlin Currie, the creation of the money supply (which implies by extension the management of the payments system) was what made banks different from and more important than any other economic actors. Others could and did lend money, but only banks created it. "Banks," Currie wrote, "derive their peculiar economic significance not from the fact that they are lenders—there are many other lenders—but from the fact that they furnish in modern countries almost the entire supply of the community's means of payment. . . . Apart from their connection with demand deposits there is no logical reason to distinguish bank loans and investments from other loans."[2]

Fifty years later, Corrigan echoed the point: "[T]he single characteristic of banks that distinguishes them from other classes of institutions is that they issue transaction accounts; that is, accounts that in law, in regulation, or in practice are payable on demand at par and are readily transferable to third parties."[3] And there is no question that from a general public point of view, what makes banks special is the payments system: "People today don't care where they get their mortgage or their car loan," says John Backus of U.S. Order, in the engine room of the electronic payments machine. "The only thing they need a bank for is a checking account."

But there are significant social and operational differences between banks and other lenders. At banks, the borrower and the lender are often one and the same: the borrower keeps his checking account at the bank, which means as a normal matter that he gives up all rights of privacy about how he spends it, because the bank as lender needs that information. ("Every good loan officer," says James Watt, president of the Council of State Bank Supervisors, "spends a little time every month leafing through his borrowers' checks.") Because he has a continuing and close relationship with his borrowers, the banker can improve the chances that his loans will be productive—to the borrower, to the lender, and to the community at large. In this view, the banker's

188

central function is not the money supply or the payments system, which can be managed by others, but its role as the first judge of the prospects of a business venture that has gone through its initial hurdle of raising start-up money and now needs a loan to get established. The banker vets the business plan, and monitors its execution.

Though neither the market analysts nor most academic economists realize it, the lending officer, geographically or industrially specialized, is the reason why diversification is a successful investment strategy for non-bankers. Investments in all business ventures across the board would show a loss, because the great majority of new businesses fail. But the pattern of start-up capital, then bank loan, then public offering is almost invariable, even for Internet companies. Once the loan officer has made the first cut, the investor knows that someone who can't afford to be wrong very often has vetted the likelihood of cash flow from this company's business. Mr. Market, as Jim Grant of *Grant's Interest Rate Observer* likes to call it, needs this summary of the banker's information before he can intelligently put his foot out the door.

"The social purpose of banking," says consultant Ed Furash, "is to create prosperity. You don't have another institution around that has the function to create prosperity." A more immediately practical point is made by Tom Cooper, once president of Bank of America, later CEO of Chase Federal Savings in Miami, which he sold to NationsBank: "B of A has a lot of stuff in the files that would not pass regulatory scrutiny today, that made Silicon Valley possible."

My own definition of banking, quite consistent with the 1970 bank holding company law and drawn in essence from Adam Smith, was that "a bank agglomerates the transaction balances of the community to lend at interest to its commercial enterprise." This does not permit savings accounts (and until the 1930s commercial banks might offer time deposits that paid interest—and usually couldn't be withdrawn until their time was up—but they didn't have "savings accounts," a business left to various savings banks, insurance companies and savings and loan associations). It does not permit loans to consumers (which were, indeed, the province of finance companies and credit unions until the 1960s). Because they are necessarily illiquid and cannot be called when money is needed for depositors, my definition does not permit the writing of home mortgages or long-term loans to anybody, which is the right way to run a bank in theory but impossible in practice. Until the National Banking Act of 1935, the only loans the Federal Reserve System would accept as collateral when discounting paper to help member banks get cash were short-term commercial loans or "bankers' acceptances." And the National Bank Examiners from the Comptroller of the Currency were instructed to classify as "slow" any loan that had more than a year to go before repayment.

Since 1980, banks as I (and Adam Smith) defined them have pretty much ceased to exist. Today, banks by and large make their loans first, and then go look for the money. The source of their funds is no longer the agglomeration of deposits. In 1961, Walter Wriston and John Exter of what was then First National City Bank of New York arranged with Discount Corporation of America to make a market in large-size certificates of deposit, which the bank would sell to raise funds, and since then the banks have not been restricted in their loans or investments by the volume of deposits that walks in the door. For the rest of that decade, while the Fed controlled the interest rates banks could pay, it was possible for Federal Reserve Board chairman William McChesney Martin to slow down lending by taking actions that would move market rates of interest above the level he let the banks pay. But first the creation of the "jumbo" (more than $100,000) CD, which the Fed exempted from interest-rate controls, and then the elimination of interest-rate controls in the early 1980s, made it impossible for the Fed to create a "credit crunch."

In April 1996, indeed, the Fed stopped the growth of bank reserves, but nobody seemed inconvenienced. As Jim Grant wrote, "[A] violent deceleration in the rate of Federal Reserve credit creation has failed to call attention to itself, much less to provoke street demonstrations against the Federal Reserve Board. . . . [T]he economy is upright and the speculative punch bowl is brimful. . . . Alan Greenspan is still being lionized on the days when he is not being canonized."4

Virtually all commercial banks today offer a bewildering variety of savings accounts, concentrating on *non*-negotiable certificates of deposit (CDs) to climax on a pre-announced date, with penalties for onanistic withdrawal. Under L. William Seidman in the 1980s and early 1990s, the Federal Deposit Insurance Corporation was willing to insure anything the banks cared to issue, up to and including accounts in foreign currencies and accounts offering interest payments hooked to stock market fluctuations. And today's banks can borrow in lots of other ways. In 1996 almost 85 percent of the banking industry's resources came from sources other than insured deposits of any kind. The advertised credit crunch of 1990–92, as indicated in the Introduction, was the result of pressure from accountants and bank examiners on valuation of loans and investments, not control of lendable deposits by the Fed.

My definition has been blown even further away by developments on the asset side of the ledger. Loans to consumers, especially on the credit card chassis, are the lifeblood of the largest banks: Citicorp makes more than $2 billion a year—more than half its profits—on such business. ("In 1992," said Joe Tripodi of MasterCard, "Citibank was technically insolvent. What kept them going was a billion-dollar profit on credit cards.") *Most* commercial-and-industrial loans are now term loans, many of them going out ten years or more. Indeed, banks write currency options that go out five and six years, which are *absolutely* illiquid.

In short, banks take their money where they can get it and use their resources for whatever the law allows that looks profitable here and now; they design "products" for sale to people and business as ways to raise funds, and other "products" as ways to use funds. As such, they are in direct competition with all the other financial services institutions, from insurance companies to stockbrokers to mutual funds to originators and packagers of mortgages to vendors of electronic payments services.

So a bank is no longer an enterprise that agglomerates the transaction balances of the community to lend at interest to its commercial enterprise. Perhaps my definition was never any good. Even before the computer changed the world, there was great authority against it and for the proposition that the functions of payments system provider and lender were easily separable. "The Bank of England," David Ricardo wrote in the early nineteenth century, "performs two operations of banking which are quite distinct, and have no necessary connections with each other: it issues a paper currency as a substitute for a metallic one; and it advances money in the way of loan, to merchants and others. That these two operations of banking have no necessary connection will appear obvious from this—that they might be carried on by two separate bodies, without the slightest loss of advantage either to the country or to the merchants who receive accommodation from such loans."[5] But the decision to link the two had been taken a long time ago.

2

J. T. W. Hubbard in his history of the New York State Bankers Association charmingly describes the business Alexander Hamilton hoped to do when he opened his bank, the Bank of New York, in 1784:

[A] storekeeper in Albany could order $1,000 worth of imported china dishes from a merchant in New York on April 15; the storekeeper would enclose with his order a written promise to pay the merchant the full $1,000 upon the safe delivery of the dishes on May 15. Without the facilities of a commercial bank, the merchant would have to dispatch the dishes and tie up his capital for the thirty days until May 15, before presenting the storekeeper's note for collection. With the Bank of New York in business, the merchant could ask its cashier, Mr. Seton, to "discount" the storekeeper's note the moment it arrived on April 15; if Seton knew the storekeeper to be a man of probity and substance then he would accept his promise to pay $1,000 one month hence, on May 15, while presenting the merchant with a sum of $995 in cash now, on April 15. . . . [This money] could now be used . . . to place an order for another bulk shipment of china dishes from Paris or London.[6]

That's banking.

Banks of this sort were the cornerstone of the American economy. Walter L. Buenger and Joseph A. Pratt of Texas A&M describe the situation in Houston:

Cotton dealers could not function without credit. They needed banks. Banks needed cotton dealers because they were their safest and most profitable loan customers. Banks needed a source of funds to lend to cotton dealers. Railroad companies and steam lines needed a place for their deposits to meet their payrolls. . . . This circle of mutual need and mutual benefit lasted from the 1880s until the 1930s.[7]

Banks allowed merchants to stock their shelves and manufacturers to inventory their raw materials and farmers to buy the seed for their crops. They also gave advice. The Levi Bank & Trust Company of Victoria, Texas, ran an ad in the local paper in the early 1910s:

PORK AND BEANS

Boston is said to be the home of Pork and Beans, but we need not go that far for them.

We really should grow our own Pork and Beans and save the freight as well as the middlemen's profits. Every one who handles a shipment of Pork and Beans rightfully expects to make a profit on them. Let's grow them at home and save these profits.

We may see six cent cotton this fall. Let's grow more hogs, beans and such like and need less cotton.

THE LEVI BANK & TRUST COMPANY
Victoria, Texas[8]

One notes in passing that the Levi family, whose sire had come to Texas as a peddler in 1848 or 1849, was Jewish, one of a small handful of Jewish commercial bankers in America before the 1980s. Also that, its last Levi board members gone, the bank in the Ku Klux Klan days changed its name to Victoria Bank and Trust. It remained throughout primarily an agricultural lender: when the fancy new building opened in 1960, ranchers were invited to bring their branding irons to the bank and 273 leather squares were branded with the neighbors' signs, to be hung behind the tellers on the main banking floor. Finally, one notes that the Victoria Bank and Trust, grown to $2.5 billion in assets, with branches through the interior of the Corpus Christi–Austin–Houston triangle, was acquired in spring 1996 by Norwest Bank of Minneapolis, which with interests in fourteen different states was already the most interstate bank in the country. Texas having decided by vote of its legislature not to permit in Texas the national branch banking Congress had authorized two years before, Norwest will not be able to fold Victoria into a larger organization, and it is by no means clear that either the seller or the buyer knew why the purchase was made. On the other hand, Norwest Corp in 1994 ranked second in the country in the fraction of its commercial loans that went to small businesses, so perhaps the acquisition was part of a pattern.

More of this sort of banking survives than academia or the media believe. William McDonough, president of the Federal Reserve Bank of New York, told a meeting of the worldwide Group of Thirty in 1995 that "smaller American communities benefit greatly from local banks, locally owned, locally managed. In New York State, small community banks continue to thrive." Community banks lend to their communities; that's their business. Communities can be geographical, or linked in a "common bond" (which is the definition of a credit union's community), or they can be self-defined. In New York City itself, the Merchant's Bank, about a hundred years old and having about a billion dollars of footings (only 40 percent the size of the Victoria Bank, one-third of 1 percent the size of the new Chase), lends to middling-size manufacturers in the New York metropolitan area. Its CEO, Spencer Witty, white-haired, erect and gracious like a banker, still expects its borrowers to do "a technical clean-up" at least once a year. What he means is that, in the old-fashioned way ("we're an old bank") he expects his borrowers to have at least a few days a year when they've paid off their debts to his bank—or, at least (technically), have more money in their account in his bank than they owe him.

More than two-thirds of the Merchant Bank's loans are to companies that have done business with this bank for more than ten years. It is, of course, a considerable saving of money to do repeated business with the same borrower: the lending officer needs spend much less time gathering information. Witty's biggest customer is General Foam Co., which makes swimming pools for the summer and plastic Christmas trees for the winter; General Foam owes him money for about four months of the year, and for eight months, it doesn't. That was the classic rhythm of banks, years ago: the farmer needed money for seed in the spring, and paid you back at harvest time; the retailer needed money for inventory in the fall, when Christmas was coming, and paid you back early in the new year.

Everybody sets his own risk profile. In the garment industry, Manufacturers Hanover (now part of Chase) lent to the dressmakers, as did specialist banks like Sterling National. Witty lends to the "greige goods," the textiles, where the value is less controversial ("After you dye it and print it, people have to like it"). Letters of credit for exports and imports are a big business. Witty's grandson is his chief investment officer. Witty dislikes fads. "When oil was thirty dollars a barrel," he remembers, "the guy who ran Midlantic [a New Jersey bank that got into desperate trouble and was eventually absorbed by City National of Cleveland] ran ads with him looking down a well. The ads said, 'The Hungry Banker.' We've never been hungry."

Witty's secret is that he doesn't take big losses. Bankers don't have enough profits on their good loans to support serious mistakes. In late 1995, the Merchant's Bank of New York sent out a note with its quarterly dividend check: "Enclosed is our Two Hundred Fiftieth consecutive quarterly cash dividend. It has never been skipped nor cut since 1933. A record few if any other American banks or companies can match. We are pleased to have you as a shareholder."

Witty and many others still make what are now called "character loans." The small-town banker who survived was a man who knew which potential borrowers would and which borrowers would not beat themselves up to pay their debts. And he could charge lower interest rates than computer models might tell him to charge because he had that human confidence in his borrowers— and, of course, he had *all* their business. Until the 1980s, when the Wall Street transaction mentality took over much of the banking world, it was common wisdom that relationships were the heart of banking. The most common benefit appears to be that the borrower can borrow more from a banker who knows him. And the banker gains by lending larger pieces, the personnel costs of lending being relatively fixed over a large range of loan values.

Mitchell A. Petersen and Raghuram G. Rajan of the University of Chicago Business School have demonstrated convincingly that "Attempts by a firm to widen its circle of relationships by borrowing from multiple lenders increases the price and reduces the availability of credit."[9] Where the lending takes the form of a line of credit against which the borrower can draw as needed, Allen N. Berger of the Fed and Gregory F. Udall of the Stern School at New York University have found that "borrowers with longer banking relationships pay a lower interest rate and are less likely to pledge collateral."[10] One should note that personal acquaintance cuts both ways. Don Stevens, chairman of the Bank of San Francisco, said he's always been a real estate lawyer, never sat on the loan committee of his bank. "Of course, if the borrower was somebody I knew, I might tell the committee, 'Don't lend to him. Every time he comes to San Francisco the burglar alarms go off.' "

George Moore of Citibank remembered his time as a "district calling officer" in the 1930s and 1940s:

> I carried address books, in which I wrote not only the man's name and business address, but the home address and the names of all his family if I had a chance to meet them, and of course the name of his secretary. . . . If people were going to Europe, I'd send them a note about a tailor in London or a hotel in Athens. Or I'd send them answers to business questions that had come up inconclusively at our meeting. The idea was to find something to send him that he would be glad to get: he looks at it, and he says, "This is from that smart young fella who was in here last week." It's even better if you send it through his secretary, demonstrating that you remember her name, too. I've actually heard a secretary say to her boss, "That nice Mr. Moore would like to see you. Can you fit him in today?" . . . You can't get quick results with such things, of course, but the bank doesn't need quick results—and if

you come to think of it, neither do you. . . . These principles apply to any business that sells. And I have yet to find a business that doesn't have to sell to survive.[11]

The real banker was the lending officer, and it was the lending officer who became chairman and CEO of the bank. He knew his borrowers' businesses. Before the 1930s, the expertise was almost always a matter of geography: banks lent in their own bailiwick. (When savings and loan associations were federally chartered for the first time, the law prohibited them from making loans more than fifty miles from their home office.) The First National Bank of Chicago, one of the nation's ten largest but restricted by state law to a single unit bank on a single city block, had to send its lending officers around the Midwest, and was probably the first bank to make its lenders industry specialists, in the mid 1930s. Chase followed, with emphasis on oil companies and insurance. Citibank didn't get there until 1954.

Specialist lenders could expand the character loan to the "cash flow" loan, looking not to the inventory that would be sold to repay the cost of its acquisition but to the ongoing use of the equipment and material to be bought with the loan. Moore remembered sending one of his lending officers to a truckers' convention when he was a middle-management man at Citibank, and being told, "We've never liked trucking, George"—and responding, "That's cash flow again—depreciation. They can pay off on those trucks even if they're not making money, you know."[12] It was also typical of Citibank that he was given the authority to make the loans. Not everyone is on Moore's side. Donald G. Simonson of the University of New Mexico reports a conversation with a finance company official who described the banks' willingness to lend against capitalized cash flow as "an exercise in fictitious capital formation."

Historically, character lending showed two faces, offering opportunity for some, discrimination to others. It's the people who live in your town—geographically, or culturally, or ethnically, or religiously, or educationally—whose character you know, or think you know. Thus you tend to lend to the members of your club, and not to those who speak differently or have a different color skin or a different sex. Even after American law had decisively ruled that women could own property in their own name and did not have to turn it over to their husbands, it was especially difficult for women to get loans—though sometimes even in the old days the bankers came through: Martha Graham at age ninety gave her special thanks to the Bank of New York and Francis Stella, "who went on the loan with me for a thousand dollars, so I could give my first recital." (The First Women's Bank that got started in 1976, though ensconced in a premier location on East Fifty-seventh Street, never made it; the Comptroller of the Currency eventually closed it down and the FDIC gave it to Spencer Witty's bank, in a deal that left the FDIC, not Witty, with the problem of disposing of the loans.)

The Bank of Italy that became the Bank of America is of course the most famous of the ethnic lenders, but the tradition survives, sometimes hidden because the Congress has written laws against favoring one ethnic group over another. (The single exception is African-American banks, which are permitted to favor African-American borrowers.) The Korean community eschews bank loans, borrowing from self-help cooperatives with roots in the mother country, which don't have to satisfy U.S. bank examiners. Taiwan, by contrast, has been the more-or-less acknowledged source of funds and direction for Chinese-American banks that serve the Chinese immigrant community and some native Chinese-American businessmen; but these Chinese banks do not welcome visitors. Hong Kong and Shanghai, which owns Midland Bank in England and Marine Midland in New York State, also has two branches in Chinatown, facing each other across the street. One is for Mandarin speakers, the other for speakers of dialects. The most cohesive of all the ethnic groups is the Cuban community of Miami, which is served by a handful of little banks and the branches of big holding companies like First Union, SunTrust and Barnett.

"Our market," said Carlos J. Arboleya, vice-chairman of the Barnett Bank of South Florida, with forty-two branches and about $5 billion in assets, "is fifty-one percent officially, fifty-five percent really, Hispanic. We cater to the needs and idiosyncrasies of the community. It's not the John Doe, motherhood and apple pie sort of community." Even the second-generation Cuban, Arboleya's assistant Barbara Rose comments, will give preference to Hispanic bankers: "They are perfect in both languages," she says, "but they *buy* in Spanish." This is, however, classic small-town commercial banking: "To have an effective relationship, you must have his term debt, his line of credit, his commercial mortgage, his cash management, his home mortgage, his business retirement plan, his IRA and his family checking account."

Arboleya, a large man with a fine gray mustache, came to the United States in the first flood of refugees from Castro, in 1960, and started his own bank. Sixteen years later he sold his bank and joined Barnett Dade County as president of what was then one of five Miami properties of this Jacksonville-based holding company. "I came to this bank," he recalls, "because they had lent me the money to open *my* bank. Nobody knew them. When I told friends I was going to Barnett, they said, 'Barnett *office systems*?'" Now Arboleya is sufficiently well known that the street on which Barnett's thirty-three-story skyscraper stands is called Arboleya Plaza. Spanish, incidentally, is not the only language useful in Miami. An entrepreneurial Haitian community wants French-speaking bankers, and Tom Cooper reported from his time as chief of Chase Federal Savings that his branch for the Art Deco end of Miami Beach needed a German-speaking manager, because the money that has transformed the South Beach is German money.

Some of this gap between the social status of the potential borrowers and the social status of the bankers could be bridged by hiring a variety of bank lending officers, or at least by assigning them to specialist work, so they got a feel for the industry. Bank of Boston lent to the movie industry, where Serge Semenenko had honed his very special perceptions of what Americans wanted to see, and then to the early electronics industry on Route 128 because MIT and Harvard were the progenitors and protectors of the industry. Texas Commerce lent to cotton farmers, ranchers and then the oil industry. It is by no means clear that the information on the computer screen can ever compensate for failure to know the people involved. An old-fashioned banker like Spencer Witty will never allow a loan to go out of his bank until somebody visited the plant "and kicked the tires."

Real estate lending was and is the most dangerous. One way to judge whether a bank knows what it's doing in real estate is to visit that department, see how many lenders are in fact in the office rather than out visiting the sites, and look at the shoes of those present. A real estate lending department where people have clean shoes is going to be in trouble. From 1985 to 1991, Citicorp doubled its involvement with commercial real estate investors and builders who by late 1991 were bankrupt already or rapidly getting there. The commercial real estate portfolio totaled $12 billion, much more than the bank's total capital, and virtually all of it was under water, with very little the bank could do to preserve itself. "Once a building has been started," Lowell Bryan of the consulting firm McKinsey & Co. notes rather dreamily, "it needs to be completed. Raw land is more valuable than a hole in the ground and a poured foundation. A half-built building . . . may even have negative value."[13] Describing Citi's relationship with 1540 Broadway, a Times Square office tower for which Citi had provided a $280 million construction loan (and which chairman John Reed himself went to visit when it became obvious that the building was never going to pay back its costs), Jerry Adler in his hilarious book *High Rise* notes that "it would have been easier for Citibank to foreclose on Brazil."[14]

Lending officers have always been management consultants, making sure the books make sense, carrying the "best practices" of an industry from borrower to borrower. In the 1970s, Citicorp acquired a management consulting firm, and the Federal Reserve Board forced it to throw back its catch on the grounds that management consulting was not a business "incident to banking." Walter Wriston, then CEO, blew his stack: "The first management consultant," he said, "was a banker on the banks of the Euphrates, telling a guy he had to build a wall around his inventory. That's all a banker is, really, a management consultant." Ex-chairman George Moore in 1984, age seventy-nine, was summoned to Minneapolis to advise Control Data Corporation, which was both a financial services and computer company, on how to dispose of its Commercial Credit subsidiary; he suggested that Control Data sell the computer company and keep Commercial Credit. They didn't think he was serious, but it was Commercial Credit that became the vehicle by which Sanford Weill took over Smith Barney, Shearson Lehman, Travelers Insurance, and Salomon.

In an adoring tribute to the small-city bankers who help smaller businesses, *Inc.: The Magazine for Growing Companies* stressed the consulting role of the lender: "A small-business person today can find not only someone willing to lend but a lender who at once is efficient, knowledgeable, generous, supportive, protective, instructive, accessible, appreciative, patient, reasonably priced, and an active small-business advocate as well."[15] This experience is less common than *Inc.* contends, but the magazine lists no fewer than twenty-six nice banks, several of them subsidiaries of big banks (First Union gets mentions in Florida and North Carolina). And big banks dealing with big international customers sometimes make similar claims. "We put ourselves in the client's position," said Marcus Rollbacher of the

Union Bank of Switzerland, the largest retail bank in that country, owner of one of the more successful British brokerage houses, and an unseen presence in the United States. "What keeps him awake at night? What makes him a winner?"

John McGillicuddy, who ran Manufacturers Hanover and then, briefly, after the merger, Chemical, said that one of his strengths as a banker was that "people knew that if they were talking to me and I said this is something we are going to do, we would do it—whatever anybody down the line might say. Goldman [Sachs] got a lot of business because people knew that if something was wrong they could call John [Weinberg]."

A. P. Giannini's Bank of Italy, later Bank of America, grew by serving the farmers and industry of California, by far the fastest-growing economy in the world for most of the period of Giannini's life. California permitted branch banking—at its peak in the 1980s, Bank of America would have more than twelve hundred branches in the state. The farmers needed money at one season, the storekeepers at another. The deposits gathered through the state from its workers and farmers and small businessmen, Giannini's customers, could be employed year-round, profitably. The Golden Gate Bridge, the oilfields of the southern basin, the Shasta Dam, the aerospace industry, the irrigation of the Imperial Valley, the Kaiser aluminum and steel and shipbuilding empire, the Napa Valley vineyards, Silicon Valley on the farmland—all were facilitated by Giannini's bank.

Still, B of A was a *practical* organization. Branch managers were in many ways the captains of their ships, but headquarters had to know exactly what they were doing, so everybody had to report on the same forms. The forms were designed by A. P.'s son Mario, physically weakened by hemophilia and the frequent transfusions the condition required, whose mind ran to organizing rather than buccaneering. The books of forms Bank of America developed under Mario Giannini were very highly regarded— when the Federal Reserve wanted to educate foreigners in how a bank should be run, it sent them to San Francisco to be walked through Giannini's *Standard Practices Manual*. And the fact is that while the Gianninis and their immediate successors were running the bank, there weren't that many bad loans. "B of A," said John Heimann, Comptroller of the Currency for Jimmy Carter, "was a confederation of community banks, and nobody is a better judge of credit than a community banker."

Because of the rigid reporting schemata, the bank could lift people with no special education or training through the branch system by the judgment of their immediate superiors. The disadvantage was that a lot of economically uneducated men were out there committing the bank's resources; the advantage was that they knew what they were doing. A senior man who left the bank as part of a 1970s reorganization argued that the downfall of the bank in the 1980s began with the reduction in the branch manager's responsibilities. "The old guys had been Mr. Bank of America in Tulare and Modesto," he said, "and they had a developed intuition. They read the trade papers, they went out drinking with the wine makers, they'd say, 'Gee, I see there's a glut of European grapes, maybe we'd better pull back awhile, prices will be coming down.' The new guys who came in to control them were all out of the analytical credit school; all they knew was the numbers—yesterday's numbers."

Frank Lourenso of Chemical (now Chase), which claims (but cannot document) status as the nation's largest lender to middle-market companies, says that he has a total field contingent of 1,300 people. "Relationship managers," he says, "go to people's weddings and bar mitzvahs. I want my officers out. Go visit the customers, check in on Friday. Why should you come in every day? With the laptop, you can access all your phone numbers anytime. You can generate documents on the laptop. A mother likes the doctor to feel the kid's head, ask him how he feels. Nobody wants one hundred percent clinical. I don't want you to look at my book of business. I want you to come to Brooklyn, look at the line, see the new product, look at the building next door that we want to buy, talk to my son—you were at his bar mitzvah—he's going to take over the business. We have customers who have been with us more than a century, three generations."

Lourenso is a gray-haired man with a gray mustache, wearing a regimental tie on a yellow shirt with a white collar. He has large rimless glasses and lots of enthusiasm. "Other banks," he says, "come in and out of this market; we're always there. We've focused on this business since 1972, we were the first bank to carve out a middle-market department and take it out to the branches. We have eighteen billion dollars outstanding." He likes to recall the day in February 1992, a month after his bank's previous merger with Manufacturers Hanover became final, when the chairman and president of the bank joined him and his sales force in making 2,500 calls on borrowers in a single day, as a demonstration that the new giant was still interested in middle-market business.

Some degree of idealization may flavor this report. The "call reports" Chemical filed with the Federal Reserve did not back up Lourenso's claims. His $18 billion of loans to small business turned out to be the total of all the bank's commercial-and-industrial loans retained in the bank's portfolio, and in June 1994, according to the *Wall Street Journal*, only $2 billion of that was in loans of less than $1 million.[16] Nineteen banks, virtually all of them smaller than Chemical, had more small-business loans outstanding than Chemical did. The 1,300 people Lourenso claimed for his small-business operation were mostly lending officers in the branches who put more time and attention into large loans than into small loans. Lyndon Comstock, a First of Chicago lending officer who came east to start the Capital Community Bank in Brooklyn, reports that he hired one of the Chemical lending officers who specialized in small-business loans to businesses in

Queens, the borough with the most manufacturing in New York. He was one of only two such on the Chemical payroll in Queens.

Even in an age when the structuring of income streams is dominated by Wall Street sharpies, an inventive banker can find new, safe business for banks. Darla Moore, Chemical's beautiful South Carolina blonde vice president (who greatly enjoyed coming to the office every day as a sight for sore eyes), invented the DIP—for "debtor in possession"—financing that kept bankrupt American companies in business through their Chapter 11 reorganization. When she came to Los Angeles at the request of Philip Hawley to make her presentation to the Carter Hawley Hale board of directors—"stroking noises," she says: " 'You're not going to fall into the Pacific; I know this is the worst thing that ever happened to you, but in six months you won't feel so bad' "—perhaps the most impressed was the eighty-one-year-old Prentice Hale, who came up to her afterward and said, "You are unlike any banker I have ever met. So *lovely*—and bright." To which she replied: "There are lots of lovely girls at Chemical Bank, and we're all bright."

A year beyond trainee status at the bank in the late 1970s, Moore had seen that the new bankruptcy code just enacted by the Congress gave prior claim on assets to a lender that backed a company which had won bankruptcy court protection against its previous creditors. The new lender would be paid in full before the old lenders saw a penny. There was thus no need for a lender to a bankrupt to tie up all the assets as collateral before advancing the money, which had been the normal practice in the banks. DIP loans could be unsecured, and very quick.

Moore was soon empowered by top management to make loans in the hundreds of millions of dollars entirely on the basis of her own judgment sitting at the table with the lawyers as the bankruptcy was negotiated. "I spent the weekend with Harvey Miller," she said, batting her eyelashes, referring to Macy's lawyer in the forty hours of negotiations in a large committee that produced the Macy's bankruptcy and an $800 million line of credit from Chemical. "It was *fabulous*." This became a giant business, but Moore ran it with a staff of seven, including secretaries. "I started this up with a blank desk. They tried to stuff me with people, but I wouldn't have it."

The way this game plays, it should be noted, Chemical rarely had to put up any money: once vendors were guaranteed that their future bills would be paid, they were happy enough to extend trade credit to the bankrupt with the Chemical commitment. "The irony was," Moore told Jim Grant, "that if we put it up, they never used it. If we didn't put it up, they would have been in a tailspin."[17] Shortly before leaving the bank for marital and other partnerships with Richard Rainwater, the Texas investment planner who made billions for the Bass family and hundreds of millions for himself, Moore commented on Lourenso's middle-market operation. "It's great for public relations," she said. "It breaks even, just barely. It's a hugely expensive business to begin with. And the risk profile is *profound*."

7/ **The Money Lenders**

The force of securitization is unstoppable, because it is driven by fundamental economics. Bluntly put, the securities business system is more efficient than the banking business system. As a nation, we should accept the fact that in the future anything that can be securitized will be securitized.

—LOWELL L. BRYAN, McKinsey & Co., 1991[1]

Back in the mid 1980s, I testified on the problems of lending to "less-developed countries" before a subcommittee of the House Banking Committee chaired by Congressman John LaFalce, a Democrat from Buffalo, New York. The other panelists were Raoul Prebisch, the Argentinian economist who developed and promoted the (false) theory that nations could prosper by substituting their own production for imports, and Tom Johnson, the rather grim-faced, squared-off president of Chemical Bank, who some years later would make himself very very rich as chairman of the little Greenpoint Savings Bank, which he converted from mutual to incorporated status with large issues of stock for the officers. I spoke critically of the banks' willingness to lend in Latin America and play games with government bonds and exotic instruments while ignoring their social function of lending to enterprise at home. Johnson finally blew up at me: "Look," he said. "There *is* no plain vanilla lending any more."

Commercial lending by banks was devastated by the information revolution. Once upon a time a network of information providers was required for a lender to learn the panoply of market interest rates at different maturities, foreign-exchange rates, creditworthiness of importunate borrowers, and so forth. Only a bank, which could spread the costs of gathering this information over a variety of customers and transactions, could maintain the necessary, constantly changing library of facts and figures. Small-city bankers needed large-city correspondents not only to clear the checks and share the larger loans and give the customers tickets to the ball games and other entertainment when they came to town, but also to provide news from the larger world of finance. Economics professors taught that banks earned their profits by measuring and taking risks, but in truth banking was a safe and steady enterprise, most of the time, because banks could count on income from using the information they had and others did not have. Banks were paid as intermediaries between those with money to lend and those who had to borrow because their routine work gave them access to so much information lenders needed and could not take the time or trouble to uncover.

In the second half of the twentieth century, these advantages disappeared at an accelerating rate, and virtually none of them survive at the end of the century. For trivial expense, anybody—large banker, small banker, non-banker—can have on his desk all the information about today's financial markets anyone might need to make a loan, and all the statistical information anyone can have about the creditworthiness of all but the smallest corporations. The squeezing out of the banks began in areas like automobile finance, where manufacturers found that rather than borrow from banks they could sell their IOUs as commercial paper (used to finance dealer inventories and consumer car purchases) to non-bank people and companies with spare cash to lend. With ventilation so much better in office buildings, commercial-paper dealers didn't even need windows, let alone marble floors and teller windows and high-ceilinged bank lobbies. The elimination of the banking middleman saved money in itself—and the ability to arrange and rearrange financing terms provided marketing opportunities.

As information improved, and the number of commercial-paper dealers increased, companies much smaller than automobile manufacturers found they could get their money more cheaply from the market than from the banks. The money market mutual funds that began in the 1970s were denounced by the banks for "disintermediating" the banking system by drawing out deposits that could be lent, but the more important "disintermediation" was the funds' purchase of the commercial paper that replaced bank loans. As consultant Edward Furash puts it, "the intermediation process has shifted away from institutions that take principal risk by taking loans and investments on their balance sheets ... toward placement facilitators who manage funds for others."[2]

By the 1990s, total commercial paper and total bank loans outstanding were neck-and-neck, at $550 billion to $600 billion each. Banks clawed back a bit of the proceeds by offering standby lines of credit that guaranteed repayment to purchasers of commercial paper, but that was a commodity business if ever there was one, and the Japanese banks grabbed their targeted market share in America by offering these lines at prices that made them unprofitable. To the extent that lending to giant corporations survived at the banks, it was on the borrower's terms. "Somebody once said to the head of oil at Chase," Wolfgang Schoellkopf of First Union/Fidelity recalls, " 'You must have an exciting job—talking to all these big people.' He said, 'Yeah, they call up, they say we want a hundred million dollars and we'll pay five percent for thirty days.' "

As commercial paper replaced short-term bank lending to the

best customers, banks increased the longer-term component of the loan portfolio. "By 1989," Lowell L. Bryan of the consulting firm McKinsey & Co. reported, "the net interest income from commercial real estate and highly leveraged transaction loans contributed nearly 50 percent of the industry's $27 billion in pre-tax profits."[3]

Home mortgages grew in importance, then shrank as "mortgage bankers" operating essentially from the offices of real estate brokers exploited the economies of government-sponsored (and thus obviously if not legally government-insured) enterprises like the Federal National Mortgage Association.

Mike Milken of Drexel Burnham, the second-best banker I ever met (when he told you the ways Stone Container Corp. could pay back its borrowings, it was like Homer reciting the siege of Troy), found he could raise money in the market for middle-sized corporations that might otherwise have borrowed from banks. "A term loan," lawyer Joseph Grundfest, then an SEC commissioner, said in 1990, "is nothing but an illiquid junk bond." Milken begged to disagree: "A high-yield bond," he said piously—"junk" never crossed his lips—"is a better credit than a term loan in a bank, because it has faced the test of the marketplace."

Soon the big banks found themselves pushed into the corner of "mezzanine finance," taking the largest risks of Milken and Milken-type deals by providing the cash needed in the early years until more paper could be sold. This business collapsed very noisily in 1989 after the Citibank/Chemical Bank fiasco in the leveraged buyout of United Air Lines that never happened. Together with the optimistic real estate lending a few years earlier and foolish less-developed-country lending a decade earlier, the mezzanine finance phenomenon created the crisis in the banking system in 1990–92.

To some extent, the heady days of mezzanine finance came back in the mid 1990s, as the biggest banks put themselves into competition with investment banks as deal-makers, merger-and-acquisition advisers, and even as issuers of securities for their customers, using the exemptions from Glass-Steagall that the Federal Reserve has given them under that law's ambiguous Section 20. The instrument of choice has been the giant syndicated loan, the very definition of Grundfest's illiquid junk bond, which the big banks "participate out" not only to other banks but also to pension funds, insurance companies, and the burgeoning "prime rate" mutual funds formed to buy pieces of bank loans. Dan Napoli of Merrill Lynch, who sees this stuff from the other side, says that "HLT [highly leveraged transaction] loans are now more liquid than the securities."

The dean of loan syndication is Jimmy Lee at what was Chemical and is now Chase Bank, still in his early forties in 1995, a square-jawed man with bushy light brown hair who has never worked anywhere but this bank. "We don't do it," said Darla Moore shortly before leaving the bank, "unless Lee can blow it out." Lee is home-grown Chemical. "I came out of Williams in 1975," he says. "My wife was a classmate. She was a squash player, and she had to go to Princeton to play in a tournament, so I kept her appointment with the interviewers for the bank. They asked me why I wanted to be a banker, and I said I didn't want to be a banker, my girlfriend told me to take this interview. So they hired me."

Chemical trained Lee as a lender, and seven years later sent him to Australia to help set up an operation there. On his return Bill Harrison, now a vice-chairman at Chase, suggested that he start a loan syndication group. In the first six months of 1993, that group put together $95 billion of new corporate financing, a world's record. "How did we get so good at this?" Lee asked rhetorically. "We focused on it as a *business*. We said, 'Let's see if we can build the largest single pot of liquidity in the world. Citibank, Bankers Trust and Manny Hanny had built large originating businesses, but they didn't have the distribution business. We started in 1983 with Japanese bank X, which we knew needed assets, and by the end we had the relationships with all the leveraged-buyout firms.

"Citicorp killed their investors," Lee said enthusiastically. "They sold their customers all the leveraged-buyout deals of the 1980s—Allied Stores, Federated, Carter Hawley Hale. People said, 'I'm not going to do business with you anymore, you killed my career.' If you went around town now, you wouldn't find anyone who's had my job more than a year, maybe two. Their predecessors got blown up. You have to have high credit standards—we can sell almost anything, but just because we can sell it doesn't mean we think it's a good deal. I and my guys watched what happened to all the people who created bad assets. We're good at big things; the Mayo Clinic things. We've put banks back into the big corporate business; we put together the largest loan in the history of the world, twenty-five billion dollars for General Motors. Now that they've got it, of course, they won't have to draw it."

Lee has a staff of about sixty people, and they meet every morning at 7:45, which is five minutes later than it used to be. "When the merger [with Manufacturers Hanover] came, I called my people in and I said, 'Everybody says I'm such a tough guy. I'm going to move the meeting. The bad news is, I'm going to move it only five minutes.' This is a business that commands Wall Street compensation, but you don't want arrogance. By making people get up the same time as the farmers, you stamp out arrogance. I believe that having people with a well-rounded value system is good business. People get the best skills in the world and an honest, open, well-rounded person. Customers [not, note, the mealymouthed term 'clients'] do business with people they like. People don't do business with you because you're a geek and you can do regressions in your head. They come to do business with you because they like you."

Standard & Poor's has developed a new kind of rating for

tradable leveraged loans, a "BLR" (for bank loan rating) that runs from an excellent 1 to a deplorable 10. Like any income stream, the interest payments and repayments on these loans can be bundled into different tranches that pay off on different schedules (see Chapter 10). Ellen Leander of *Global Finance* reports that the rating "measures the potential for recovery in the event of a bankruptcy," and quotes the opinion of Steve Bavaria of S&P that "Investors want their risks unbundled."[4] The borrowers, Leander adds, are cable-TV, high-tech and health companies.

This semi-lending, semi-securities-issuance business has brought total bank lending back near the numbers of the late 1980s, but the numbers are misleading. The 1990s have indeed seen a sea change. Between 1963 and 1990, deposits in banks and thrifts varied between 63 and 73 percent of the gross domestic product. In 1990, the line dropped out of the band, and by the end of 1994, deposits in banks were only half of GDP. During that five-year period, the total indebtedness of American corporations rose by $573 billion—but the total commercial and industrial loans in American banks *fell* by $30 billion.[5] The enormous loan losses of 1988–91 forced dramatic cutbacks in bank personnel, and the cadre most seriously cut back was the corps of lending officers. They were not rehired.

By 1995, though C&I loans rose smartly through the first three-quarters of the year, only about one-fifth of the borrowings of American business were from banks. But half the borrowings of *small* businesses were from banks; as Allen Berger, Anil Kashyap and Joseph Scalise put it in a paper for the Brookings Panel on Economic Activity, "banks are a particularly important source of funds for small, information-problematic borrowers that often have little access to other sources of external finance. Based on a survey of about 1.7 million individual loans to domestic businesses by U.S. banks over time, we estimate that there was a 39.2% contraction in loans to borrowers with bank credit of less than $250,000 during the first half of the 1990s."[6]

Philip E. Strahan and James Weston of the New York Fed argue that Berger's estimates are misleading, especially when applied to a likely future when large bank holding companies acquire more and more small banks and convert them to branches. The Berger study, they say, omits the likelihood that if big banks reduce their small-business lending, the surviving smaller banks will find it profitable to fill the breach. The New Yorkers find evidence for their thesis: "Between 1993 and 1995, a period of rapid consolidation [in banking], the share of total assets invested in small business loans rose by about 5 percent for banks with assets under $100 million."[7] Berger and company don't see the same numbers.

Some of the difference between the two divisions of the Fed lies in the definition of a small-business loan, which is under $250,000 for the Board economists and under $1 million for the New Yorkers. The matter is also complicated by the fact that when a large bank holding company acquires a small bank with a strong portfolio of small-business loans, the fraction of small-business loans reported by the large bank holding company automatically rises. When NationsBank North Carolina consolidated the loans from its South Carolina acquisition, its apparent investment in small-business loans rose by 118 percent.

The *Wall Street Journal* did a compilation of loans to small business, and even with the trigger set at a million dollars, 47.7 percent of all small-business loans were made by banks with less than $1 billion in assets, which have only half that proportion of the nation's bank assets.[8] The number of independent banks—banks not owned by a holding company—dropped from 9,482 in 1980 to 2,920 in 1993, while the number of holding companies (only some of which are small banks) rose only from 2,886 to 5,455; the share of assets in banks with less than $100 million dropped from 19.2 percent to 9.1 percent.[9] Most observers (and most small businessmen) feel that as banks consolidate, there are fewer and fewer answers to the question of where small businesses get their small loans—the central function of the banking system.

2
_____

David Apgar, a tall, slightly stooped young man with longish hair and large horn-rimmed glasses and a diffident, patient, contemporary manner, came to the Office of the Comptroller of the Currency from investment banking at Lehman Brothers (and moved on, in 1996, to the consulting firm of McKinsey & Co.). Like Bank of America's Alan Rosenthal before him, he had a mission to expand the pool of money available for certain kinds of investment—Rosenthal's, to housing; Apgar's, to small business.

Rosenthal's idea was to package mortgages that were not government guaranteed (all previous mortgage-backed securities had enjoyed some form of government sponsorship), and sell them on the market to provide funds for more housing loans. Rather than collect interest on the mortgages, which was greater than their cost of funds (making a living on the "spread"), banks would earn fees for originating the mortgages, for putting together the packages and for servicing the coupons, and let the purchasers of the securities make what money was to be made from the interest payments themselves.

Mortgages paid higher interest rates than bonds of equivalent safety sold in the market; there would be a margin the banks could capture, and also, probably, for this was a commodity business, a benefit for the householder in the form of slightly lower rates. If the packager wished to sacrifice some of his interest income, insurance companies could offer a "credit enhancement" guaranteeing the payment of most or all the interest on the mortgages and the repayment of the principal.

Similarly, Apgar wanted to package small-business loans into securities that would represent a pro-rata share of the revenues from the repayments of those loans. "Over-collateralization" would give the face value of the loans in the package a greater value than the initial selling price of the package. The existence of many loans in the package would make the package less risky than the loans individually and permit the sale of the package at a lower interest rate than the rate on the loans. The government would get involved not as a guarantor of the loans but through schematic publication of examiners' reports on the accuracy of each participating bank's own ratings of the riskiness of its loans.

"Under this Business Loan Underwriting Evaluation (BLUE) initiative, the OCC would offer a bank a statistical summary of the way the bank's credit grading of reviewed loans correlates with the OCC's credit grading of the same loans." This would "lower the information costs associated with selling small business loan pools."[10] Customers for this paper would be easy to find among other banks, because the scheme would allow banks to gain the advantage of lower capital requirements for loans to small business—mandated by Congress in 1994—without actually incurring the expense of making the loans. Again, someday, somewhere, somehow, at some price, private insurance would be available to buttress the safety of the security, and non-bank customers could be added to the roster of buyers. And the bank originating the loan would pocket an origination fee—indeed, most banks charge a fee loan applicants must pay to apply, whether they get the loan or not.

Apgar's argument started from a theory that the only money banks would be willing to commit to commercial and industrial lending was the money that came their way in the form of insured deposits. They would not and maybe could not—fund their business loans by their own borrowings in the market. Properly done, business lending is a fully customized activity, with loan terms drawn up to meet the circumstances of the borrower, monitoring costs, payment delays, renegotiations, and so forth, all time-consuming and expensive. It therefore has to be matched against the cheapest money in the bank, which historically has been the transaction balances (the money depositors *must* keep in the bank in the normal course of business) and the savings accounts the government has insured at bargain rates. To the extent that the bank as intermediary borrows in the market the money it uses for business loans, the bank will be a loser, because the margin between its costs as borrower and its receipts as lender will be insufficient to yield a profit over and above the expenses of the lending activity. There has been a steady and persistent decline in the fraction of bank liabilities—of the sources of the banks' money—that comes in on a chassis of insured deposits. By 1996, that fraction was less than one-sixth.

Practical bankers as well as theoreticians hold the view that deposits and commercial loans should balance. Bud Baker, CEO of North Carolina's (and Georgia's) First Wachovia, notes with annoyance that "Deposits have been flowing out like crazy to mutual funds. I have more loans than deposits now—people have been looking at us. We recently [this was fall 1995] had a deposit sale, of ten-month and three-year CDs. We wanted to test the deposit market, and get our people thinking about selling deposits. We paid seven percent interest for ten months and eight percent for three years, and we got a billion dollars in one day. We did publicity on it—'a great bank offering a great rate'—because we were trying to get a sense of the power of the franchise. People came into the branches and sat on the floor and waited; they wouldn't take rain checks and come back another day. In one day, we opened seventy-eight thousand accounts, thirty thousand of them new." And all of them, at those numbers, selling their money to Wachovia at higher prices than Wachovia would have had to spend to buy it in the market.

If the banks are to be kept in the C&I lending business, by this argument, ways have to be found for them to replenish their funds for that purpose by reselling the loans. Baker says resignedly of the middle-market and smaller loans on Wachovia's books: "You're not making money—or you're making only a little money—on *any* loans these days. We'll probably move more of these loans off the books"—that is, find a way to make them into securities and sell them.

Not all of this is new, and maybe not all of it is true. Clearly, lenders that are *not* banks can borrow from the market and make a good living on lending what they have borrowed. GE Capital, The Associates, Commercial Credit and others make C&I loans profitably with borrowed money and greater investments of their own capital than can be found in the funding of a bank loan. "Our business is helping yours," says the brilliant GE slogan, and the list of clients and products is dazzling. One browses through the 1993 annual report: a proprietary billing system for Sam's Club; easier ways to pay for mortgage insurance; financing for a printing press equipment maker in Canada, Mexico and Europe; phone service in Alaska through Alascom; Ringling Brothers Barnum & Bailey clown school; private-sector finance for the Washington Metro; new ordering and repair systems for Xerox and FMC railroad cars; leasing for the Delta Airlines hub in Portland, Oregon. The Commercial Equipment Financing division is "the world's largest supplier of middle-market financing," Retailer Financial Services is "the world's leading provider of consumer and commercial private label credit programs, with ... 75 million cardholders in North America, Europe and Asia."

People with charge accounts at Harrod's in London are really borrowing from GE. So are people who lease cars from Avis in Europe. All the ratings are triple-A. "Rates on commercial paper offered by GE Capital, GE Capital Services and General Electric may be obtained by calling one of the regional offices shown below...." The company's average daily paper issuance is over $7 billion.

In 1994, despite writing off losses from its badly managed Kidder Peabody subsidiary, GE Capital had over $2 billion in earnings. The company earns over 18 percent return on equity through good years and bad, mostly as a lender. In the first quarter of 1996, GE Capital made about $600 million, 42.8 percent of the total profits of the largest corporate enterprise in the world. And these profits are mostly in loans GE Capital books and holds— even after washing out the Kidder subsidiary, GE Capital had more than $120 billion in assets. GE Capital, in short, runs a very successful banking business built on lending money all of which has to be bought in the marketplace.

"We have a finite capacity," says its chairman Gary Wendt, an engineer turned financier, "based on the leverage the market will let us use." What makes it possible is the triple-A rating. In 1986, nine U.S. banks (and eight Japanese banks) had a long-term triple-A rating from Moody's; by 1993, Morgan was the only one from the United States, and there were none at all from Japan.[11] The banks were trying to earn a spread by intermediating between the people who had money to lend and borrowers who had better credit ratings than the banks; it's not really surprising that banks found it hard to make a profit. "Banks go down to Washington a lot," says Wendt, whose reputation for intimidating both customers and employees grows in large part from the purity of his contempt for inefficiency, "because they get into trouble." When GE's borrowers get into trouble, Wendt has access to hands-on capacity that can take over the hapless company and run it. Its leasing contracts include not just money but service for the equipment. "We have a different attitude," Wendt told *Business Week*, "because we're part of an operating company."[12]

While the banks still had very strong credit ratings and could borrow in the market at competitive rates, there was no theory that C&I loans had to be funded from deposits. In those days, banks required borrowers to leave in the bank, as "compensating balances," from 10 to 20 percent of the deposits created for them when the loan was made. (Loans that permitted the borrowers to take all the money were called "clean credits," and were rare.)

The theory was that these interest-free compensating balances were the way the banks loaded onto borrowers the reserves against deposits required by the Fed. Alex Pollock, then the planner and thinker for Continental-Illinois (later CEO of the Federal Home Loan Bank of Chicago), argued that when you took the compensating balances out of the total deposits in a big money-center bank, what was left was "essentially zero." Later, a more sophisticated generation of bankers and borrowers came to realize that a compensating balance was simply a form of higher interest rate, and this nonsense stopped.

Bank sales of loans, moreover, are nothing new. What made Franklin Roosevelt's federally insured mortgage plan fly in the 1930s was the energy of Walter Bimson of Valley National Bank in Phoenix, who carried his bank's mortgages back east to the big insurance companies and persuaded them to buy the paper, thus giving Valley additional funds and setting an example for others. Big-city correspondent banks have always purchased the "excess lines" from their small-city and country correspondents.

Efforts to securitize diversified packages of small-business loans have been up and running since 1981, when W. Mack Terry led half a dozen planners and lending officers from their jobs at Bank of America to a new Tavistock Financial Services Company in San Francisco. They had been the brightest thirtysomethings at the bank, they were disgusted by what had happened to it, and they were going to build a brave new world in a nest of folding aluminum chairs and tables in windowless space in one of the older Montgomery Street office buildings. The operation was named Diversified Corporate Loans. Banc One in Columbus, Ohio, already seeking to spread its wings, provided the backing and some of the loans for the packages.

"We were a co-op, like a bunch of farmers," Terry says reminiscently. "You grow tomatoes, you bring 'em in, we give you a share of the grocery store. If you grow lettuce, you bring that in. We were naive in expecting a high degree of cooperation in a situation where egos were on the line. Each loan was attached to a lending officer, and he was all for the concept, but he was offended that *his* loan would be part of the package. Everything you put in the package, you had to offer some discount, and he didn't think his loan should be out there at a discount."

3

The drive toward securitized small-business lending has taken a different direction in the mid 1990s. Instead of taking the time to learn about the small entrepreneur and his enterprise, banks are now attempting to "score" small-business loans the way they score auto loans and mortgage loans, on a standardized form with places for machine-readable pencil marks. Over a certain threshold of comforting qualities, the bank makes the loan; under that threshold, it doesn't. At Seafirst in Seattle, where Bank of America plans to consolidate its consumer lending, and at Texas Commerce Bank in Houston, the approval of small-business loans of up to $100,000 has been consolidated with the approval of unsecured personal loans.

Clerks can do the work of filling out the forms for scored lending in a "branch" that occupies four hundred square feet of a supermarket—or over the telephone. At Texas Commerce Bank, such loans can be ordered by telephone—dial 1-800-221-LEND[5363]. In December 1995, a few months into the service, there were 230,000 calls, which resulted in 2,300 applications and 650 loans. I watched a cheerful young man thumb through some faxed pro forma statements in his cubicle with shoulder-high walls in TCB's processing center off the toll road at the edge of inner ring Houston. The legend on his screen read, "Faith Builds Character." He was shaking his head. "Looks like," he said, "I'm gonna say, 'Harvey, you'd better keep working at the grocery store and not buy this business.' " Oley Williams, who runs the department, says that the bank has relations with 52,000 small businessmen (defined as under $3 million in sales). "Banks have come to realize that small business is very profitable, because of the deposit side of the business and the products—cash management, overdraft lines of credit, business bank cards and such."

California's Wells Fargo, hastening to eliminate its brick-and-mortar branches, has instituted a program of loans up to $50,000 on application by mail or fax. Nor does scoring necessarily exclude more conventional analysis: Hibernia Bank in New Orleans decided to give a $300,000 line of credit to a galvanizing factory after a hurricane mostly because the owner scored well, but the lending officer also went out to look at the place. The point of scoring, said Robert Kottler, who runs small-business lending for Hibernia, is to reduce the break-even point on the size of loans: "Before we started credit scoring, we lost money on any loan of less than $150,000. But 82 percent of businesses in Louisiana have less than $1 million in revenues, and the average loan to them is $25,000."[13]

All this has to be done pretty delicately, of course, because answers to questions of race, gender, physical disability and age (Federal Reserve Regulation B prohibits "age-split credit scoring systems") cannot be scored. Discarded applications must by law be kept twenty-five months, so gumshoes can search for signs of discrimination. Texas Commerce keeps them forever, on general principle, the Sony "jukebox" of optical disks that holds the records having essentially unlimited capacity.

John Medlin, recently retired from running First Wachovia, resents the drive to securitization and the whole idea of "one-size-fits-all lending." Once such a loan is made and sold as part of a package into the market, there will be nobody to monitor the progress of the business, to change the terms of the first loan to make a larger loan feasible for a growing enterprise, or to work out something that looks to go sour. Unfortunately, this judgment-free procedure meshes well with the reorganization now shaking up and shaking out the banking industry, and it's going to get a whirl.

As the number of bank branches shrinks and the lending function becomes more centralized, small businesses will need other sources of loans. The *Wall Street Journal* suggests that suppliers and customers may be replacements for banks as sources of loans for established partners, and that "wealthy corporate executives are a growing source of capital." Among the side benefits of getting help that way, the article suggests, is "some of the mentoring and boardroom expertise that fledgling companies desperately need."[14] Governments help some: California, Connecticut, Massachusetts and Pennsylvania all have set aside public pension-fund money for small-business loans. The federal Small Business Administration has a "low-doc" (for low-documentation) loan guarantee program that picks up any losses above 10 percent of the loan where the borrower meets small-business definitions. In February 1996, the Comptroller held a conference in Washington on community-development lending, and 550 bankers attended. Almost, in other words, as though the company had a bank lending officer to talk to. In some big cities, banks that need regulatory approval for mergers or acquisitions may set up subsidiaries to improve their reputation. In New York, an eleven-bank consortium committed $10 million, primarily for equity investments in new businesses.[15]

Bill Clinton while running for president in 1992 promised help for "community-development banks," which would greatly improve the availability of credit in depressed neighborhoods both urban and rural, modeled after the success of Chicago's South Shore Bank. Purchased in the 1970s by a group of urban activists supported by the Ford and Carnegie foundations (perhaps in penance for their previous support of Saul Alinsky's in-your-face Woodlawn Organization, which had left the neighborhood devastated by juvenile gangs and the flight of retail businesses),

South Shore served the area along Lake Michigan below the University of Chicago. Its purchasers also got some help from the First National Bank of Chicago, which had been compelled by a city law to publish its deposits and its loans by zip code, and had been embarrassed by the revelation that against $24 million of deposits from this area it had made only $1 million in loans. South Shore Bank, which had been around a long time—for this area had been developed at the turn of the century, when the World's Fair was at its northern border—had also pretty much stopped lending to the neighborhood as it decayed, which had one positive side: the new owners found a fairly clean balance sheet with few loan losses. It had to be a stand-alone bank under what were still severe Illinois unit banking rules (one bank, one office), but by the terms of the Bank Holding Company Act of 1970, it could incorporate a subsidiary community-development corporation.

The progenitor of South Shore was Ron Grzywinski, who was president of the Hyde Park Bank & Trust in the university-sponsored urban redevelopment district just to the north. To run it, he hired Milton Davis, a calm, bespectacled, round-faced black graduate student at the university's business school, who insisted that he would be interested only if the bank was to be a business: "In a society like this," Davis said, "you have to have a profit-oriented institution." If a bank is going to make profits, it must collect on its loans—a Black Muslim bank not far away was in process of disintegration for failure to recognize that truth.

The improvement of the neighborhood could not be wrought by reestablishing the retail storefronts on Sixty-seventh Street, which had been the first hope, because the atmosphere on the street was too discouraging. Instead, South Shore concentrated its efforts on lending to buyers of single-family homes—and, most importantly, to the craftsmen who worked on refurbishing those homes. Nonprofits, especially hospitals, came for lease financing; South Shore hesitated, then went along, profitably. When South Shore needed money, First National Bank of Chicago bought $1 million of loans. Walter Heller, one of the big finance companies, took loan participations.

When the big downtown S&Ls began to make single-family loans on the south side, Davis shifted his attention to small multi-family dwellings—up to six flats—but only where the owner is in residence, and only on a complicated loan contract that sets up a rehabilitation reserve jointly controlled by the bank and the borrower. The next step was to condominium conversion, very profitable to the bank. By the 1990s, no less than a quarter of all the housing in Woodlawn had been rehabbed, mostly with money from South Shore. Then there was enough middle-class occupancy to make a case for redevelopment of the shattered shopping street on which the bank had been at one time the only well-maintained building. Among the bank's contributions to the revitalization of Sixty-seventh Street was paying for street patrols to provide protection and comfort to merchants. By the early 1980s, the bank had about $80 million in assets and was making something like a quarter of a million dollars a year despite the high interest rates. A minor but important fraction of its lendable funds came from foundations, which took marginally lower interest rates on their deposits.

What had brought the Clinton campaign into the picture was the first expansion of the South Shore enterprise, in 1987, to Elkhorn Bank and Trust in Arkadelphia, Arkansas. Hillary Clinton's Wellesley roommate Jan Piercy was working for Southwest Regional Development Bank. She had brought to the Clintons the story of the Grameen Bank of Bangladesh, the pioneer of lending to the very poor, which had become a truly inspiring success story. Founded in 1976, Grameen by 1995 had made more than half a billion dollars of loans to more than two million women, at an interest rate four percentage points above the rate charged by the Central Bank of Bangladesh in lending to privately owned banks.

Grameen Bank is a monument to an individual, the economist

Mohammed Yunus (Vanderbilt Ph.D., 1971). On his return home, he found that the market ladies and textile spinners of the villages around his university were being horribly exploited by local moneylenders, who provided the pennies a day they needed in working capital and took virtually all the proceeds of their labor. "A decade later," David Bornstein reported, testifying before the U.S. Congress Select Committee on Hunger in a hearing devoted to micro-enterprise credit, "[Yunus] recalled what had gone through his mind: 'I felt extremely ashamed of myself being part of a society that could not provide twenty-six dollars to forty-two able, skilled human beings who were trying to make a living.' "[16] Yunus's trick was to lend to these women only in the context of their participation as a group: *everyone* in the group guaranteed all the loans. And 97 percent of the borrowers repaid their loans.

Two points have to be made here: one, that this is real banking, with a group of borrowers doing some of the work of lending officers; two, that it has little relevance for the American economy. But President Clinton was not wrong in thinking that its success could be an argument for the creation of community-development banks in the United States. Among the items his administration got through Congress in its first, brief spring was the creation of a Community Development Financial Institutions Fund, supposedly $382 million over four years, to support the chartering and activities of community-development banks in America. No money was voted for this activity before the Republicans took over Congress, and community-development banks were among the many programs the Republicans "zeroed out" in the budget resolution. But after Clinton vetoed that, somehow $50 million for the banks was snuck back into the Treasury Department appropriation, and the money, administered by Treasury rather than a separate institution, began to dribble out in early 1996.

Among the godfathers of the community-development bank was Clifford Rosenthal, an overweight middle-aged former political activist with curly hair and a cheerful countenance, who heads the National Federation of Community Development Credit Unions. These are easier to start than banks (but harder to grow, because the only source of capital is retained earnings), and in some ways they fit better with the self-image of the movement. (Grameen is "owned" by its borrowers.) Rosenthal's organization has been helped by, among others, J.P. Morgan, which gave a $300,000 grant. "I said, 'We like to keep accounts where we get grants,' and they almost blushed. Three hundred thousand wasn't *near* the minimum balance for an account at Morgan." Technology has helped: "A credit union can buy a 486 computer and set up the whole share draft process for less than ten thousand dollars. We give people access to the payments system and small-business loans, and we teach them about thrift. Promoting thrift is historically a function of credit unions."

The shock for those who have taken the job seriously is how difficult it is to find good borrowers. Running a financial institution has been highly educational for this politically motivated cadre. Mark Griffith, very black, dreadlocks framing a handsome face with glaring eyes, graduate of Brown University, came from the Central Brooklyn Credit Union in Brooklyn's Bedford-Stuyvesant section to a meeting of the Levy Institute, and listened scornfully to the academics, and ultimately broke down: "You don't understand," he said sorrowfully, shaking his head. "A lot of these people have had too much credit already." And yet . . . if you build it, they will come.

Of greater immediate importance to small business has been the growth of factors, which are not lenders to their clients but purchasers of accounts receivable—in effect, lenders to the purchasers of their clients' goods. This is an old ("already common by the time of Hammurabi"[17]) and not always honorable occupation, with a history especially in the garment industry of extravagant "interest rates" to be paid by the borrower, and strong-arm tactics to compel payment by the purchasers of the borrower's goods. The business was legitimated in the United States by the Contract Assignment Act of 1940, which allowed vendors to the government to assign their claims to third parties as part of the drive to increase financing for expanding defense contractors. In the 1960s, as part of his crusade to increase the earnings potential of banks, Comptroller of the Currency James Saxon authorized the purchase of factors by nationally chartered banks, and in 1970 the Bank Holding Company Act listed factors among the appropriate subsidiaries of a holding company subsidiary.

The banks' experience was not entirely happy. One of the things that forced Britain's Midland Bank to sell (really, give) Crocker Bank to Wells Fargo in the early 1980s was Crocker's mistake in buying United Factors, then the largest American factor, as it fell into the hands of a bankruptcy court. By late in that decade, however, banks had learned how to evaluate factors, and by 1992, 94 percent of factoring volume in the United States was done by the subsidiaries of bank holding companies.[18] Factors became prominent in the late 1980s and early 1990s as the proximate cause for the bankruptcy of retailers—department store chains went under, the newspapers reported, because the factors were no longer willing to give suppliers cash for their prospective payments. Factors have also become important in the medical care industry, where both government programs and insurance companies (let alone the occasional individual consumer) have become very slow to pay.

Dimitri Papadimitriou, Ronnie J. Phillips and L. Randall Wray of the Levy Institute at Bard College have promoted the idea of community-development factors, which by vetting customers and taking over the bill-collecting function would solve what are usually the most problematic aspects of a relatively new small business. Factors also enhance a company's balance sheet by eliminating both accounts receivable on the left and debts on the right, thereby improving the debt-to-equity ratio. And instead of negotiating a new loan when the company grows, a manufacturer using a factor simply watches his resources rise with his sales. The Levy Institute authors argue that "niche factors," which have expertise matching their clients' businesses, are growing rapidly; nobody knows how rapidly, because they are private companies. As banks shut down branches or take lending power from branch managers, one would expect niche factors to fill some of the void. The Levy Institute authors (and Hyman Minsky, emeritus senior fellow at the institute) have proposed that banks be permitted to satisfy their Community Reinvestment Act obligations by providing funds to a community-based factor.

By separating the payments system from lending, technology has struck a blow at one of the vital organs of capitalism. The strongest argument for easing government regulation of community banks is the hope that if they saw easier entry and were promised less paperwork, more people might try to be bankers. It doesn't require a license. When securitization becomes habitual, there will be packagers of loans who will need loans to buy. And a friendly bank in a neighborhood, giving its depositors access to ATMs through the service bureaus, should have plenty of money to get loans started and seasoned.

8 / The New Mergers: Technology and Size

The challenge for all of us is to understand that the user has realized he doesn't need *a bank.*

—JAMES McDERMOTT, president of Keefe, Bruyette & Wood, the largest broker of bank stocks, 1994

"You know what we need if we're to get consolidation in this business?" said William Isaac, formerly chairman of the Federal Deposit Insurance Corporation and then CEO of the Secura consulting group under the umbrella of the Washington law firm of Arnold and Porter. This was 1991, when the banks were under heavy pressure, and the occasion was a small dinner at the New York Yacht Club, staged by the consulting wing of *Institutional Investor* magazine. I was there as a paid speaker. I had been warning that there was income to justify only a much smaller number of large money center banks than we already had in the United States, and that the government should let the market force the consolidation of the industry instead of force-feeding a bunch of dinosaurs.

Isaac was, I think, a regular in the group of fifteen or so. "What we need," he said, "is for a certain number of bank CEOs to get up in the morning, look out the window at the rose garden and say, 'I'm tired of having a limousine pick me up every morning and take me to work. I'm tired of spending the day in a big office on the fiftieth floor, having all those people come in and bow and scrape. I'm tired of these gourmet lunches with filet or swordfish and fancy wines. I'm tired of being on the phone with congressmen and telling them what bills to pass. And I'm tired of making all that money—I don't know what to do with it all.' If you get enough bank chairmen saying things like that, then you'll have a lot of mergers of big banks. Until then, forget it."

Also in the group was the CEO of one of the nation's twenty-five largest banks, New Jersey's First Fidelity. With about $25 billion in assets and more than six hundred branches, First Fidelity was a power in New Jersey and in the Philadelphia area, where it had recently acquired Fidelcor, owner of the separate Fidelity Bank there. Tony Terracciano, tall and lean, a long-headed matter-of-fact man with very dark eyes and very black eyebrows, had come to First Fidelity the year before from three years with Mellon Bank and twenty-three years at Chase, but he had always been in New Jersey, born in Bayonne (apparently a hotbed of economists, also home to former Federal Reserve chairman Arthur Burns and future Council of Economic Advisers chairperson Laura Tyson). "I live three blocks from my mother's house where I was born, and one block from my wife's mother. My kids are growing up with the kids of the people I grew up with. I remember when I was at Chase somebody said I'd better move, living in Bayonne was going to ruin my career. I asked [Willard] Butcher [then CEO of the bank], and he said, 'Is there a whorehouse upstairs?' I said, 'No,' and he said, 'Then it's nobody's business where you live.' "

Chase, it should be noted, now just the name for Chemical Bank, had after the departure of George Champion in the 1960s the poorest reputation of any of the New York money center banks. David Rockefeller, whose family was tightly identified with the bank (his uncle Winthrop Aldrich had pulled it out of the Depression), loved to go around the world and hobnob with heads of state—Bill Moyers did an adoring television profile of Rockefeller on his travels but he didn't pay much attention to the bank. And there was in any event some doubt about his capacity. Shortly before the purchase by Chemical was to be consummated, a former middle-management officer wrote a letter to the *New York Times*: "Having joined Chase with ten years' experience, I was shocked at how behind the times it was. While other institutions were downsizing, cutting expenses and competing for customers, Chase was operating as if it were still the 1950s. Infighting was rampant, with customer needs the last things on anyone's mind. Management spoke of the corporate 'franchise' as if customers were required to bank with Chase."[1]

Terracciano, by contrast, is still deeply loyal: "David wanted a mixed workforce, he made me a senior vice president after only seven years at the bank, and he gave me the opportunity to go on the board of the New York Philharmonic when I was thirty-five years old. I never would have met any of those people without him." After Rockefeller left, Terracciano adds, "Butcher put together a great comeback. Then in 1982 we had Drysdale [a government securities scam, where Chase extended credit to a fraudster], and Penn Square, and Lombard-Wall [another government bond scam], and the LDC debt. As a boy, I set up pins in a bowling alley, and sometimes I'd fall off the wall and get hit by the pins. They don't all hit you at the same time. It's bong-bong-bong. That's what it was like in 1982."

Terracciano listened to Isaac, as he had listened to my talk about why big banks were doomed, without much reaction. He had significantly increased the size of his bank in the preceding year, but he was not yet one of those moguls. New Jersey was an interesting place to have a bank. ("I *love* New Jersey," says Richard Bianco, who came out of Dillon Read to run Carteret Savings there, until Office of Thrift Supervision director Tim

Ryan, on his last day in office in December 1992, closed the place down. "It's the most densely populated state in the union, and everybody's wife has to have her own checking.") But New Jersey real estate was in trouble, and Newark, Terracciano's headquarters city, was in terrible trouble. Jim McDermott of Keefe, Bruyette & Wood deplored Fidelity's main office as "a horrible building," and while the location was worse than the building—a nondescript 1950s office tower—the visitor does feel negative vibes when his host finds someone to stand with him waiting for a cab, to make sure he doesn't get mugged on the sidewalk between the bank and the street. At ten in the morning.

Terracciano had decided that to build his own operation and take advantage of the low prices on small banks around the New York and Philadelphia metropolitan areas, he needed foreign capital. He went to Banco Santander, then the fourth-largest bank in Spain (now the largest), which had divested itself of all its industrial assets and had cash from the sale that might be—and was—available for overseas investing. Santander owned the second-largest bank in Puerto Rico and was about to make a partnership deal with the Royal Bank of Scotland. Gonzalo de Lasperas, an austere, elegant figure who combines Spanish aristocracy with English education and training as a Morgan banker, negotiated the deal.

"The European Union meant the internationalization of the Spanish financial market," de Lasperas said, "and we couldn't make progress without a chunk of assets in the United States. The history of European involvement in the United States is dismal. You need first-class locals, and you can't get that with a branch. We thought there was a window of opportunity, to acquire a minority stake. American banking was consolidating. Many banks were in dire straits, in serious need of capital. The availability of capital was most likely to ensure the survival and success of the recipient, because its competitors didn't have it." Santander hired Goldman Sachs to explore the market, and looked at more than a hundred banks "Terracciano," de Lasperas said, "was open to good ideas."

With $400 million from Santander on its books, First Fidelity set off to establish itself on the Atlantic corridor from Maryland to Connecticut. The acquirer was Wolfgang Schoellkopf, German-born and educated in the United States, who had come to Chase in 1963 from a job as a lecturer in economics at Princeton. He is First Fidelity's chief financial officer; he and Terracciano go way back. "The job of the CFO," he said, "is to do what the CEO doesn't want to do. Many CFOs are accountants, and don't know asset-liability management. The asset-liability manager runs to the Fed Funds desk, and says we need two billion, three billion a day, in Chicago five billion dollars a day. If you find Fed Funds are getting expensive, buy Eurodollars. Here we have a guy called the treasurer. Reporting to him is a funding group, a portfolio group [loans] and an investment group [securities]. And he reports to me.

"The question for us," Schoellkopf continues, "is what to pay for *deposits*. What advertising do we do? We sell CDs and commercial paper to commercial customers, at twenty-five basis points below the market, as a convenience to the customer. We never call a Eurodollar broker. We have about five billion in swaps [see Chapter 9]; in all cases we receive fixed [rates] and we pay floating [rates], because we have a preponderance of fixed-rate assets. When we feel we have enough mortgages, we sell the new production.

"Fifty-three percent of our loans are consumer loans. Our liability composition is unique. Out of $27.4 billion [this was as of January 1, 1994], we have $6.9 billion in transaction [checking] accounts, $6.4 billion in savings accounts, $8.8 billion in CDs, and only $1.5 billion in market funds. When we came in 1990, they had $5.8 billion in market funds, with a smaller bank." Reducing the amount First Fidelity had to borrow from the market every day was a remarkable accomplishment, because the bank had experienced a "tremendous outflow of consumer savings" in the early 1990s. Schoellkopf in his role as the acquisitions man had bought other banks' core deposits, especially savings accounts, getting the local bank's franchise as a lender thrown in. By 1995, First Fidelity was the second-largest bank in the New York suburbs of Westchester and Rockland Counties in New York State and Fairfield County in Connecticut.

Santander had made it possible. "Nobody could figure out a way to buy Union Trust in Connecticut," Schoellkopf says, "because of all the nonperforming assets. We had the capital to take the loss on the assets. We just sold them and filled the hole with our own money.

"We like suburban markets. You have enough branch density to give advertising its maximum effect. Tony pushes the concept of 'market managers'—people who were born there and grew up there, mostly the people who worked for these banks before we acquired them. Tony goes [to the counties mentioned earlier] every three months to show the flag, meet with a couple of customers. But there isn't much difference between banks. You put your rates a little lower, you get more business; you put them a little higher, you get less business. The size of the branch is a combination of advertising for deposits and rate-setting for loans."

Terracciano, who had been on the assets and liability committee at Chase, took large views of the industry and First Fidelity's role in it. "You have to ask, 'Why does this industry step on a rake every three or four years?' The reason is that starting in the late 1970s we moved into an operating environment that meant our techniques for evaluating risk had become obsolete. We'd had micro techniques—we looked at an industry and decided which firms you wanted to lend to. That works in a benign operating environment where risk is determined by micro variables. Starting in 1980, risks were determined by macro variables. If you'd asked a banker in the seventies whether he had a diversified portfolio, he would have said, 'Yes'—shown you SIC codes and maybe countries. Then the price of oil goes to ten dollars a barrel, and all the risk segments go at the same time. You had to aggregate—ask, 'Are we long oil or short oil?' And it takes a while to develop the techniques to do that. People couldn't quantify risk because the nature of the risk had changed.

"If you're a banker, you have to be ambivalent about technology. It creates new products for the customer. But we're middlemen. We make a living out of inefficiencies in the system, and technology eliminates inefficiencies, reduces our spreads. And it drives you crazy on timing—if you're too early, it's very expensive, and if you're late you can lose the franchise. Our risks go up and our spreads go down at the same time. Unless you concentrate on productivity, you're not going to survive."

Terracciano drove the branches hard, concentrating on consumer lending and on loans to companies with sales of less than $50 million, where "the spreads are still good. You're their only bank. But it's hard to find them unless you have a presence on the ground." By mid 1995, his bank had $38 billion in assets. Santander bought Banesto, the largest bank in Spain, laid low by its direct investments in nonbanking enterprise, and First Fidelity graciously contributed $22 million to the purchase funds. Terracciano took a seat on the Santander board, and expanded First Fidelity's reach to Chile, where Santander had a branch that needed more capital. Santander expanded its share of First Fidelity to almost 30 percent.

And then, in June 1995, First Union of North Carolina bought First Fidelity, paying $5.4 billion of market value of its own stock, more than twice the book value of First Fidelity, a third more than the price of the stock a week before the deal. It was, briefly, the largest bank merger ever in the United States. Word on the street was that Terracciano had been agreeable to selling—Goldman Sachs had been casing the field for purchasers—but wanted the deal made with Bank of Boston, which would have signed him on to become CEO of the joint enterprise. Santander, however, had always been most interested in the Southeast. It could not acquire or invest there originally because by the terms of the International Banking Act it had to take the state of its original investment as its home state, and for "state" purposes, Puerto Rico was New York, which a compact of southern states had agreed to bar from acquiring banks within their borders. The deal offered by First Union left Santander with 11.4 percent ownership of what became the sixth-largest bank in the United States. A Santander spokesman told the *New York Times* that his bank had only two of twenty-eight seats on the First Fidelity board, and no power to tell Terracciano what to do.[2]

First Union, a North Carolina bank, blanketed the Southeast from Maryland to Florida; First Fidelity had a small presence in Maryland, but was basically north of there. There wasn't much overlap, and there wouldn't be much downsizing. Terracciano and all his senior executives were given employment contracts by First Union—Terracciano would be president of the combined banks, and a member of a three-man "office of the chairman." The initial announcements said that at most 5 percent of the employment roster would be gone—an amount obviously manageable by attrition. The argument for the merger appeared to be no more and no less than a belief that in banking's brave new world there wasn't a place for a stand-alone regional bank with $37 billion in assets.

2

Historian, lawyer, regulator, consultant, bon vivant Carter Golembe, before his gradual retirement in the 1990s, was one of the most interesting and informative sources on the banking scene as observed from a base in Washington. One of his clients before he sold his firm and went to partner with Bill Isaac was Barnett Banks of Florida; indeed, he got so enthusiastic about Barnett that he joined the board of the holding company and participated in the planning hands-on. In the late 1980s, I went down to Florida to see what it was Golembe liked so much.

We start from the premise that like politics, lending is local. As Terracciano said, you have to have somebody there on the ground. Florida had been until the 1960s a rigid unit banking state, where each office was its own bank. When the state approved a holding company structure, Guy Botts, a Jacksonville lawyer turned banker who organized the Barnett holding company and became CEO of the bank, started a campaign of acquisition. He bought banks to get their people as well as to get their assets and liabilities, and one of the people he got, in 1966, was Charles Rice, the smart son of a convenience store manager in Orlando. A graduate of the University of Miami, Rice had done an apprenticeship at the First National Bank of Orlando and at Merrill Lynch, and at the age of thirty-one had been promised the presidency of the First National Bank of Winter Park, the suburb of Orlando where the rich folks lived. A year later, young Rice, having become president of what had become the Barnett Bank of Winter Park, set up a lending office in Orlando, where Barnett did not then have a bank, to exploit the opportunities arising out of the building of Disney World. "This was a bank founded in 1917," Rice recalled twenty years later, speaking of Winter Park, "and between 1965 and 1971 it roughly quadrupled. This was before the days of jumbo CDs, when you had to earn deposits. I put in a calling officers program, with quotas for everybody. We benefited from a certain lack of energy among our competitors."

It is not an accusation that could be leveled against Rice, whose energy level could not be concealed by his handsome, slow-spoken, broad-shouldered Rotary Club appearance. In 1971, at thirty-six, Rice was summoned to Jacksonville to be executive VP, and eighteen months later he was president and COO of the holding company. He carried Barnett through the real estate depression of the mid 1970s, and when Botts turned sixty-five in 1979, the Barnett board installed Rice as CEO. Barnett's share of the Florida market was then something like 15 percent; by 1987, it had almost 30 percent of the state's retail market, and 22 percent of its deposits, and growing.

In the holding company structure, each of what were then sixty Barnett banks had its own president and its own board. Golembe thought that was a good idea: "In a state like Florida, you want somebody there who cares like hell how he recruits newcomers. We have one bank president who goes out every night and cooks barbecued chicken for new arrivals in town. A branch manager won't do that; he would suffer a loss of pride." But Rice couldn't handle sixty presidents reporting to him, and because so many of the banks had been acquired lock, stock and barrel, with managements in place and retained, there was no common Barnett system to handle any of the problems. Stephan Hansel, a roly-poly and very smart New Englander who came to Jacksonville with a University of Virginia MBA as a kind of apprentice the same year Rice became president, remembers that in 1971 there wasn't even a prospective annual budget for each bank in the holding company. One of Hansel's first jobs was to create forms for such upstream reporting.

In 1976, Florida law was changed to permit branching, and Rice reorganized the holding company into thirty-two separately chartered banks, each of which would have and operate its own branches. Every summer (not a very busy time of the year in Florida) the president of each of these banks would set out his goals for the succeeding year. The president's remuneration was a function of how well he met those goals. Bonuses for meeting and exceeding those goals could be as much as half a president's compensation—"They make it interesting," said Charles "Pete" Gross, who ran Central Florida from a headquarters in Orlando.

Depending on the market involved, the goals fell into one of three categories: market share, earnings improvement, or profitability on an absolute scale. "In Indian River County or Port St. Lucie County," said holding company vice-chairman Thomas Jacobsen, who came from Chicago to manage Barnett's technology and sat on the goals review committee, "we're more concerned about getting a high share of growing markets; in Jacksonville and Tallahassee, we may be happy with a stable market share of slower growth, but we want a higher profit." These goals were negotiated through the fall, some presidents promising the moon, others trying to sandbag headquarters and ensure themselves a grander bonus.

Once the goal was set, the banks within the holding company had a great deal of freedom in finding ways to meet them—the bank presidents chose the managers of their branches without interference, though headquarters supplied a training program for them, and loans that were within the legal lending limit of the individual bank could be made without consulting Jacksonville. Virtually all bank presidents had been promoted from inside the organization. The local boards of directors had to approve the choice, but they didn't participate in the selection, because, Rice said, "they don't know the talent pool in the state. These people are too valuable for us to let them think they're making the decision when they're not." Reports to headquarters were sent monthly, and the three or four banks that were falling furthest behind in their quest for their goals received visits from Jax. "The bank president," Rice said, "is at risk for his performance." Golembe, who participated in the goal-setting exercise and did a biennial review of the results in his own shop, described the visiting groups as "SWAT teams."

The heart of Barnett's operation was continuous research on the demography of Florida, the most rapidly growing of the larger states. "Obviously," Rice said, "we're in the right place at the right time. To get business in this state, you don't have to take it away from anybody else." Vice-chairman Albert Lastinger, who came out of a Tampa bank Barnett had acquired, noted that in the 1970s Florida had one of the highest ratios of people to banking offices in the United States—one bank office for every 13,000 or 14,000 people, as against a national average of about one office for every 3,000 people. "You could throw a dart at a map of Florida and open an office wherever it struck, and you'd do all right." Total deposits in a Barnett branch rose an average of $425,000 a month in the mid 1980s, as the number of branches increased by about fifty a year. By 1987, the average Barnett branch had $37 million in deposits, more than double the rule of thumb of what you need to justify such an operation. "People," Rice said, meaning Wall Street analysts, "say we're building too many branches, but these are small buildings on appreciating property, and meanwhile they are gathering deposits."

The fight for market share was intense in Florida, especially after a southeastern states compact permitted a bank chartered by any of the states to start or acquire a bank in any of the others. But Barnett won it. In 1995, its total assets pushed $40 billion, and it could claim a banking relationship with 40 percent of the state's households. In 1993, Barnett was second only to Citicorp in the proportion of its total loans that were consumer loans: 63 percent. And if you took the securitized credit card receivables off the Citicorp books, Barnett would have been first.

"Our advantage," said Steve Hansel, "is that we're close to the customer. The presidents live and work in their communities, which know them from church and Little League. That's much better than the guy who flies in with a suitcase and looks for all companies with more than fifty million in sales. I've been involved ten years here with asset quality, which is the one area we think can derail the train. This is an interesting market. The hustlers of the world come here. In West Florida, Pensacola, Panama City, in what's referred to as the redneck division, you get the good old boy hustlers who are more dangerous than any garment district types. We're trying to professionalize asset quality. We've recruited a number of people from the New York State Banking Department and some national bank examiners, keep them here [at the Jacksonville headquarters] for a while and then move them into the banks. The difference in this business is people. If we get the right people, we'll be fine. If we don't, we're—well . . . there are no systems that are that good. You need people who are creative and have a good moral core.

"There was a time when everybody in the Barnett world reported to Charlie Rice. You had a fairly pure management-by-exception situation. New acquisitions and banks that weren't doing well got to see me. It was great fun and it usually worked. One of Charlie's best qualities as a manager is that he has a lot of tolerance for diversity in the people around him. Now we do less of that. We have central systems that are pretty damned serious. All the information comes out of the machine. I can tell you how many exceptions were granted last week on consumer loans in the Warrenton branch of the West Florida bank."

Every year Rice, his three vice-chairmen, Hansel and Golembe met with nobody else in the room to develop a five-year plan for the bank that nobody else would hear about. Mostly, the plan did work out, and did guide the bank. The stress was on keeping earnings up while expensing the costs of expansion. The Palm Beach branch opened one of the first bank-operated discount brokerages in Florida, and by the mid 1980s Barnett's brokers were doing three hundred trades a day. Barnett made a big investment in ATMs, and was a pioneer member of the Honor ATM network, which generated fees from non-Barnett users of Barnett machines. Barnett was the first bank in Florida to charge a fee to its own cardholders when they used ATMs in supermarkets and other banks. Fee increases had to be sold to the banks, which would have to live with them, by the holding company.

The advantage of the holding company structure with initiative in the field was that each bank knew the range of services it was providing to the commercial customer, and could successfully price accordingly without worrying too much about the competition. The basic measurement was profit as a percentage of core deposits. "Profitability as a percent of total assets is not a meaningful number for me," Al Lastinger said. "In a high-growth market, we don't want to suboptimize the future by too much concentration on the bottom line." Among the discouragements to unfettered growth was the fact that holding company expenses were assessed against the individual banks according to their total assets, which raised the marginal cost of going beyond core deposits.

All this worked: Barnett grew and, by the more conventional measures of Wall Street, maintained profits that fluctuated very slightly around 1 percent of assets.

Barnett's success in the 1980s and early 1990s, when many other banks became deeply troubled, made the stock popular with pension funds and mutual funds, and suddenly the institutional stockholders were upset about Rice's "efficiency ratio"— non-interest expenses as a percent of revenues. Growth by branching inevitably increases expenses before it gains revenues, but Barnett's history had indicated that the long-term benefits were there. On a low time horizon, however, it was clear in 1995 that an acquirer could cut costs at Barnett by abandoning the holding company structure and the now twenty-eight separate banks with their presidents and boards. A 1988 Florida law had permitted banks to go to statewide branching for the first time, but Barnett had ignored it. "A branch bank structure is inherently less expensive to operate," Larry Werz, CFO of the Florida end of First Union, told *Institutional Investor*. Thomas Hanley of the securities house CS First Boston (formerly the star bank analyst at Salomon Brothers) said at a conference that "within two years" Barnett "will be gone."[3] It should be noted that in summer 1996 Hanley developed a fancy derivative contract for Union Bank of Switzerland, his new employer, to sell to its clients. The derivative involved stock prices for ten banks Hanley considered most likely to be acquired by other banks. Barnett was not on the list.

Hansel had left the Barnett team in 1992 to become CEO of Hibernia Bank in New Orleans, that city's number two bank. It was a basket case, with $191 million in equity capital and $320 million of nonperforming assets. It was in default on a $90 million loan from a consortium of other banks, and the bank was operating pursuant to a memorandum of understanding with the Fed which required its executives to raise their hands if they wished to go to the bathroom. Hansel quickly sold off the company's Texas bank subsidiary, convinced creditors to take stock in the bank, and raised capital through a subscription rights offer. He cut staff and briskly cleared out an underbrush of bad loans, picking up in the process $100 million of future tax benefits. By 1995, Hibernia had paid off its loans, earned out the tax credit, and created an equity ratio half again as high as what the regulators required.[4] It was one of the most profitable banks in the South, a prime takeover candidate if Hansel could get his price. (Hibernia *was* on Hanley's list in 1996.) His pioneering effort, alas, had been the computerization of small-business-loan scoring. Still, Hansel's Barnett experience had taught him not to be a slave to the computer: "We have bankers who know their customers because their kids go to the same schools or they go to the same churches, but there is no payoff for that if you don't make loans you wouldn't otherwise make."[5]

Rice brought in a Wall Street operations man to reorganize Barnett's information systems, and centralized some of the pricing and lending authority—and especially the collecting and processing roles—once delegated to the banks. The Comptroller of the Currency released a study showing that the *announcement* of a switch from multibank holding company status to branch banking stimulated a rise in the price of a banking company's stock.[6] In late 1995, Rice bit the bullet: Barnett would abandon the holding company form geographically, turn its existing banks into branches of the Jacksonville main office, and make the boards of directors of those banks nothing more than advisers to the branch managers. Applications for small-business loans would be scored in the machines, and the customer's contact often enough would be through the telephone lines rather than person-to-person at the branch. And then he sold the bank to First Union.

3

Not long before Barnett abandoned the holding company structure, Banc One of Ohio and many other states, the seventh-largest bank in the country, had moved to centralize an enterprise that had been built on almost total autonomy for the subsidiaries. Most of Banc One's eighty-eight banks had been acquired with Banc One stock on an arrangement its chairman John B. McCoy liked to call "the uncommon partnership." There were 147 checking account plans offered in the system, and different levels of technological sophistication were to be found at every bank. The largest single source of savings from geographically spread banking—the conversion of checks from items that had to go through clearinghouses to "on us" items—had never been implemented. Even local collection and loan files were different from bank to bank.

Then the flagship in Columbus got itself involved with large purchases of collateralized mortgage obligations and index-amortizing swaps, which knocked the stock price down a quarter, and the number of banks interested in uncommon partnerships diminished. With the evaporation of the derivatives profits, Banc One also showed a terrible "efficiency ratio" (which is, after all, a derivative itself, being merely the operating profit divided by operating expenses). Among McCoy's acquisitions in 1992 had been Arizona's Valley National Bank, a great statewide franchise destroyed mostly by the federal government's failure to police the S&Ls, which drove interest rates up for deposits and down for loans in their mad rush to oblivion. Its chairman was Richard Lehman, and on welcoming him to the Banc One family McCoy suggested that he might wish to break Valley National into pieces, chartering separate banks for Tucson and Flagstaff. Lehman thanked him for the advice and continued to run his centralized shop, as the uncommon partnership gave him every right to do. In February 1995, McCoy summoned Lehman to Columbus and made him president and chief operating officer, to plan for the introduction of nationwide branch banking when the Riegle-Neal Interstate Banking and Branching Act of 1994 took effect on June 1, 1997.

The other big-time acquirers had been centralizers from the start: NationsBank (originally North Carolina National Bank, a mid-sized bank for the largest corporate borrowers it could corral), Fleet Bank of Providence, Rhode Island (grown from the Industrial Bank of Providence, which had started out financing textile and costume jewelry businesses), and Key Banks of Albany, New York, which acquired banks on a northern tier from Maine to Alaska, left them very much in local hands for lending but centralized the operations end to a remarkable degree, becoming pioneers of electronic check presentment. A suspicious lawyer who represented a bank selling out to Key Banks for stock in the 1980s did a due diligence on the Key New York State portfolio and said it was the cleanest set of loans he had ever seen in his life. But after the merger of Key and Cleveland's Society Bank, loan-scoring procedures came to Key Banks, too.

One of the earliest mergers across state lines (the state of Washington had to pass a law to make it possible) was organized in 1982 to allow Bank of America to take over Seattle First, which had bought baskets of bad loans from Oklahoma's Penn Square Bank. B of A was almost as sick as Seafirst—but nobody was admitting it, and its still optimistic CEO was eager to expand to Seattle. Seafirst stockholders, remarkably, got $15 a share in cash and market value of a new issue of 11.5 percent preferred stock.

Like Texas Commerce, acquired by Chemical Bank three years later, Seafirst soon seemed worth much less than its purchase price. The only deal the Washington state legislature would have approved left the bank freestanding, with B of A simply its owner on a holding company basis. Luke Helms, who would later run the B of A branches from an office on the fortieth floor in San Francisco, was then in the international department of Seafirst. "I was running around the world trying to raise Fed Funds. B of A was very nice to us. [Sam] Armacost came up and said, 'You guys have a fabulous franchise. Look at B of A as a candy store. Tell us what you need, otherwise run your own show.' " Seafirst continued to hemorrhage money for another three years: the first quarter when the bank got more customers than it lost did not come until 1986.

Still, Helms says, "Best thing that ever happened to Seafirst was that we went bankrupt. You realize who your customers are. You walk around with a sack on your head. You have to explain why you were in Oklahoma lending money to Penn Square. You're not traveling to London—you're seeing your real customers—the farthest away you go is Yakima. Cooley [Richard Cooley, who had been chairman of Wells Fargo and had been hired away to run Seafirst when the crisis came] would walk around, take the doors off the offices, put glass walls on the conference rooms. This became probably the most profitable large bank in the world. Last year"—Helms was speaking in 1994—"we made three hundred million on a fifteen-billion-dollar bank. Ninety-five percent of our business was in the state of Washington. We had twenty-seven percent of the deposit market, sixty percent of the small-business market, and seventy percent of what big stuff there is."

By then, while still using its own name and retaining its own board of directors, Seafirst was very much part of Bank of America. The big California banks don't believe in drive-through teller windows; they all dropped the service at the same time. Seafirst not only had drive-through teller windows, it had a rule that the teller was to throw a dog bone through the window if there was a dog in the car. "We were," Helms recalls, "the largest purchaser of dog bones in the state of Washington." Now Seafirst, too, has dropped teller drive-in stations, and installed B of A's Versateller ATM machines. Almost half the Washington customers are on a plan whereby deposits or withdrawals at any kind of teller windows incur a fee, while ATM deposits or withdrawals are free.

Helms, a large man about fifty years old with gray eyes under blond eyebrows, considers himself a marketer first of all. "Mentally, I work for Ford Motor Company. My job is to design, do the image advertising. Those guys out there own the business." He goes to Pepsi-Cola and Coca-Cola bottlers' conventions. Daniel Yankelovich designed a day in a San Diego shopping mall, a "safari," to help B of A's branch managers get a better grip on the services people were offered and buying. "We're running a factory," Helms says. "The factory has to know the orders. The managers have to commit to the orders—twenty-five home loans a day, thirty car loans a day. Then we can build the factories."

The home mortgage factory is in Portland, Oregon; the consumer loan factory is in Seattle; the factory for auto loans through dealers is in Reno. Seafirst itself has become one of the eighty districts into which B of A divided its supervision, and everybody was selling the same products and reading from the same page—including the wholly owned subsidiary Bank of Arizona, the Nevada bank, the Colorado bank, even the recently acquired Continental in Chicago.

"Rosenberg's theory," Helms said, referring to the bank's CEO, "is that checking accounts lead to other business. We do a Saturday special somewhere every weekend. This year we'll have a gross million people opening checking accounts at B of A. It's the Fidelity approach. Come in. We'll buy your home equity line, give you a fifty-dollar credit for transferring your credit card, lock you into our products and penalize you if you leave early. We measure net new checking accounts by district and customer service scores, and publish the results every quarter. If you're a manager, you don't want to be at the bottom of that list twice. The only thing the managers are held responsible for is sales. We provide the products. We're behaving as though we already had interstate banking." On the corporate end, Rosenberg's philosophy was that you make the loans to get the other business: "If you're not lending money," he said, "you're not in the cash management business or the derivatives business. Corporate lending is the price of entry."

The consumer lending center had about 170 employees, 145 of them processing applications. The credit bureaus were on line, and a collateral evaluation unit made independent judgments about home equity. Auto loans get approved in an hour or two, but turnaround time for home equity credit is necessarily two to three weeks, because B of A can't do the title searching or appraising itself. This is not state of the art: in 1994, a lot of the output was still paper, zipping through laser printers. "Even as we speak," said supervisor Ann Mix, "we are working on automated entry, which I've been screaming about for a year and a half." But it's far from your grandfather's bank.

Texas Commerce, when Chemical Bank set the price for its acquisition in 1986, did not appear to be a troubled bank: Chemical paid a billion dollars for it. Two years later, it probably could have got the bank for nothing. "You have to give credit to Walter Shipley," says TCB chairman Marc Shapiro, a dark, lean Texan who became successor to the storied Ben Love while still in his thirties. "He made a billion-dollar acquisition, saw it do much worse than he'd expected; he got severely criticized in the media, and he left all the people in place. We had the incredible advantage that all our competitors failed, an extraordinary thing. We thought we'd been conservative, but we lost a quarter of our capital, which Chemical replenished. What killed us was the land; land lost eighty percent of its value in Texas." TCB was a corporate bank—"a narrow base," Shapiro says, "but it turned out to be wide enough." When the in-state mergers all failed—First Republic, Interfirst, M Corp, First City—the corporations turned to Texas Commerce. In early 1966, Shapiro claimed that his was the primary Texas bank for 55 percent of all Texas companies with more than $250 million in sales.

Chemical will have to leave Texas Commerce substantially self-managed: Texas, as was its right, has opted out of the Riegle-Neal interstate branching law. Chemical does the credit card business, and with one significant exception handles the international work; Jimmy Lee takes care of the syndication on the biggest stuff. But, Shapiro says, "if we were a stand-alone bank, we would be the eleventh-largest syndicator of loans in the country." The international exception is trading in Mexican pesos. Texas Commerce is the payroll bank for 75 percent of the *maquiladoras*, the factories where cheap Mexican labor assembles components from the United States and elsewhere, on an arrangement which excuses from any U.S. duties both the export of material to Mexico and the import of finished products.

The workers in these plants are not people who have bank accounts or ATM cards, and in the eastern section of Mexico, where the unions are strong, the wages have to be distributed in cash. (Further west, where the unions are weak, employers can get away with paying by check, which is cheaper, and load the costs of cashing the checks onto the workers themselves.) The employers, especially the Asian companies, want to keep their money in U.S. dollars and have American banks make the conversion into pesos and deliver the pesos to the workers. In 1995, TCB had $18 million of revenues from this business, and half of it dropped down to the bottom line.

"We deliver cash to seven hundred plants," Shapiro says. "All the GM plants, and plants in Baja California and Monterrey. We buy it from Banamex in Mexico City and sell it to Banamex in Nuevo Laredo and we make a spread. It's a business based on service; we've got to be open on a holiday when it's not a holiday in Mexico." There is, of course, more to it than that. Jack Borland, a low-keyed, middle-aged man who supervises the always-young currency traders at a station with ten or twelve screens, explains that he buys his pesos from Banamex because under Mexican law he is technically permitted to buy currency only where he has an account. "The rule is from 1984, and it's applied on a selective basis by the Mexicans," he says; "it doesn't apply to the banks that helped refinance the debt, but it does apply to us. We are very efficient. We know where all the buttons are, who to call in the Mexican bank if the money's lost. If you call us up at ten in the morning and say, 'My money's not there,' we don't say, 'We'll research it,' which is the usual thing in foreign exchange, and it doesn't go to the back room to operations, we do it up here at the desk. We know everybody in Mexico City. We do not take huge positions in the peso market, but we time our position. On any given Thursday I will do a hundred-odd transactions for x million dollars. I'm naturally short pesos and long dollars, I can wait." Elsewhere on the desk, TCB is financing Texas importers and exporters who do business through the very busy ports at Galveston and in the Houston ship channel; Borland says he makes more money on "middle-sized trades involving imports and exports that don't tend to get paid for all at once. It's a business based on commercial flows." And essentially it has nothing to do with Chemical's very extensive foreign-exchange trading.

Perhaps the most centralized of the multistate banks is NationsBank, built on the chassis of the old North Carolina National Bank of Charlotte. In a state where branching had always been permitted, NCNB had gone after corporate rather than consumer business (in the early 1980s, the bank didn't even write

home mortgages, except for its employees and its best customers).
I visited its London branch in 1973, when the annual rental of
space in the City was higher per square foot than the cost of
building a branch in North Carolina: these fellows were ambitious
from early on. In 1983, when ex-Marine Hugh McColl took over
as chairman at the age of forty-eight, NCNB had $7 billion in
assets. In 1995, NationsBank was ranked twenty-fifth in the world
and third in the United States in *Institutional Investor*'s annual
summary of the banking industry, with $170 billion in assets and
(more important) $14.5 billion in capital.

What exploded NCNB into the national limelight in 1988 was
its FDIC-organized takeover of First Republic, created a year earlier by an FDIC-organized merger between Republic Bank and
Interfirst, which had become the largest and most insolvent bank
in Texas. This transaction, in which the Internal Revenue Service
and FDIC chairman L. William Seidman increased the government's deficit and the national debt by about $500 million, has
never been satisfactorily explained. Its foundation was a ruling
from the Internal Revenue Service that even though the FDIC
would buy several billion dollars of assets from First Republic for
$1.3 billion more than they were worth, NCNB as acquirer of the
bank could claim as a deduction from its taxable income in years
to come a billion dollars of the losses that the FDIC had in fact
absorbed. The news that this tax dodge would be legal was given
to NCNB alone in a private letter from the IRS.

The staff of the Task Force on Urgent Fiscal Issues of the
House Budget Committee reported to Congressman Charles
Schumer on this deal:

> The IRS, as confirmed by its former Chief Counsel William
> Nelson, understood that the tax rulings were "novel" and "broke
> new ground." Nelson, therefore, put the "best people" in charge
> of responding to the requests. Mr. Nelson realized that "time was
> money" when dealing with failed bank situations and he custom-

arily insured that the IRS paid "special attention" to "agency agendas." He insisted, however, that the IRS not "give the appearance of giving away the store." . . . The IRS officials did not recall specific discussions with FDIC officials about details of the First Republic bailout but did confirm that there had been previous discussions with FDIC, OCC and FSLIC officials about "general patterns" in resolving or restructuring failed financial institutions. The FDIC, as confirmed by Roger Watson, Director of Research, had an internal discussion about whether to treat the NCNB letter rulings as proprietary information or disclose them to other bidders. It was decided not to disclose them, and the FDIC did not internally discount the value of the tax benefits in weighing the competing bids.[7]

The FDIC's defense rested on the argument that the law enjoined the *agency*—not the *government*—to get the best price when it sold off the carcass of an insolvent bank. If losses could be sloughed off to the IRS, the fact that taxpayers as a whole would have to bear them was no skin off the FDIC's back. As a practical matter, what happened here was that the FDIC fund, which was the responsibility of the banking industry and would eventually have to be replenished by the banking industry, was spared about $300 million because the tax-advantaged NCNB could bid more for the bank, while taxpayers had to make up the hole caused by the disappearance of $500 million NCNB would otherwise have had to pay in federal taxes. *Fortune* called the NCNB-assisted takeover "the deal of the century," and quoted NCNB chairman McColl that "Candidly, I think we paid zero for First Republic."

Absorbing First Republic's losses eventually cost the FDIC more than $3 billion, and NCNB in addition to getting the bank got management fees for administering a Special Asset Division, into which were slotted the loans on which losses would be borne by the FDIC. Businesses whose loans were sent to that Siberia found themselves cut off from credit. Moreover, many other corporate customers of First Republic found themselves cold-shouldered by NCNB Texas. Some Texans said the initials stood for "Nobody Cares, Nobody Bothers"; others, more pragmatic, believed they stood for "No Cash for No Body." NCNB within thirty days of taking on the deposits of the Texas bank became the nation's largest holder of collateralized mortgage obligations issued by Fannie Mae and Freddie Mac, a category in which they had occupied a trivial position before. Marc Shapiro says they came into Texas with the attitude that all Texans were "crooks or stupid," which gave Texas Commerce a considerable edge in poaching their commercial and industrial business. But NCNB in the glamorous Dallas tower built by First Republic remained the biggest bank in Texas—twice the size of TCB—and eventually the NCNB Texas branch became a big seller of NCNB's standardized loan products.[8]

Later NCNB acquired the merged bank made from Atlanta's Citizens & Southern and Richmond's Sovran, stimulating the new name NationsBank, then Boatmen's in Missouri, Kansas, and Arkansas, itself recently a major acquirer, as noted below on page 257. It entered into a deal with Dean Witter to put brokerage offices in its two thousand branches (a deal later broken off, after Wall Street salesmanship got the bank in trouble without generating much business), and acquired Chicago Research and Trading, a fascinating firm that had pioneered the invention and pricing of options. Resident high up in one of those silly skyscrapers Chicago built in the years when the Japanese were willing to finance anything in that city, CRT despite its five hundred employees was still the creation of two Mennonite brothers-in-law, Gary Ginter and Joe Ritchie, who lived in the Chicago slums, tithed to their church, and taught Sunday school to kids who would terrify just about any other banker. In summer 1996, McColl was worrying in public that all he had achieved could be blown away by a single wrong call in technology.[9] There is a cheering section for that.

4

A staff study from the Federal Reserve makes the point that the 1990s wave of mergers and acquisitions had a precursor in New York in the 1950s, when wholesale bank Chemical merged with consumer bank Corn Exchange; wholesale bank First National merged with National City; wholesale bank Chase merged with retail Bank of the Manhattan Company; and wholesale Hanover Bank merged with consumer bank Manufacturers Trust Company.[10] Some of the more recent mergers have also brought together deposit gatherers and lenders. Most of them, however, are not questions of fit, or even of geographic expansion. (From the first loosening of the law in 1988 through 1993, the Federal Reserve Bank of New York reports, 75 percent of the interstate expansion of bank holding companies was into adjacent states.[11]) They are simply ways to get rid of excess capacity. And they handle Bill Isaac's problem of the CEO who doesn't wish to discard the limo and the forty-foot office by letting the older boss become the nominal head of the merged organization, with all the perks (and no small bonus) for a little while, after which the younger boss takes over.

The model for this sort of merger is Wells Fargo's takeover of Crocker Bank in 1986. Crocker had a presence in southern California, having taken over the failed U.S. National Bank of San Diego (owned and jackpotted by Richard Nixon's buddy C. Arnholt Smith), but it was basically a San Francisco bank, like Wells Fargo. Wells was not that much bigger than Crocker—$30 billion to $20 billion—but it was a lot smarter and tougher, and it gutted its acquisition, closing three-quarters of the branches and dismissing three-quarters of the employees. But it kept most of the deposits, and all the business it wanted to keep.

Two years later, Bank of New York, Alexander Hamilton's original bank, which had developed a niche in data processing for mutual funds to supplement its specialty as a trust company for the city's high society, took over Irving Trust, a bank of equal size, which had pioneered corporate electronic payments, in a hostile tender that tripled the price of both stocks before the battle was over. Bank of New England collapsed under the weight of real estate lending in Florida as well as Massachusetts, and the FDIC awarded it to Fleet, which soon bit off Shawmut, where chairman Joel Alvord, who had doubled the size of his bank in 1988 by acquiring Connecticut National Bank, had vowed to fight on the beaches. In 1991, Chemical bought Manufacturers Hanover, guaranteeing Manny Hanny's John McGillicuddy two years as chairman of the new bank before Walter Shipley took over, and four months later, Bank of America acquired Security Pacific, closing four hundred branches, leaving part of the price contingent on the value of SP's assets, which turned out to be worth a lot less than either side thought at the moment of sale.

In 1995—the litany continues—Bank of Boston bought Bay Banks for $2 billion and a promise to BayBanks chairman William Crozier that he could serve as chairman of the united bank for three years. First Chicago merged with National Bank of Detroit, which had a fortress balance sheet, which First Chicago did not (in the first quarter of the merger, the combined bank took a $210 million loan loss reserve). Boatmen's Bancshares of St. Louis acquired Worthen Bank in Arkansas (fief of the Stephens family that had bankrolled Bill Clinton) and Bank IV in Kansas, making itself the largest holder of deposits in Missouri, Kansas, Arkansas, New Mexico and Oklahoma. Before the year was out, Chemical and Chase announced the blockbuster merger that would make by far the largest bank in the United States, with the leadership of Chemical and the name of Chase. Early in 1996, Wells Fargo won its California rival First Interstate, fighting off a challenge from First Bank Systems of Minneapolis, which First Interstate management and employees wanted as its acquirer for obvious reasons. The Chemical-Chase merger was advertised to cost 12,000 jobs, reduce gross revenues but increase earnings thanks to cost-cutting; the Wells–First Interstate merger was announced as a loss of 9,300 jobs.

In the first five years of the 1990s, employment in banking dropped from 1,560,000 to something under 1,400,000, and the number of banking organizations dropped from 9,200 (already down from 12,200 in 1980) to less than 7,500. Banks' share of financial intermediation, which had been over 50 percent in the years right after World War II and 37 percent in 1979, fell below 25 percent in 1993 despite the collapse of the S&Ls (down from a 25 percent share of financial intermediation in 1979 to 11 percent in 1993), which should have fattened the banks.[12] Always the optimist, the Federal Reserve in 1996 published a pamphlet suggesting steady-as-you-go, pointing out that the number of banking offices (banks plus branches) is up since 1980 (we ignore the fact that there has been no gain in the 1990s): "The demand is large for 'old-fashioned' banking. . . . Given banking offices' potential as retail platforms for new products, their unique presence in the financial services sector, and the excruciatingly slow progress of general retail electronic banking, the most profitable strategy may be to streamline these offices to take advantage of their unique strengths. . . . [T]he industry has just received legal power for nationwide geographic expansion and appears on the verge of receiving it for product expansion, which may ensure a bright future for banking."[13]

5

Before 1980, economists generally believed that there were economies of scale in banking—the larger the bank, the smaller the unit cost of doing a piece of work. In 1982, George Benston, Gerald Hanweck and David Humphrey published a paper showing that the results those economists had deduced from their studies were an artifact of their procedures, and that in the real world, economies of scale were exhausted at a low level— between $10 million and $25 million per office—and that above this level banks began to suffer *dis*economies of scale: unit costs rose.[14] Later studies indicated that for banking companies economies of scale were exhausted somewhere between $100 million and $200 million in assets. Still later, economists looking at large banks began arguing that the economies of scale might go up to something more than a billion dollars. But nobody said that banks got more efficient as they got bigger over that rather modest level.

When mergers began to proliferate in the 1980s, the Bank Research Office of the OCC did a study which indicated that acquiring banks were almost always more efficient than the banks they acquired, and that the stock market reacted to the news of a merger by pushing up the stock of the acquirer in expectation that it would improve the operating ratios of the bank it bought. And this did happen, to some degree, about two-fifths of the time. It did not happen in the other three-fifths. This improvement, moreover, was a function of superior management replacing inferior management rather than any economy of scale. The authors of the study also looked at the literature on economies of scope—that is, did expanded product offerings reduce the cost of operating a banking office? and concluded that "offering a wide range of products does not give a bank a significant cost advantage over its less diversified rivals."[15]

Buoyed by such research and by my own observations, I wrote a cover story for *Forbes* to which editor Jim Michaels gave the title "Too Big Not to Fail." My central criticism was of the banking regulators, especially the Fed, for giving the banks regulatory accounting procedures like those previously given the S&Ls—not to mention structuring a steeply sloping yield curve that benefited banks at the expense of borrowers and made the 1991 recession worse than it should have been. "Today's global economy," I wrote, "does not offer a congenial climate for banking dinosaurs. . . . They are so weakened that the best course for the regulators probably is to knock heads together in the nation's dozen largest banks until only half of them—not much bigger than they are today—are still offering their services to the public. The real strength of our banking system is not in the giant banks but in the myriad of middling-sized banks. Using the taxpayers' money and credit in a futile effort to keep the whole herd alive could create another tragedy for the federal budget and for the future efficiency of financial intermediation in the United States."[16]

This was right in theory but wrong in practice: there can be no question that by keeping the big banks alive to buy each other out after the government had restored them to profitability, the Fed achieved the necessary results with the least shock to the system. Some of this has been dirty pool: the Fed's war against electronic payments has meant that multistate banks can save quite a lot of money converting checks to "on us" items instead of sending them on to the Fed, while independent banks are stuck with the cost of the service bureaus that do their demand deposit accounting. One of the reasons most mergers don't produce economies of scale is that the acquiring bank continues to use the old payments-processing system for the operations end of the bank that has been bought.

The spread of detailed regulation—much of it the fault of the Congress, in the aftermath of the S&L disaster and disturbing evidence about racial discrimination in lending—has given advantages to larger banking institutions that can pay the relatively fixed cost of a compliance officer from a larger base of earning assets. And there is no way to count the economic or social cost when the smaller banks that do the information-intensive lending are displaced by branches of holding companies run from headquarters in the money centers on a Keep-It-Simple-Stupid chassis. The Fed's clientele, in addition to its check-processing employees, is the big banks, and the Fed serves its clientele.

The proprietors of today's mergers do not expect the joined banks to keep total assets as high as those of the institutions before they were merged. The day of worrying that our banks cannot compete with the enormous Japanese banks ended when the Japanese banks began to go bust. Citicorp, which has not been in the acquisition market except for random S&Ls to create a presence in another state, has been buying back its stock with excess capital instead of using it to support expansion. Wells Fargo is closing down most of First Interstate; the new Chase will hold 25 percent fewer assets than the old Chase and the old Chemical combined. Bank of Boston and Fleet will hold fewer assets than used to be in the two of them plus Shawmut and New England and BayBanks. Bank of America and Wells Fargo, both cutting back traditional branches, will have fewer deposits than the two of them plus Security Pacific and First Interstate, and B of A expects to keep only the most profitable parts of the business done by Continental in Chicago.

The big banks, in short, may not be much bigger when the merging is done, and there will be fewer of them. Because the banks stopped bidding against each other for deposits, their cost of funds came down in the 1990s by comparison with money market rates. This widened the spread between their cost of funds and the rates they could charge for loans, and explains the improvement in the industry's profits in the mid 1990s.

But all these banks expect to be much less dependent on banking for their earnings. Ed Furash suggests that the successful among the three hundred largest banks "will be structured to produce superior returns with net operating income of 40 percent from intermediation [what I have called banking], 20 percent from capital markets [securitization, trading, and financial engineering], and 40 percent from fee business [consumer finance, investment management, mortgage banking, credit card processing]."[17] He leaves out some important sources of earnings such as foreign exchange, various forms of correspondent banking to win fees from smaller banks, "controlled disbursement" to help customers play the float (Texas Commerce arranges for *Fortune* 100 companies to pay their bills through San Angelo, Texas; Dallas-based EDS paid me for a speech in 1996 with a check drawn on Ithaca, New York), and administering mutual fund accounts.

State Street in Boston, run by former IBM salesmen, the original banking partner of Fidelity Investments and of the originator of the NOW account, has more than half its earnings in fees for managing data associated with mutual funds and pension funds and trust accounts. Bank of New York would never have been able to acquire Irving without the revenues from processing for mutual funds, especially Dreyfus; no less than Morgan bank sold its master trust business to Bank of New York because it was more efficient at it. And individual banks will have individual specialties: Morgan, for example, runs the basic clearinghouse for dollar-denominated bond trades in Europe, and helps launch casualty insurance companies in Bermuda, investing their reserves for a fee and eventually taking them public at a whopping profit.

Some of the reach for fees is resented; some is not. People will pay $20 and $25 for bouncing a check (fees for bouncing checks are the single largest source of profit in some branches) because they feel guilty, but they dislike charges for writing a check—as supermarkets hate the charges banks impose on their deposits. "It is not only the nickel-and-dime approach to service charges that annoys the customer and makes him think of moving the account," writes banking professor Paul Nadler. "It is also the feeling that he gets as charges are applied, one after another, that his account is looked at as a sheep to be shorn rather than a solid relationship."[18]

Banks still hope to make money as stockbrokers, an activity

that has been permitted to many small state-chartered banks for-
ever—there being no other point of access to the financial
system in many towns—and to large banks since Bank of
America acquired Charles Schwab in 1982. Citibank followed
with Quick and Reilly, PNC in Philadelphia offered a Cash
Management Account to compete with Merrill's, and then
NationsBank made a marriage of convenience with Dean Witter.
For one reason or another, all of these arrangements collapsed.
The variety of the disasters may have hidden a more fundamental common fault: people go to banks to *preserve* their
wealth in savings accounts, not to *increase* their wealth in the
stock market. Banks have done somewhat better selling mutual
funds than creating brokerage customers, but even here most
customers tend to buy money market funds or bond funds from
banks, and stock funds elsewhere.

Trust operations, long a source of fee income for banks, have
deteriorated in earnings power as the mutual funds have grown
and as brokerage houses like Merrill Lynch have increased the
range of the financial services they offer. When Bankers Trust
decided to offer a service to employees whose retirement money
was going into fixed-contribution 401(K) plans, it found that
Fidelity Funds could provide important features (like over-the-
phone net asset value figures) that the Bankers computers could
not be programmed to match. Corporate trust work, mostly the
transfer of shares in a company from one owner to another, has
virtually disappeared from the banks with the rise of the Depository Trust Corporation. This creature of infinite efficiency, operated today essentially with the New York Stock Exchange but
launched originally by John M. Meyer, Jr., when he was chairman for J.P. Morgan, does trust work for virtually every traded
company.

The big banks hope and expect to make money at both ends of
the quantity scale: they want to get fees for volume processing,
where obviously there *are* major economies of scale, and they

want to establish "private banking" relationships with rich clients who ideally would do *all* their financial business with the bank—checking, investments, credit cards, mortgages, estates, foreign involvements both personal and commercial. Historically, "private banking" was essentially a payment to the bank to extend the cloak of legally recognized bank secrecy over the activities of an individual client, and there is still an element of jiggery-pokery to some of the services the banks provide, especially but not exclusively to the rich in the poor countries. But financial counseling has become a recognized specialty if not a profession, and it fits neatly into the relationships of a bank with its larger customers.

Furash expects *both* large and small banks to make 20 percent of their future operating income from "capital markets," and in the case of the larger banks, that means trading, making money with money. The model for some years was Bankers Trust, which the deceptively southern gentleman Charles Sanford pulled out of conventional banking in the 1970s, organizing it as what a consultant to the bank described as "a lot of little nests of entrepreneurship, letting people make their own businesses and make profits at them." By 1994, two-thirds of the assets on the Bankers Trust balance sheet were trading-related, and BT, which had been one of the first banks to move to midtown Manhattan to be near its customers in the 1960s, was moving back downtown to be near the markets. Vice-chairman George Vojta said, "We're not a lender to hold to maturity. Banks get in trouble when they get locked into loans." Dick Rosenberg at Bank of America watched Sanford in the 1990–91 recession with mingled distaste and awe: "Ten percent of his loan portfolio was nonperforming," Rosenberg recalled, "and it had zip impact on their performance."

David Berry, research director of the bank stock firm Keefe, Bruyette & Wood, testified to the House Banking Committee in October 1993 that "Trading is a growth business. Combined trading revenues for the largest trading banks have grown at a 17 percent compound annual rate over the last five years. . . . Variations in trading results have caused less bottom-line earnings volatility than have variations in credit costs." And "trading is consistently profitable."[19] Berry summarized 373 quarterly observations of trading results at nine money-center banks, from the first quarter of 1983 to the third quarter of 1993. There had been four loss quarters for individual banks in that period, totaling $19 million, and 369 profitable quarters, totaling $35.9 billion in earnings.

The key to bank profitability in the modern world of large banks, then, would be trading revenues. Lending is just the entry: "If you're not lending money," said Dick Rosenberg, "you're not in the derivatives business." The elevator door opens onto the third floor, and the visitor sees literally an acre of enormous bullpen, dimly lit because people are reading from cathode ray tubes rather than pages, hundreds of traders sitting at more hundreds of screens, pushing buttons, talking on the phone, yelling to each other and throwing spitballs. On another floor, the researchers are working on the math, for this is not *supposed* to be a risk activity. But it is.

9 / Trading: The Zero-Sum Game

We have two formal meetings every week, Tuesday after-noon and Friday morning. I say, "What's making you nervous?"

—DAN NAPOLI, chief risk controller, Merrill Lynch

One fine afternoon in spring 1994, I got a telephone call from a man in Texas who wanted advice. He was, he said, a retired builder, seventy-five years old, with a nest egg that had been about one and a half million dollars. He had been living nicely on the interest earned by this money in bank CDs and money market funds, until the Federal Reserve began hammering rates down in 1991. As six-month CD rates fell to 3 percent, his standard of living was squeezed.

One pauses in midstream to note that he was in fact nowhere near so badly off as he thought. When the rates had been 8 percent, inflation had been 5 percent, and the prospective purchasing power of his nest egg had been shrinking fast. He could have supplemented his 3 percent interest income in 1992 by taking another 3 percent out of his capital and been just as well off as before. But not many people have that kind of sophistication about money.

Anyway, someone had put my caller in touch with a brokerage house, Murchison and Company, which advertised instruments "guaranteed by the United States government" that would actually *increase* in yield as rates went down. These were "structured notes," otherwise "inverse floaters," issued by GE Capital, the Federal National Mortgage Association and, especially, the Federal Home Loan Bank Board (which put out *$30 billion* worth in 1993). Such bonds came in many varieties. The easiest to understand is the bond which paid some fixed percentage *minus* the prevailing short-term rate, normally the London Interbank Offered Rate, otherwise Libor. If Libor was at 5 percent, the inverse floater might offer 10 percent minus Libor. That was 5 percent on the day the bond was issued. If Libor went down to 4 percent, the bond paid 6 percent; if it went to 3 percent, the bond would pay 7 percent. Of course, if Libor rose, the bond would pay less. If you wanted to *speculate*, you could get a structured note based on a constant minus Libor doubled—still 5 percent on the day you bought it, when you were entitled to $15 -$ Libor $\times 2$. But now if Libor went to 4 percent you would get 7 percent on your money; and if Libor went to 6 percent, you would get only 3 percent. One of the notes in the portfolio Bankers Trust greedily put together for Gibson Greeting Card actually involved Libor *squared*. In the world of financial engineering, all things are possible.

The most dramatic instrument of this kind was the collateralized mortgage obligation (CMO) that had been split into interest-only (IO) and principal-only (PO) strips. The average pass-through mortgage security, where the investor receives each month his pro rata share of everything paid last month by the homeowners whose mortgages are in the package, is likely to be paid off in about twelve years, because the average homeowners sells his old house and buys a new one every twelve years. The security is priced to reflect the expected monthly cash flow from the mortgages. The owners of the PO strip bets that interest rates will go down, which will persuade lots of homeowners to refinance their mortgages, paying off the principal ahead of time. The owner of the IO strip bets that rising interest rates will slow home sales, giving him continuing mortgage interest payments on a larger amount of mortgages. In October 1993, Fannie Mae issued a $2.6 *billion* CMO structured into no fewer than 130 different "tranches" of payout; Merrill Lynch marketed the paper. For the entire year 1993, more than $300 billion of CMO paper was issued, most of it by "government-sponsored enterprises" like the Federal National Mortgage Association and the Federal Home Loan Mortgage Corporation.

Academics defend such instruments as hedges. A man content with 5 percent, after all, can guarantee himself the continuation of that 5 percent by putting half his portfolio into simple variable-rate note holdings and the other half into inverse floaters. In real life, however, these instruments are sold mostly to retired Texas builders and their friends (and to college and hospital and museum treasurers and county financial officers hard put to deliver on their promises of income to their bosses), who are hoping to profit rather than lose by what look to them like permanently declining rates. Promoted with a good sales pitch ("Government Guaranteed!"), the more volatile strips of mortgage payments can really *get* them. They are in general a pretty easy mark for bond salesmen.

Murchison and Company relied on a Wall Street house to handle the payments and deliveries and clerical details of its work, and my Texas builder got his monthly statements from New York. One had just come in. It listed his holdings and the price he had paid for them, and in the column for current market value there appeared the message "N. A." What, he inquired, did that mean? It meant, I told him, "Not available"—there were no bids in the market for his structured notes and CMOs. He thought maybe he should sue. I thought maybe he should.

A few weeks later, I happened to lunch with someone connected with the Wall Street house that had sent the statement to the Texas builder. My friend said there wasn't much hope for a lawsuit—Murchison was already bankrupt, and his Wall Street firm had no liability for what Murchison might or might not have done. Anyway, he said, "N.A. isn't so bad. Most of these things we send out " 'Y.D.W.T.K.' "

What the hell is that?

"Stands for, 'You don't want to know.' "

Welcome to the world of "derivatives." Counting everything that might be placed under that rubric, the "notional value" of derivative contracts passed the $25 *trillion* level in 1995. Something like a fifth of the total 1993 profits of the largest American dealers in such instruments—J.P. Morgan, Bankers Trust, Chemical-Chase, Citibank, First Chicago, Bank of America, Merrill Lynch, Salomon, Goldman Sachs, Bear Stearns, Morgan Stanley—came from creating, selling and trading the great zoo of futures, forwards, options, structured notes, CMOs, swaps, swaptions, collars, range forwards, and so forth that carry the label "derivatives." Some of the "end users" whose risks were supposedly being controlled by these instruments suffered losses of more than a billion dollars each. The list includes Showa Shell in Japan, Bank Negara in Malaysia, Barings in England, Metallgesellschaft in Germany, Orange County in California, Sumitomo and the New York branch of Japan's Daiwa Bank. (The Orange County, Sumitomo and Daiwa losses were not suffered in the derivatives market, but without derivatives contracts the gamblers who lost the money could not have concealed what they were doing from public view.)

One large fund that was using these instruments to make itself "market neutral"—profiting through clever hedges whether interest rates went up or down—was devoured in 1994 by sharks who wouldn't roll over its debts or pay a fair price for the paper it had to sell; the loss was $600 million to its investors, who included the Rockefeller Foundation with a $50 million piece.

Merrill Lynch itself once lost $350 million in less than a week on collateralized mortgage securities. Regional banks like Pittsburgh's PNC and Banc One in Columbus, Ohio, were damaged if not crippled in 1994 by wrongheaded investments in structured notes.

But banking, securities and commodities market regulators worldwide have rallied round to defend the creation, use and trading of derivatives. Financial economists have even abandoned their long-standing advocacy of marking-to-market in valuing the portfolios of financial institutions, because a regime of daily valuations of hedging instruments might make derivative players look bad. Market prices, the academics argue, can compel recognition of the losses on derivative contracts at a time when the presumed gains in the position being hedged are still "unrealized."[1] Warning that "A legal vacuum is preferable to a bad legal regime enacted out of hysteria and ignorance," one academic commentator in spring 1994, just before Orange County went under, cited as an example of hysteria the fact that "In Orange County, California, the derivatives trading activities of the treasurer is a controversial issue in that treasurer's re-election campaign."[2]

2

Trading activity by the banks for their own account begins as a significant matter with the discovery in the 1960s that funding the bank was not just an expense but could be a source of profit. The central action was what I once labeled the revolution in banking—the development of the negotiable certificate of deposit in 1960 by John Exter and Walter Wriston of National City Bank of New York. Before then, banks' ability to lend had been mostly at the mercy of the customers who did or did not bring them new deposits. Forbidden to issue bonds or commercial paper, and pretty much forbidden to downstream money to the bank from a bank holding company (which *could* issue bonds and sell commercial paper), banks were limited in their capacity to borrow from the money markets.

But a negotiable certificate of deposit, which the purchaser could resell into the market if he needed his money back before the CD expired, was a neat and repeatedly useful way for banks to get cash when needed. After the revolution, banks with access to the money markets could make their loans first and look for the money later. "If a depository institution wasn't sure it could borrow funds, it would behave very differently," former Federal Reserve vice-chairman George Mitchell said from beneath his trademark gray crewcut in 1980, when the new systems were firmly in place. And the effective money supply rose sharply. George Garvy of the Federal Reserve and Martin R. Blyn noted in their pamphlet on *The Velocity of Money* that thanks to "the introduction of the negotiable CD, . . . a large part of the funds which in earlier literature were not improperly referred to as 'idle' has shifted into the high-turnover category, being continuously invested and reinvested in the money market."[3]

Even before the introduction of the negotiable CD, big banks had begun to make arrangements with their smaller correspondents to borrow from them on an overnight basis any reserves they might have beyond what the Fed required from them. This was fairly small potatoes, because a loan is a loan, and restrictions on how much a bank could lend to any one borrower prevented the correspondents from lending more than about 1 percent of their deposits in this way. Still, it was important money for Morgan Guaranty, which lacked a large base of customer deposits to fund its loans, and which pioneered these relationships with correspondents around the country as early as the 1950s.

And in 1963, John Kennedy's swashbuckling Comptroller of the Currency James Saxon ruled that because the proceeds were used to increase the larger bank's reserve balance at the Fed, this sort of transaction was not a loan but a *sale* of Fed Funds by the correspondent bank. There were no restrictions on what a bank could *sell* to another bank, and thus there would be no restrictions on the quantity of Fed Funds a big-city bank could acquire in this channel. The Federal Reserve Board repeatedly voted that Saxon was wrong and that banks should not pay attention to what he was saying, but Saxon in effect said, "Sue me." (Carter Golembe in an article in the *University of Virginia Law Review* suggested that Saxon was sometimes "motivated by an impish desire to shake other regulatory agencies out of their accustomed routines."4) Eventually, the Fed gave up. Out in the countryside, especially when pressure by the Fed was pushing interest rates beyond what local borrowers wanted to pay (or could safely be asked to pay), selling Fed Funds to the money-center banks became a major source of income.

The certificate of deposit as a liberating device was not fully effective while the Federal Reserve retained its power to limit the interest rates the banks could pay on their CDs. When Fed chairman William McChesney Martin imposed a true credit crunch on the country in 1966 to limit the inflationary harm the Vietnam War would do the country, his yank on the string was made even more effective by the large volume of CDs outstanding from the money-center banks. Not only were new sales of CDs automatically choked off because the Fed did not permit the banks to pay money market rates of interest for the money, but old CDs could not be rolled over, compelling the banks to sell investment securities and even call loans as their funding well ran dry.

But in 1970, the Penn Central Railroad collapsed with $83 million of unsecured commercial paper in the hands of investors. The collapse did not happen all at once, because President Richard Nixon searched frantically for some way the government could keep Penn Central afloat, including a Navy Department loan of $200 million (still a lot of money in 1970) on the grounds that the railroad was essential to national security. Unfortunately, the law that authorized the loan required the Federal Reserve to certify that the condition of the borrower was such that the Navy would get its money back, and Thomas Waage of the New York Fed, the officer on the case, could not do that. This horror story spooked the holders of Chrysler commercial paper, which Chrysler had to roll over to stay in business.

Informed on a Sunday that Penn Central was going to be in bankruptcy court on Monday, the operators of the discount windows at the twelve district Feds got on the telephones to the heads of the larger banks in their bailiwicks to push them into helping Chrysler. ("By Monday night," commentator "Adam Smith" reported, "phone calls had gone out through the twelve Federal Reserve Banks to every bank in the system—not just to big-city banks, but to small-town banks all over the country. The Fed's index finger was beginning to bleed from all the dialing. The message was the same: if anybody comes into your bank and wants a loan, *give it to him*. Then if you're all loaned out, come to us and we'll see that you have the money."[5] As a quid pro quo for agreement to maintain Chrysler's lines of credit (which, incidentally, cost the banks a bundle before the decade was out), the Fed agreed to exempt large-denomination CDs (over $100,000) from interest-rate controls. Now banks could meet their funding requirements in various ways: borrowing Eurodollars in London, purchasing Fed Funds in the market or from correspondents, or selling large-denomination CDs to the market.

The purpose of freeing the CD from interest-rate controls was to permit banks to compete against other financial institutions, not each other. Underlying the 1970s system of bank funding was an assumption by the regulators that on any given day the market would see to it that all large banks paid the same interest rate on CDs of the same duration. Big banks didn't fail; lending to them was essentially risk-free. In the late 1970s, the Chicago Board of Trade created a contract for futures on bank certificates of deposit. A bank could use that market to lock in the rate it would have to pay for money in sixty or ninety days by selling a contract—or, conversely, could protect itself against falling yields on its loans by buying a contract. Speculators would gamble on interest rate movements to provide liquidity. These contracts, it should be noted, contemplated possible delivery of the money commodity being traded, just as the wheat contract contemplated the delivery of wheat.

So the CD contract assumed a standardized bank certificate of deposit which would be delivered to anyone who held such a contract on expiration date. The Board of Trade contract identified ten American banks all of which were assumed to pay identical interest rates to borrow money for a year on the chassis of a certificate of deposit.

One pauses to note—as nobody would have done in 1979— that this notion that the ten biggest banks would all pay exactly the same interest on their CDs was the product of massive government intervention in the banking business. Left to a free market, interest rates paid by the big banks would vary to some degree— as indeed they do today—simply because the banks would be to some degree differently situated, in different places, with different ease of access to other funds, with different risk profiles, having made different bets earlier that week or month on the course of short-term rates in this period.

But through the 1970s the Federal Reserve controlled the maximum rates banks could pay to consumers on their savings accounts, and absolutely prohibited the payment of interest to corporations on their transaction balances. It was assumed not only by the regulators but also by the traders in the commodities markets that in the over-$100,000 category, where rates had been free from controls since 1970 (as a reward to the banks for maintaining their guarantees of Chrysler's commercial paper in the aftermath of the fiasco at Penn Central), a similar uniformity would prevail. All markets rest on a legal order, for contracts are unenforceable without one, and the establishment of weights and measures to be used by everyone in a market is a governmental function, as Napoleon demonstrated. The more likely a man is to wear a T-shirt proclaiming (as they do in Chicago) that "free markets make free men," the more likely he is to be working in a government-protected environment.

John Heimann had come to the Comptroller's office in 1977, having been Commissioner of both banking and housing in New York State, hoping to conduct bank supervision at a new level of sophistication. John and I had known each other since the 1940s, and one day in 1979 when I was in Washington he set up a sandwich-and-Cokes lunch in his conference room so I could meet a group of his younger people. One of this group, a sandy-haired young lawyer with the memorable name of Chuck Muckenfuss, arrived mid-lunch with a message for Heimann that he was clearly somewhat concerned about delivering in the presence of a stranger, especially a stranger from the press.

Heimann told him not to worry, and he gave his news, which was that one of the ten banks with CDs that could be presented in satisfaction of the Board of Trade futures contract was being compelled to pay a higher rate than the others for the money it needed. This was, necessarily, Chicago's Continental-Illinois, the "Morgan of the Midwest," crippled at a time when the Fed was tightening the money supply by the nutty Illinois "unit banking" law that forbade a bank in that state from having more than one office. A Bank of America or a Wachovia in North Carolina could have branches all over the state to gather deposits from its local customers, but Continental was stuck with one magnificent headquarters in Chicago (a twenty-three story office building and a grand annex from the early days of the Chicago School, the two linked across the street by an aerial bridge, so that the unit bank could be said to be in one building). Only about ten percent of the money it had to lend or invest was provided by insured depositors; everything else had to be bought one way or another in the market— from Europe (where the bank did not have a major presence), through large-denomination CDs of the kind traded in the futures market, or in interbank loans of one sort or another.

Among Continental's major sources of funds was the "correspondent balances" country banks all over the Midwest kept at Continental in return for the Chicago bank's services in clearing their checks, taking "surplus lines" when they were asked to make loans above their legal lending limits, providing a back-up line of credit, investing their surplus cash, managing trust services, giving big-city hospitality to their customers, and so on. Basically, the country or small-city bank paid for correspondent services by leaving a minimum deposit at the bigger bank. Correspondent balances had been a big part of Continental's funding since the world was young. Writing of 1933, Jesse Jones, chairman of the Depression-era Reconstruction Finance Corporation, which saved Continental from collapse after Roosevelt's bank holiday, argued that "Continental was a great correspondent bank—a bankers' bank—in which a large proportion of the country banks of the Middle West and many in the South and Southwest kept accounts. Had it collapsed, the effect would have been frighteningly felt in fields and towns and cities over a large area of the country."[6]

Irvine Sprague served eleven and a half years as one of the three directors of the Federal Deposit Insurance Corporation. One of those years was 1984, when Continental had to be bailed out with $9 billion of federal loans and grants and $4.7 billion from a "safety net" of other large banks, which advanced their money under pretty strong guarantees from the FDIC that they wouldn't lose it. Writing about this event, Sprague gave the same argument for what was done in 1984 that Jones had given for what was done in 1933: "Best estimates of our staff, with the sparse numbers we had on hand, were that more than two thousand correspondent banks were depositors in Continental and some number—we talked of fifty to two hundred—might be threatened or brought down by a Continental collapse. (We later computed that 179 banks had more than 50 percent of their capital in Continental; 66 of them more than 100 percent.)"[7]

In 1979, in Heimann's office, such problems were either forty-five years behind us or five years ahead of us: the simple explanation that Continental was being victimized by the unit banking law sufficed to explain to Heimann and his colleagues the emergence of "tiering" in the CD market. It simply did not occur to any of us bright people sitting around the Comptroller's conference table that a bank would or should have a competitive advantage or disadvantage because the market required it to pay lower or higher interest rates than were demanded from other banks. *Regulators*—not markets—knew all about banks; there was no reason for them to pay attention to market signals. It would be another three years until the collapse of Penn Square Bank revealed that Continental, growing like Jack's beanstalk, had bought a billion dollars of bad loans from Oklahoma cowboys. The market then refused C-I CDs at *any* price, and presently the FDIC had to take over the bank. It could be argued that by its solicitude for the miner's canary in 1979, the Comptroller's office was an accessory to the immolation of lots of miners in the 1980s.

3

Investment banks like Goldman Sachs and Morgan Stanley and the rapidly rising Salomon Brothers had long financed their inventory of bonds by entering into "repurchase agreements" ("repos"), a means of borrowing that left the lender almost totally secure because for the duration of the loan he owned securities roughly equal to the value of the loan. The arrangement was that the investment bank sold, say, $100 million of government bonds to a big corporation holding cash to meet a coming tax payment or other commitment, under an agreement to buy the bonds back for the same price plus the interest rate on overnight borrowings—or longer, if the repurchase agreement ran more than one day. This wasn't really a *market*—it was a set of continuing lending and borrowing relationships between the big Wall Street investment houses and the big banks. (In the Drysdale affair of 1982, Chase Bank found a way to lose money in what credit risk remained to repos, but the details are too technical for exposition here,[8] and everyone's computers were rejiggered to make the duplication of Drysdale impossible.)

Financing with repos took organization, because the bonds had to be delivered to the purchaser and reclaimed. And it was a New York business: FedWire was not fully computerized until 1973, and until 1978 FedWire was an overnight system, with credit to the recipient of the payment blended in with the check processing at the clearinghouse the next day. The Federal Reserve itself conducted its interventions in the "open market" mostly through repurchase agreements, providing cash *to* the market temporarily by bidding for bonds that would be returned to their owners at a later date, taking cash *from* the market temporarily by offering some of its own portfolio for sale and repurchase. But the Fed until the 1980s would not do a repurchase agreement directly with a bank, because that would be too quick and easy a way for a bank to take care of a shortfall in its reserve position when the Fed was trying to cut back.

Technology made the distinction between bank and non-bank dealers ludicrous by eliminating the physical, parchment-and-engraving government bond and the attached coupons that people clipped and took to the bank to cash. By the 1980s, virtually all U.S. government paper had been "dematerialized" and "immobilized" into "book entry" on at least two and probably three Federal Reserve computers (one considered secure from nuclear attack). Ownership of government securities was transferred from one investor to another over the same FedWire that completed payments. The procedure was untouched by human hands: bonds were transferred out and payment in through the same wire today, with everything in place to reverse the transaction first thing tomorrow morning.

Now banks could in effect carry large inventories of government paper without increasing their deposits or their other borrowings, because the paper could be financed with repurchase agreements. Moreover, because even medium-term government paper usually paid higher interest than the overnight rate on repurchase agreements, the banks could make a little money on their inventory, which gained in value overnight more than the cost of the money used to buy the bonds. One of the arts of running a trading desk in a brokerage house or a bank became the construction of a "matched book" of "repos"—securities sold to be repurchased tomorrow (the repurchase agreement) and securities bought to be returned tomorrow (the "reverse-repurchase" agreement). By sitting at the center of the spider web, bringing together customers for money and customers with money to lend, banks could create a risk-free steady income in dealing government securities. And they did.

With the expansion of international trade, corporate customers increasingly asked their banks to handle the job of converting one currency to another on some future date certain at a known exchange rate, so the company could set its prices intelligently and plan its activities. An April 1977 survey by the New York Fed showed that the forty-four U.S. "banking institutions" most active in this market "had gross turnover—the sum of all foreign exchange sales and purchases—of more than $100 billion that month."[9] By 1983, when the Fed did another study, turnover in the foreign-exchange market had risen to more than $500 billion a month—of which, Federal Reserve Board governor Henry C. Wallich reported, 85 percent was trading between the banks themselves and only 15 percent was "customer-related."[10]

In 1995, foreign-exchange sales and purchases that passed through the CHIPS computer in New York were something more than $900 billion *per day*, and the Bank for International Settlements estimated that the total worldwide had passed $1.3 trillion a day. Only $244 billion of that, the Fed reported, was New York based; another $464, according to the Bank of England, originated in London; $161 billion, $116 billion and $85 billion were done in Tokyo, Singapore and Frankfurt, respectively.[11] Certainly no more than 5 percent of that was "customer-related." And there was in addition an unknown volume of such trading that was settled privately between corresponding banks on a basis of bilateral netting, with nobody else the wiser.

It should probably be noted that for all the trading, this is an opaque market: the screens carry information on what banks are bidding and asking for currencies (always in dollars: if you want to buy yen with marks, you buy dollars and then use the dollars to buy yen), but not the actual price or size of transactions. Reuters brings the two sides together, and then its computers become a straight wire that simply carries and does not record messages while buyer and seller do business in the privacy of their own offices, leaving no records anywhere else.

In 1977, "spot" transactions—purchases and sales of currencies for what was then immediate delivery—were for "value" two days after the transaction (that is, the actual exchange of dollars for marks and vice versa happened two days after the dealers hung up their telephones). Transfers of money occurred almost entirely by banks crediting or debiting the accounts of their correspondent banks abroad in response to "cables." Late that year, the Belgians launched the Society for Worldwide Interbank Financial Telecommunications, or SWIFT, for the purpose of taking these cables out of the message rooms where they were routinely screwed up and putting them directly onto bank computers. In 1995, virtually all messages to pay or receive on international transactions passed through SWIFT, a communications system probably as secure as anything the private sector can boast, and virtually all foreign-exchange transactions were for settlement that same afternoon, either by bilateral netting or through the multilateral clearing at CHIPS.

What remained the same through the passage of time was the system for "forward" transactions, involving an agreed-upon date in the future when the currencies would be exchanged. Banks did forwards with their customers, assuring an importer that he could use his dollars to pay the required foreign currency at a known exchange rate when the television sets or shirts he was importing arrived in ninety days, guaranteeing an exporter that he would receive dollars at a known exchange rate when his customer paid him a foreign currency on delivery of the x-ray machine or ton of wheat. But banks did not enter into forward transactions with other banks. Within their own community, banks did swaps, exchanging marks for dollars today with the transaction to be reversed in ninety days. They made their money as a markup, guaranteeing for themselves that they would have the currency their customer needed to complete his transaction on the day he needed it, at a rate somewhat better than the rate they had promised him.

But the existence of these swap mechanisms had importance beyond the banking focus. Because currency swaps were easy, it became possible for companies to raise money *for domestic use* in markets other than their own. The pioneering venture of this kind was done by Salomon Brothers in 1979, for the World Bank and IBM. IBM, which needed dollars, had little paper outstanding in the Swiss market, and thus could borrow francs at a lower rate than it would have to pay in the United States, where it had just sold a large new issue of bonds. The World Bank, which wanted Swiss francs, had borrowed for years in Swiss francs, and Swiss customers already had a good deal of World Bank paper in their portfolios. (Differences in the national interest rates were of course taken care of by countervailing differences in the exchange rates looking ahead for the length of the borrowing.) So the World Bank borrowed dollars in the New York market, IBM borrowed francs in Zurich, and they swapped both the proceeds of the bond issues and the obligations to pay interest and eventually principal on the bonds. Both parties borrowed cheaper than they could have borrowed in the domestic market for the currency they wanted.

"In essence," the Salomon Brothers bond market research department explained in early 1986, "the currency swap allows entities to arbitrage across differing relative credit standings in different markets. If a borrower wishes to receive funding in the market where the terms available to that specific borrower are relatively less favorable, it may be less expensive to issue debt in the market where the terms are more favorable and swap into the otherwise less-favorable market." In 1985, "swap-driven primary issues" accounted for 25 percent of all non-dollar bond issues, and the total dollar value was about $20 billion. These were normally zero-coupon instruments—"bullet maturities"—to make the foreign-exchange calculations simpler and to postpone tax payments.[12]

Swap mechanisms profoundly altered the relationships of banks and markets and the ability of money markets to transcend national boundaries even while some major countries were still attempting to control the international use of their currencies. By their nature, however, swaps are bilateral instruments, requiring correspondent banking relationships. They have to be settled between the parties, not in a clearinghouse. The bank trader who does swaps enters into transactions quite different from those of a trader who buys and sells in the spot market. He establishes a relationship with his counterparty that will persist until the swap is closed down. The International Swap Dealers Association Master Agreement does contain a provision under which one party with the consent of the other can assign his rights under the swap to somebody else, but the usual procedure is to do the switch by "novation," with a new contract between the somebody else and the original counterparty. Usually a dealer gets out of his position not by selling what he has bought or purchasing what he has sold, but by acquiring a countervailing instrument (a swap in the opposite direction) from another counterparty. The record-keeping on all this is complicated and could not have been done before the computer delivered on its promise of perfect storage and instant retrieval.

Despite the Master Agreement, swaps by their nature are more subject to negotiation—the payments by the party with the floating-rate obligation can be Libor or that day's market rate on Treasuries with five years to run or rates in a foreign currency or the closing price for ninety-day deliveries of light crude, for that matter. *Traders* work in enormous rooms at consoles that may or may not have a quasi-private low-walled space around the screens. *Swaps dealers* usually have a little room of their own as well as a place in the trading room, because they need to negotiate. "In FX [foreign exchange]," says Citibank vice president Gordon Clancy, "customer transactions are one in twenty. In derivatives, it's more like one to one." Meaning that Citibank might lay off a customer's swaps contract with Morgan, but the expectation would be that Morgan would then keep it in portfolio.

And swaps are fundamentally *private* instruments, secret treaties secretly negotiated. They are accounted for "off–balance sheet," frustrating normal accounting practice. Don Layton of Chemical Bank explains: "With this stuff, changes in market value go right to net worth without passing through income." Thus swaps present risks to a system where credit must be extended on the basis of incomplete information—at a time when the political pressure from taxpayers who have been stung by bailouts is to remove the government guarantees that were a sturdy substitute for information.

All that was still ahead in 1977, when most currency trading was done through specialized foreign-exchange brokers, because Fed Funds trading was done through money brokers and government bond trading was done through interdealer brokers. Each of these was a different occupation, tapping different expertise. The information systems walked in the front door and took the elevator up to the trading floor every day. By 1995, "anomalies" between spot and forward prices—taking into account the different interest rates being paid at different maturities in the two currencies—were profit opportunities to be spotted not by people but by computers programmed to do nothing else. And the bank sent out its own quotes to be displayed on screens all over the world, proclaiming this bank willing to buy Fed Funds or currencies or government bonds at this price, or sell them at a very slightly higher price, all day long. Instead of arriving from an interdealer broker (though a few do survive in the government bond market), information about prices and quantities in foreign exchange and bond and overnight money markets is continuously available on the several different screens that glare at the trader all day long. The computers also know what the bank owes for delivery today in different markets, what it will have to borrow and what it can lend.

Three aspects of this story are especially important and easy to overlook. The first is that trading activity at the big banks grew out of the central function of funding the bank. Thus the trading operation was not (as in the brokerage houses and at corporations like the oil companies that manage immense books of foreign exchange) a separate division of the operation but a central aspect of management. And derivatives trading was supposed to blend into securities trading. In its application for a license to trade and broker derivatives, the Swiss Bank Corporation promised that "derivatives transactions will be integrated with Company's trading activities in the underlying securities markets and other cash markets and will not function as an independent unit seeking separate profits solely from the derivatives markets."[13]

Acquiring the liabilities banks use to buy their assets had always been a cost center: you gave people toasters for opening accounts. As the 1970s became the 1980s, increasing numbers of banks began to regard their funding operation as a profit center.

Describing the duties of Executive Vice President and Deputy Cashier Ray Peters, who supervises the bank's trading, Bank of America lists them as "managing the Corporation's global funding and interest rate as well as capital funding. He also manages the Bank's Federal Reserve accounts, Central Money Bank and the Investment Securities portfolio." Speaking in 1994 of Chemical Bank's young cashier Pedros Sabatacakis, who had been passed over for promotion three years earlier and had moved on to the insurance group AIG, Darla Moore said, "Pedros had funded us short two years out [i.e., at a time when interest rates were falling, Sabatacakis saw to it that the bank had a minimal proportion of its liabilities that ran any length of time at higher rates], made us *hundreds* of millions of dollars. But he had no political skills; didn't care about it."

Trading, however, is a peculiar activity to lie so near the heart of a banking enterprise. Banks traditionally benefit when their borrowers do well. Every successful businessman had his banker, as he had his lawyer and his accountant. Of course, there were conflicts of interest between banks and their customers, even in the best of times. Borrowers typically wanted more money than the bank wanted to lend them. When funding costs were fixed, banks liked interest rates higher and customers liked them lower. Banks wanted borrowers to keep "compensating balances" in their accounts at the bank, so that the deposits created when the bank made the loan would not require the bank to pony up additional reserves at the Fed. Borrowers might like to keep for their own use (or as security for other borrowings) assets that the bank wanted to see pledged to its loan. At the end of a long day, however, the lending officer's career was hostage to the success of those whose loans he had taken to the committee at the bank.

Trading, by contrast, is a zero-sum game: the bank trading financial instruments with its customer profits when the customer loses. The matter is not necessarily as stark as that, because the bank is an intermediary, not a principal, in many of its money market trades with its corporate customers. Its revenues in those transactions derive not from price movements that benefit the bank and harm the customer but from small dealer markups that can be taken when two customers have opposing needs and do their business through the bank. Moreover, Sabatacakis argued in the early 1980s, while still with Chemical, "Funding is like lending—it has relationships and customer business." Blowing up customers is dangerous work here, too. Still, many of the instruments the banks have created for this trade are custom-designed for specific customers and are held by the bank as counterparty in the deal—and in constructing these instruments the bank has an enormous information advantage over its customer.

"This is the ultimate thieves' market," says Michael Bloomberg, inventor and proprietor of the Bloomberg business news services that have been beating up Dow-Jones and Telerate and the broadcasters. "You take the customer to the hoops and pucks and you get him laid, and he pays you another two points."

A lawyer who represents "end-users" told Karen Spinner of *Derivative Strategies*, "When a dealer is out there, it's an arms-around-your-shoulder relationship. They say, 'You can trust me. I'm the wizard from New York.' Then as soon as the deal goes sour, they switch into a different mode and it's an arms-length relationship."[14]

The extent to which these information advantages could be exploited at the highest levels of the banking industry was horrifyingly revealed in 1994, when Bankers Trust consented to findings by the Securities and Exchange Commission and the Commodity Futures Trading Commission that it had lied to and cheated Gibson Greeting Cards in a series of transactions from November 1991 through March 1994. The parade of names given the instruments Bankers created for this purpose was a circus in itself: "Ratio Swap," "Periodic Floor," "Spread Lock 1, 2 and 3," "Wedding Band." All these involved correlations between interest rates for different maturities of Treasury instruments, interest rates in the London dollar-denominated interbank market, and so forth. The procedure for calculating the value of the deal was so complicated that it existed only in the form of a computer program. Only Bankers Trust had that program. Calling to ask how things were going, Gibson's treasurer was entirely at the mercy of what BT said.

Things could get even more complicated than that: one of the swaps county treasurer Robert Citron put in the Orange County portfolio involved relative changes in the interest rates on Swedish kroner and Finnish markka. A note for $225 million issued by the Federal National Mortgage Association in 1992 was designed to make its owner a fortune if by any chance the Italian lira became more valuable while the Swiss franc became less valuable. (Indeed, it yielded 12.35 percent if the Italian lira held its own against the Swiss franc.) Because the Swiss franc appreciated and the lira devalued, Fannie Mae got $225 million of somebody's money interest-free for eight years. Unlike the swaps, which are private promises to pay and are complicated to sell, the Fannie Mae notes were traded. *Grant's Interest Rate Observer* reported in January 1995 that they could be bought for 72.5 cents on the dollar.[15] "What's risky for one investor is not risky for another," said Sharon Stone, head of Fannie Mae's CMO program, explaining what were comparable disasters for investors in that paper.[16]

Trading rooms, like the Oval Office in the White House, are places where tape recordings of conversation are routine. Recordings are needed in the trading rooms because so many transactions are achieved over the telephone, without paper records or even computer verification. The tape machines capture everything a trader says, to his supervisors and colleagues and subordinates as well as to his counterparties. Thus we know that Bankers Trust routinely gave false information to Gibson about how much it was losing on the instruments the bank had tailored for the company.

In one remarkable instance, on January 13, 1994, a BT

salesman told Gibson that it would "not go 'further in the hole' by entering ... new positions when, in fact, Gibson immediately incurred an additional unrealized loss of approximately $4,954,000." The managing director at the securities affiliate of the bank that was handling Gibson's purchases from the bank told his supervisor a few weeks later that "from the very beginning, [Gibson] just, you know, really put themselves in our hands like 96 percent. . . . And we have known that from day one. . . . [T]hese guys have done some pretty wild stuff. And you know, they probably do not understand it quite as well as they should. I think that they have a pretty good understanding of it, but not perfect. And that's like perfect for us."[17] Bankers Trust paid a fine of $10 million to the government, and settled for another $28 million the lawsuit Gibson had brought in federal court in Cincinnati. It should perhaps be noted that when Gibson first brought suit in September 1994, Bankers Trust issued a statement that all its actions had been "legal, proper and appropriate." [18]

Because the typical foreign-exchange forward contract took the form of a swap, banks became conscious that other money market business could be done on a swap basis. Reduced to its essentials, a foreign-exchange swap was the exchange of the interest to be earned over the life of the contract in one currency for the interest that could be earned in that period in another currency. Obviously, the same principles could be followed by a bank that wished to remove a mismatch between the interest stream it received on a loan and the interest it had to pay the suppliers of the funds for that loan. If the loans paid a fixed rate of interest (like an old-fashioned home mortgage) and the bank had to borrow at the fluctuating market rate, a contract could be negotiated by which the bank received a fluctuating payment from another bank or insurance company or corporation while making a fixed payment to that counterparty. Interest-rate swaps like repurchase agreements were essentially without credit risk, in this case because the principal of the "loan" never changed hands.

And like the foreign-exchange swaps, they were "off balance sheet," not accounted for with the banks' assets and liabilities.

All these things became important very quickly. As late as 1988, observers as sophisticated as Professors George Benston and George Kaufman, writing a "staff memorandum" for the Federal Reserve Bank of Chicago, could present a long report entitled *Risk and Solvency Regulation of Depository Institutions: Past Policies and Current Options*, in which the only off-balance-sheet assets or liabilities discussed were letters of credit and loan guarantees.[19] Only seven years later, the "notional value" of off-balance-sheet derivatives in the portfolios of the dozen largest American banks was more than $25 trillion, and the admitted "gross replacement value" (GRV) of these instruments (the money the bank would have to pay to replace the contract if its counterparty reneged on the deal) was reported as more than $250 billion. Though less than two dozen banks were significantly involved, the profits earned from these "derivatives" were seen as so important to the future of the industry that all the banking regulators turned themselves inside out to keep Congress from establishing limits on what the banks could do in swaps, forwards, futures, options, swaptions, structured notes, "tranches" of mortgage bonds, securitized credit card receivables and the like.

4

What is a "derivative"?

The conventional definition says it is a financial instrument that "derives" its value from changes in the prices of other financial instruments. Thus an interest-rate swap by which one party pays a floating rate and the other party pays a fixed rate will be profitable to the former if rates go down and to the latter if rates go up. Similarly, a currency swap has value if the currency to be paid out at its maturity falls in value against the currency to be received at its maturity. All option contracts are derivatives; so are all futures and many forward contracts.

But the conventional definition is misleading, because *most* financial instruments turn out on examination to change in value as a function of what happens to other financial instruments. Harvard's Robert Merton has argued amusingly if not very convincingly that a nineteenth-century banknote was a "derivative" because it derived its value from the gold to which it could be converted.[20] A fixed-rate mortgage is worth more to its holder in times of falling interest rates and less in times of rising interest rates—but nobody would consider a normal fixed-rate mortgage to be a "derivative." A mortgage is in fact an investment by a bank to secure an income stream in the form of payments by the householder. A derivative is a *bet*, not an investment—a bet on the direction, dimension, duration and speed of changes in the value of another financial instrument. And like any bet, its value is entirely a function of the creditworthiness of the man who wrote it. (Merton's banknote example works when the bank is out among the wildcats and you're taking your chances on whether there is any gold behind it.) The International Swap Dealers Association standard contract permits a participant in a swap to cancel the deal anytime one of the credit-rating services takes away his counterparty's A rating.[21]

Eugene Rotberg, who was treasurer of the World Bank and thus a party to the first bond-related swaps, says, "I do not think it useful to define derivatives. I find it more helpful to describe why they are different and potentially dangerous. First, they can be used to leverage risk—interest rate risk, currency risk, share prices—without putting up a lot of money. That simply means that during a period of volatility, losses or gains are magnified 50-fold. . . . Often the leverage is asymmetrical: that is, potential gains are sometimes limited while potential losses can be multiples of the maximum gains."[22] For Rotberg, too, in other words, a derivative is a bet.

The word "bet" has a pejorative quality, but the intent here is descriptive, not judgmental. The publisher who contracts to pay marks for a German printing press to be delivered and paid for in six months has made a bet that the dollars in his budget will buy him the amount of marks he will need when the machine arrives. It is the reverse of gambling when this publisher makes another bet that will compensate him for any losses he might suffer if the mark strengthens over that period of time. Similarly, a banker who writes a fixed-rate mortgage has made a bet that the interest rates he has to pay for his funding will not rise above the rate on that mortgage too often during the course of the bank's possession of it. The banker is prudent, not reckless, when he buys an interest-rate contract that assures him against loss in the market.

Futures markets have a long history, going back to seventeenth-century Japan. At one time they existed in large part as a way for farmers to make advance arrangements to sell the produce they were in process of growing to the food processors who would use it: a significant fraction of the trades in the futures market produced actual delivery of the commodity traded. But it can be a considerable nuisance to find a customer who will agree to buy your crop in however many months are required to grow it. And in the context of agricultural commodities, the relatively small number of food processors who purchase the grain are likely to have too much bargaining power if the relatively large number of farmers with grain to sell must find them one at a time.

The commodities exchange gives producers, processors and market-makers a place to meet, standardization of contracts, and convenience in delivery. Indeed, the quality and efficiency of the storage and delivery facilities associated with the exchange were among the selling points for the use of futures contracts. Only 0.64 percent of outstanding futures contracts were settled by the physical delivery of the products involved in 1993, but the *possibility* of physical delivery (and it should be noted that the seller can always force some buyer to take delivery) underlies the trading.

These contracts, too, were bets, and both winnings and losings could be very high. Because what was traded required *future* purchase and delivery, there was no need for purchase prices to be paid in total when the deal was struck. Purchaser and seller both put down deposits as evidence of their bona fides to participate in the market, and the clearinghouse which held their stakes could call on either to put up additional "margin" if prices moved against him. To the extent that these exchanges were regulated at all, it was by the Packers and Stockyards Division of the Department of Agriculture.

By the twentieth century, the clearinghouse of the exchange where the commodity was traded had itself become the counterparty on all trades, guaranteeing delivery if necessary but making it easy for both sellers and buyers to extinguish their obligations by making a countervailing trade at the same exchange. Every transaction produced one contract between the buyer and the clearinghouse, and one contract between the seller and the clearinghouse. Sellers did not have to find the buyers with whom they had done business to fulfill their contracts, and buyers did not have to find the sellers in order to get out; they could buy to or sell from anybody trading on that exchange, and the clearinghouse would take care of their problem. Tone Grant, an elegant ex–Yale quarterback, ex-Marine, ex-lawyer who became president of Refco, the largest broker on the commodities exchanges, likes to say that "we guarantee our customers to the clearing corporation, and we guarantee the clearing corporation to our customers." Membership in the market does not give traders the right to go on the floor and trade; a trader also needs a guarantee from one of the eighty or so "clearing members," who handle his cash. About the only activity required from banks in these markets was holding the cash balances of the clearinghouses and the clearing members, and processing the checks.

But in the end these markets would be the mechanism by which technology made banking in the last years of the twentieth century a business entirely different from banking in any other time. Indeed, a liberated historian, able to see the world round, would have to say that the two most important people in the history of banking in the 1970s were Leo Melamed and Richard Sandor, neither of whom ever worked a day of his life in a bank. For they were the creators of the financial futures markets.

Melamed has had the greater publicity, and is in fact a far more unusual fellow. Born in Bialystok, Poland, he was the only child of teachers in a Yiddish-language school who fled just ahead of the Germans. They made it across the Soviet Union to Japan, moving on to Chicago just before Pearl Harbor. "As a small boy," Melamed recalls, "I lived for two years holding my mother's hand." As Melamdovich, in the Slavic patronymic, young Leo went to Chicago public schools, then to the Chicago campus of the University of Illinois on the old Navy Pier, then to John Marshall Law School in the afternoon program. As a law student, he thought he should have a morning job with a law firm, and at the age of twenty he answered an ad from Merrill Lynch, Pierce, Fenner and Beane (as it then was), which sounded like a law firm to him. They hired him, and sent him to work for their man on the floor of the old, shabby Chicago Mercantile Exchange. The Merc then traded futures contracts for butter and eggs and onions, and the place was a scandal. "They'd allowed corners and squeezes and whatever else," Melamed says. "I had to watch. It was a lesson." But he was hooked on trading from the first day.

A year later, he borrowed $3,100 from his father ("all the money he had, I think") and bought a seat, and traded eggs. And went to law school, and drove a cab at night. And went broke three times. Meanwhile, the Merc had added livestock contracts—pork bellies (bacon), live cattle and feeder cattle. Melamed, amusingly for the child of Yiddish teachers, made his first real money in the pork bellies pit. In 1967, which was only his third year as a full-time trader, he organized a group of younger members, who elected new officers, who in turn appointed committees to explore what the exchange could do. Melamed made his reputation by redesigning the delivery system for the live cattle contract, and in 1969, at the age of thirty-seven, he became chairman himself. He was a nervous, dark, darting creature, but there wasn't much doubt he had leadership qualities. Almost from the beginning, he urged his executive board to organize a trading pit in currency futures.

In 1969, the world's central banks and the International Monetary Fund were still locked into the "gold/dollar" exchange system that had been established in the Bretton Woods agreements of 1944. Exchange rates between the dollar and other currencies had been fixed within a 1 percent band, and the gold value of the dollar had been permanently pegged at $35 an ounce. But these agreements were already under unbearable pressure from the asymmetrically changing economic status—rates of inflation and trade balances—of the different countries. The British pound and French franc had gone through repeated devaluations; the German mark and Swiss franc had been revalued upward. After each such earthquake, the fixed-rate agreements had been reinstated, but there was handwriting on the wall. And as the Belgian-American economist Robert Triffin had pointed out as early as 1959, any national currency used as a reserve currency by other nations was going to face a dilemma without solution, because the deficits it had to run to supply the demand for its money would eventually force the devaluation of that money.[23]

In 1968, the United States had abandoned its foundation-stone offer to sell gold to all comers at $35 an ounce, restricting such sales to the central banks of other countries, which in turn would agree not to sell *their* gold onto the private market. And, as noted, Congress had removed the gold "cover" from the Federal

Reserve's American paper currency. Milton Friedman, among others, had denounced fixed exchange rates because they led to excessive government interference in the economy for no better purpose than the maintenance of these artificial ratios. The remedy, he had told a congressional committee as early as 1963, was floating exchange rates, "an automatic mechanism for protecting the domestic economy from the possibility that [trade] liberalization will produce a serious imbalance in international payments. . . . It is not the least of the virtues of floating exchange rates that we would again become masters in our own house."[24] In August 1971, at the end of an emergency meeting of his economic advisers at Camp David, President Nixon slammed closed the gold window and demanded from the international community the right to devalue the dollar, in terms of gold and in terms of the other major trading currencies.

Melamed went to Milton Friedman and commissioned a paper on the advantages of a futures market in currencies as part of the liberalization of exchange trading that was now clearly in the cards. On May 16, 1972, under a corporate umbrella called the International Money Market that was effectively part of the Merc and traded in the Merc's pits but could be separated out if it got into trouble, exchange trading of foreign currencies began in Chicago. The *Wall Street Journal* carried a comment by a banker who said he was "amazed that a bunch of crapshooters in pork bellies would have the temerity to think they can beat some of the world's most sophisticated traders at their own game." It rankled Melamed for years.

The banks wanted no part of foreign-exchange futures contracts. "Without participation by the banks," Melamed remembers, "we ran a risk that our transactions might not have any connection with reality. Was our price for Swiss francs the real price, or just a Merc price?" There had to be an arbitrage between the Merc market and the banks' own prices for currencies. "So I said to the banks, 'We'll insert someone who is a customer of yours. He will buy D-marks from you in the cash market and sell D-mark futures in our place, or vice versa. I will let you look at his position every day, so you can assure yourself you are never at risk, and he will have the backing of the commodity firms at the Merc, who are your customers."

On this basis, the Chicago banks went along, allowing themselves to be picked off by this odd congeries of friends of Leo who worked in the currency pits at the Merc, making markets well inside the prices the banks were charging their customers. Eventually, the banks realized what they were giving away, and became members of the International Money Market at the Merc. The first to join, in 1982, was not a Chicago bank but New York's Morgan Guaranty. Bank forwards and options took over as the dominant instruments, too: the Merc estimates that only about 4 percent of the dollar volume of foreign-exchange trading in the United States goes through the standardized futures and options contracts in the exchanges. But that 4 percent is what sets the prices.

Interestingly, though the currency futures and options markets quickly became crucial to banking in an electronically interconnected world, they have never been front-and-center in the discourse of business. As late as 1984, the astonishing strength of the dollar—up 44 percent against the German mark in three years—made it difficult for American manufacturers to sell abroad. The volatility of exchange-rate movements meant that profits or losses in international trade were as likely to be a function of currency prices as of manufacturing costs. The *Wall Street Journal* printed a split-page article about the problem, stressing that "To protect themselves, corporate treasurers often hedge their foreign exchange exposure in the forward market." Nowhere in the long article was there a mention of exchange-traded futures or options as a way to hedge such risks: everything was the banks.[25]

In 1976, Melamed moved on to interest-rate futures with a contract on the ninety-day Treasury bill. These instruments are sold on a discount basis—that is, if the market interest rate on ninety-day paper is 6 percent a year, $985,000 is paid today for a T-bill that will be worth $1 million in ninety days. Thus Melamed was not out of the market's thinking about the subject when he designed his contract to be one that compels the purchaser to buy (and the seller to sell) ninety-day T-bills at certain expiration dates in the future. People who think interest rates are going up can sell the contracts; people who think interest rates are going down will buy them.

The other shoe dropped in 1981, with the introduction of the Eurodollar contract, which replicates the T-bills contract except that its subject is the interest-rate for ninety-day loans to the most creditworthy borrowers in the offshore dollar market. Here there were no T-bills to deliver or accept at expiration, and no way to structure the endgame so that actual delivery would be an option. This contract required "cash settlement"—that is, the seller could not compel purchase and the buyer could not compel delivery, as he could with the wheat or soybeans or cattle or T-bills, but would have to accept a cash payment for the difference between the discount price of the ninety-day Eurodollar loan and the price he contracted to pay in the futures contract.

This contract, Melamed says, "changed history. It was the first instrument where the buyer didn't have to take delivery in kind." In 1994, the Merc's Eurodollar contract traded 105 million contracts of a million dollars each (a nominal value of $1.05 quadrillion for the year)—as against 91 million contracts for all currency contracts on all exchanges anywhere in the world.[26] The Eurodollar contract also opened the door for what the banks would do in future years. The banks' swaps are best seen as non-traded, private, cash-settlement futures contracts.

Melamed is and has been throughout an active trader, never without communications devices that keep him in touch with the course of the market and enable him to place his bets from whatever restaurant or meeting room or congressional hearing room he happens to be in. He is in every part of his life except the Yiddish background an autodidact, a man who has taught himself what he has to know. He was a champion bridge player, he reads Yiddish poetry at commemorative occasions and acts in the Yiddish-language theater, and he has written a science fiction novel entitled *The Tenth Planet*. In his autobiography, *Escape to the Futures*, Melamed reports a friend's comment that he is a legend in his own mind.

Richard Sandor, Melamed's co-founder in these markets, was by contrast a young professor at the University of California at Berkeley, striding daily through the detritus of the 1960s revolution he had not made. Malamed was looking to expand the opportunities for trading. Sandor was enlarging the capacity of the financial system by inventing synthetic instruments that could be traded more easily, with more efficient "price discovery" in the market, than the instruments from which they derived. He had studied the Board of Trade and its contracts, and he knew that there was no such thing as "wheat." There was durum wheat and semolina and soft winter wheat and Red River Valley wheat. From the point of view of the cereal manufacturers and spaghetti makers and bread bakers, they were interested in only one kind of wheat. Thus there were inefficient premiums and discounts, and buyers and sellers argued with each other about quality. The wheat contract could be satisfied with various mixtures of different kinds of wheat—there were "quality substitution" factors. (This also prevented squeezes.) Grain elevators where the different grades of wheat were stored were said to "originate grain." Both farmers and users could trade wheat on the Chicago market because the contract bridged the differences among the grades of wheat.

Similarly, U.S. Treasury bonds were issued for different maturities, expired in different years, and paid different interest coupons fixed in the terms of the bond. Someone who held a bond issued in a year when the Treasury had put out lots of them might.

have difficulty selling that bond to the life insurance companies that were his usual customers, because the companies already had as many bonds expiring that year as their actuaries told them they needed. Billy Salomon, who ran the then upstart trading house of Salomon Brothers, liked to say as late as the late 1960s that the bond market was much more dangerous than the stock market. You can get a bid on almost any stock by cutting the price a few percentage points—but if the insurance companies already have all they want of bonds coming due in 2001, prices will have to drop much further before anybody calls you up to ask for quotes on that maturity. And there were bonds of other years where relatively small orders could push the market way up, because relatively few bonds had been issued to mature in those years.

Sandor designed a standard $100,000 face-value U.S. Treasury bond with an 8-percent coupon. Any bond with more than fifteen years to go could be delivered to satisfy the contract. This was accomplished by the creation of "conversion factors," like the "quality substitutions" in wheat. The higher the coupon on the bond, the lower the total of face values; the longer the bond had to run, the greater the discount that would be applied to compensate the purchaser for the years his cash was tied up. "We had to normalize all bonds," Sandor recalled. "Everybody said they wanted yield equivalence [i.e., every package of bonds that could be delivered to fulfill the futures contract would pay the same interest rate]. We had a crazy factor system that made higher coupons and longer bonds the cheapest to deliver. Every time we gave the short something [i.e., applied a grading factor that made the deliverable bonds cheaper], we had to give the long something [apply a grading factor that made the deliverable bonds more expensive]. But we couldn't make the contract so perfect it became a cash instrument—you had to leave room for arbitrage." The T-bond contract at the Board of Trade was launched in 1977, and by the early eighties it had surpassed the wheat contracts as the most heavily traded instrument in the world. The Merc's Eurodollar contract displaced it in 1994, but at 100 million contracts traded it was still a strong number two.

The intellectual achievement of this contract has not received as much attention as it deserves. The cash market for U.S. Treasury bonds looked like a well-oiled machine, but in fact it was not, because each bond had its own market, and one bond could not be substituted for another without risk. Sandor's futures contract created a synthetic bond that everybody could trade, and that would relate to the instrument he owned or wished to buy in a known manner. Moreover, because a futures contract can be purchased with a down payment of a few pennies on the dollar, the T-bond contract allowed anyone with interest-rate risk in his portfolio (which means the entire community of investors) to hedge that risk at relatively low cost.

The popular and perhaps slightly overadvertised example was the Salomon Brothers underwriting of IBM bonds just before the bond market was decimated by Fed chairman Paul Volcker's Saturday night massacre of 1979. Morgan Stanley had been IBM's investment banker, and Solly had priced the issue fine to win it away. When Volcker announced new Fed procedures that would violently raise interest rates, the value of the IBM paper Salomon still held would drop pretty deep. But Solly was safe, the story says, because Jon Rotenstreich of its investment banking division had sold a bundle of T-bond futures contracts. When the price of the contracts dropped in response to the higher interest rates, Rotenstreich, who owed the contracts, could buy them back and make a profit that canceled out what he had lost from the drop in the value of the IBM bonds he still held.

Without these contracts—currency, interest-rate, and long bond—none of the "derivatives" activity in the banks would be possible. Banks absolutely must have the opportunity to lay off their bets with the big bookmakers in Chicago, and to "discover" what the prices of their contracts ought to be by reference to a public market where transactions are put on the wire very soon after they occur. "Over-the-counter derivatives and aspects of the mortgage-backed market," Gene Rotberg said, "are idiosyncratic, ad hoc, unpublicized and illiquid. That means that derivatives are difficult, if not impossible, to price or value. It means that if they are held as collateral, there may be no buyers in the event of a forced sale, or the spreads between the buyers and sellers may be so wide that even hedges are ineffective. That means that the dealer who holds such instruments may have to sell short, say, plain vanilla government bonds in very large amounts to protect himself, thereby creating tremendous pressure on the bond market."[27]

In 1994, relatively small moves by the Fed to raise interest rates produced spectacular declines in ten-year government bonds, because the holders of collateralized mortgage obligations premised on continuing declines in rates could protect themselves only by going to the public market and taking large short positions in bond futures. (The ten-years did worse than the others because of the assumption that mortgages in a stable interest rate environment had a twelve-year duration; the math behind the models told the traders to find the closest match to the mortgage assumptions.)

If possible, banks would rather do their business behind closed doors, where they can exploit their information advantage. But when trouble comes, nobody picks up the telephone at the banks. When the British pound collapsed in 1992, and George Soros made his billion dollars with safe leveraged bets on its decline, the volume of currency trading at the Melamed's IMM quintupled overnight. Most of that was banks trading with each other in public, in markets where the purchases and sales were guaranteed by the clearinghouse, because they were scared to do business in private.

Commenting on the clean bill of health the Fed gave the futures and options exchanges in 1985 (responding to congressional queries in the Futures Trading Act of 1982), Leo Melamed chastised the banking regulators for their failure "to distinguish between *futures*, which are standardized contracts traded on commodities exchanges that guarantee both sides of the trade, and *forwards*, which are customized off-exchange arrangements with no guarantor standing in between. . . . [M]ost financial catastrophes involving trading for future delivery have occurred in the forward market, *not* in the futures market. . . . The reason for the difference is largely one of accountability. In futures, all gains and losses are settled in cash at the end of every business day. . . . [B]ank traders cannot hide losing positions or unrealized losses from management. Therefore, from the standpoint of control, futures are far superior to forwards. Bank regulators such as the Fed should appreciate this distinction."[28]

But they don't.

10 / Derivatives: The Computer Rules

There are some causes, which are entirely uniform and constant in producing a particular effect. . . . Fire has always burned, and water suffocated every human creature: The production of motion by impulse and gravity is an universal law, which has hitherto admitted of no exception. But there are other causes, which have been found more irregular and uncertain; nor has rhubarb always proved a purge, or opium a soporific to every one, who has taken these medicines. . . . [W]hen we transfer the past to the future, in order to determine the effect, which will result from any cause, we transfer all the different events, in the same proportion as they have appeared in the past. . . . As a great number of views do here concur in one event, they fortify and confirm it to the imagination, beget that sentiment which we call belief.

> —DAVID HUME, *An Enquiry Concerning Human Understanding* (1748)

In the middle ages, you had a battle, you killed five hundred people, it was a big deal. You had to do it one at a time. Now, you have this guy in Singapore. Fewer and fewer people can kill more and more. I'm in the business of seeing to it that when everything screws up, it will continue to work.

> —ISRAEL SENDROVIC, executive vice president, automation and systems services, Federal Reserve Bank of New York

Derivatives are something out of Robert Louis Stevenson: the very useful Dr. Jekyll and the very dangerous Mr. Hyde. The availability of cheap, effective hedging instruments in the financial markets has served functions not unlike those played by money itself in the larger economy. Bankers committing money to future mortgages in an environment where they run all the risk—farmers selling their grain now for delivery three months hence, at today's price—importers agreeing to pay in a foreign currency in six months (or buying that currency now for use six months later)—are engaged in barter transactions. Inserting interest-rate options and futures and currency options and futures into that market system provides the same anonymity and extended utility that money offered when institutionalized several millennia ago.

A Citicorp executive told Carol Loomis of *Fortune* in 1994 that derivatives were "the basic banking business of the 1990s."[1] Asked what a bank could do for its customers these days, Don Layton of Chemical Bank gave as his second example "Control his risk; that's a core banking product." Andre F. Perold has argued that derivatives are part of the payments system, with contracts substituting for currency in the bilateral relations of correspondent banks.[2] Efforts to *eliminate* derivatives would be foolish as well as futile, as utopian efforts to run communities without money were foolish and futile in the nineteenth century.

"Derivatives are essential to our strategy," said Marcus Rollbacher of the Union Bank of Switzerland, the largest or second-largest player in the market. "We work on transactions where a series of derivatives permit a company to change its whole risk profile. Derivatives allow you to decompose the company into random parts and reassemble them at will."

"Derivatives," said Bankers Trust vice-chairman George Vojta, who went from Citibank to Salomon to Bankers and thus has touched all the bases, "is a different way of looking at the world. Markets, clients, franchises, countries—you look at all of them in terms of the risks embedded in the operation. We've tried to take this firm away from the traditional dumb banker's mistakes. The derivatives are the tools to solve the problem. As

Sanford [BT chairman Charles Sanford, who built BT as a trading bank and walked the plank after its derivatives problems surfaced] said, 'we're trying to build a particle theory of finance.' "

But just as a John Law could debase the currency of France, a major player in leveraged derivatives could shake the banking system if he got on the wrong side of the interest rates or (like Nicholas Leeson of Barings) underestimated the possible volatility of the market.

John Plender, chief leader-writer for *The Financial Times* and not a flake, wrote that "derivative instruments such as swaps, futures and options appear to be the most fiendish of new-fangled booby traps."[3] His advice to users was "be boring . . . it pays to play safe."

Grant's Interest Rate Observer quoted an anonymous trader as saying that "the head of the derivatives department isn't going to go to the chairman of the firm and say there is a one-in-100,000 chance that he could blow the firm up. You'd never be in the business if you were willing to admit that it may happen."[4]

The (then Republican) minority report of the House Banking Committee analyzing hearings on this subject in 1993 pointed out that the use of derivatives by banks had "grown dramatically" after 1989, when the world's banking regulators adopted the risk-based capital standards approved by the Bank for International Settlements in Basel. "As off-balance-sheet items," the report notes, "derivatives may be used by institutions to increase their leverage."[5]

Moreover, this is a market where a dealer who can put a brand name on his product may have some days' advantage before his competitors catch up. Scott Pardee, an MIT Ph.D., then chairman of Yamaichi International in New York, previously the chief foreign-exchange trader for the Fed and chief interest-rate trader for Discount Corporation of America, told a meeting in 1993 that "each derivative product is an exercise in product differentiation. As sellers of futures and options products, we are always seeking new strategies which will generate more commissions or trade at a wider bid-spread than we can earn on the underlying product."[6]

This truth puts the correct real-life spin on the Federal Reserve Board's reply to the House Banking Committee's question about whether regulators should seek to put a limit on bank exposure to derivatives. Any such regulations, the Fed wrote, "would also tend to stifle or discourage market innovations. Such innovations add greatly to the competitiveness and profitability of U.S. banking organizations."[7] Nor can one expect private sector correctives. Rich Sandor, inventor of the T-bond futures contract, noted while head of the Drexel Burnham Chicago office that "I've never seen an accountant's opinion qualified because there were unauthorized trading profits."

The common practice is to label some derivatives as "hedges," meaning "good," and others as "speculations," meaning "naughty." The hedger is a fellow who has already made a bet, committing himself to enter into a mortgage, or provide or accept a foreign currency, or pay a creditor at some future time. By entering into a derivatives contract, the hedger can relieve himself of any worry about price movements, exchange-rate changes, interest-rate increase or decline in the period before his obligation comes due. In its 1996 *Proposed Statement* on accounting for derivatives, the Financial Accounting Standards Board ruled that changes in the value of derivatives held for hedging purposes had to be reported only to the extent that they exceeded the countervailing gains or losses in the value of what was being hedged.[8] The speculator, by contrast, is assumed to have no prior interest in the matter: he simply places and books his bets. The vague implication is that speculators may feed buckshot to people's frogs or somehow manipulate the market, because their only interest is to stir up some action. Speculators are the source of volatility, market prices that move up or down more than they "should."

An alternative taxonomy divides the participants in the market into "dealers" and "end users." Good dealers don't gamble any more than good bookies gamble: they construct a matched book, financing their ownership of instruments that pay 5 $3/16$ by the sale of instruments that commit them to pay 5 $1/8$. When their own customers don't supply them with enough supply or demand to balance their books, they go to other dealers and lay off their excess positions—just as a professional bookie goes to the "bank" in Las Vegas to unload his risks. If they can't lay off their bets and balance their books, they change the odds and keep changing them until demand balances supply.

At a conference in New York in early summer 1995, Walker Todd, maverick lawyer and historian from Tennessee who had been assistant general counsel of the Cleveland Fed, called attention to the losses some midwestern banks had taken on their portfolios of structured notes. Speaking as the supervisor of the New York banks, Ernest Patrikis, formerly general counsel and now first vice president of the New York Fed (who had been Todd's boss some years before), replied that it was really important for the government not to interfere too heavily with the growth of the derivatives market, because if the money-center banks couldn't deal in derivatives, they "might do something really risky, like making loans."

But banks, including money-center banks, are end users of derivatives as well as traders. Given the tiny margins they earn on the money they lend, they cannot afford to see drastic changes in the value of the government bonds and long-term loans in their portfolios. And like the treasurers of the corporations, the CFOs of the banks are under pressure to reduce the cost of funds by trading. It isn't terribly important to the world at large if end-user banks take a view of where interest rates or exchange rates are going, and get it wrong: the failure of a bank here or a bank there doesn't damage the system. But as dealer banks devise more and more sophisticated instruments for their customers, they must find more and more ingenious ways to lay off their exposure—or, in effect if not in intent, keep the risk on the instrument themselves.

"The only perfect hedge," says Gene Rotberg, the former World Bank treasurer, "is in a Japanese garden." Dealers gain additional confidence in keeping the risk because they have an information advantage over the client to whom they sold it. But if big dealer banks get in trouble because they have bet the wrong way, the financial markets could seize up before the regulators know that anything has gone wrong.

This in fact happened in the Herstatt situation in 1974, when John Lee was president of the New York Clearing House, and didn't go to the Federal Reserve Bank of New York for help until two days later, when the volume of transactions in his CHIPS computers had fallen by more than 40 percent. Regulators and academics now talk learnedly of "Herstatt risk," which occurs when delivery is made in one time zone and payment in another. But the real problem is that the perception of Herstatt risk diminishes willingness to trade, and especially in markets where transactions are privately settled ("netted") between the parties, nobody will know a significant failure has occurred until it is too late to remedy the damage.

Probably the most useful division is that of Henry Hu at the University of Texas, as elaborated by Lynn Stout, law professor at Georgetown University. Hu and Stout separate "alpha risk" and "beta risk." Alpha risk is an unavoidable business risk, and normally affects both parties to a transaction. The airline risks having fuel become more expensive, the oil company risks a decline in petroleum prices. Obviously, they can contract with each other to establish prices for future delivery (in effect, barter), but it's much more convenient to access the universe of suppliers and purchasers through an oil futures market. The relative bargaining power of the two is thereby determined by their status with reference to the general expectation of the marketplace rather than differences in resources or information. Portfolio theory says investors have no interest in the management of alpha risk, because anybody can buy stock in both the airline and the oil company; but it's useful for the managements of both companies, and probably beneficial to the society over time, for them to plan ahead and use a public market.

Beta risk, by contrast, is the risk of changes that affect all participants. Stout prefers "uncertainty" to "risk" as the label: risk is measurable, uncertainty is not. In fact, however, most uncertainties can be converted to alpha risks that affect economic actors differently, and most derivatives written to protect against the risks that affect everybody—interest-rate changes, for example—do find hedgers on both sides of many transactions. Even the "diff swap," which rewards or punishes its holder according to the *difference* in the movements of, say, German and U.S. short-term interest rates, can be a hedge for a multinational company. But now we are nearing the underworld of swaps and option contracts and structured notes, which are bets without economic utility for the bettor, and which are proposed to "protect" the player, not against rising or falling prices, but against volatility itself, the danger that rates will move rapidly in either direction.

Underlying all pricing of derivatives is a model for valuing options on common stocks or currencies developed in the early 1970s by the mathematician Fischer Black and finance professor Myron Scholes. The subject is very important, because economic life is full of imbedded options, and the model is very clever. But it rests on two uncertain assumptions. The first is that the current price is the right price for today, because markets are "efficient" and all the available information has been processed into the price by the players. The second is the validity of the statistician's bell curve as an expression of the likelihood of different changes in that price. Given those assumptions, the "correct" price of an option can be calculated. If the option is not selling for that price, it is because the market expects volatility different from that predicted by the bell curve.

At best, expectations of volatility are a crapshoot. The computer has in its guts the historical record of volatility in the instruments that underlie the swap (and if your computer doesn't have that stuff, you can push first a button and then a mouse and J.P. Morgan will supply the information for free on the Internet). But that merely tells you the *frequency* with which certain price movements have occurred in the past. And as John Maynard Keynes pointed out in his *Treatise on Probability* in the early years of this century, frequency and probability are not the same thing. The computer doesn't know from Kobe earthquakes.

Lisa Polsky of Bankers Trust observes, explaining the disastrous decisions so many users of derivatives made in 1994, when the Fed unexpectedly raised interest rates: "Since historic volatility and correlations don't change dramatically with only a few months' new data, investors didn't change their expectations of returns and didn't adjust their positions."[9] Morgan's RiskMetrics, in fact, weights recent events much more heavily than earlier events, which means it forgets what it learns.

The truth is that instruments which derive their value from expectations of volatility—whether they are IO and PO strips of collateralized mortgage obligations, or structured notes, or interest-rate swaps, or "collars," or currency options—are gambling devices as much as the video games in the casinos. It is rare that an external economic interest motivates the seller of a "cap" (protecting the purchaser against a price or rate rise) or a "floor" (protecting the purchaser against a price or rate fall)—though such instruments are, of course, hedges for their purchasers. Halsey Bullen of the Financial Accounting Standards Board, a rather earnest, square-jawed accountant now in his forties, who has given his life to finding ways to value financial instruments and financial institutions, talks about "the jack-in-the-box swap. You get a better spread, and the swap sits there and sits there and doesn't do anything until finally the top springs open and the boxing glove jumps out and hits you in the face."

Some people can handle this sort of thing; most cannot. Comptroller of the Currency Eugene Ludwig, a banking lawyer with the big Washington law firm of Covington and Burling before coming to government with Bill Clinton, likes to speak of "culture risk." A good example of people from the wrong culture can be found in the contract with Bankers Trust that cost Procter & Gamble $157 million, which set up a textbook illustration of the jack-in-the-box swap. It involved the interest rate on five-year Treasuries, the interest rate on thirty-year Treasuries, and the difference between the two. The maximum benefit P&G could get was a ³/₄ of 1 percent reduction on its quarterly interest payments on $225 million, but that benefit would hold true for most interest rates anywhere near the rates prevailing on the day the swap was arranged. Unfortunately, once the rates turned against P&G, the *increase* in what the soap company would have to pay was a very steep curve. By the time P&G bought its way out, it was paying 16 percentage points *more* annual interest to Bankers Trust than Bankers Trust was paying to P&G on its leg of the swap.

Here again, by the way, the tape recorders on the traders' phones tell a story. The Bankers Trust managing director who made the deal called his fiancée to say, "I was so smooth. It was like, yeah, no problem. . . . I said, you know, let me just talk to my trader. . . . We set 'em up." He told a colleague, "You're looking at an $8 million trade." The colleague said, "It's like our greatest fantasy." The managing director said, "I know. It is. It is. This is a wet dream." His boss, told that P&G had decided to do a $200 million rather than a $100 million deal, said, "I think my dick just fell off." Later, the director's fiancée warned him about a separate deutsche mark deal he was peddling to P&G: "I hope that these people don't get blown up. 'Cause that's the end of the gravy train." And the managing director said, "Yeah, well. I'll be looking for a new opportunity in the bank by then anyway."[10] In May 1996, after swearing that it would fight on the beaches, and bringing suit to keep *Business Week* from publishing transcripts of the tapes, Bankers Trust settled the Procter & Gamble suit, paying out an estimated $150 million.

The central problem with bank-created over-the-counter derivatives is their valuation. There are so many simple interest-rate and currency swaps written every day that presumably the computer screen can tell the trader (and, more importantly, his boss) whether a given swap is making or losing money. Unfortunately, the presumption is wrong. Accountants have approved four different ways to value swaps, and they give four different results.[11] When the derivations of the instrument trace back to more than one source, and especially when the payments are a function of the relative movements of different indices—interest rates at different maturities, different currencies, stock market price movements, commodities prices—there may be no simple way to value the note or the swap. Such instruments cannot be "marked to market"; they must be "marked to model."

As the Gibson Greeting Card case revealed, dealers have regarded these valuation models as proprietary to their firms, and have refused to give customers access to them. In *its* settlement with Bankers Trust, written more in sorrow than in anger ("In recognition of their common goals to ensure the prudent operation of the leveraged derivative transaction business," the document begins[12]), the Federal Reserve Bank of New York required the bank to establish a policy of giving customers access to valuation models. "The Gibson case," says the Fed's Ernest Patrikis, waving off its relevance to anything else in banking, "was *fraud*."

In fall 1994, fund managers told *Institutional Investor* that "dealers quote them one price for daily mark-to-market valuations of their derivatives positions and another, significantly lower price for unwinding that same position. 'We bitch and moan and remind ourselves that we will be cautious in the future,' [Douglas] Lempereur [of the Templeton Emerging Markets funds] says. *In the dealer's defense* [italics added], other observers note that the mark-to-market value is intended only as an indication of the price, not as an actual bid."[13] In the securities markets, anybody who quotes a price to a customer is required to do business at that price—the NASDAQ market got into just terrible trouble because dealers violated that rule—for the reason that any other procedure invites fraud.

Oddly enough, the "Code of Conduct" proposed by the industry and the Federal Reserve Bank of New York puts the onus on the customer to "clearly state the desired characteristics of the requested valuation (e.g., mid-market, indicative close-out or real close-out," and even then suggests that the "Participant . . . should recognize that the valuation may include adjustments . . . and may not be representative of either (i) the valuation used by the counterparty for internal purposes or (ii) a theoretical model based valuation." Moreover, "if a Participant wishes to rely on another Participant *to any extent*, it can justifiably do so only if prior to entering into a Transaction involving such reliance (i) it has put the Participant on notice in writing that it is relying on the Participant. . . ."[14] In other words, remember that you've entered a den of thieves, and keep both hands on your wallet. Highlighted selections from the document should be printed in every over-the-counter derivatives contract, like the warnings on a pack of cigarettes. In late 1995, Douglas Harris of the Comptroller's Office shocked the derivatives world by refusing to accept adherence to this code of conduct as a prophylactic against regulatory action alleging cheating by a bank.

Such problems arise not only from fraud, and not only in the relation of dealer and end user. Within the end-user firms, pricing can be done however the people who run the portfolio wish to do it. In the case of Askin Capital Management and Granite Capital, the "market neutral" hedge funds that went down with a loss of $600 million, David Askin in February 1994 substituted his own "manager's mark" for quotes received from dealers when estimating the value of his positions. His fund then had 550 positions in various CMOs, and he dropped the dealer quotes he had previously fed to his model and substituted his own estimate of value for 268 of them. Some 126 of these estimates differed from dealer prices by more than 10 percent. The result was to change the values he reported to the investors in his funds (and used in his presentations to potential new clients) so dramatically that losses ranging from 20 to 28 percent in the different funds could be presented as one fund with a gain of 0.71 percent and the others with losses ranging from 0.85 percent to 1.68 percent.[15]

Vice-chairman George Kenny of Merrill Lynch reports that his risk controllers take prices from the traders, but they must independently sign off that the prices are okay: "If a trader has a bad week, he'll start to shade some prices, two basis points here, three basis points there, and it's hard to catch. But the next week he'll do it again, and then it begins to show up in the computer as a widening spread. People are fired *automatically* when that happens."

Citibank deliberately uses for its internal purposes two separate valuation models, one for traders to keep track of their own accounts, the other for the comptrollers who keep an eye on the traders. The traders cannot change either model. Gordon Clancy, vice president for Citibank's Global Derivatives, says that "risk management now reports away from the profit center, like the corporate auditing function; it's independent of the line units." This still leaves open the interesting question of which model controls the profitability Citi reports to (*a*) the Internal Revenue Service, (*b*) the banking regulators, and (*c*) its stockholders. By the rules of the Group of Thirty, the international omnium-gatherum of bank chief executives and central bank governors who periodically pronounce the private sector's views on what should be done about publicized problems in the financial markets, profits from derivatives creation and trading should be taken into the bottom line "periodically" even though there is no agreement on the accounting procedures that should be followed.

A dealer said, "Let's say I think an IAS [index-amortizing swap] is worth $15, so I'll pay $10 for it, but there's no way I can sell it to prove that it's worth $10. The accountants come to me and say, 'How much is it worth?' I say I think it's worth $15, but I can't sell it so there's no way to prove it. But from day one, I've got to show profitability, and I'm still asked every day to report my profits. So I put down a profit of $5 and everybody pats me on the back and I think I've made five bucks. Then you get somebody else at another firm who thinks the value is $10, not $15, so he'll pay $10. If there's that much discrepancy . . . should they let me book that money, when there's no outside market to prove it? If I were management and the trader says, look here, there are two caps and this is how you determine where the value lies, and it's all theoretical, I'd be very careful about booking those profits."[16]

When Kidder Peabody fired its Treasury bonds trader Joe Jett and alleged that Jett had booked $350 million of "false profits," commentators wondered how such huge sums could be hidden. But GE Capital, Kidder's parent company, had a $3.2 billion "reconciliation account" which expressed the difference between its valuation of its inventory and the cost of that inventory, and all the profits of the enterprise were in those valuations. The banks are the same. "Models are smart," says William Broeksmit of Merrill Lynch, "but they are only as smart as their architects. I am always concerned about buying an instrument at prices that no human being is willing to pay, but a box of electrons bouncing around will pay."[17] Tony Terracciano, head of what was then First Fidelity Bank, put it simply: "If you can't break it down into a bond yield equivalent in a few minutes, you don't understand it and you shouldn't do it."

The General Accounting Office reported in early 1994 that banks' financial reports "may be inconsistently presented, unrepresentative of the substance and risks of derivatives activities; and misleading to investors, creditors, regulators and others."[18] David Folkerts-Landau of the International Monetary Fund and Alfred Steinherr of the European Investment Bank write,

[T]he creative use of derivatives has given intermediaries tools that are much more powerful and effective in disguising their true financial position. By marking derivative positions to proprietary pricing models losses can be shifted very far into the future, whilst current income and profits can be generated through the skillful structuring of in-the-money options. As a result, *insolvency has become a more tenuous concept*. Essentially it has become necessary for counterparties, supervisors and regulators to rely on the intermediary's interest in protecting its franchise value. Given that banks have privileged access to central bank facilities—including liquidity support—and that they are still playing a key role in the financial system in delivering the bulk of credit and payments, this situation is far from satisfactory.[19]

Nevertheless, the Group of Thirty in their very influential 1993 report on *Derivatives: Practices and Principles* recommended that "Dealers should account for derivatives transactions by marking them to market, *taking changes in value to income each period*."[20]

Comptroller of the Currency Eugene Ludwig told me in response that "There's a difference between an examination and an accounting. If you ask me, 'Are *we* getting an accurate picture?', I'd say, 'Yes.' If you ask me, 'Is *the public* getting an accurate picture?', well . . ."

Enormous amounts of money are involved here. In 1987, Howard Sosin and his friend Randall Rackson left Drexel Burnham to start a derivatives trading operation for Maurice "Hank" Greenberg and his American International Group. They installed themselves in lavish offices (including a fifty-foot saltwater fish tank) near their homes in Westport, Connecticut. The deal was that 38 percent of the profits from the new AIG–Financial Products company would go to Sosin and 62 percent to AIG, which was supplying the financial guarantees. This was presumably a completely hedged operation: every night, a proprietary computer program named Value Hedging evaluated the portfolio (in 1992, according to the AIG annual report, no less than $82.4 billion of swaps), and Sosin personally typed in the letters "VHGO," to get automated marching orders on the hedges his fund should purchase.[21]

Rackson's lawsuit against Sosin for what he considered his share of the profits claimed that in the five years 1988–92 AIG-FP made more than a billion dollars—"and, absent certain accounting adjustments made by AIG after termination of the venture in order to bolster its litigation position, 1993 was far and away AIG-FP's best year ever."[22] Sosin's settlement on the dissolution of the venture was, Rackson reported, $200 million. AIG later took a $172 million charge against previously reported earnings to eliminate alleged overvaluation of the AIG-FP portfolio.

Banking regulators around the world have recommended "gross replacement value" (GRV) as the measurement of the loss a bank would suffer if a counterparty successfully backed out of a swaps deal, and "value at risk" (VAR) to control the danger that a rapid change in interest rates or currency values would kill the profits already booked from a deal. What is especially interesting about VAR is that it applies only to the derivatives where banks hold what seems to be a winning position. In 1993, Veribank, a commercial service that ranks banks according to their profitability as indicated in their semiannual "call reports" to their regulators, issued a statement claiming that all the worry about bank involvement with derivatives was just foolish or worse: banks were *coining* money on derivatives trading. Then someone pointed out that Veribank had no way to know whether banks were making money on derivatives, because the only derivatives positions covered by the call reports were winners that left the bank with value at risk. The losing derivative positions, which might be bigger than the winners, were not declared.[23]

In 1995, the Federal Deposit Insurance Corporation changed its rules and began to report global results in derivative trading. *New York Times* reporter Keith Bradsher was told in June that "for those derivatives held for trading purposes and priced at the end of the first quarter, banks had accumulated gains of $289.48 billion and losses of $285.03 billion, for a net gain of $4.44 billion."[24] The careful reader notes that the FDIC priced *only* "those derivatives held for trading purposes and priced." From this statement, it is by no means clear whether the banks as a group had made or lost money on their derivatives holdings in the first quarter of 1995. Given the normal tendency to price more of the winners and carry more of the losers at historic cost, it seems at least possible that American banks were in a net loss position with reference to their derivatives in spring 1995.

J.P. Morgan has published and updates daily its "RiskMetrics" data on interasset correlations that can help dealers calculate how much damage changes in interest rates will do to their positions. At best, Morgan believes these correlations to be accurate to a 95 percent confidence level—which means that on one day a month they will probably be misleading. That's not a problem for Morgan, said Jacques Longerstacy, a dark-haired young man with large round eyeglasses, a striped shirt and Paisley tie, who helped develop and operates the RiskMetrics model, because Morgan has so many different swaps and notes out covering virtually every possible price movement in virtually every market. If the correlations fail in one direction for the one set of instruments, they will probably fade in the opposite direction for another set. "And the best we can say," he adds, "is that *if* historical patterns hold, this is the risk you're running."

Longerstacy does not deny that it would be on the twentieth day, while Morgan rests, that the customer, far less diversified in his positions, would get his margin calls. "The question is," said Tanya Beder of Capital Markets Risk Advisors, "how much can you lose during that five percent of the time? . . . These relationships can change dramatically in a period of dislocation. . . . Risks which once tracked each other may not longer move in sync."

"Value at risk," unfortunately, is an inherently deceptive measure. The world is discontinuous: measurements that expect prices to remain within two or even three standard deviations are an abuse of statistical analysis. The bond market in February 1994 moved *fifteen* standard deviations, as did the exchange value of the Italian lira. Dan Napoli of Merrill Lynch says that stock prices in "the emerging markets" moved *thirty* standard deviations. The invasion of Kuwait moved oil prices by ten standard deviations in one day. And even if you want to sell at the new prices, there are often no buyers—at any price. "The worst thing that can happen to you as a trader," says Bank of America's Ray Peters, "is that you can't get out of it. That's the ultimate sin for a trader." Ron Dembo, president of Toronto's Algorithmics, Inc., and proprietor of RiskWatch, a PC-based risk-monitoring product, told *Derivatives Strategy*, "Liquidity is the biggest risk, but VAR numbers don't take liquidity into account at all. . . . If [David] Askin was going to calculate the VAR on his $600 million in exotic mortgage backed securities, he could have based his numbers on the historical volatility in the mortgage market and come out with a VAR of $15 million."[25]

In fall 1994, *Euromoney* reports, "a handful of swap-dealing banks in various countries were asked by the Basle Committee on Banking Supervision to run the same sample derivatives portfolio through their internal risk management models and come up with a number for value at risk. . . . The portfolio consisted of a hundred or so swaps, swaptions, caps and floors, bonds and bond options, in various currencies. . . . There were four variations of the portfolio. . . . Two were unbalanced. . . . The unbalanced portfolio with options was understandably the most risky and the most difficult to predict. Even so it was a shock to learn that, according to one bank supervisor, the banks' VAR numbers for this portfolio varied at the extreme ends by a factor of eight. Exact numbers aren't available but if, for example, the bank at one extreme had calculated a maximum loss in 10 days of $30 million, the bank at the other extreme was predicting $240 million! This was not very encouraging."[26] On the most rudimentary level, the market may simply be wrong. "Wall Street got caught with its pants down in 1993," says David Lerach of the Mortgage Bankers Association. "They missed the prepayment speed when interest rates went down. They stayed with their models based on history, and we were writing new history."

Christine Cummings, a large, cheerful lady who keeps an eye on these matters for the Federal Reserve Bank of New York, says with just a touch of annoyance that "too many people are in options who can't measure the risk. But measurement can only give you an idea. If the sub is sinking, it's good to know what the water pressure is, but it won't save you." Her colleague Ernest Patrikis speaks of "intellectual risk"—the danger that the only man in the organization who understands the portfolio will be hit by a bus or bought away by somebody else. "You don't keep control by *numbers*," says Marcus Rollbacher of the Union Bank of Switzerland. "You keep control by dialogue."

2

Presumably, markets are self-correcting: if too many people are losing money, customers shy away. In August 1995, the *Wall Street Journal* ran an article headlined "Derivatives Could Hedge Career Growth," which presented quotes from funds managers and research directors to the effect that everyone was now shying away. "You don't want to find yourself in a boardroom," said John Carroll, who manages a $12 billion pension fund for GTE Corporation, "explaining why you've bought some kind of odd-ball product. If you made the right call and used derivatives, you might get a small additional return. But if you make the wrong call, you could wind up unemployed, with a big dent in your credibility as an investor." It's humiliating, another manager told reporter Suzanne McGee "to get labeled as someone who got snookered by an investment bank."[27]

The obvious citation here is to the collateralized mortgage obligation market, which dried up in the aftermath of the Askin fiasco. Kidder Peabody had been by far the largest dealer, and went bankrupt. Bear Stearns had been next, and cut back by more than 50 percent. J.P. Morgan ate losses apparently approaching $120 million, and closed down its CMO trading department for good. But the reason these CMO departments were destroyed did not really have much to do with the losses taken on the instruments. The reason was that index-amortizing notes could be written to have almost the characteristics of a CMO, and more attractive to end users because changes in its pricing were not dependent on extraneous factors like householders' decisions to refinance their mortgage. Russell Janeway of the investment banking house Warburg Pincus likes to draw a simple graph in which the x axis measures the length of time before the bond or swap or option matures and the y axis measures the extent to which human rather than mechanical action determines the price. In the area near the intersection of the x and y lines, mathematical analysis works. The farther up the diagonal—the longer the time, and the higher the human component—the less likely it is that the rocket scientists have any contribution to make.

In fact, this market will not be self-correcting. The collection of publicized derivatives disasters in 1994 made barely a hiccup's worth of difference in 1995. "The derivatives holdings of American banks soared in the first quarter of the year," The *New York Times* reported in June 1995.[28] A year later, the International Swaps & Derivatives Association reported, according to *Financial Times*, that "activity in over-the-counter (OTC) financial derivatives soared to record levels last year."[29] Eighty percent of the growth in foreign-exchange trading in London, the Bank of England reported, was in swaps.[30] The riskiest sector of the market—long-dated swaps of currencies (where the parties do in fact exchange the principal) was the fastest-growing sector in late 1994 and 1995. There is absolutely no liquidity here: Michael Hawker of Citibank in London says that "it can take up to a year to do one deal, the counterparties are so scarce." But the profits are great, when there are profits: "Instead of getting three to four basis points at the short end," Hawker says, "you can get three to four percentage points at the long end."[31]

What has been happening in the derivatives market is an illustration of Hyman Minsky's "financial instability hypothesis." Entering a new business—lending to movies, buying interest-rate futures, financing shopping centers, writing long-dated currency options—banks are cautious, worried about their counterparties, insistent on limiting their risks. The worst thing that can happen to a young man is that he makes money on his first trip to the race track. The banks find that they can make money from an "innovation." Management begins to wonder how long this has been going on. Euphoria arrives.

The British magazine *The Banker* heralded the 1993 creation of a joint venture in derivatives by Abbey National, a big mortgage bank, and Barings: "Abbey's key contribution will be its strong credit rating while Baring will provide its long established expertise in the risk management area."[32] Barings' experience was growing fast: the bank in 1993, en route to its billion-dollar loss and final collapse, would win the Singapore Monetary Exchange award for the greatest volume of business done by a single member.

The industry acquires new geniuses, and new heroes. The early products become commodities, and, as Scott Pardee points out, competitors seek product differentiation, something salable at a good markup. Safety considerations vanish into the background. Everybody still talks a good game, but in fact the increased profits are being bought by hyperbolically increased risks. The brokerage function, through which dealers write instruments for one customer and then sell them to another, slides imperceptibly into a trading function, in which some substantial part of the risks are held.

But beyond the obvious euphoria, something more dangerous has happened here. Barring government intervention, future developments in the banks' end of the derivatives markets will be controlled by Mayer's Laws of Financial Engineering. I put my name on them because, though they are transparently true, I seem to have discovered them.

- *First Law: When the whole is valued at a price less than the sum of the prices of its parts, some of the parts are over-priced.* Debt instruments can be profitably cut into separate tranches because there are unsophisticated buyers, like my Texas builder, who will buy the tranches where large possible rewards deflect attention from even larger probable risks. In the collateralized mortgage obligation business, these tranches were called "toxic waste." The strongest of the arguments against the issuance of such fancy paper by government-sponsored enterprises like Fannie Mae and Freddie Mac and the Federal Home Loan Bank is that their imprimatur helps salesmen conceal risk from purchasers.

- *Second Law: Segmenting value also segments liquidity.* Trading volume rises, but a crisis in any part of the segmented market conveys contagion rapidly to other markets. "The basic principle behind all financial risk management," writes Gary Gastineau of the Swiss Bank Corporation, "is the exchange of one set of risks and rewards for another set that fits a market participant's utility preferences more closely."[33] When that market participant's utility preferences move away from this instrument, he will require great good fortune to find another market participant whose utility preferences have moved toward this instrument, so he can sell it at anything like the price it carries on his books. The more reasons in the community to buy a given instrument, the more likely that instrument will find customers when its owner no longer wishes to hold it. The more narrowly tailored the instrument to specific needs, the less salable it will be in a crunch. "Market risk" is made much more dangerous by segmentation risk. "Stripping the coupons off a 30-year U.S. government bond," says Scott Pardee, "creates 61 separate sub-markets, one for the principal and 60 for the twice-a-year coupons. They are all linked by means of arbitrage, but anyone holding just one piece and trying to get out of it may lose a lot of money before he can find a buyer."[34] "Dynamic hedging" tactics, by which a holder sells derivatives into a declining market to compensate for accelerating losses in a portfolio, quickly absorbs whatever liquidity may be available for segments of an instrument.

- *Third Law: Risk-shifting instruments ultimately shift risks onto those less able to bear them.* The obvious illustration is the S&P 500 futures pit at the Chicago Mercantile Exchange, where a couple of hundred ex–taxi drivers working as "locals" were expected to carry the dynamic hedging of "portfolio insurance" when the stock market broke on October 19, 1987. The logic here is inevitable: those who got, want to keep, and hedge; those who ain't got, want to get, and speculate.

The dealers' first line of defense is insistence that counterparties have impeccable credit, but this line quickly erodes as competition for the business of the triple-A participants knocks down the margins and (worse) educates these fellows in what they are doing. As early as 1992, Robert H. Litzenberger, president of the American Finance Association, had occasion to note that "In practice swap spreads are not sensitive to credit rating differences between counterparties (at least for entities rated single A or better)."[35] When AIG took over Howard Sosin's derivatives operation, it reportedly found deals with very marginal people like the Bronfmans' troubled Edper conglomerate.

And the banking regulators are moving to make this risk worse, by encouraging bilateral "netting" between the participants of trades. The clearinghouse of an exchange knows the total position of every trader—and, indeed, the commodities exchanges in 1995, in the aftermath of the Barings collapse, put in place a mechanism for worldwide exchange of information about the positions participants have acquired in similar contracts in different markets. Each clearinghouse, moreover, places the entire resources of its membership behind the settlement of the contracts traded on that exchange, and by the imposition of "variation margin" prevents any participant from running up debts to the clearinghouse.

But banks do not know what contracts their counterparties have signed with other banks, or what exposures they have to price movements. And while the bad news of 1994 persuaded some banks to require collateral from counterparties, most derivative trades are entirely on credit. Indeed, one of the advantages Douglas Harris of the Comptroller's Office claimed for bank-traded derivatives was that they eliminated the "administrative expense and nuisance of maintaining margin at a clearinghouse." Not to mention the administrative expense savings related to the fact that exchange-traded derivatives must be marked to a public market price every night, while bank-created derivatives can be carried at whatever valuations the bank's own computers assign them.

In November 1994, a "working group" of central bankers meeting at the Bank for International Settlements acclaimed the growth of derivatives. "To the extent that risk is shifted from agents less capable of bearing it to others more able to do so, there is likely to be a reduction in the fragility of the financial system. There is, in other words, a net gain to the economy, as greater financial market resilience, both domestically and internationally, should help disperse shocks."[36] The premise being diametrically wrong, the conclusion must be reversed. Because derivatives will inevitably shift risk to those less able to bear them, their extension will *increase* the fragility of the financial system, with a net *loss* to the economy. In 1996, researchers at the BIS found that delayed payment or settlement of foreign exchange swaps had left individual banks with credit exposures to other banks as high as $2 billion, which in some cases was more than the entire capital of the bank at risk.

3

George Soros has suggested that "all derivatives traded by banks ought to be registered with the Bank for International Settlements in Basel through the various national regulatory agencies. The BIS could study them, gather data, establish capital requirements, and, when necessary, discourage them by raising capital requirements or ban them altogether."[37] Soros particularly wants to ban the "knock-out option," which allows its purchaser to hedge cheaply against a small price movement, at the cost of losing his hedge entirely if the market moves decisively against him. (With the market at 100, the purchaser buys an option to sell at 95 on the expiration date of the option, but if the price goes below 90 at any time before that date, the option "knocks out." This produces remarkable trading volumes in the underlying security or commodity as the price nears the knock-out trigger.) Given the published enthusiasm of the BIS for customized derivatives, the Soros proposal looks flawed.

I argued in testimony to the House Banking Committee in fall 1993 that it should be public policy to discourage over-the-counter derivative contracts and encourage the use of exchange-traded instruments instead, because the systemic risks created by custom-made derivatives were overwhelmingly greater than the very marginal benefits to be gained from such "innovation."[38] A year later, David Folkerts-Landau of the IMF and Alfred Steinherr of the European Investment Bank won the annual American Express Bank Review Essay Competition with a paper concluding that

> the apparent tilting of the playing field in favour of the OTC markets, implied in the current regulatory structure, should be re-examined. By increasing capital requirements for OTC derivative positions and thereby making them more costly relative to exchange/clearing house positions, it is possible to induce a shift towards the exchange/clearing house market structure. In terms of the various risks generated by OTC derivative activity, credit risk would be reduced by marking to market with margining, transparency of price discovery would increase, liquidity risk would be reduced by the fungibility of contracts, legal risks would be eliminated under existing laws, and operational risk would be reduced.[39]

Banking regulators do not understand the extent to which they invite fraud in highly leveraged situations when they protect trading activity behind the veil of bank secrecy. One of the more aggressively promoted swaps in 1995 was the one between Libor and the commercial-paper rate in the United States. The Federal Reserve publishes the index of CP rates on the basis of reports from a cross-section of seventeen broker/dealers, nine big banks and eight big securities houses. But the big issuers of commercial paper, like General Electric Capital Corporation and General Motors Acceptance Corporation, complain that this index is biased upward by dealers who "misrepresent the level at which commercial paper is being sold, to curry favor with customers. If the benchmark CP index is quoted at an artificially high level, then dealers can look like heroes by calling up corporate clients and in silken voices offer to place their commercial paper below the benchmark." Jeffrey Werner of GECC told the newsletter *Deriva-tive Tactics* that he looked forward to the construction of a separate index that would not involve reports to the Fed, "as opposed to this fictitious number . . . of questionable integrity."[40] The big profits were made by those who knew the CP numbers were being inflated, and could buy Libor/CP swaps with a certainty of win-ning. Eventually, the spread between Libor and CP widened, and the manipulators of the market moved on to other things.

Scott Pardee has suggested "a Federal Drug Administration approach to new products. . . . I don't want to create a new bureaucracy or stifle creativity, to the contrary. But the Fed, the SEC, the CFTC and the SRO's should make a practice of asking what this new derivative product would look like five years from now and what can go wrong as a result. The creators of such prod-ucts should be prepared to demonstrate that their inventions will not prove to be a financial form of thalidomide. They would be liable for the results, both as firms and individuals, even if the individuals are now basking comfortably on their yachts in Florida, having taken the money and run."[41]

But there is an easier way to "tame," as Folkerts-Landau and Steinherr have it, the derivatives monster. The first opinion Justice Oliver Wendell Holmes, Jr., wrote as a Supreme Court justice upheld a California constitutional provision that forbade the enforcement of "contracts for the sales of shares of the capital stock of any corporation or association, on margin, or to be deliv-ered at a future day." In a previous case, *Booth* v. *Illinois*,[42] the Court had upheld a state law making all options contracts illegal. "[I]f a man can buy on margin," Holmes wrote, "he can launch into a much more extended venture than where he must pay the whole price at once. If he pays the whole price he gets the purchased article, whatever its worth may turn out to be. But if he buys stocks on margin he may put all his property into the venture, and being unable to keep his margins good if the stock market goes down, a slight fall leaves him penniless, with nothing to represent his outlay, except that he has had the chances of a bet. There is no doubt that purchases on margin may be and frequently are used as a means of gambling for a great gain or a loss of all one has."[43]

The first significant derivative in American finance was the contract the bucket shop sold the customer who thought he was buying a real stock through a real broker. Instead, the customer got a piece of paper that gave him a claim on the bucket-shop proprietor if the price of the stock went up, and lost him his money if the price of the stock went down. Like today's derivative, the bucket-shop contract was a leveraged instrument—a "10X," as today's dealers would say, meaning that the customer normally puts up only 10 percent of the price of the stock. In the early years of this century, most individuals who "played the stock market" did so at bucket shops. If the market went up enough, bucket shops closed and snuck away to avoid paying their customers.

Most states passed legislation making bucket shops and their instruments illegal, and that legislation is still on the books. The New York State law says, "Any person, copartnership, firm, association or corporation . . . who shall: 1. Make or offer to make, or assist in making or offering to make any contract respecting the purchase or sale, either upon credit or margin, of any securities or commodities, including all evidence of debt or property and options for the purchase thereof, shares in any corporation or association, bonds, coupons . . . or anything movable that is bought and sold, intending that such contract shall be terminated, closed or settled according to, or upon the basis of the public market quotations of or prices made on any board of trade or exchange or market . . . without intending a bona fide purchase or sale of the same . . . shall be guilty of a felony."[44]

When Melamed pushed the first cash settlement contracts, he had to get the Commodity Futures Trading Commission (CFTC) to authorize it specifically, because otherwise many brokers ("futures commission merchants" is the term of art) could have been in danger of criminal prosecution. Banks do not have that protection, and in 1991 sought a blanket safe harbor from Wendy Gramm, Senator Phil Gramm's wife and then chairman of the CFTC. She gave one, but it is by no means clear that derivatives lacking any legitimate hedging purpose can be protected from state law even by the CFTC. There are those who believe Bankers Trust settled with Gibson Greeting Cards and Procter & Gamble rather than risk a judicial decision that Ohio's anti–bucket shop law voided these contracts. For 1994, Bankers Trust reduced its claimed profits from derivatives by more than could be explained by the Gibson and Procter cases, arguing that the bank was also settling with others in an unpublicized way. One that did get publicized in 1996 was a settlement with Air Products and Chemicals, Inc., which cost the bank $76 million.[45]

The most important common law precedent, after all, goes against the banks. In England, the borough council (county, in American terms) of Hammersmith had entered into interest-rate swaps with London banks, and had refused to pay off when the swaps turned sour, arguing that playing in derivatives was something they had no legal authority to do, and the banks should have known it. They won their case in the House of Lords, costing British and American banks about $600 million.

When banks speak of "legal risk" in the derivatives business, what they usually mean is the danger that if a counterparty goes bankrupt, a bankruptcy judge will declare the entire notional amount of a swap part of the assets to be distributed to creditors, with the bank somewhere down the queue. They are entitled to and in the United States have (probably) achieved protection from such disasters. What they are not entitled to is the services of a court to enforce a gambling contract that would be illegal if anybody but a bank promoted it.

This is the one weapon the bank regulators have to control the proliferation of highly leveraged derivatives that are without redeeming economic purpose: they can simply announce that unless the instruments have been registered with a securities or commodities market regulator or a banking regulator, a bank that sells them will have to take its chances on collecting what the contract says the customer owes. Registration with a securities or commodities regulator would meet current criteria (which are pretty minimal) for approval of trading. Registration with a banking regulator would require a statement of the utility of the instrument, a model for its valuation, and a commitment by the bank to repurchase from the customer at the price quoted as market value if the demand for repurchase follows immediately on the declaration of the mark-to-market price. Failing such registration, a court believing that the instrument was simply a bet could decline to compel payment, as the Michigan Supreme Court in 1994 declined to enforce a marker a citizen of that state had given to a Las Vegas casino.[46] It should be noted that this procedure also eliminates the incessantly uttered threat that if the American authorities seek to compel honesty in their markets the miscreants of finance will simply take their business overseas. Markets are *entirely* the creatures of a legal order, and overseas courts could not compel payments by foreign counterparties.

Banking regulators react in horror to the idea that any OTC derivative contracts might be declared unenforceable under the gaming laws. But as William McDonough, president of the New York Fed, said in a speech in Geneva in March 1995, "Experience has shown repeatedly that prudent risk management and controls need not hamper creativity."[47] Prudence cannot be left for the eye of the beholder or the "supervisor." As we shall see in Part III, the system of bank regulation established in the New Deal and pretty much sustained into the mid 1990s does not encourage prudent risk management—indeed, it creates perverse incentives and encourages cowboy behavior.

Leaving the decision on legitimacy to the courts in private lawsuits makes sure that banks *always* have money at risk when they create private, highly leveraged instruments for sale to customers. There is no need to adopt rules or unleash the bureaucracy. Banks need not be prohibited from writing gamey instruments—and need not be required to ascertain whether a derivative sold to a customer is in truth a "suitable investment" for that customer. They would merely have reason to consider, taking into account their enormous information advantage, whether the fact that they can sell something means any customer really has a reason to buy it.

11 / The Bad Example: Barings

"Nick had an amazing day on SIMEX.... Baring Singapore was the market. I mean, he just has a corner there. So everybody wants Nick to do their business.... He's just absolutely the centre, the vortex of the information curve there.... He just sees opportunities that are phenomenal, and he just takes them."

> —RON BAKER, head of the Financial Products Group at Baring Bank, in a phone call from New York to London, four weeks before Leeson's trading losses sank the bank.[1]

Telephones began ringing in the homes of the leaders of major American banks and investment banks at six in the morning on Saturday, February 25, 1995. The caller was the Bank of England, often enough its governor Eddie George himself. It was noon in England, and the bank had learned that Baring Brothers and Company, the longest-established and until two days before apparently one of the most solid merchant banks in London, was hopelessly insolvent, with losses that were at least twice its capital.

This bank was 233 years old, founded by the Dutchman-turned-German Peter Baring, whose direct descendant, with the same name, was now the shocked chairman of a terminally stricken bank. In 1818, the Duc de Richelieu had said there were six great powers in Europe—France, England, Prussia, Austria, Russia and Baring Brothers. Barings had been there before Rothschilds, and if you'd asked people in London to bet, they'd have bet that Barings would still be there after Rothschilds. The family roster was full of earls and barons, including Lord Cromer, who had been governor of the Bank of England, British ambassador to Washington (and buddy of Jack Kennedy), and head of the largest nongovernmental television channel. When the leaders of London banking had been summoned to the Bank of England the previous afternoon to put together what the British call a "lifeboat," they knew that some bank was in trouble, but they didn't think it was going to be Barings. Then they found that they couldn't build a big enough lifeboat. Now the New World was being called in to redress the balance of the Old.

The Learjets and Challengers rolled off the runways and landed in London that evening, and the Americans met late at night with Eddie George, who had himself been called back the day before just as he arrived in Switzerland for a skiing vacation. There were assets in the Baring Group to be bought—a successful investment management group serving pension funds and life insurance companies, a banking group with a major presence in Asia, and a great brand name.

There was even a track record of recovery after disaster, for Baring Brothers had failed 105 years earlier, brought down by large and unwise lending in Argentina—and had been snatched from the brink of default by a consortium of British banks led by the then private Bank of England, with a partial, secret guarantee from the government. The family had been impoverished, for the bank was then a partnership and all the partners were liable, but within a dozen years Baring Bank, reorganized as a corporation but still wholly owned by the same people, had regained its position. John Baring, second Lord Revelstoke, successor to his father as head of the bank, proposed to Nancy Langhorne: "Do you really think that you could fill the position that would be required of my wife? You would have to meet kings and queens and entertain

334

ambassadors." She turned him down and presently married Waldorf Astor, becoming the Lady Astor of 1930s fact and fiction.[2]

But in 1995 nobody could save them. The losses the bank had suffered in its Singapore and Osaka trading of futures and options on Japanese stocks and government bonds had overwhelmed the value of the assets. Worse: some of those positions were still open, and it was clear that when the market opened on Monday there would be new and heavy losses. There were, in fact, an additional *$370 million* of losses in the Barings position on February 27.

Andrew Buxton, chairman of Barclays Bank, leader of the lifeboat builders, told the international cadre of bankers on Sunday afternoon that "the future of the banking industry" was at stake. Apparently he won a commitment from London banks for $900 million for three months, during which time the Barings assets could be sold piecemeal. But nobody was willing to carry the contingent risk. Judith Rawnsley in her book about the fall of the bank describes the octagonal room where the bankers met, sitting under an eighteenth-century chandelier at a hollow square formed of blue baize-topped tables. She adds the nice touch that when the meeting ended, the London press corps, having been tipped off to the problem by a distraught Barings executive, let the casually dressed bankers go and pounced on the formally attired lawyers and accountants.[3]

The Bank of England was glad to host the meetings and pay for the pizzas, but politically it could not put public money into rescuing Barings. The Chancellor of the Exchequer was asked, and said No—if he tried that, the Labour Party MPs and no small fraction of his own backbenchers would have him for lunch. Barings was not a very big bank; its capital was something less than half a billion dollars, its assets something less than $9 billion. Eddie George and the British Treasury believed that the bank simply wasn't big enough to pose a systemic risk. BCCI had been more than twice that size, and its closure had barely made a ripple in international commerce.

This was awkward for the Bank of England, however, because what had gone bust, after all, was Baring Securities, a severable arm of the bank, and Baring Bank was insolvent because it had advanced so much money to Baring Securities for margin calls on futures contracts. This sort of lending to one's own subsidiaries was something the Bank of England should have been watching, and it had been blindsided—in large part because it had been willfully or at least negligently blind. A call was put out to the Bank of Japan, which referred the matter to the Ministry of Finance, which disapproved of any derivatives trading in Japanese equities or government bonds, and had strong views of such trading in Singapore. Maybe the sultan of Brunei, who was the biggest client of Barings' asset management subsidiary and had once, at the request of Ronald Reagan's national security adviser, put up $10 million for the Nicaraguan Contras, only to have Swiss Bank Corporation credit it to the wrong account. . . .

But it was not to be. At exactly 8:36 on Sunday evening, with the market about to open in Singapore, Barings was put into the "administration" of the British equivalent of a bankruptcy court, and the accounting firm Ernst and Young were appointed administrators. At about the same time, the Singapore exchange declared Barings in default on a margin call for its losses the previous Friday, and the High Court appointed Price Waterhouse as judicial managers of the Barings futures operation, which was a Singapore corporation.

2

The official report to the House of Commons on the Barings matter was made by a Board of Banking Supervision, an ad hoc body chaired by the governor of the Bank of England but including outsiders (one of them in this case being Sir Dennis Weatherstone, the Australian banker who rose to be chairman of J.P. Morgan worldwide). These nine experts concluded that "Barings' collapse was due to the unauthorized and ultimately catastrophic activities of, it appears, one individual that went undetected as a failure of management and other internal controls."[4] In other words, when Peter Baring told Eddie George that the problem was a "rogue trader," he had it right. It's sort of an accident, like "drunk driver."

The description does fit this case better than most in which it is used, because Nicholas Leeson, the twenty-seven-year-old trader and director of trading operations at Baring Futures Singapore (BFS), did in fact cook his books to hide what he was doing from his nearby supervisors in Singapore and his faraway supervisors in London. (Barings had recently shifted to a fashionable "matrix management" mode, in which activities were accounted for both geographically and by function—which meant in practice here as in many other corporations that the man in the field could do as he pleased.) But in fact the first lesson of management in financial services is that you have to worry about the guy who's making all the money. This is counterintuitive in business, particularly where departments are rated by their contribution to profit and the boss of the department gets a bonus if the profits are high. The tendency is always to intensify the supervision of the man who is *not* making profits, and, indeed, to get rid of him. But the real danger to the firm is likely to be the person, especially the trader in highly leveraged markets, whose profits are extraordinarily high.

Vincent Murphy, who was the partner in charge of keeping the books straight at Salomon Brothers in the 1970s, before the computers kept all the accounts, cherished a set of keys to all the traders' desks and stayed at the office very late every so often to see whether there were any slips in those drawers that spoke of trades not reported to management. He looked especially carefully through the desks of the traders who were showing the best results. With the arrival of computers, and payment by bonus for performance, these disciplines were forgotten.

When Kidder Peabody claimed that its trader Joe Jett had caused the accounting system of its parent company to book $350 million of "false profits" from the obscure activity of trading strips of government bonds in 1992–94, a veteran investment banker in a firm that does such trading commented that Jett's figures "were like your daughter comes home and says, 'Daddy, we had a great day at the lemonade stand.' You say, 'Yes, dear, that's nice,' and she says, 'We made a million dollars.' Wouldn't you want to sit her down and say, 'Dear, *how* did you make a million dollars at the lemonade stand?' " The Kidder claim was not true, by the way: Jett did not know the system was crediting him with unrealizable profits.*

Nicholas Leeson was supposed to be arbitraging the prices of futures contracts on the Nikkei index of Japanese stocks as traded at the Singapore International Monetary Exchange (SIMEX) and on the Osaka Stock Exchange, and to a lesser extent the prices of contracts on the ten-year Japanese government bond (JGB) future as traded in Singapore and in Tokyo. The theory was that because identical contracts were subject to different domestic pulls and tugs they could trade at different prices at exchanges in two different countries. A firm like Barings, with offices both in Japan and Singapore and an open phone line between the trading floors and those offices, could take advantage of these disparities by purchasing cheap in one market and selling dear in the other— instantaneously, no risk, guaranteed profit. Leeson's *net* position—shorts in one market subtracted from longs in the other—was

---

* I was Jett's "expert witness" in June 1996, when the Securities and Exchange Commission brought a proceeding against him for civil fraud.

supposed to be zero at the end of each trading day. This is a legitimate business from which respectable money can be made, assuming not too many people are in it. But even if one "legs" this trading—buying a little earlier in the day if the prices look to be rising and selling on the other exchange a little later to take advantage of the trend as well as the intermarket price differences—there is no way it could make the group that does it the most profitable single division of a large banking company, and the individual directing the group the largest single contributor to corporate profits.

And, of course, this sort of business—where the trader is supposed to have a "matched book" at the end of the day, no net exposure at all—cannot possibly require the *billion dollars* in margin deposits at the exchanges which Leeson had drained from his employers before February 23, 1995, when he left an ongoing meeting with a couple of the bank's money men and slipped off, never to return to the office, for a long weekend on the beach with his wife Lisa to celebrate his twenty-eighth birthday.

Baring Bank had not been long in the securities, let alone the derivatives, business. It had acquired the Far East division of the brokerage firm of Henderson Crothwaite in 1984, and set it up as a separate firm named Baring Far East Securities; the "Far East" was dropped after the Big Bang of deregulation in London in 1986 freed banks to own and operate domestic securities firms. In 1988, Baring Securities Japan (BSJ), a subsidiary of Baring Securities London (BSL), became a member of the Tokyo Stock Exchange, and perhaps the most successful Western stockbroker in Japan. It was definitely a broker: its basic sales pitch to clients, especially from America, where professional money managers were sick of having their orders front-run by securities firms that traded against their customers,[5] stressed that the firm acted *only* as their agent and did no trading for its own account. A company that had only fifteen employees grew to a staff of more than a thousand in 1991, with offices in Hong Kong, Singapore, Malaysia,

Thailand, Taiwan, South Korea, Indonesia, the Philippines and Australia.[6] All these offices dealt mostly with Japanese securities and derivatives. What trading BSJ's customers did in Singapore was funneled by Baring through Chase Manhattan Bank, which was a clearing member of SIMEX. Baring Securities London decided to get its own clearing membership in SIMEX in 1992, because the Japanese government had restricted futures trading with enough regulation to drive business south.

The Singapore International Monetary Exchange was a clone and protégé of the Chicago Mercantile Exchange (CME, or "Merc"), which had helped set it up in 1984, contributing the golden bell that first rang after the lion dancers had circled the floor to bring good luck, and then rang to open and close each trading day. Chicago also, more importantly, contributed the procedures that allowed Merc contracts to be created or extinguished in Singapore through a shared clearinghouse. The basic rules of SIMEX were those of the Merc, including gross margining (that is, everyone was supposed to put up margin for every contract, even if one hedged another) and the segregation of client and house accounts, a total Chinese Wall (if one may) that guaranteed no broker could use customer money to meet margin requirements on its own trading.[7]

Leeson had been hired by Baring Securities in 1989, to work as a settlements clerk in the back office. With no education beyond high school, he had done similar work at Coutts Bank and at the London office of the American Morgan Stanley. He met his wife at Barings, and they apparently established their relationship when they were both sent to Jakarta to straighten out back-office problems in Barings' Indonesia office. When Baring Futures Singapore was organized in early 1992, Leeson was sent to "head up our SIMEX operation and also act as floor manager. . . . He will report to Simon Jones [operations manager of the Singapore office] and to Gordon Bowser [head of futures and options settlements in London]."[8] At about this time, Ron Baker, an Australian with experience at Bankers Trust in *debt* derivatives, was hired by Barings in London as head of a Financial Products Group that would supervise trading in *all* derivatives, including equity exotica like the Nikkei 225.

Nick and Lisa, now married, went off to live the luxurious life of the expatriate banker in the city that arguably enjoys the highest urban standard of living in the world. There was, of course, no career future in the back office. Leeson, who had failed to become a trader in London (*everybody* in a trading house back office wants to become a trader), seems to have suggested to his bosses that if he was going to hire and supervise traders, he should take the SIMEX exams and "wear the badge" on the trading floor.[9] Soon he was on the floor every day, and loving it.

Tall and trim in Barings' purple and gold striped jacket, he became a feature of the market—and also general manager of BFS, continuing to run the back office while trading vigorously for five accounts: Baring Securities Japan, Baring Securities London, Baring Futures Singapore, Baring Securities Hong Kong and (for a while) the Tokyo office of Banque Nationale de Paris (BNP). He executed the orders phoned in to his floor clerks at SIMEX from Tokyo and Osaka and Hong Kong, and soon, to conduct his arbitrage business, he began sending orders to Tokyo and Osaka. Almost immediately, he formed a separate account 88888, "8" being the Chinese lucky number. This account was identified to SIMEX as a client account, and to London as one into which he would shovel trades that had somehow gone wrong, which happens with considerable frequency in these frenetic trading rooms. From July 3, 1992, Leeson was in a position to report different numbers to different people.

Leeson reported all his trades by computer every night to London—except that he did not need a London account for 88888, which, after all, was an error account that would be washed away in time. The computer in London therefore sloughed the 88888 trades into a suspense account that was not reconciled with the

Barings positions—though it was part of the calculation to determine how much margin BFS had to deposit at the exchanges. Baring Futures Singapore and Baring Securities both had offices in the Overseas Union Bank Building on Raffles Place—Futures on the fourteenth floor, Securities on the twenty-fourth floor. The management of the Singapore office of Baring Securities (which had general responsibility for South Asia) thought Leeson was reporting to Mike Killian, an American who was chief of all Barings' equity derivatives trading, and who divided his time between Tokyo and his home in Portland, Oregon. London and Killian thought Leeson was reporting to the managers of Barings in Singapore. Nobody worried, anyway, because Leeson's rules of engagement did not permit him to carry a position overnight.

Rawnsley's book reports that in their desperate effort to close out a rescue, the Bank of England and the assembled bankers building the lifeboat for Barings called the counterparties of Leeson's trades and tried to get them settled before the markets could open on Monday. Stephen Fay reports that calls went to Bankers Trust, Goldman Sachs and Morgan Stanley, asking them to settle for the profits they already had on their short positions in Singapore.[10] Tape recordings of these phone calls will be among the most entertaining items discovered when the Bank of England Archives are explored to the historian of the next generation.

The number of bankers who understand how commodities exchanges work is very small. In fact, Leeson, once his trades were over, *had* no counterparties as the word is normally understood. The rules of the commodities exchange are that each transaction produces two contracts: one between the exchange's clearinghouse and the buyer, the other between the exchange's clearinghouse and the seller. Because nobody ever extends credit to anybody else, the futures markets are open to all. As Terence Martell put it while research director of the New York Commodities Exchange (COMEX), "futures markets are designed to permit trading among strangers, as against other markets which permit only trading among friends."[11] The traders who had sold to or bought from Leeson were mostly long gone from these trades, and most of those whose open interest matched his had not acquired their positions in trades with Barings.

The other side of this coin is that these markets settle every day. Because these are contracts for future delivery, nobody has to pay or deliver at the time of the trade, but both sides must make a down payment. If the trade is at $100 and the margin is 5 percent, each side puts $5 into the clearinghouse. If the price goes down $5, the buyer must put up another $4.75 (5 percent of $95)—and the seller can take out all of his $5, because he's now $5 in the money. Similarly, if the price goes up $5, the seller must put up $5.25—and the buyer can take his $5 back. To the extent that an arbitrageur has a matched book—that he's long the same value of the same contracts in Singapore that he's short in Osaka, which is what we are told Barings London believed Leeson was doing—he never needs additional margin, because he can take out of the exchange where he is a winner what he has to pay into the exchange where he is a loser.

Yet on December 31, 1994, Leeson's BFS required $350 million of funding to meet its margins—and by February 24, 1995, the total was more than $1.1 *billion*, more than twice the reported capital of the Baring Group.[12] How could a man who was supposed to be running a matched book—and was showing an exact balance of contracts bought and contracts sold in his daily reports to the home office—need so much margin?

The *Report* suggests with some embarrassment that some of the margin Leeson required might reflect "front-running" Barings clients. In the internal Barings audit done in the autumn of 1994, Leeson offered as one source of his profits "proprietary positioning on the back of larger orders . . . on one of the exchanges, using the order as a stop-loss. For example, if BFS had a large buy order from a client for SIMEX Nikkei contracts, BFS could buy up to the equivalent value of OSE Nikkei contracts for its own account and if the market went up, simply sell them out for a profit on OSE. If the market went down, then they could simply execute the client's order by selling SIMEX contracts to the client (or the other broker with the order) themselves, leaving BFS with an arbitrage position that could be unwound later. . . ."[13] That's riskless trading, just like arbitrage, but it does require margin.

Then there were more technical explanations. Margin requirements were different on the two exchanges. Singapore margin calls and credits required payment the next day in dollars or two days hence in yen, while Osaka allowed three days. Thus a price movement that logically ought not to have imposed a demand for additional margin might for technical reasons leave Leeson with a need for money, a need that would increase as his positions grew, even though he remained hedged.

Leeson claimed client accounts—indeed, 88888 was presented to inquirers as a client account. The rules of the exchanges prohibit brokers from lending margin to their customers, but they don't prohibit other members of a financial group from lending money to the clients of their colleague. They should, but they don't. When London or Tokyo was asked to "top up" Singapore's margin at the futures exchanges, the assumption was that some of it was for Tokyo's proprietary trading, and some of it was for clients.

"From November, 1994," the *Report* proclaims, "the US Dollar funding requests usually split the amount being requested (itself usually a round sum amount) 50:50 between a request for client accounts and that for the house positions. . . . If the US Dollar funding requests had been in relation to genuine positions taken by clients and house, on any one day we consider it unlikely for the margin requests for these two sets of positions to be identical; as for having the requests split 50:50 most days, this in our view is beyond all possibility. Tony Hawes [of Barings' Treasury Department] appears to agree with this view. He told us that: 'It was just one of the factors that made me distrust this information. . . . It was too much of a coincidence."[14]

344

John Gapper and Nicholas Denton of the *Financial Times* say Leeson's losses began because he shaved prices for his customers to build up his trading volume. The truth is that Leeson was a bad trader. Bad traders lose money, but that doesn't mean they don't love trading. They find ways to disguise their losses and to counterfeit profits, and increasingly they go for the big score that will bring them back to even. In the last months before their disguises fall, their depradations become enormous. Leeson's basic tool for concealment was faking transactions between his semi-secret 88888 (now presumably the account of a large but hidden trader) and the accounts of Barings subsidiaries. Almost every day at the close of the market, when additional trades could be made at the closing price, Leeson would "cross" transactions between two of his accounts on the floor at SIMEX. Then as the master of the back office he would enter the transaction for the Barings subsidiary at a lower price (showing an immediate profit) and the transaction for 88888 at a higher price (adding to the humongous losses in that account, which was not being tracked by the Barings computers in London).

Meanwhile, he tried three strategies for generating profits that might get him out. One was to sell exchange-traded options, which in theory lay beyond his authority, but he was keeping the books. He sold both call options, giving their purchaser the right to buy the underlying security or index contract at a predetermined "strike" price at any time for the life of the contract, and put options, giving their purchaser the right to sell the underlying security to the options writer at the strike price at any time for the life of the contract. The most the options seller can make is his premium; if the price goes up, however, he can lose limitlessly on the call, and if it goes down, he can lose almost limitlessly on the put. Leeson usually chose a strike price for both puts and calls very near that day's price for the underlying security. If the market remained stuck at that price, he would have a cash cow, pumping out two sets of premiums; but if it moved substantially in either direction, he would have a black hole. The term of art is "selling volatility." Some commentators have argued that Leeson adopted this strategy to get the cash flow from selling the options, but in fact Singapore required option sellers to leave their receipts as margin. If the market moved strongly, however, the option seller could be required, as Leeson was, to fill the black hole with additional margin.

Meanwhile, despite the fact that he was not authorized to hold net exposure overnight, he built enormous long positions in the Nikkei futures contract (betting that the Japanese stock market would rise) and enormous short positions in the Japanese government bond futures contract. It is conceivable that he had a hedging strategy. One could make a case for the argument that the Japanese stock market, down more than 50 percent from its 1991 highs, was a good bet to recover, so long as interest rates, already low, stayed low. If interest rates rose, however, the stock market might be in trouble. Thus a short position in JGBs (which would be a winner if interest rates rose) could be seen as a sophisticated—well, semi-sophisticated—hedge against a long position in the stocks.[15]

These proprietary positions, of course, would have to be margined. Brenda Granger, the liaison in London's futures settlements office who sent most of the money, told the Board of Banking Supervision that she assumed "Treasury was lending money to Singapore to fund Tokyo's business. As a company I am sure that it is allowable: it just bothered me the way that the money was flowing, that it should all come through the house."[16] But Leeson had no authority to borrow from anybody else, except Citibank in Singapore for intraday margin needs.

In January 1995, Coopers and Lybrand (Singapore) came to do an external audit of Leeson's shop, so that profits for the year 1994 could be certified and bonuses paid. Auditor Khoo Kum Wing found an oddity: a discrepancy of about $78 million between the SIMEX settlement account on the BSF ledgers and the balance for the account in the SIMEX statement. Leeson, after several requests for information, told C&L that the difference was a receivable due to BFS from Spear, Leeds and Kellogg in New York from a transaction between Baring Securities in London and what C&L identified as "SLG." The accountants queried London, which said they had never heard about it. Leeson then confessed to the manager of Baring in Singapore that he had engaged in an unauthorized transaction—that he had brokered an over-the-counter option between SLK and his friends at Banque Nationale de Paris in Tokyo, and he had goofed, paying the $78 million price of the option to BNP before receiving the payment from SLK. Nobody checked on whether a payment to BNP had ever gone out from BSF, which had no source for such money except other parts of the Baring Group.

From an American point of view, this is perhaps the most peculiar moment in the entire Barings story. Spear, Leeds and Kellogg is the dominant market-maker in American equity securities, controlling three specialist posts on the New York Stock Exchange, four on the American Stock Exchange, and two of the four largest dealers in the over-the-counter market. Peter Kellogg, though little known to the public, would be almost everybody's nominee on Wall Street for the most influential man in American stock markets. He was both the hero and the villain of the October 1987 market crash—the hero because he was on the floor on Tuesday October 20, offering to lend money to his specialist colleagues at a time when the banks had turned tail; the villain because his house as specialist in IBM gouged purchasers in the early-morning rally that day by charging them more than $20 a share over the price SLK had paid for IBM the afternoon before. (The New York Stock Exchange as punishment assigned IBM to another specialist.)

Among the securities on the American Stock Exchange for which an SLK firm is the specialist is the Japanese put warrant, a form of option giving its purchaser the right to sell the Nikkei index, which has been at various times among the more actively traded securities on the AmEx. It is not unreasonable to believe that Leeson as the largest trader in Nikkei futures and options had some dealings with SLK.

Barings London apparently had never heard of SLK, told Coopers and Lybrand that this American firm had a capitalization of about $2 million, and that its limit as a counterparty for a trade with BSL, established in 1993 at Leeson's request, was $5 million. (The British Board of Banking Supervision notes scornfully in its report that as of September 30, 1994, SLK had a capitalization of about $268 million.)

In any event, Leeson presently told the auditors that the problem was solved. He had a fax from SLK confirming the receivable and announcing an intention to pay immediately (the fax, on SLK stationery, has an origin imprint "from Nick and Lisa" on it), a fax from Ron Baker of Barings' Financial Products Group that he had okayed the transaction, and a Citibank statement showing a wire transfer of $78 million to the BFS account. All of these, the Singapore police say, were forged. But something had happened at Citibank, which was extending intraday and probably overnight credit to Baring Futures Singapore. The week after Barings' collapse, Citibank chairman John Reed went ape, called in all his senior executives, denounced sloppy credit standards in the international section of the bank, and announced that in the future he would expect "obedience."

Coopers and Lybrand certified the BFS statement on February 3. Leeson could play his game for another three weeks. But the Kobe earthquake had happened a few weeks before, driving the stock market down and the bond market up, decimating all of Leeson's positions. He was already trading so heavily that he routinely won or lost several tens of millions of dollars every day. The three weeks after his brush with C&L saw few winners. His losses in February would total another $500 million, and absolutely doom the bank. Meanwhile, the audited statements showing large 1994 profits, implying a bonus for Leeson of about a million dollars, and more for his London supervisors, worked their way through the Barings bureaucracy, and the bonuses were about to be paid when the bank went belly-up.

3

The Singapore authorities were much less charitable than the British to the explanations offered for this preposterous but true scenario. "Mr. Leeson's product managers," the Inspectors of Baring Futures (Singapore) PTE LTD reported in October 1995, "accepted the reports of his considerable profitability with admiration rather than scepticism. . . . [Top management] discussed the issue of funding BFS on at least six occasions in January and February 1995. . . . However the preoccupation of these meetings was to arrange adequate funding lines to meet Mr. Leeson's large requirements, rather than to investigate the causes underlying these requirements."[17]

There had been an internal audit in the third quarter of 1994, the inspectors reported, which had noted the dangers inherent in the fact that Leeson both traded and supervised the back office. Still, the auditors concluded, "insofar as Mr. Leeson's trades were almost all executed for other Baring Group entities, these trades would be subject to reconciliation controls." In fact, the inspectors noted grimly, "no such reconciliation controls existed. BSL's claim that it was unaware that account 88888 existed, and also that the sum of [$600 million] which the Baring Group had remitted to BFS, was to meet the margins required for trades transacted through this account, if true, gives rise to a strong inference that key individuals of the Baring Group's management were grossly negligent, or willfully blind and reckless to the truth."[18]

Leeson's SLK story was incredible on its face, and if true was grounds for dismissal. Leeson did not have authority to broker over-the-counter options, and certainly not to advance $78 million to anybody to complete such a transaction. (A management committee meeting in London on February 13 accepted Leeson's story, and noted that "The trade expired on 30th December, but the amount was [not] recovered until 5th February. We have yet to claim interest."[19]) Instead, Peter Norris, CEO of Baring Securities, protected Leeson from further investigation, and indeed leaned on Coopers and Lybrand not to include any mention of the episode in their report. The British investigators thought the reason for that was probably to avoid calling this peculiar story to the attention of SIMEX and the regulators of the Singapore Monetary Authority. The Singapore investigators probably agreed with that diagnosis, which may explain their fury at Norris.

They argued that senior management at Barings had lied to them, especially Norris, who had recently become CEO-designate of the Baring Group. Norris had come to the top at BSL after a disastrous year in 1992, they noted, and he needed profits to show he had been the right choice. (Not that the family gave him that much credit: in a conversation in September 1993 with Brian Quinn, executive director of banking supervision for the Bank of England, Peter Baring said that the "amazing" recovery in profitability at BSL that year led him "to conclude that it was not actually terribly difficult to make money in the securities business."[20]) The British report had said that Norris had passed through Singapore on February 16 on other business, and Norris told the inspectors that he had met with Leeson only socially for a few minutes. The inspectors did not believe him.[21]

But what keeps recurring in the Singapore report is puzzlement over how England could conceivably have shipped all that money to BFS: "Some of the funds used by Mr. Leeson to finance the transactions booked in account 88888 were requested from BSL ostensibly to fund client positions. These funds were recognised by BSL as 'loans to clients.' In these circumstances, Credit Control would have been expected to take steps to verify the identities and creditworthiness of the 'clients' receiving these loans. Any such attempt would have revealed that there were no such 'clients.' However, no such attempt was made. Credit Control explained that this was because it was never informed by Settlements or Group Treasury that large remittances had been made to BFS on account of 'loans to clients.' "[22]

The Bank of England had "Large Exposure" rules, limiting any loan to a maximum of 25 percent of a bank's capital, already more generous than such limits elsewhere (in the United States, the limit was traditionally 10 percent, raised to 15 percent in the 1980s, just in time to make trouble). In January 1993, Barings wrote the Bank of England requesting an exemption from the rule for margin at the Osaka Stock Exchange. Such exchanges, Barings argued, were "quasi-sovereign." Anyway, the clearinghouses had many members, and if you divided the total margin by the number of members of the clearinghouse, it was well under 25 percent to each. "Our argument," Norris told the supervisors, "was that you should not regard the exchange as a single counterparty for large exposure purposes."[23] The Bank of England played possum. Tony Hawes, group treasurer at Barings, told the board that "It had been agreed with the Bank of England that until the policy on whether exposures to the Exchanges were a single exposure . . . the limit was a soft limit so Credit would not have been concerned."[24]

George Maclean, director of the bank group, told the investigating board that he had called Christopher Thompson, Barings' direct supervisor at the Bank, to report that Barings was over the 25 percent limit at Osaka, "and to enquire where the BoE stood on exposure to the Japanese exchanges. . . . Thompson said he was aware he owed us a response but that the matter was buried reasonably deep in his in-tray. He said, however, that he was relaxed about the exposure on the basis of our view that the exposure was in effect an exposure to all the individual members of the Exchange."[25] The board noted laconically, "We understand that the Bank does not have a record of this telephone call." If it was good for Osaka, of course, it was good for Singapore and Tokyo, too; by the end of December 1994, total exposure to the three exchanges was well over 75 percent of the bank's capital. Two months later, it would be well over 100 percent.

In the meantime, the Bank of England *had* come to a decision, and on February 1, 1995, had notifed Barings that indeed the clearinghouse of an exchange was one borrower, and total margin should not exceed 25 percent of capital. Of course, it would be a lot of trouble for the bank to cut back immediately. "In view of the nature of the exposure and its importance to your business activities in Japan, instead of instant compliance we would propose that you explore urgently whether it might be possible to reduce the exposure, for example, by persuading the nonsegregated clients to become segregated or by obtaining an authoritative legal opinion that margin provided to the exchanges to cover clients' positions was not an exposure to Barings."[26] There was no mention of Singapore in the letter. Perhaps because no on-site supervisory visit had been made to Barings in the 1990s, the Bank of England still didn't know from Singapore.

4

"[Q]uietude," the director of studies at the Council on Foreign Relations in New York wrote in the council's invariably pollyanna magazine *Foreign Affairs*, "followed the collapse of Barings Bank in late February 1995. . . . Many chicken littles had predicted during the late 1980s and early 1990s that trading in derivatives—futures, swaps and options—would trigger the next global financial crisis. But they overlooked the important role that derivatives have played in moderating systemic risk, providing banks with increased opportunities to diversity their portfolios and protect themselves from sudden market shifts. The Basle Committee has amended its accord to account for derivatives trading. Significantly, the Bank of England did little to reassure markets during the Barings collapse."[27]

The truth of the matter is that the Bank of England didn't begin to understand what had happened at Barings or what its impact might be. There *was* a systemic risk in the Barings collapse, and if the matter had been left with the banking regulators, a disaster scenario might well have played out. Though most derivatives are traded over-the-counter, the public exchanges set the important prices. And they could have frozen up if Singapore and Osaka were unable to pay out the variation margin to which the winners in their casinos were entitled on Monday.

There was blood in the water: everyone knew that the Singapore Nikkei contract had to trade way down on Monday, and the Osaka JGB contract had to trade way up. The Barings positions were going to accrue enormous additional losses. As of Monday morning, SIMEX and the Osaka exchange were responsible for those losses. Most—with luck, almost all—of these losses were covered by the margin already paid in by Barings before its demise. But there were lots of sharks. Simply selling Barings out of its positions could involve additional losses far beyond the margin on deposit. Who would pay them?

Freezing the Barings accounts as part of the bankruptcy order, the British administrators made it impossible for American commodity brokers to get at $350 million of deposits that had been left with one or another Barings entity—some of which Leeson had used and lost as part of his margin—or to get out of positions they held for which Baring had been the clearing broker. Singapore was umbilically linked to Chicago, still. Nobody knew what went on inside Osaka, which was by far the larger exchange. If those exchanges failed to open on Monday or Tuesday, the

Chicago and London and Paris and São Paulo markets might well have failed to open on Tuesday or Wednesday. Japanese city banks, already reeling from bad real estate loans, had a potential loss of $690 million on their advances to Barings. BIS in spring 1996 reported that in fact more than $250 billion of transactions could have been blocked if the Barings failure had blocked these payments.

Writing of the October days in 1987 when single-handedly he saved the world, forcing the New York banks to lend to the demoralized specialists at the New York Stock Exchange, E. Gerald Corrigan, then still president of the Federal Reserve Bank of New York, told the Williamsburg Conference on the U.S. payments system, "Many observers, myself included, are of the opinion that the greatest threat to the stability of the financial system as a whole in that period was the danger of a major default in one of these clearing and settlement systems. . . . [D]efault in one of these systems has the potential to seriously and adversely affect all other direct and indirect participants in the system, even those that are far removed from the initial source of the problem. Unlike many other types of financial problems, a major disruption in one of these systems can occur suddenly and can spread rapidly. . . . [A]ll too often their legal, technical, and operational characteristics are so complex that the direct and indirect users may not fully understand the nature and scope of the risks and exposures—including intraday exposures—that they are incurring."[28] But the Bank of England, significantly, as the Council on Foreign Relations says, did little to reassure markets.

Fortunately, Mary Schapiro of the Commodity Futures Trading Commission in the United States did quite a lot. She worked closely with Elisabeth Sam, director of SIMEX, to find the right assurance to American firms that SIMEX remained solvent, and that the doubling of margins on Nikkei contracts on Monday—clearly justified by the anticipations for increased volatility—was not a way to get other participants in the market to put up cash to cover Barings' losses. (The increased margin did mean of course that people who might otherwise have been able to take out cash could not do so, which was undoubtedly part of the purpose of the exercise.) SIMEX at American urging went out and got an additional $250 million loan from international banks active in Singapore to buttress its claims that everyone who had a winner in its casino would be paid.

Then, Schapiro told the Twentieth Annual Futures Industry Conference three weeks later, "we were able to turn our full attention to the problem of moving U.S. customer positions and funds that had been frozen as a result of the U.K. administration proceeding, and by informal steps of the Japanese exchanges. For five days, virtually eighteen hours a day, we talked, cajoled, and pressured foreign exchanges and regulators to transfer positions from various Barings accounts. We made extensive use of the good offices of the U.S. embassy in Tokyo, and we imposed upon all of our personal and professional relationships within the Japanese Ministry of Finance, the U.K. Securities and Investments Board [Schapiro had been a commissioner of the Securities and Exchange Commission before becoming chairman of the CFTC], and Securities and Futures Authority, the Bank of England, and the Monetary Authority of Singapore, as well as the Federal Reserve Board and the U.S. Treasury Department. Time differences required us to arrive at the office by seven a.m., and often not to leave until midnight or later. We spoke regularly with officials at the Osaka and Tokyo stock exchanges and the Tokyo International Financial Futures Exchange. We worked particularly closely with the Chicago Merc in one of the best demonstrations of a government-industry partnership I have ever seen. . . .

"The CFTC and regulators from Japan, Hong Kong, Singapore and the U.K. each established a command center that operated around the clock. Through these command centers, regulators communicated with each other, the various markets, the bankruptcy administrators, and multiple customers and clearing firms. Extraordinary efforts were made ad hoc to permit the transfer of positions at exchanges that had no rules for such transfers. The Asian markets designated firms to manage trading out of Barings' proprietary positions. . . . And, of course, we cannot forget"—and this was what ultimately saved the situation, Schapiro added—"that in the end, a White Knight arrived on the scene."[29]

Stephen Fay reports that on Monday Merrill Lynch decided not to meet the margin call SIMEX was preparing, which would have resulted in Merrill's expulsion from SIMEX, the immediate sale of Merrill's positions in all SIMEX contracts, and the departure of all the other American brokers. At three o'clock Tuesday morning Singapore time, Schapiro called Ko Beng Sang, chairman of the Monetary Authority of Singapore, to alert him to the dangers. Ko dressed, went to his office, and before dawn issued a statement that MAS would guarantee the payment of customer margin deposits at Barings, and Schapiro convinced Merrill to back off.[30]

The White Knight, the Dutch insurance company ING, looking for a way to expand its foothold in the banking business, especially in Asia and Latin America, paid the administrators one pound as the price for all Barings' assets, and pumped in an additional billion dollars to pay off the debts of the operating companies and restore a capital position. The American firms with frozen deposits at Barings did not in fact get their hands on their $350 million at Barings until ING took over.

Barings plc, the holding company for all the banks and the securities houses, had not long before sold $600 million of subordinated debt, and the holders of that paper were told to go whistle. Then it turned out that many of Barings' best and biggest customers were holders of the paper, and ING was on the hook for lots more.

Leo Melamed, whose child SIMEX was, set up a commission to advise the Singapore exchange and got the London end of the Merc's law firm, Mayer, Brown and Platt, to bug the British regulators and courts to release traders' money so business could continue. This was no easy task: concerned about what this episode might (and did) do to the status of British merchant banks, the British took an attitude that lawyer Eric Bettelheim (son of the great psychologist) described as "fuck the U.S.A."[31] Most observers have been highly sympathetic with SIMEX, which had twice in January and February asked Barings in London whether it knew the enormous risks to which Leeson was subjecting it—and had twice been told, Get away from me, boy, you bother me, our positions are fully hedged elsewhere. "It is tempting to suggest with the benefit of hindsight," wrote the Singapore inspectors, "that SIMEX placed undue reliance on the Barings name and the assurances given in that name. However, given the tone of BFS's letter of 10 February 1995, it is difficult to imagine circumstances in which such assurances given by any reputable merchant bank would not have been accepted."[32] Leo Melamed, for all his affection for Singapore, is less charitable: "When SIMEX called Leeson and he said, 'I'm hedged in Osaka,' you think you'd pick up a telephone and find out? If you don't talk to Osaka, you can call the Monetary Authority in Singapore and ask them to call the Ministry of Finance in Japan.

"But the first line of fault," Melamed says, "is the Barings executives themselves. Here's a guy who's twenty-seven years old and you have no controls on him at all. On a comparative negligence basis," Melamed adds, harking back to his days in law school before he became a commodities trader, "you can make a case for Leeson. I wouldn't give him more blame than maybe forty percent."

Melamed is too much of a gentleman to say so, but the Bank of England can probably take an equal share. There have been scapegoats. Christopher Thompson, who directly supervised Barings, was sacrificed quite early in the investigation. Brian Quinn, director of supervision for the BoE, retired in early 1996. But the Board of Banking Supervision found no fault with the Bank of

England itself, its rules or procedures. If it had been thought that they would, there would not have been a board.

In fairness, it should be said that there is no reason to believe that in a comparable situation, the Federal Reserve would be any more alert or effective than the Bank of England was. If, as Dennis Weatherstone observed, the capital markets have overwhelmed the credit markets, then the banking regulators are on a sinking ship. They just don't know it.

PART

III

GOVERNMENT INTERVENTIONS

12 / Government Gone Mad: The S&L Disaster

> "A company with $11 million in assets lost $800 million. With perhaps $500,000 in equity, it destroyed $800 million of insured deposits.... This anecdote is tantamount to a news report that a drunken motorist has wiped out the entire city of Pittsburgh."
>
> —JONATHAN GRAY, bank stock analyst for Sanford Bernstein, writing about the collapse of American Diversified Savings & Loan in California.[1]

The saddest story in the long history of the relationship of American government and American banking is the collapse of the savings and loan industry in the 1980s and early 1990s. The cost to the American taxpayer, counting interest on the debt the U.S. government had to assume to pay down the obligations of the Federal Savings and Loan Insurance Corporation, was *at least* $300 billion before one begins to estimate the damage done to the Texas, California, Florida, Arizona and Arkansas economies by the land boom of the early 1980s and the construction collapse at the end of the decade. But the greatest damage done was in the corruption of the regulatory and legislative processes, which invited the thievery that characterized both the boom and the bust.

When the depository institutions subcommittee of the House Banking Committee came to hold hearings on this disaster, its chairman, Democratic congressman Frank Annunzio of Illinois, having been himself a faithful servant of the S&L lobbyists, arranged to have a banner reading "Jail the S&L Crooks!" flung across the wall stage right in the chamber. Fittingly, the banner covered the portrait of former chairman Fernand St. Germain, who had grown rich on his investments in several International House of Pancake franchises financed by a failed S&L. This is a truly wondrous tale, full of colorful characters, greedy fools, doctrinaire knaves and egregious crooks.

But the real story was the systematic, sometimes ignorant and sometimes deliberate misdiagnosis of the disease that was wasting the business, and the administration of quack remedies in response.[2] As federal judge Jack B. Weinstein put it, throwing out a criminal case against a criminal S&L executive, "Congress and the Home Loan Bank Board are directly responsible for what happened here. The government, in removing adequate controls, . . . led to the activities now complained of."[3]

The 1980s were by no means the first time that the viability of the S&Ls had been called into question. They were originally voluntary associations, part of the national social capital Robert Putnam of Harvard has written about so eloquently in deploring the decline of parents' associations, Lions Clubs, bowling leagues and the like. People pooled their money to make it possible for members of the association to get mortgages on their houses without falling into the hands of loan sharks. (Banks, which had short-term deposits, were not supposed to make mortgage loans; nationally chartered banks were forbidden to lend on the security of real estate until the Federal Reserve Act of 1913, which presumably made the banking system safer, and heavily restricted in the kind of real estate they could support until the McFadden Act of 1927.) If any number of members needed their money back, the mortgage-lending association was not very likely to have it, because it couldn't call its loans.

Thus S&Ls were cooperatives in which members bought non-negotiable shares, not "banks," which took deposits. Normally, the terms of share purchase provided that the association could delay for up to one year the members' access to their money when they wished to return the shares. Thousands of these state-chartered associations went bankrupt in the Great Depression, when a quarter of the country lost their jobs and the general deflation meant that houses were worth less than the mortgages their owners had taken to buy them.

Seeking the revival of the housing industry, Herbert Hoover's administration (with a Democratic Congress) formed the Federal Home Loan Bank system, a dozen district public-purpose "banks," owned like the Federal Reserve banks by their member institutions but controlled like the Fed by a national "board" appointed by the president and confirmed by the Senate. These banks, which still survive with $150 billion in assets (funded in part by the kind of crazy note that was Y.D.W.T.K. when my Texas builder tried to find out what it was worth), were empowered to borrow money with what looked like (but wasn't quite) a federal guarantee, and to onlend that money to its member S&Ls. To keep them in business when the S&Ls began to sink, Congress authorized an expansion of their membership to include all banks that held more than 10 percent of their assets in home mortgages.

The New Deal added a Home Owners Loan Corporation, which bought mortgages from S&Ls to keep them liquid, and a Federal Housing Administration to insure home mortgages and make them marketable nationwide to insurance companies and the like. The Housing Act of 1934 also empowered the Federal Home Loan Bank Board to issue national charters for S&Ls—which despite their national charter were restricted to the state of their origin. They were permitted to lend only within a radius of fifty miles of a branch office.

The organizing principle remained the share, not the deposit, a fact that had interesting corollaries. S&Ls could not promise a rate of return on their shares, because they could pay "dividends" only out of their profits. Milton Friedman's and Anna Schwartz's *Monetary History* as late as 1963 (indeed, in the paperback editions printed as late as 1979) consistently referred to people's money in S&Ls as "shares." By the same token, S&L shares were not subject to the interest-rate controls that the government imposed on banks in 1933, and the S&Ls could advertise a current dividend that usually ran considerably higher than what the banks were paying. Share drafts, as the credit unions came to call them, were not permitted—people could take cash out of their shares at the S&L, but couldn't write checks against their value for payment to third parties.

But the truth was that the purchase of an S&L share was very much like a deposit in a bank. A horror of bank runs had been so instilled in everyone who had anything to do with such institutions that no one was willing to risk the publicity associated with a delay in cashing in S&L shares. So in fact shares at S&Ls could be cashed on demand, though they couldn't be used for third-party payments—no checkbooks.

After 1934, a Federal Savings and Loan Insurance Corporation stood behind the shares if the S&L didn't have either money or paper to discount at its regional Home Loan Bank. The FSLIC couldn't give the shareholder cash for his shares, but it could give him an account at another, solvent insured S&L, from which, presumably, he could withdraw cash. Oddly, the law provided that alternatively, at his own motion, the shareholder could take an FSLIC non-interest-bearing "debenture" rather than an account elsewhere.[4] In 1950, the FSLIC guarantee was put on a par with the Federal Deposit Insurance Corporation guarantee at the banks, and the shareholder in a failed S&L could get cash "as soon as possible," which was also the language of the FDIC Act. From 1934 to 1981, total losses at FSLIC ran only $630 million.

But as early as 1966, maintaining the viability of the S&Ls had taken some fairly fancy footwork. In December of 1965, Federal Reserve Board chairman William McChesney Martin had decided that the inflationary pressures from the Vietnam War were such that the Fed would have to restrain the economy by raising interest rates. (He had actually made this decision in the summer, and was about to announce it in October when "I was hauled over to the White House by [President Lyndon] Johnson. . . . He said, 'You know, Bill, I'm having my gall bladder out. You wouldn't do it while I'm having my gall bladder out, would you?' All I could say was, 'I've had my gall bladder out. It isn't so bad.' But I went home to my wife and I said, 'Well, suppose the President is in the hospital and I raise the discount rate and he dies. . . .' " In early December, when Johnson was safely recuperating on his Texas ranch, Martin moved.[5]

In the shibboleth of a later time, S&Ls borrowed short (paid interest for deposits that could be withdrawn at will, or for CDs that ran six months to a year) and lent very long (wrote thirty-year mortgages). When interest rates rose, the value of a long-term fixed-rate mortgage fell fast, to something not far from the price of a new investment that would yield the same cash flow at these higher rates than this mortgage yielded at the old lower rates.

California S&Ls were buying money all over the country in 1966, bidding higher future "dividends" than banks could offer under the Fed's interest-rate restrictions, or would have offered if they could have. Suddenly a number of S&Ls were at least technically insolvent. Two sizable associations failed.

As part of the bail out arrangements in 1966, S&Ls were allowed to describe what customers did when they put money into the association as a "deposit" rather than a "share purchase." In return, the Home Loan Bank Board agreed to control the interest rates insured S&Ls could pay, allowing them a one-quarter percent "differential" over the maximum rates the Fed permitted to the banks. There was, however, as the economist Andrew Carron pointed out, a further trade-off in the marketplace. The operating expenses of S&Ls rose as "nonprice competition (in the form of more service) . . . replaced price competition (in the form of higher interest rates)."[6] And the dangers of borrowing short and lending long were not diminished by the imposition of interest-rate ceilings on consumer deposits, especially after money market funds made it possible for consumers to get higher rates elsewhere. Now, if S&Ls couldn't pay market rates for money, their deposits would bleed away to the money market funds, and they would have to sell mortgages to pay back the depositors.

In the case of mortgage lending, these risks were heightened by the fact that the householder who took a mortgage had a one-way option: if rates went up, he hung onto his low-rate mortgage, and if rates went down, he could pay off his high-rate mortgage by taking a new low-rate mortgage. This was a major source of the extraordinary inflation in home prices in the 1970s and 1980s, when volatility in inflation rates and interest rates made such an option increasingly valuable to its holder.

So the S&Ls would be losers when rates went up, but their winnings would be limited when rates went down. They suffered a double whammy. As President Reagan's National Commission on Housing put it, the "system for mobilizing consumer savings for housing . . . required either a currency of relatively stable value, or the absence of competitive repositories for personal savings, or both."[7] Once inflation took hold, the only obvious solution was the adjustable-rate mortgage, and in 1970 California passed a law permitting such mortgages for state-chartered institutions, which meant most of the larger California S&Ls. But the Home Loan Bank Board, advised of congressional opposition, prohibited federally chartered S&Ls from offering mortgages with interest rates that fluctuated according to changes in market rates.

To ride out such storms, the Nixon administration decided, S&Ls would need the power to borrow money in the bond market, which mutual associations could not do. Preston Martin, a lean and cynical academic turned politician and later entrepreneur, was then chairman of the Home Loan Bank Board. He started a drive to persuade S&L managements—a self-perpetuating group subject to discipline neither from the market nor from stockholders—that they should convert their associations to joint-stock organizations. Martin worked to preserve some of the benefits of these conversions for the depositors, but increasingly the easy way to induce a conversion was to let the executives of the association profit substantially by it, awarding stock to themselves and their directors. Though some of the more extravagant failures in the S&L industry occurred in mutuals (like California's Eureka Savings, where a pistol-packing CEO installed a two-story-high indoor waterfall as part of the decor of his office suite), most of the worst gambling was done in the joint-stock S&Ls.

In 1975, Maurice Mann was president of the Federal Home Loan Bank of San Francisco—a jovial, balding Bostonian Ph.D. in economics, a Republican because he couldn't see why not, who had served at the Federal Reserve Bank of Cleveland and as assistant director of Richard Nixon's Office of Management and Budget. He offered the California S&Ls an index to which the rates on adjustable-rate mortgages (ARMs) could be linked. This was the average cost of funds to S&Ls in the Eleventh District, incorporating California, Nevada and Arizona. To that rate, the S&L in Mann's formula could add 225 basis points (2$\frac{1}{4}$ percentage points) to cover its expenses and profit. This was inflexible and backward-looking (the S&L didn't get a chance to raise rates until six months after its cost of funds had gone up), and most people hated and still hate the idea that they would not know from year to year what their mortgages would cost them. It would be necessary to tempt people with very low teaser rates for the first year to get them to commit to an ARM in later years—and there remained a kind of one-way option, for when rates went down people would lock in a fixed-rate mortgage.

Moreover, not everybody could hack it on 225 basis points of gross revenue. Mark Taper, the grand old man of California S&Ls (born in Poland, seasoned as a home-builder in pre-war England, triumphant as a banker in postwar America), had laid it down as a rule of life that an S&L's G&A (general and administrative) expenses had to be less than 1 percent of its assets. He was a total skinflint, decorating his branches with orange curtains and carpets because the color orange faded more slowly in the sun, and taking care of the worn carpet beside his own desk by having a piece patched in from under the couch.[8] He had his successful followers. Herbert and Marian Sandler, joint CEOs of World Savings in Oakland, were transplanted New Yorkers who came out of investment banking and could measure the costs of a business very accurately. (Marian remembers that her first job was with Leon Levy at the Wall Street house of Oppenheimer and Company in the 1950s. "Leon," Marian Sandler said, "thinks in *decades*. That's my education. We're the country's third-largest thrift, because the others went under.") But most S&L operators were builders, and many of them were cowboys like Charles Knapp, who bought Taper's American Savings and Loan to merge with his State Savings, and wanted all the perks of big-time corporate life for himself and his buddies. The public unraveling of the S&L swindle can be said to have started in May 1984, when a Home Loan Bank Board that was still considered a pussycat of a regulator took public steps to prevent Knapp from issuing $225 million of debentures to get cash to prop up the price of his stock.

Efforts to get adjustable-rate mortgages on a national basis were frustrated by politicians. Jay Janis, a New York homebuilder of some sophistication, became chairman of the Home Loan Bank Board in the Jimmy Carter years. He was told by Senate Banking Committee chairman William Proxmire that under no circumstances would he be allowed to tamper with the fixed-rate mortgage. His compromise, in which he devoutly believed, involved "Canadian roll-over" mortgages written for a five-year term, which would in theory be matched by five-year CDs sold to the public. This sort of "maturity matching" would take the risk (and, as Janis did not entirely understand, most of the

profit) out of mortgage investment. S&Ls could earn fees for originating mortgages and servicing the coupons homeowners had to
pay every month, but those revenue streams were equally available to "mortgage bankers," agents of money pools like Fannie
Mae and Freddie Mac—or the big regional banks as intermediaries to Fannie and Freddie—which had much lower expenses
than the S&Ls.

Everything had been made worse for the S&Ls by legislation
in California and a dozen other states that prohibited the enforcement of the standard "due-on-sale" clauses in American home
mortgages. These clauses required the purchaser of a house to pay
off the seller's mortgage and take a new one at whatever rates
were in the market. It should be noted that when rates rose, the
benefits from prohibiting due-on-sale went not to the buyer but to
the seller of the house, who could charge a higher price if the purchaser could be promised lower mortgage payments from the
lower interest rates of prior years. In 1980, in the case of
Wellenkamp v. *Bank of America*, the law was upheld by the
Supreme Court of California, the biggest state, where the most
new mortgages were written every year and the biggest S&Ls
were located. The prohibition of due-on-sale clauses did not necessarily restrain federally chartered S&Ls, because the Federal
Home Loan Bank Board in 1976 had adopted a regulation pre-
empting such state laws—and in 1982 its authority to do so was
upheld by the U.S. Supreme Court in *First Fidelity Federal Savings and Loan* v. *de la Cuesta*.[9]

Quite a lot of future trouble was caused by the contrast
between the permanent mortgage the state-chartered S&Ls were
compelled to offer and the mortgage extinguished on sale which
was available to the federally chartered S&L. The fees paid
by state-chartered S&Ls supported a large California thrift-
supervision department, which would be decimated if these S&Ls
switched to federal charters. The state legislature in bipartisan
comity (there was only one vote against the bill in each house)

decided that the way to level the playing field was to give state-chartered S&Ls enormously expanded asset powers—the right to develop property themselves, make commercial loans, buy junk bonds, make direct investments in nonfinancial businesses, and so forth.

This Nolan Act, named for the Republican leader of the state assembly, permitted S&L operators in effect to own stock in and lend money to whatever business ventures they might like to attempt. Charles Knapp told financial analysts in New York that his American Savings and Loan was going to use insured deposits to buy up Merrill Lynch, and it did become at one point the largest shareholder in American Express. Charles Keating acquired Lincoln Savings and Loan with the help of Mike Milken of Drexel Burnham, and promptly became a prime customer for his junk bonds. This expansion of asset powers meant that the taxpayer through deposit insurance was to be a co-venturer with an incredible crew of speculators, incompetents, and thieves. It set up the Federal Savings and Loan Insurance Corporation (FSLIC) for unimaginable losses in the succeeding years. One of its great innocent advocates was Alan Greenspan, then a private consultant, who accepted a $40,000 fee for writing a letter to the Federal Home Loan Bank Board praising the business acumen of Charlie Keating and the theory that said it was fine for Keating to use insured deposits to fund Milken's paper mill.

The background to this nonsense was that during the key years of escalating interest rates, 1978 to 1982, many S&Ls were stuck with long-established mortgage portfolios that on average yielded less than their cost of funds. They had losses on their gross receipts—on what they had to pay for money next to what they made by lending it out—even before they counted their expenses. CEOs of savings associations went to conventions with cards tucked in their shirt pockets, on which were written the dates at which their institutions would become insolvent.

In the meantime, the rules of the game were dramatically changed on the federal level by the Depository Institutions Deregulation and Monetary Control Act of 1980 (DIDMCA). A judge had killed off NOW accounts at the savings banks and S&Ls (and the automatic transfer accounts that had given the banks a competitive product, sweeping money out of a savings account whenever it was needed to honor a check). He gave Congress until December 31, 1979, to change the Federal Deposit Insurance Act if it wished to legitimize such interest-bearing transaction accounts. The House Banking Committee could not agree on a bill before that date, and Congress gave itself a three-month extension.

This was to be the last term in Congress for Henry Reuss, chairman of the committee, who thought he was seriously ill. (He wasn't: the country would have been lots better off in the 1980s if Henry Reuss had gone to a less alarmist doctor.) He wanted to leave a substantial piece of legislation as his legacy from his time in the banking committee chair, and he refused to approve a stopgap bill that would go beyond March 31, 1980. *Real* change in American banking laws was politically impossible: Jimmy Carter was running for reelection, and remembered vividly the fuss and feathers that had greeted his suggestion when governor of Georgia that something might be done about that state's unit-banking law. But at least the foolishness of government-regulated interest rates could be eliminated.

Reg Q, the Federal Reserve's interest-rate controller, was not without its supporters. Anthony Frank, CEO of Citizens Savings and Loan in San Francisco (which he later built into First Nationwide Savings, before departing to be postmaster general), told a meeting that for the S&Ls to "meet our function in this society," the first requirement was "long-term extension of Regulation Q with a rate differential. There is no number 2 because the space between Q and everything else is so great."[10] Smaller banks throughout the country worried that liberating the money-center banks to pay whatever interest they wished would enable them to drain the countryside of funds.

Reuss agreed to permit a six-year phase-out of interest-rate controls (which quickly created a new bureaucratic instrument of banking regulation to haggle over how fast the relaxation should occur). But it really didn't make sense to continue limiting the interest rates the depositories could pay. When short-term rates were higher than long-term rates, it was duck soup for the money market funds to put together a very safe investment portfolio of Treasury bills and AAA-rated commercial paper that yielded a higher return than the government permitted banks and S&Ls to pay. They could then advertise higher rates and equal safety and take the money out of the banks and S&Ls with minimal marketing expenses.

Indeed, the regulators had been compelled to permit banks and S&Ls to sell fixed-term certificates of deposit (penalty for "premature withdrawal") at market rates. A rising proportion of S&L funds—the total would reach 50 percent in 1981—were being secured with such CDs. What the continuation of Reg Q really meant was that passbook savers, predominantly older people and poorer people, would get less interest on their savings, while more educated consumers would get the market rate of return.

The S&Ls did not begin to understand the danger they were in. George Mitchell of the Federal Reserve Board, who had midwestern roots and a strong understanding of how financial institutions operated, went around the country in the late 1970s urging the S&Ls to sell the longest-dated certificates possible, and do their other borrowings at the longest available terms, but long-term debt still cost more than short in those days, and almost without exception the S&Ls took their chances.

California S&Ls had enormous political clout; the California delegation to the conference that was to reconcile House and

Senate versions of the new banking bill, fighting the targeted end of Reg Q, prevented the committee from reaching an agreement. Among the issues on the table was the difference between a Senate provision that would lift the maximum insured deposit to $60,000 and a House provision that would leave that maximum where it was, at $40,000. At midnight, Senator Alan Cranston of California, number two in the hierarchy of the Democratic leadership, came to the conference with an offer from his paymasters: if the committee would raise the maximum amount for insurance to $100,000, the California delegation would vote for the bill. And so it was done.

But the worst single aspect of the DIDMCA was noncontroversial in Congress. This was, in the words of the builder-scholar-mortgage banker Ned Eichler, "the authorization of commercial real estate loans. Banks and insurance companies were already aggressively offering this kind of financing, and pension funds were buying commercial properties for cash. How did commercial mortgages, historically a high-risk form of lending, solve the maturity mismatch? Were not thrifts, which had no experience in this area, likely to be plagued by commercial bank and insurance company rejects?"[11] The question answered itself—pretty quickly, too.

Not long after the DIDMCA was passed, Eichler, a San Francisco native, visited Cranston to tell him that the S&Ls were in an all-but-terminal crisis. Cranston took a minute off from dunning him for a political contribution to ask more or less idly what Eichler thought should be done about it. "The industry has to shrink," Eichler began, and Cranston cut him off. "I would do *anything*," he said, "to prevent that."

Behind all this turmoil lay the unpleasant truth that the S&Ls were losing their social and economic function. Part of the original New Deal legislation in the housing area had been authorization for establishment of a Federal National Mortgage Association, which would sell bonds and use the proceeds to buy mortgages.

Private enterprise in the 1930s did not respond to the invitation, and the government itself started Fannie Mae as a customer for the mortgages the Federal Housing Administration would insure. In the 1960s, new federal budget rules inadvertently put Fannie Mae on budget, which meant that its mortgage purchases would balloon the deficit. Lyndon Johnson then privatized the association, keeping the social-purpose, subsidized part of its lending in a newly formed Government National Mortgage Association (GNMA, or Ginnie Mae). These organizations related mostly to mortgage bankers—S&Ls were lenders which held the mortgages they originated.

In 1970, the Home Loan Bank Board formed a Federal National Mortgage Corporation, otherwise Freddie Mac, which would offer the public "pass-through" securities—bonds that "passed through" to their holders every month what homeowners paid on their mortgages—so that S&Ls could improve their liquidity by "securitizing" and selling some of their mortgages. With their easy and quick access to funds from the markets (Fannie and Freddie securities do not have to be registered with the SEC), these "government-sponsored enterprises" were by 1980 becoming by far the largest mortgage holders in the country.

On the other side of the teller's cage, S&Ls were losing their grip on consumers. Banks were offering savings accounts, and mutual funds were offering a range of high-yielding uninsured alternatives for the people who used to put their money into S&Ls. There were about 4,000 S&Ls, but there were 14,000 banks, and not many communities where there was an S&L but not a bank. The question of who *needed* S&Ls was there to be asked. Nobody asked it.

2

When Ronald Reagan came to office in 1981, he found a terribly—indeed, terminally—sick S&L industry. Even by the highly permissive accounting standards of federal regulators, the S&Ls were supporting $650 billion of assets on a net worth of $32 billion—and would lose more than $4.5 billion of that net worth in Reagan's first year. If the assets were marked to their market value, the industry had a net worth of *negative* $80 billion.[12] Among the advisers to Reagan's campaign had been a House Banking Committee staffer named Robert Feinberg. After the election, Feinberg put through a memo saying to the President-elect's transition team what Eichler had said to Cranston. He received the same reply, too. Instead of Feinberg, Reagan appointed as his liaison with the Home Loan Bank Board Ed Gray, a former newspaperman and press secretary for Reagan when he was governor of California, who had subsequently signed on to direct public relations for a San Diego S&L. And as chairman of the Home Loan Bank Board, he chose Richard Pratt, forty-three years old, a professor at the University of Utah, who had a doctorate in business administration but had all his working life been an academic or a staff economist for the U.S. Savings and Loan League.

Black-haired, bull-necked, muscular, unscrupulous in controversy and terrifyingly intelligent, a rider of motorbikes, Pratt quickly saw that deposit insurance, which he had previously considered a given in the situation, was in reality what made the situation hopeless. Deposit insurance enabled proprietors to draw deposits from the public after they were insolvent beyond the hope of rescue. Once they no longer had any of their own money in the institution, they had reason to gamble as wildly as they could: if they won, they would keep it; if they lost, the government would pay back the depositors. Extension of asset powers would simply extend the number of casinos to which such proprietors could take their money.

But nothing could be done about deposit insurance. So the Home Loan Bank Board would have to take a gamble, doing what it could to keep the S&Ls going until interest rates turned down and their hoard of mortgages became profitable again. Capital requirements were lowered to 3 percent of assets: for every dollar of capital, an S&L could increase its size by $33. Not many S&Ls could keep recruiting additional cash in their own communities, and prior to 1981, deposits bought from brokers had been permitted only to a total of 5 percent of all deposits; now the fraction of deposits which came through paid brokers would become unlimited. Charles Keating of Lincoln Savings and Loan paid Prudential-Bache as much as 4.68 percent commission to bring him money.

Pratt has denied vigorously and to my face, in a debate the group of the one hundred largest S&Ls staged at the La Costa resort in 1991, that he ever believed the industry could "grow out of its problems." But the fact is that in Pratt's second year at the Home Loan Bank Board the industry's assets *did* grow by more than 17 percent, and that the changes in rules that he put through his board greatly facilitated that growth. And the Garn–St. Germain Act of 1982, which began its progress through Congress as "the Pratt bill" and mostly codified the regulatory changes Pratt had already put through at the Home Loan Bank Board, really opened the barn door to allow all the animals to escape.

There were literally dozens of regulatory relaxations, most of which contributed to the later raid on the taxpayers, but four stand out.

The first was the relaxation of capital standards. The Federal Home Loan Bank of San Francisco calculated that under the new rules a man with $2 million in hand could start an S&L and get himself $1.3 billion of insured deposits—$99.85 of other people's money for every 15 cents of his own—to invest as he pleased. In the first year and a half after the Nolan Act, a California S&L commissioner chartered no fewer than 210 new S&Ls in that state alone: enterprising law firms held seminars up and down the state of California, drumming up business in new S&L charters. California law, one notes in passing, permitted state-chartered S&Ls to contribute to political candidates. Pratt in later years did not defend this change in regulations: "Lowering the capital standards," he conceded, nodding briskly, "did allow the problems to increase. No question about it."

The second disastrous change involved procedures for rescuing insolvent S&Ls through merger. Pratt changed the bank board's accounting rules to permit an S&L that acquired another S&L to capitalize as "goodwill" the difference between the net worth of the acquired institution and the price paid for it—and to write off that "goodwill" over as many as forty years. The logic of "goodwill" as an asset is that businessmen are rational, so when one company pays another company more than the net asset value of the business being bought, that business must have "intangible assets"—a franchise, a location, a brand name, a customer list—that will generate income in the future.

But the intangible asset of a money-losing S&L is its deposit insurance, which the government sells it cheap. Thanks to deposit insurance and the Home Loan Bank Board's permissive capital standards, every dollar of goodwill booked into the acquiring S&L would make possible the acquisition of at least another $33 of other people's money in the form of insured deposits. As the game played, an insolvent, money-losing S&L with mounds of low-rate mortgages and bad loans would be "worth" more to an acquirer than an S&L which was still above water, because the goodwill that could be booked by purchasing it gave greater opportunities for expansion. In fact, one insolvent S&L could acquire another such, and the two combined would suddenly show enough capital to keep operating.

Depreciating this goodwill over forty years legitimated fraud, because the average duration of a mortgage was twelve years. As the low-rate mortgages were paid off, the S&L instead of writing off the goodwill it had acquired by purchasing them at a price below their face value could take a profit and pay dividends to its owners—forgetting about its obligation to write off what was still after twelve years the surviving 70 percent of the goodwill on its books. Because each year's reduction of the "asset" goodwill produced a one-for-one reduction in the "capital" goodwill on the liability side of the balance sheet, the continuing write-offs of that 70 percent doomed the S&L to severe shrinkage or eventual insolvency.

When Congress got wise to the S&L scam in 1989, it yanked all "supervisory goodwill" off S&L balance sheets in one swoop, making several dozen institutions instantly insolvent. Several of them sued, led by Glendale Federal of California, which had counted as capital more than a billion dollars of goodwill acquired when the Home Loan Bank Board talked its directors into buying some doggy S&Ls in Florida. Their argument was that the bank board had promised them the accounting use of this fiction and the government could not six or seven years later require them to live in a nonfiction world. The cases wended their way gradually through the federal courts, and in 1996 Glendale Federal won, which will cost the taxpayers several billion dollars more as the former owners of the other S&Ls seized by the regulators for insufficient capital bring their own lawsuits. What the Supreme Court did not recognize was that Congress had not killed but had merely accelerated the demise of these institutions, which were doomed in any event by the need to continue writing off this "goodwill" at the rate of 2.5 percent per year.

The third ruinous regulatory change was Pratt's masterpiece: "Memorandum R-49," approved in September 1981, which encouraged "loss deferral." Under the terms of this rule, S&Ls could sell loans on which they showed a loss and amortize the loss over the life of the loan. There would, of course, be an immediate loss—and that loss the S&Ls could show in the set of books they kept for the Internal Revenue Service. The 1981 tax bill, passed the month before, had set up a crazy "safe harbor" system by which companies could carry back to any and all of the five previous years losses taken after 1980, which meant that the IRS would have to give an S&L conducting this activity a refund on past taxes.

At the beginning, Memorandum R-49 was a tax dodge pure and simple: the S&L exchanged whole mortgages for Fannie Mae and Freddie Mac pass-through paper of the same market value, and was allowed to take as a loss for tax purposes the difference between the face value of the mortgage and the market value of the paper for which it was exchanged. This generated about $1.5 billion of tax refunds, which the IRS disputed, but the courts came down on the side of the S&Ls, on the grounds that the losses were real, which they were.

But Memorandum R-49 could serve another function. Pratt and the Bank Board staff—and the staff of Reagan's Housing Commission, and my colleagues on its finance committee—were fully convinced that the salvation of the S&Ls lay in diversification. By encouraging S&Ls to cash in their underwater mortgages, Pratt was helping them find funds for new and different investments. After the first months, the trick of swapping mortgages for Freddie Mac paper became boring, and the S&Ls discovered the wonderful world of exotic investments.

Herbert Sandler of World Savings vividly remembers what happened. "The tin men," he says, affecting the accents of a movie con man while making reference to the movie about aluminum-siding salesmen, "came out of Wall Street. They said, 'Pssst. You dere, you wit da S&L. Yer in trouble, yer board's upset, because yer showin' a loss, ya got too many low-yield mortgages. But we can package doze mortgages for ya into mortgage-backed securities, and we can sell doze securities, and ya won't even have to show a loss onna sale. Den we can take all da money ya get from da sale and put it inta some high-yield paper we're underwriting, and yer gonna be a hero—yer gonna show a profit.' And," Sandler adds in his own voice, "everybody took those deals." Under the new rules the ambitious S&L operator could buy loans other than mortgages, and junk bonds were loans. Among those who used the invitation offered by the Home Loan Bank Board's approval of loss deferral was "the candy man" (to use the label pinned on him by Robert Monks of Institutional Shareholders Services): Michael Milken of Drexel Burnham.

Even insiders in the S&L disaster still have little sense of how much damage was done by the consequent eruption of Wall Street into the little world of the S&Ls. The debilitation of the industry is in large part the result of its contact with a more intelligent and more predatory form of life. It was like the Indian tribes when the white settler brought them measles. A real estate developer in Dallas describes the scene: "When the salesmen from Wall Street worked over the S&Ls here, it was like the rocket scientists selling to drivers of Conestoga wagons. And all around the encampment were the regulators, scratching their heads and wondering how the wagon drivers had managed to get those blocks of wood so they could roll." For once they had this paper that Wall Street sold them, the proprietors of the S&Ls could trade it, following the wonderful, guaranteed models of "risk-controlled arbitrage" that these brilliant people on Wall Street had designed just for them. Just like the derivatives the corporate customers were sold in the 1990s, after the S&L market dried up.

The Financial Accounting Standards Board wouldn't accept loss deferral for S&L accounting, and Pratt made a pilgrimage to what was then their parklike monastery in Greenwich, Connecticut, to plead with the seven board members. "Do you," he asked in peroration, "want the demise of this industry on your conscience?" FASB, which would later compromise with Pratt on the crazy forty-year amortization of goodwill (allowing only amortization over the twelve-year average duration of mortgages), could not compromise here. But the great accounting firms felt themselves protected by the bank board and its "Memorandum," and gave clean statements to some remarkably dirty balance sheets.

The final villainy of Memorandum R-49 was that it sabotaged the one good argument for trying to keep the thrifts alive through the horrors of 1981–82: that when interest rates turned, they would be viable again. By encouraging the sale of the mortgages that would recover their value if interest rates dropped, as they did after August 1982, Memorandum R-49 guaranteed that the profits from the turn in the rates would go not to the S&Ls but to the Wall Street houses that bought their mortgages and sold them a mess of pottage.

The fourth and perhaps most devastating regulatory change came in November 1982, when the Home Loan Bank Board permitted S&Ls to credit themselves with "appraised equity capital." An S&L that owned commercial property, as increasing fractions did, either through foreclosure or because some important states permitted direct investment of S&L deposits, could credit itself with any increase in the appraised value of that property and take that credit into capital (allowing, once again, the recruitment of $33 in insured deposits for each $1 of appraised equity increase). Given the low professional and moral state of real estate appraisal, this rule was a direct invitation to cheating. In "daisy-chain" situations, where a number of S&Ls worked together (Empire, Alamo, Vernon, Sunbelt in Texas; Lincoln, Centrust, Imperial, Western of Dallas and San Jacinto in Milkenland), it was child's play to trade land and securities back and forth (incurring no tax liability, for the trade of like assets did not create taxable gain) at prices that grew and grew. In Texas, these procedures, developed originally to protect the value of bad loans, were called "trading the dead horse for the dead cow." In Washington, it was known as "deregulation."

3

Edward J. Kane, economics professor at Ohio State and later at Boston College, inventor of the phrase "zombie thrifts," has pioneered "public choice" theory, which holds that government regulators are motivated by self-interest, just like everybody else. They oppose all restrictions on their authority to declare their wards insolvent or keep them alive; insist on discretionary, judgment-based rather than rule-based monetary control; oppose the public reporting of bank assets (anyone who buys a money market mutual fund gets quarterly statements of how the fund has invested his money, but purchasers of money market accounts at banks never have the slightest notion of what the bank is buying); and fight the very *idea* of valuing bank assets at their market value, even when those assets are publicly traded securities. Deposit insurance is beloved by the regulators, Kane argues, because through deposit insurance the government protects banks and S&Ls from market discipline and thereby makes them totally dependent on their regulator. And to make the cheese more binding, the regulators will deliberately underprice deposit insurance to make sure their wards will have to take it.

Few programs are as popular as deposit insurance. Adopting the first such law in 1829, the New York State legislature wrote that "The loss by the insolvency of banks falls upon the farmer, the mechanic and the laborer, who are least acquainted with the condition of banks, and who, of all others, are most illy able either to guard against or sustain a loss by their failure. The protection and security of this valuable portion of our population demands from us, in their favor, our most untiring exertions."[13] Justice Oliver Wendell Holmes, Jr., in 1911 defended the right of states to assess banks for the establishment of an insurance system, "to make safe the almost compulsory resort of depositors to banks as the only available means of keeping money on hand."[14] In 1950, the Federal Reserve proclaimed that "the major value of deposit insurance is for the Nation as a whole. By assuring the public, individuals and businesses alike, that cash in the form of bank deposits is insured up to a prescribed maximum, a major cause of instability in the nation's money supply is removed."[15]

Outside a narrow group of economists, the perceived need in the early 1980s was for a *strengthening* of deposit insurance. Indeed, the Housing Commission (in large part at my urging) recommended in 1982 that "Congress act to back up the statements of the secretary of the treasury and White House spokesmen that the federal government will stand behind the repayment of all deposits in federally insured banks and thrifts, up to the legal ceiling. What is needed is not encouraging resolutions but legislation to establish a deeper line of credit for the insurance corporations at the Treasury and/or the Federal Reserve."[16]

In a matter of months, I learned better. The obvious truth was that the wider asset powers the commission recommended were incompatible with deposit insurance. If the government was going to insure the deposits, it had to control the use to which the bank and S&Ls could put those deposits. When the Garn–St. Germain Act in late 1982 vastly extended the asset powers of the banks and S&Ls without doing anything about deposit insurance, I wrote an op-ed piece in the *New York Times* about "why the old Prudential National Trust had changed its name to Crazy Louie Bank N.A. [which advertised] 'Shop the banks! Shop the savings banks! Shop the money market funds. Then take your money to Crazy Louie's. He'll beat them all! Crazy Louie's Maniacal Money Account will *always* pay the highest interest rates in town! And that interest is *guaranteed*, because Louie is a member of the FDIC, an agency of the federal government, which insures your deposits—not only the principal, but the interest, too."[17] Accepting the argument that banks and S&Ls could not make a living in the businesses to which they were then restricted required at the least major modification of deposit insurance, or the insurance funds would self-destruct.

By the time he left the Home Loan Bank Board, Dick Pratt had learned the damage that could be done by deposit insurance. His final statement, *Agenda for Reform*, submitted to the congressional banking committees in spring 1983, warned that "Under the system in place today the federal government shares in any losses, while gains accrue entirely to those who have interests in depository institutions. A rational course of action in these circumstances is for the firm to engage in activities that may be excessively risky."[18]

Pratt was succeeded as Chairman by Edwin Gray, who came over from the White House full of enthusiasm, believing that the S&Ls were pulling out of their troubles. It took Gray about six months to learn that not only were things bad and getting worse, but that most of the leaders of the industry were delighted with all the opportunities to make a quick buck that Pratt and Garn had opened up for them. Gray struggled manfully to control the looting, with no help whatever from his former friend Ronald Reagan or the Treasury Department, and left in 1988 a hero though an ineffective one. His successor Danny Wall, an irritable little man with a short beard, a former architect and city planner in Salt Lake City who had been Senator Jake Garn's chief-of-staff, was put in the job in full knowledge that he would be over his head. He was pushed out in 1989, and I went down to Washington to debrief him. "What," I asked, "are you going to do?" Wall said, "I'm going to be a brain surgeon." I said, "I beg your pardon," and Wall said miserably, "I'm as prepared for that as I am for anything else."

The Federal Deposit Insurance Corporation, which should have led the charge against the lunacy of the Garn–St. Germain Act, concentrated instead on maintaining the capital standards for the savings banks it supervised, mostly in the Northeast, preventing them from trying to grow out of their troubles, and closing them down when their capital ran out. But before he left in 1985, Chairman William Isaac had begun to tighten the screws on the commercial banks, too. Then the job passed to L. William Seidman, a lawyer and accountant who had run the Phelps Dodge copper enterprise when that company broke one of the longest strikes in mining history, and had moved on to be dean of the business school at the University of Arizona. His previous connection with banking had been as a director of United Bank Corp. of Arizona in 1982. The bank went bust after various unsavory involvements with local real estate types. "As I looked at the record of the lawsuit," he wrote some years later, "it became clear much to my chagrin that the bank which I thought I had served so diligently as an independent director had been guilty of a great many unsafe and unsound lending practices not revealed to us directors. But how an outside director could have learned about this is beyond me."[19] He was an amusing, intelligent, irresponsible fellow with a colorful persona and appearance and a love for attention. He began making a series of speeches that described bankers as "our clients, our customers and our constituents." A veteran FDIC staffer says he was tempted to sneak into Seidman's office and take the "c" key off his secretary's keyboard.

"During meetings with FDIC staff just after Mr. Seidman took over . . . in 1985," the House Committee on Government Operations reported, "he routinely made the following statements: 'bankers are our friends'; 'the FDIC should be a friend of the industry'; and it should be like a 'trade association for the industry.' To FDIC staff, the message was clear: 'Go easy on this industry.' "[20]

The truth was—strange as it sounds a decade later—that in the mid 1980s the banks envied the S&Ls their power to create assets for themselves. In 1987, the FDIC for the first time in its history permitted the state-chartered banks it supervised to make equity investments in real estate. Asked by *New York Times* reporter Jeff Gerth how this squared with his statements some years later that the great error of bank regulation in the late 1980s had been to permit the expansion of bank lending on real estate, Seidman said, correctly but perhaps disingenuously, that it wasn't the 5 percent of capital he had let banks put into real estate investments that created the later insolvencies.

In 1989, the FDIC circulated a draft document on *Deposit Insurance for the Nineties*, which acclaimed deposit insurance as a "merit good," something that costs the society nothing (because it prevents runs and therefore need not be used) but benefits all parties. In fairness, this was not a new argument, and it had been made on both ends of the political spectrum. Milton Friedman and Anna J. Schwartz had written that "Federal insurance of bank deposits was the most important structural change in the banking system to result from the 1933 panic, and, indeed, in our view, the structural change most conducive to monetary stability since state bank note issues were taxed out of existence immediately after the Civil War."[21] J. K. Galbraith wrote even more lyrically: "With this one piece of legislation, the fear which operated so efficiently to transmit weakness was dissolved. As a result, one grievous defect of the old system, by which failure begot failure, was cured. Rarely has so much been accomplished by a single law."[22]

Because deposit insurance was such a universal benefit, the FDIC was prepared to extend it far beyond the intent of Congress, which had merely guaranteed deposits up to a maximum amount, in domestic branches. Under Seidman, the FDIC if possible would not simply liquidate a bank and protect the insured depositors, letting the uninsured carry their piece of the risk. In 1988, when First Republic of Texas failed, Chairman Seidman sent a letter to the bank's chairman and suggested he share it with the bank's customers. What he wanted to do, he wrote, was "to assure all depositors of the banks, insured and uninsured, and all general creditors of the banks, that valid and enforceable obligations of the banks will be fully honored, regardless of the nature of the long range solution that may be announced."[23] Then, as noted in Chapter 8, he organized the sweetheart deal by which NCNB got First Republic for nothing.

The next year, *Deposit Insurance for the Nineties* proclaimed in a self-satisfied way that "the 'too-large-to-pay-off' doctrine in all probability is here to stay. There will always be certain situations where an individual bank will be perceived to be too important to macroeconomic or international stability to allow to be handled in a way that would inflict losses on bank creditors. This becomes increasingly true as other countries provide de jure or de facto 100-percent coverage to their banks and as banking and finance become more international in scope."[24] In fact, it didn't have to be a big bank for the FDIC to waive the congressional guidelines on bailouts and hold all the creditors harmless. In 1990, the National Bank of Washington failed, and the FDIC paid out more than $200 million to the depositors in and lenders to its branch in the Bahamas, though deposits in foreign branches paid no insurance assessment and presumably were not covered by insurance. The 1991 U.S. Treasury report *Modernizing the Financial System* noted that "from 1985 to 1990—the period of the highest number of bank failures since the 1930s—over 99 percent of uninsured deposits have been fully protected in bank failures."[25]

In one respect, however, the FDIC's presentation of the international aspect was correct: in a number of developed countries, banking regulators had fallen into the careless habit of assuming that large banks would not be allowed to fail in ways that subjected their creditors to loss. Before the first half of the 1990s was over, Swedish, Finnish, Spanish and French taxpayers would be compelled to pick up large tabs to pay out the losses of their largest banks when deregulation opened up new "investments" that banks could make. The loss in Finland was on a per capita basis larger than the American losses in the S&L disaster.

And the Japanese financial system teetered on the edge of total collapse in 1996, because the Japanese banks had expanded ludicrously in the 1980s. At one point Japan was headquarters for nine of the world's ten largest banks (and the tenth was a government-owned French agricultural lender) on the strength of its government's assurance that no Japanese bank would ever default on its obligations. A "bubble economy" pushed real estate and stock prices to fantastic heights as Japanese banks competed for business that could always be financed because those who provided funds to the banks had a government guarantee.

Japanese banks were a world unto themselves. In the back offices, ant-heaps of traders and clerks were jammed into enormous rooms with dirty, cream-colored walls, working on folding chairs at picnic tables on which the screens were anachronisms. In smoke-filled little meeting rooms across the wall from these back offices, decorous tea ladies in uniforms served cigarettes and tea while young vice presidents in white shirts and striped ties did business. On the executive floors, forty floors up, slightly overweight older and smaller men sat at massive desks in Mussolini-size high-ceilinged offices with marble walls, giving the effect often enough of Egyptian tombs into which someone had intruded the most glorious of Oriental carpeting. Forbidden like American banks to do business on the domestic stock exchange or as underwriters of domestic securities, the Japanese had expanded the scope of banking activity to new dimensions.

In the 1980s, the Japanese banks took business from everyone everywhere in the world, cutting margins on everything from letters of credit to municipal bond guarantees to leveraged-buyout loans to construction finance from the Arabian Gulf to the shores of Lake Michigan. From Hawaii to London to the French Riviera, their clients always bought the best, and paid the highest prices, because their banks were behind them. In Japan itself, they financed credit unions and *jusen*, specialized lending institutions for housing, which like the American S&Ls turned out to be engines for the enrichment of their officers, who were in no way restricted from becoming property developers themselves. And then, quite suddenly, it was all gone, sunk in a miasma of bad loans that even the government admitted totaled at least $500 billion.

In America, Congress bit the bullet with the Financial Institutions Reform and Recovery Act of 1989, and put the taxpayer (and the deficit) on the line to pay the costs of shutting down hundreds of insolvent insured institutions. In 1991, the Federal Deposit Insurance Corporation Improvement Act limited the discretion of the regulators in deciding when to close down a bank or thrift institution that was operating with insufficient capital. But the Japanese Diet did not have the investigatory powers to find out what lay behind the disaster in the Japanese banks, or the guts to tell the Japanese taxpayer the truth that he was stuck with big losses.

A team of television journalists came from a Japanese network to visit me in Washington. Someone at home had said that the accelerating collapse of Japanese banks was very much like the American S&L fiasco. Was that true? my interviewer asked, the eye of the camera upon me. Yes, I said, that was true: in both cases, foolish governments had guaranteed the liabilities of financial institutions that used other people's money in an undisciplined way. And it could happen, I added, to others.

A year later, it *did* happen.

13 / The Fed and Other Regulators

We had a bad banking situation. Some of our bankers had shown themselves either incompetent or dishonest in their handling of the people's funds. They had used the money entrusted to them in speculations and unwise loans. This was of course not true in the vast majority of our banks, but it was true in enough of them to shock the people for a time into a sense of insecurity and to put them into a frame of mind where they did not differentiate, but seemed to assume that the acts of a comparative few had tainted them all. It was the government's job to straighten out this situation and do it as quickly as possible and the job is being performed.

—FRANKLIN ROOSEVELT, first fireside chat, March 12, 1933

The French view: regulators are good, so optimal mechanisms can be designed and will work.
The American view: regulators are evil. They will maximize their own self-interest. They are also invertebrate so they will do whatever is expedient ex post.

—RAGURAM G. RAJAN, University of Chicago, 1995

In 1989, the Senate Banking Committee, coming to grips reluctantly with the disaster in the S&Ls and beset with rumors about the losses the banks were suffering in their real estate portfolios, held a public hearing to quiz the three federal regulators about how the banks were doing. All three—Alan Greenspan from the Federal Reserve, Robert Clarke from the Office of the Comptroller of the Currency, L. William Seidman from the Federal Deposit Insurance Corporation—assured the senators that there was nothing to worry about in the banking industry. Senator

Donald Riegle asked them point-blank whether the real estate loans in the banks' portfolio were better or worse than they had been the year before. One after the other, the three regulators answered: "Better." "Better." "Better."

Richard Carnell, a young man with a fine brown beard who was then counsel to the Senate Banking Committee, later an assistant secretary of the treasury, commented on the occasion. "It goes down in the history books," he said, "as the 'Three Blind Mice' hearings."

1

Robert E. Litan and Richard J. Herring write that "three broad reasons appear to have motivated countries to subject their financial institutions and markets to regulation and supervision: preventing disruptions in financial markets ... from posing wider systemic risks; protecting consumers from excessive prices and opportunistic behavior by providers of financial services ... ; and achieving various social objectives."[1] But a fourth point is crucial. The most significant purpose of bank regulation is to protect bankers from themselves. Because banks create money, the normal operations of the market will not police their activities. The willingness or reluctance of banks to create credit money by lending has been so important to the economy over the years, and the behavior of bankers has been so subject to what Charles MacKay called *Extraordinary Popular Delusions and the Madness of Crowds*, that governments have felt themselves compelled to control their banking systems.

Ed Furash argues that "Risk is a narcotic. It's a rare CEO that can go cold turkey. In situation after situation that we've seen here, it's been an inability to sober up. Frank Morris of the Federal Reserve Bank of Boston was retiring in the late 1980s. He gave valedictories all over New England, told the bankers they were hooked on real estate. They laughed at him. He warned them they were making too many real estate loans out of town, where they didn't know the market. They said, 'We're just following a local builder who's going there.' "

What sank Bank of New England beyond hope of resuscitation was its Florida real estate lending. I had known about it some months before it happened, by accident, because I'd had drinks in New York with a bunch of people from Barnett Banks who had come from Florida to the big city to make their pitch to the Wall Street securities analysts. I said, "I bet you guys are going to take a bath in real estate." And one of the Barnett officers said, "Nah. We would have, but Bank of New England came down and grabbed off all the worst deals for itself."

"Banks are actually no more accident-prone than other businesses," Martin Taylor, CEO of Barclays Bank, wrote in a 50th anniversary tribute to the "Lex" column in the *Financial Times* (a column he had written himself before he became a banker). "It's just that their gearing makes it more likely that mistakes will be fatal; poorly capitalised banks are like haemophiliacs on an assault course. . . . The greatest danger to banks still comes from other banks, whether in the urge to copy each other's behavior or in the spread of trouble through the dry underbrush of the payments system. Perhaps the very low regulatory weightings for interbank business encourage indiscriminate exposure (in which case blame the banks, not the regulators). The International Monetary Fund is a haemophiliacs' convention. Think of those sharp elbows at cocktail parties. Sorry, did I knock you?"

2

In the United States, for historical reasons, government supervision of banks is split among several agencies, and to date all efforts to concentrate this work have fallen afoul of interest groups strong enough to immobilize the Congress. In 1791, Alexander Hamilton as secretary of the treasury won legislation in Congress to charter a privately owned Bank of the United States, mostly to place in safe hands as much as possible of the national debt acquired in the Revolutionary War and the eight years of enfeebled government that followed it. Shareholders could buy their shares by exchanging U.S. government debt at par.

The First Bank of the United States in theory served the public purpose of policing the issuance of currency by other banks, mostly chartered by a state government. The federal government's revenues in those days were almost entirely from the customs house, and required payment in specie. To the extent that these receipts remained with the branches of the Bank of the United States (one of its few extant balance sheets shows $5 million in specie in the vaults as of 1809), state-chartered banks could find their ability to issue notes diminished by shortages of gold and silver. The shares of the Bank of the United States were owned to a large extent in England. This did not have much to do with policy because stockholders could vote only in person, but it was unpopular. In February 1811, the charter expired, though the bank was not formally wound up until 1852, by which time it had returned to its shareholders 109 percent of their investment, over and above the dividends paid while it was in business.[2]

The Second Bank of the United States, chartered in 1816 in large part to mop up the inflationary consequences of the War of 1812, became a bone in the throat of the rising commercial classes in the seaboard cities. The history textbook tale that it was the farmers who resented tight money reads back into the 1830s the attitudes of the late nineteenth century, when deflation made debts much harder to service; Bray Hammond gives chapter and verse for the cheap-money attitudes of 1830s businessmen in his great *Banks and Politics in the United States Between the Revolution and the Civil War*.

In the mid 1830s, President Andrew Jackson's dislike for the Second Bank deprived it first of its benefits as the repository of choice for customs duties and then of its federal charter, and state banks flourished. As noted earlier, many of them were irresponsible in their issuance of banknotes, and only in New England and to a slightly lesser extent in New York were the older state-chartered banks in position to maintain the value of the paper currency. Litan and Herring estimate that as much as four-fifths of the banknotes printed in the United States in the heyday of "free banking" (when bank charters were available to anyone who would buy a specified quantity of state bonds) were in fact worthless.[3] The violent fluctuations of the business cycle in America from the late 1830s to the Civil War persuaded the states to create banking commissions or departments that sought to "supervise" the conduct of each state's banks.

During the Civil War, as noted, Abraham Lincoln hit upon the issuance of "greenbacks" as a means of paying the armies, and federal chartering of banks as a way to create a captive market for government bonds. The banknotes issued by federally chartered banks would have to be backed in full (in fact, 110 percent) by the banks' holdings of Treasury bonds, valued at par. To force existing banks to convert to federal charters (and buy Treasury paper), the law taxed the issuance of notes by any but federally chartered banks. The requirement that note issue be backed by ownership of government bonds did not greatly hamper the operation of a bank. Depositors' money had to be invested in government bonds, but they paid interest, too, and the bank could earn an income from the investment of the banknotes it issued. The emerging clearinghouses enabled banks to exchange each other's paper rather than redeem the bills with specie. To control the issuance of bank charters and police the operation of the federally chartered banks, Congress established within the Treasury (where it still is, though no longer in the same building) the Office of the Comptroller of the Currency, and Lincoln appointed as Comptroller the banking superintendent of the state of Indiana, Hugh McCulloch.

The state banks did not, however, wither away. McCulloch was a tough regulator with a conservative philosophy of banking and a strong distaste for "financiering." The fact that a nationally chartered bank had to back its notes 110 percent with Treasury paper meant that before establishing the liquidity reserve that would enable the redemption of some banknotes with specie, a bank had to put aside 10 percent of its resources as what we would now consider a capital ratio. There was a federal tax on banknotes issued by state-chartered banks, but in the metropolitan centers, banks did not have to create banknotes to make loans: they could create deposits and give borrowers checkbooks.

Originally established in the 1850s to enable banks to net out their claims on each other from the presentation of their banknotes at other banks, the clearinghouses could easily be adapted to netting out their claims on each other from the presentation of checks. Country banks could be brought into this clearing and settlement system through the maintenance of correspondent interbank accounts in the metropolitan banks. The advantages of universal membership in clearinghouses were apparent to all, and both state and national banks could be part of a common clearinghouse. The clearinghouse itself would automatically police the extension of credit money by its member banks, which had to settle their accounts at the clearinghouse nightly.

Nationally chartered banks were forbidden to lend on the security of real estate, and they were forbidden to operate a trust business, accepting and investing funds for the benefit of third parties. State banks were subject only to state regulation, which might well require less capital to back the bank's deposit issuance and permit loans against a wider range of collateral for longer periods of time. Though most states restricted banks to a single office (Colorado did not abandon "unit banking" until 1991), state law also could permit branching within the state, while national charters originally were tightly restricted as to place. State laws also permitted bank holding companies—or, for that matter, individuals—to own more than one bank, provided each bank in the group was legally separate from the others.

At the beginning, federally chartered banks had to be numbered in each location, as the First or Second or Third National Bank of the city of operation, a strange requirement that survives in strange names like Cincinnati's Fifth Third Bank, an amalgamation of two numbered institutions. (The law no longer requires federally chartered banks to have "National" in their names, but a nationally chartered bank that wishes not to do so must keep the initials "N.A.," for "National Association," as a suffix to the corporate moniker.) Under the McFadden Act of 1927, national banks in a state were given the same branching rights that state-chartered banks enjoyed, but the ultimate control remained with the state.[4]

From the 1860s, then, banks have had a choice of state or national supervision. Some of the very largest banks have chosen to remain with state rules, especially in New York. The tale of Chase is tangled enough to be worth telling. Founded as a nationally chartered bank (named, of course, for Salmon P. Chase, secretary of the treasury when the National Banking Act was passed), Chase became state-chartered in the 1950s, when it acquired the Bank of the Manhattan Company (Aaron Burr's bank) in a complicated deal which left the acquired bank as the operating shell—with a state charter. In the 1960s, when James Saxon as Comptroller was liberating federally chartered banks from regulatory constraints and the Fed was wringing its hands, Citibank as a nationally chartered bank was out there pushing the envelope and Chase as a state-chartered Fed member was being held down. Walter Wriston of Citibank remembered a meeting of the International Monetary Conference, the international club of big bankers that meets once a year for purposes of self-congratulation. This meeting in the mid 1960s was in Puerto Rico. The vice-chairman of the Fed announced that his board would *never* allow the sort of thing Saxon was permitting. "[David] Rockefeller [the Chase CEO] went down to Washington right after the meeting was over," Wriston said gleefully, "and applied for a national charter—after saying he thought Saxon was crazy. I would have liked to sell tickets to that meeting." For thirty years, then, it was Chase-Manhattan N.A. Chemical through all this time had kept its state charter. Now Chemical has acquired Chase lock, stock and barrel, and the two together are called Chase—but the bank will be a state bank.

Some of this reflects rather interestingly the fundamental divisions of American polity. The Tenth Amendment to the Constitution reserves to the states ("or the people") those powers not enumerated as federal powers. It does not take great cleverness to extend the interstate commerce powers of the federal government to cover banking, and the most famous Supreme Court decision curbing state powers (*McCullough* v. *Maryland*) was written to deny a state the power to promote state banks by taxing federally chartered banks ("The power to tax," John Marshall wrote, "implies the power to destroy"). In 1996, in an opinion largely neglected outside the industry because the wisdom of the media says that the Rehnquist Supreme Court is intent on returning powers to the states, a unanimous Court forbade states to interfere with the congressionally granted powers of federally chartered banks to act as insurance agents in towns of population five thousand or less. (A holding company in a big city can then, of course, sell insurance to everybody through its subsidiary in the itty-bitty town.) But even today it remains true that federally chartered banks can be licensed to operate across state lines only if the states involved have awarded similar powers to their own banks.

This system did not provide a sufficiently flexible or expanding money supply, especially as trading in financial instruments grew in the 1890s and early 1900s. This trading was concentrated in New York, which was also where the banking system kept its reserves. The use of bank reserves as a source of finance for the stock market—Andrew Carnegie noted with the annoyance of a man who was a steelmaker, not a financier—gave the nation the worst banking system in the world. The early 1890s especially saw great economic hardship in the country, dictated in large part by deflationary pressures that made debts harder to pay. The discovery of the cyanide process for South African gold mining was especially important because it broke the back of deflation throughout the industrializing world.

But a fragmented and disconnected banking system was also unsuited to the needs of a continental nation with rapidly expanding transportation and communication resources. The panic of 1907, when the New York Clearing House had to issue scrip—private money—to keep the banks afloat, convinced President Theodore Roosevelt and Senator Nelson Aldrich of Rhode Island that something had to be done. It should be remembered that in the early years of this century, senators were still elected by the legislatures of the states they represented, not by popular vote, and were therefore even more susceptible than they are today to local pressures. The Aldrich-Vreeland Act of 1908 created a National Monetary Commission to work on the nation's banking problems.

The commission found some boils to be lanced—especially the banks' ugly habit of discounting checks from other banks not members of their own clearinghouse. A $100 check on a bank in Atlanta might be accepted by a bank in St. Louis for only $97, and it was not uncommon for the Atlanta bank to have to honor the check by sending $100 in currency or even gold to St. Louis. These payments inefficiencies added to the cost of doing business at a distance, which was becoming more and more common. In 1910, a group of Wall Street bankers headed by George Baker of First National and delegates of the Morgan empire met secretly on Jekyll Island in Georgia. Bill Ford, an economic historian with practical experience as president of First Nationwide and the Federal Reserve Bank of Atlanta, said sourly that "they met to create an independent authority that could keep them from screwing each other all the time." The bill that came out of these meetings proposed a central bank with some powers to control government chartered but privately owned regional banks that would be bankers' banks, run clearinghouses and serve as lenders of last resort in time of trouble to avoid bank runs. This was scuppered by the Democrats in 1910 but served as the foundation for the bill written mostly by then-congressman Carter Glass of Georgia, which created the Federal Reserve System in 1913.

In 1933, the failure of the Fed to stop the economic decline that led to the Depression—in part because a weak leadership feared that low interest rates would lead to a loss of gold—provoked Franklin Roosevelt to kill the gold standard and seek rising prices. Congress created a Federal Deposit Insurance Corporation to make people feel safe about their money in the bank (at least the first $2,500 of it). This FDIC would get its initial capital from the government and would have a line of credit at the Treasury, but would be funded by premiums the banks would pay. Thus there developed the strange tripartite federal regulatory structure—the Comptroller, chartering and supervising national banks; the Fed, making monetary policy for the country and providing payments and emergency services; and the FDIC, insuring deposits and examining all insured banks that don't report to the Comptroller (which now means all state-chartered domestic banks that are not members of the Fed, plus those state-chartered branches of foreign banks, mostly Irish and Israeli, that seek domestic consumer deposits).

3

Regulators are to be found today in three very separate organizations.

The operations of the Fed are highly decentralized through the twelve district banks established by the original Federal Reserve Act of 1913. These district banks are a remarkable hybrid, "owned" by their "member banks," each of which must buy stock in the district bank pro rata to its deposit base. A third of the directors are appointed by the Board of Governors in Washington, a third are elected by the bankers of the district, and another third are businessmen chosen by the other directors. One of the Washington-appointed directors is the "fiscal agent," who alone can authorize orders to the mint to print the Federal Reserve notes, which are the paper currency of the country. The president of the bank is elected by his own directors, but the board in Washington has and uses its veto power. Both Paul Volcker and Alan Greenspan as chairmen of the Fed have been, in fact, rather heavy-handed in telling the district banks who should be their presidents.

Most of the Fed's functions and powers—operating the discount window where solvent banks can borrow (with good security) when they need cash, running check-clearing operations and other aspects of the payments system, controlling credit to the securities markets—are related to its role as creator and controller of the money supply. But the banking acts of the 1930s, 1956 and 1970 gave the Fed regulatory powers with relation to permissible activities for banks and for holding companies that own banks, and these responsibilities have confused the institution's sense of its own mission. The Fed must approve mergers and acquisitions, and enforce a whole series of regulations with which it has little institutional sympathy: fair lending laws, community reinvestment laws, truth-in-savings laws, antitrust laws, and securities laws for bank securities affiliates which have not chosen to register with the Securities and Exchange Commission.

400

The Board of Governors and its staff preside in a marble palace on Constitution Avenue near the State Department, behind a large portico topped with the biggest and fiercest stone eagle in Washington. (Another, more modern building stands behind, linked by a tunnel under the street.) The seven governors, appointed to thirteen-year terms to insulate them from politics, each have a splendid high-ceilinged room on the second floor of headquarters. They can decorate their room and the anteroom for their secretary from a collection of American art on loan from the nation's museums under a program launched a generation ago by Chairman William McChesney Martin (also a backer of Broadway shows and the inventor of the National Tennis Foundation that runs the national championships; there is a tennis court on the Fed's property because for Martin, ninety-two years old in 1996, a day without tennis was like a day without sun).

Martin is an interesting man: from St. Louis originally, he had become "the boy wonder of Wall Street" representing A. G. Edwards on the New York Stock Exchange floor. The arrest of former president Richard Whitney for embezzling money from the fund that provided death benefits for survivors of deceased exchange employees forced the exchange to hire a full-time professional president. Martin got the job at the age of thirty-four. He became chairman of the Fed in 1952, arriving from a job in Harry Truman's Treasury Department to implement the "accord" of the previous year that had released the Fed from its former obligation to support the price of government bonds and keep the government's interest expenses down. He was a democrat by temperament: he always let the other governors vote first. He avoided publicity; he liked to say that the central banker's job was to take the punch bowl away just as the party was getting good.

Martin's successor, Arthur Burns, was a heavyset, German-born academic economist with an Oom Paul pipe, very smart, a protégé of the economist Wesley Mitchell at Columbia University, never in doubt of the correctness of his opinions. In Burns's time, the chairman voted first "to make sure the others won't go wrong." Under Burns, too, the staff acquired the habit of believing that it worked for the chairman, not for the board. Paul Volcker, two years after Burns, was also an economist, but despite a few years at Chase Manhattan and a few years of teaching he was basically a civil servant, like his father before him (city manager of Teaneck, New Jersey, a municipality on the edge, which he saved from bankruptcy in the Great Depression). For all his admirable qualities, Volcker also was not a man to encourage dissent, and the staff became even more a service agency for him alone than it had been for his predecessor, but unlike Burns he was never deceptive.

One of the issues that dogged Volcker in the mid 1980s was the "non-bank bank," usually an institution that took deposits but did not make commercial loans, thus escaping the 1970 congressional definition of a bank as an enterprise that did both. Nonfinancial corporations like Gulf and Western and Parker Pen and Sears Roebuck and Automatic Data Processing were using this loophole to acquire banks and thus access to FedWire, and Volcker—a firm believer in the separation of commerce and banking—was highly distressed. I once had occasion to listen to a tape of a meeting of the board during which the staff, currying favor, proposed to get rid of non-bank banks by defining repurchase agreements for government bonds as commercial loans. There was a rumble on the tape, like Mount St. Helens getting ready to let go. Soon it became apparent that this rumble was the voice of the chairman. "We make repurchase agreements all the time," the voice said finally. "We don't consider them commercial loans." Paul Volcker was—still is— ready to fight; but he fights fair.

Alan Greenspan, Volcker's successor, is owlish, with thick glasses and a rather shy smile. His Ph.D. in economics came relatively late in life, after he had dabbled in the politics of Ayn Rand. I have a precious copy of a truly nutty piece he wrote for her magazine, *The Objectivist*, in 1966, when he was in his mid-thirties. Entitled "Gold and Economic Freedom," the article opens with the statement: "An almost hysterical antagonism toward the gold standard is one issue which unites statists of all persuasions. . . . In the absence of the gold standard, there is no way to protect savings from confiscation through inflation. There is no safe store of value. . . . This is the shabby secret of the welfare statists' tirades against gold."[5]

Despite Greenspan's instinctive deference to wealth and power, he was married briefly to a woman who embodied the spirit of revolt: the beautiful and talented abstract expressionist painter Joan Mitchell, whose first husband had been Barney Rosset, the publisher of Samuel Beckett and Giovanni Verga and D. H. Lawrence. I met Greenspan in the late 1960s on Wall Street, where he ran a well-regarded small consulting firm that did what he called "statistical espionage."

For a man with his political beliefs, Greenspan has had a surprising career: no major success in the private sector (a mutual fund he started had to be closed up because it did so poorly) but an excellent record in government. He was an outstanding chairman of the council of economic advisers for Gerald Ford, setting the country on track for the recovery that was well under way when Jimmy Carter won election by proclaiming Ford's unconcern. Two months after he became chairman of the Fed in summer 1987 the stock market fell out of bed in the biggest one-day decline in history, a situation he handled with courage and aplomb (it wouldn't have worked without Gerald Corrigan as president of the New York Fed, but that was not Greenspan's fault). He fed out liquidity at a proper pace in the delicate winter of 1987–88, and called it back before it could do much damage. Unlike Arthur Burns, who triggered the great inflation of the 1970s by pumping up the economy to help Richard Nixon, Greenspan avoided politicizing the Fed in 1992. He made a welcoming gesture to Bill Clinton by sitting beside Hillary Clinton at the new president's first State of the Union address in 1993. Being a governor to his chairmanship, however, has been no fun at all, unless you like to make speeches written for you by the staff; his Fed is a one-man operation.

Chairman of the Fed is by popular report the second-most-important job in the government of the United States, a half-true claim that is one of the unintended consequences of the rational expectations theory that won Robert Lucas his Nobel Prize in 1995. (Everybody knows that the Fed can't *really* control even medium-term interest rates or the money supply, but an action by the Fed to change the overnight rates it does control creates expectations in the market.) The Fed does not pretend to be an efficient or effective regulator of banks: it "supervises," which in practice means that it tries to enhance their profitability and stability, especially for the larger banks. In fairness, most of the larger banks are federally chartered and are not examined by the Fed. The Fed's greatest influence on what banks do derives from its authority to approve or reject bank mergers, and its power to decide under the holding company acts and Glass-Steagall which activities are indeed proper activities for banks and their corporate owners.

The Comptroller's job has less prestige—and controls a smaller payroll, less than 3,500 employees all told—but probably exerts greater influence on the operation of the banks. In the days of James Saxon, the Comptroller had one of the superbly dignified Victorian rooms in the Treasury Building beside the White House, but the office was moved in the 1970s, first to rather fancy space at L'Enfant Plaza, now to more modest housing beside the railroad tracks behind the hideous Southwest Triangle federal buildings. Unlike Fed chairmen, Comptrollers have usually had some contact with real live banks. James Smith, John Heimann's predecessor, had been an executive of the First National Bank of Chicago, and Heimann's young successor Todd Conover was an accountant with a banking practice.

404

The job was open for the better part of a year after Conover left in 1985, and one of the deputies who served as acting Comptroller was Michael Patriarca, a tall, black-haired, very handsome lawyer who had been a career employee and would later move to thrift supervision in San Francisco to be the scourge of Charlie Keating (and then on to an executive position at Wells Fargo). Patriarca wrote an "Examination Issuance" on the valuation of commercial and industrial real estate used as collateral for a loan or acquired in the process of loan foreclosure (a category charmingly called OREO, for "other real estate owned"). The new rule proclaimed that "advances in excess of calculated current fair value which are considered uncollectable do not warrant continuance as bankable assets. . . . A doubtful classification may be appropriate in cases where significant risk exposures are perceived, but loss cannot be determined because of *specific, reasonable pending factors* which may strengthen the credit in the near term. . . . Any such troubled real estate loan or portion thereof, not considered doubtful or loss, should be classified substandard when well-defined weaknesses are present which jeopardize orderly liquidation of the debt."[6]

This examination circular was issued fourteen months before the 1986 tax act knocked a third of the value off commercial real estate. If it had survived, banks might have been saved from some of their real estate–related disasters of the 1989–92 period. Alas! President Reagan appointed a new Comptroller, Robert Clarke, a lawyer for Texas banks, who almost immediately issued a "clarification" advising bank examiners that "the OCC recognizes that many real estate values are subject to cyclical swings and that certain depressed properties can be expected to recover their value within a reasonable period of time. . . . Accordingly, 'Loss' classifications should reflect permanent value impairment, i.e., loan exposures *exceeding the undiscounted future market value expected to be realized within a reasonable period of time, nor-*

mally not to exceed five to seven years."[7] Clarke would later say he wanted to be known as "the regulator from hell," but the damage had been done.

Clinton appointed Eugene Ludwig, a compact, alert, black-haired Wall Street lawyer with a banking practice, who has built an impressively professional staff, including economist Philip Bartholomew, as director of bank research; one of Bartholomew's Most Memorable Experiences was visiting Moscow as a consultant to the emerging Russian banking authorities and being fitted for a bulletproof vest before going out to visit Russian banks.

Like Saxon before him, Ludwig has tried to open business opportunities for the banks, especially in the insurance agency area, to the great resentment of the state bank supervisors and some congressmen. In 1996, he even issued a national charter to a state bank that wished to convert to national status, authorizing it to continue to exercise all the powers it had enjoyed in its state incarnation even though those were not permitted to federally chartered banks.

At the same time, Ludwig has restored an air of big-city sophistication to the office, hiring Douglas Harris from J.P. Morgan as his derivatives expert. He considers himself a regulator as well as a supervisor: "The SEC uses enforcement actions where we address through supervisory action, but we have a lot of regulations with specified penalties. We try to do a meticulous and serious job; supervision needs a scalpel, not a meat axe." In general, the Comptroller's Office takes an expansive view of bank powers, permitting activities from stock brokerage to insurance agenting to travel bureaus to be operated by subsidiaries of the banks themselves. The Federal Reserve, by contrast, wants anything that isn't fairly plain vanilla banking to be done under the umbrella of a holding company. The Comptroller supervises banks; the Fed supervises holding companies.

The third of the regulatory organizations is the Federal Deposit Insurance Corporation. As its name implies, the FDIC is intended to function like a private-sector institution. Its three-member board consists of a chairman, the Comptroller, and one independent director appointed by the president and confirmed by the Senate. For some reason, the FDIC wound up much closer to the White House than the other banking regulators, in a square, modern, seven-story building on Seventeenth Street across from the Executive Office Building. Its top-floor conference room, with a broad terrace on three sides, has splendid views over the Mall to the river and Virginia.

Its mission is the "resolution" of banks that have been declared to have failed by their chartering authorities, state or federal, at minimum loss to the insurance fund. The FDIC cannot itself declare a bank insolvent; only the agency that chartered the bank can do that. It *can* withdraw deposit insurance from a bank, thereby guaranteeing a run that would make the bank insolvent, but there is a danger in doing that if the Comptroller or the state banking commissioner doesn't want it done, because the bank that has been put out of business can sue.

The modus operandi is not well understood. FDIC does not, as is usually said, "pay back the depositors." It purchases the assets of the failed bank at whatever price is necessary to get some successor institution to honor the deposits. Very occasionally, this may be a new "deposit guaranty bank" formed by the FDIC itself to inherit the corpus of the dead bank and gradually bury it. More commonly, it will be an existing institution that buys the franchise of the failed bank—its relations with depositors and with those borrowers the purchaser wishes to retain as customers—selling off to the FDIC for cash money, at face value, whatever loans it doesn't want to keep.

The establishment of a deposit insurance fund was strongly opposed by the big-city banks in 1933. George Moore, as an assistant to James Perkins, chairman of New York's National City, sat in on the congressional conference that wrote the Glass-Steagall Act. His instruction to oppose deposit insurance, he says, was based on the argument that "the competence of bankers is not an insurable risk." From the point of view of the big-city banks, the special vice of deposit insurance was (and still is) that it props up independent small-town and country banks which would not be rescued by other banks (or, these days, the government) if they fell into trouble. Franklin Roosevelt didn't think much of deposit insurance, either, mostly because the country bankers that would be rescued were all Republicans, and he didn't agree to go along until his leaders in the House of Representatives told him that without a deposit insurance clause there would be no banking bill at all.

The description of the FDIC's functions indicates that the agency is the least of the federal regulators. William Seidman himself writes in his memoirs that "this was not a high-prestige job."[8] The decision in 1984 to make the FDIC the senior partner in resolving the Continental problem produced a major change in its status. It was not until the telegenic and turf-grabbing Seidman took over that the press began referring to the chairman of the FDIC as "the nation's leading bank regulator." When Congress finally gave its mighty heave on the S&L mess, it made Seidman chairman of the new Resolution Trust Corporation formed to wind up these dead institutions as well as of the FDIC, and it set a sunset date after which the RTC activities would be folded back into FDIC, where they now lodge. Thanks to the S&L hangover, the FDIC in 1996 still had 9,000 employees, but the number was shrinking fast.

It should be noted that the operations of all these agencies, state and federal, doesn't cost the taxpayer a penny. States tax banks to pay for the banking supervisors or commissions. The Comptroller requires an annual fee from federally chartered banks. The Fed demands dues from its members and is enjoined by law to charge users the full cost of the payments service it provides. (Because the Federal Reserve district banks print the money everybody uses, they are hugely profitable, on the order of $15 billion to

$20 billion a year, which is turned over to the Treasury after the Board of Governors—which does not have to submit its budget to Congress—takes its cut.) The FDIC pays its expenses out of the insurance premiums the banks pay—or, in 1996, now that the deposit insurance fund has been built to 1.25 percent of insured deposits, as Congress mandated in 1992, out of the interest the government pays on the Treasury bills in the insurance fund.

Though the tribodied arrangment *is* peculiar, its peculiarity derives in large part from the constitutionally mandated separation of powers. The Comptroller of the Currency, an individual with deputies, reports to the secretary of the treasury, who reports to the president: he is part of the executive branch of government. The Federal Reserve Board has monetary policy as its major function, and is thus an agency of the Congress, even though the president appoints its governors with the usual advice and consent (and even though the secretary of the treasury was, for the Fed's first twenty years, one of them, though never chairman). Only Congress—*not* the president—can "coin money and regulate the value thereof."

The chairman of the Fed reports twice a year to each of the congressional banking committees, and under the terms of the Humphrey-Hawkins Act he is supposed to tell them what he is doing to reduce unemployment as well as what he is doing to prevent inflation. Don Regan's deputy secretary of the treasury, Tim McNamar, said at the depths of the less-developed-countries debt crisis that it had to be handled by the Fed rather than the Treasury because "the Fed is not part of the government."[9] Because the Fed is the creature of Congress, it will almost always win legislative battles against the SEC, the Comptroller or the FDIC.

One should also note peculiarities of compensation in the bank regulatory agencies. The heads of the agencies are political appointees, whose salaries run against the ceiling set by congressmen who are damned if they will have these guys paid more than they are. But the agencies need skilled and experienced people, and while they can't compete with Wall Street, they can't be ludicrously cheap. So deputy comptrollers, department heads at the FDIC and Federal Reserve senior officers are paid up to $200,000 a year (including living allowances), and the presidents of the twelve district Feds all receive more than $200,000. The General Accounting Office in 1995 found that exactly one governor of the Fed—the chairman—had the use of a limousine, but no fewer than fifty-nine employees of the twelve Reserve Banks had limousines.

4

All these institutions "examine" banks. States keep tabs on their own banks, but are not in fact allowed an exclusive jurisdiction. State banks that are members of the Federal Reserve System are also "supervised" by the Fed, operating not from headquarters in Washington but from the twelve district banks. "We are not *regulators*," says first vice president Ernest Patrikis of the New York Fed; "we are *supervisors*. There's a big difference." The Comptroller employs a cadre of National Bank Examiners, who keep track of the federally chartered banks. The FDIC examines those state banks that are *not* members of the Fed, most frequently, these days, as part of a team with the state examiners.

In the early 1990s, especially in Massachusetts and New Hampshire, these joint visits tended to be contentious, because the collapse of the "Massachusetts miracle" and the real estate boom had left New England bankers with portfolios full of loans that could be considered unimpaired only by lending officers who knew these borrowers and knew that somewhere, somehow, they would pay what they owed. State examiners, worried about the condition of the local economy, were somewhat more likely to accept such claims than the FDIC examiners, who were carpet-baggers and were under pressure from chairman L. William Seidman to protect him from the kind of obloquy that had landed on Danny Wall, chairman of the Federal Home Loan Bank Board, when his busted S&Ls fell deeper and deeper into the hole. I had spoken at an annual convention of Massachusetts bankers, and I began to get calls about what the FDIC was doing.

I lacked sympathy. My perception had been that the bank examiner is rather like the teacher in an urban school. Outsiders, especially of liberal persuasion, worry that teachers are picking on the kids, and unreasonably go to the principal to get someone out of their class when a child makes himself a nuisance or fights back. In fact, as I knew from work in schools, the teacher who goes to a principal with a problem child is not cheerfully received. She brings the principal a problem the principal doesn't in any way need and doesn't want to know about; his every wish is that teachers take care of behavior problems inside their classroom. If the child in question belongs to somebody with a position in the PTA or the school board, the teacher may get an actively hostile reception.

Similarly, the bank examiner who brings back a negative report on the First Feedbag, N.A., may be greeted by his supervisor with a yowl of "First Feedbag! Don't you know that the chairman of that bank was also chairman of Congressman Whosit's reelection campaign? Do you want to get our budget cut?" But in 1991, Seidman had told his examiners to make sure the FDIC could never be criticized for losses from permitting an endangered bank to continue in business.

The examiner's first job is to decide whether the bank is being run with due regard to standards of safety and soundness. In the old days, teams of examiners would be secretly assembled in a local hotel the night before, and would descend unannounced on a bank early in the morning to see if the ledgers balanced, count the cash in the tellers' tills and the vaults, and pull the files on the loans to make sure they were current and that any failures by the borrower to meet the terms had been noted, had been remedied, or had been considered in valuing that loan on the balance sheet. Assets also had to be examined to see if they were legitimate investments of other people's money and deposits that are, after all, government-insured. All this might take several days in a small bank, and a couple of months (every year) in a large bank. The banks paid the cost of the examination themselves, and sometimes complained, but it was part of the price they paid for public confidence.

Today the ledgers are balanced by the computers (in the case of about three thousand banks, by computers owned and operated by service companies like EDS, which not only own and lease or service the ATM machines but also keep the books on the deposits and the checks). The examiner's job is to test the inputs into the computer system and make sure they're accurate. It's not really worth a civil servant's time to count the cash. And Congress or the regulators have steadily widened the range of investments that are permissible for banks. All FDIC examiners are now equipped with notebook computers. Indeed, they were initially equipped with notebooks in the Seidman days, but except in the area of failed banks—where the "resolution division" had developed a function for valuing insolvent banks that enabled them to download all the necessary information about large institutions in three or four days—there were no programs for the notebook computers, and the examiners continued to outline information about loans on long yellow legal pads.

When Ricki Helfer became chairman of the FDIC in 1994, she brought over a computer wonk from Social Security, commissioned bank examiner software, and started a project to establish a telecommunications link between the FDIC's computers and the banks' computers, to permit major parts of the examination to be done remotely. Just married herself—to the lawyer who had represented her in her Senate confirmation hearings—she didn't like the idea of her employees on the road, away from spouses and families. "Examiners," she said, "have lousy lives. They travel Monday through Friday. If they can download here, they'll be happier examiners—and it will be easier for them to consult with colleagues; they'll do a better job."

At the end of the examination process, which includes interviews with the senior officers of the bank, the examiners from any of the agencies give the bank what is called a CAMEL rating, for capital, assets, management, earnings and liquidity (in practice, a measure of the composition of the bank's liabilities). A bank funded almost entirely with short-term borrowings will lose something in the liquidity section, because it is at the mercy of changing interest rates. If recent promotions for deposits or credit cards have crashed and burned at great expense, or long-standing relations with borrowers have been ruptured, or the general and administrative expenses have ballooned, the examiners might have some questions about management.

These days good CAMEL ratings are worth cash money, because banks rated 1, 2 or 3 are to all intents and purposes excused from paying deposit insurance premiums. Banks with a 5 rating, however, in addition to repeated visits by examiners that may add up to a trusteeship by the regulators (Citibank for two years operated under a memorandum of understanding that gave the Comptroller's people veto power over major decisions), must pay a premium of 27 cents per $100 of insured deposits to remain in business. As of early 1996, 92 percent of the nation's banks were in the better categories, and paid essentially nothing.

The FDIC Improvement Act of 1991 (pronounced *Fidishia*) mandated higher premiums until the insurance fund reached 1.25 percent of insured deposits. Former FDIC chairman William Seidman gnashed his teeth over this requirement, and said the increases in premiums would destroy the nation's banking system. In fact, the vessels filled up quickly as the economy improved, the FDIC was able to realize a little more than expected from the properties that had come into its charge during the banking bust of 1989–91, and the number of bank failures diminished. For the last six months of 1995, in fact, there were *no* bank failures, and thus no deductions from the FDIC's insurance fund to buy overvalued assets. At the end of that time, the fund had $25 billion, which even at the interest rates the government pays for its use of that money means that the fund grows by $100 million a month. In 1995, the American Bankers Association went to the Republican Congress to suggest that the bankers themselves owned the insurance fund and ought to get that money as a refund on what they've paid—and, surprisingly, sold the idea to Congressman Jim Leach of Iowa, chairman of the House Banking Committee. Mrs. Helfer fought them off fairly easily, because President Lyndon Johnson had put the FDIC on budget, and that $100 million a month put the politicians one little step closer to their cherished balanced budget.

The three federal agencies fight over turf a lot, and they all fight together against the Securities and Exchange Commission, which controls the accounting processes that must be used by bank holding companies when they sell stock or bonds or file their annual reports. There was a blow-up over Penn Square, which Paul Volcker tried to save despite the clear evidence of its insolvency (and by taking *all* the good assets of the bank as security for discount window advances, maximized the loss to the FDIC). Again, when Continental-Illinois was failing, Treasury Secretary Donald Regan, superseding the Comptroller, fought with the Fed because he thought on free-market principles that the bank should be allowed to fail and the unsecured creditors should pay for their folly.

There is a Federal Financial Institutions Examinations Council, mentioned in Chapter 5, which tries to make sure that all the bank regulators sing from the same hymnal, and which has risen occasionally to public attention. (Most prominently, perhaps, in the early 1980s, when the Deputy Comptroller for International

Banking sought to declare for all the regulators that examiners should grant less than full valuation on loans to the Italian government.) In summer 1996, they precisely agreed that they would all add an "S," for "Sensitivity to Market Risk," to the old CAMEL ratings. And every once in a while they work together operationally, too.

Note, for example, the devastation in 1988 of First Republic, a holding company for about seventy Texas banks, which had been put together a year earlier by merging First International and Republic Bank under FDIC auspices. There were state-chartered banks here and federally chartered banks. Some of them were okay and some were seriously bust, and the holding company showed no disposition to use the resources of the better banks to shore up the books of the bad ones. To give the devil his due, Seidman solved this problem by lending a billion dollars to the holding company and taking as his collateral the stock of all the subsidiaries. When all the regulators had their ducks in a row, he called his loan to First Republic, which couldn't pay, and the FDIC seized the stock, making itself the owner of the banks.

Among the solvent First Republic banks the FDIC now claimed to own was a prosperous credit card issuer and processor in Delaware. Keith Ellis, a young man who had recently left the staff of the Council of State Bank Supervisors to become banking commissioner in Delaware, saw in his law book that Delaware prohibited the pledging of bank stock as security for a loan. He told the FDIC that he could not recognize their ownership of the credit card bank, because they weren't entitled to the stock. That's all right, Seidman said, we'll have our friends at the Fed cut this bank off FedWire. Ellis found that the Philadelphia Fed, through which this bank worked, was indeed willing to slam down its receiver, and presently the FDIC auctioned off the property for something like $400 million, to Citicorp.

14 / Examining the Banks

Accounting standards ought not to conceal the reality they were established to portray.

—Letter of September 13, 1990, from Edmund Coulson, chief accountant of the Securities and Exchange Commission, and Robert A. Bayless, chief accountant of the Division of Corporate Finance, to Jack Kreischer, president of the American Institute of Certified Public Accountants

Valuing the assets is the name of the game in bank examination. Since the 1930s, banking regulators have greatly simplified the process by permitting banks to continue to carry any securities they hold at "historic cost" rather than current market value, and to carry loans at face value, whether they pay market rates of interest or not, unless they are significantly impaired. The disagreement between the Massachusetts bankers and the FDIC was on the definition of impairment, and the security of what bankers have long called "character loans."

Most modern commentators consider capital the essential measurement of banks. *Institutional Investor* ranks the world's banks by the size of their capital rather than by their assets. But you arrive at the book value of a bank by deducting all the other liabilities from the value of the asset; the remainder is capital.

Impairment of the loan portfolio or the bond holdings or the derivatives positions resulting in a write-down on the asset side of the ledger can be made up only by reducing the capital on the liability side of the ledger. The same numbers will turn up on the profits-and-loss statement as the admission of a loss. A solidly profitable bank will have more capital when you return next year (provided it doesn't pay excessive dividends), and an unprofitable bank will have less capital.

Bank regulators typically have permitted banks to avoid fluctuations in reported capital (and reported earnings) by creating "loan loss reserve," which may be considered part of capital, leaving the assets valued as before. Reductions in reported assets occur only when there is an actual write-off, which is then balanced on the liability side by a reduction in the loan loss reserve. This allows banks to smooth out their earnings for presentation to stockholders and the public—for it is the public, through its deposits in the bank, that is the largest creditor of the institution, and the public must be kept comfortable. Uncontrolled, it could also lead to a "smoothing out" of corporate tax payments, and the IRS has rules to control how much a bank can deduct from its taxable earnings for the purpose of increasing the loan loss reserve.

The procedures that should be followed in valuing bank assets are perhaps the most contentious argument in finance. Reviewing proposals to reform deposit insurance in 1990, the Congressional Budget Office found seven authorities and organizations (including two district Federal Reserve banks) in favor of market-value accounting, and four authorities and organizations (including one district Fed) opposed.[1] The Federal Reserve Board and the SEC were at daggers drawn during the incumbency of Richard Breeden as chairman of the SEC. Breeden, a lean, vigorous, abrasive lawyer, especially strong at the SEC because he was known to be a protégé of President George Bush, thought market-value accounting was necessary for banks. Alan Greenspan, chairman of the Fed, thought it would be the ruination of the country. The banks and Greenspan argued that if the paper was good paper, with no defaults on covenants or interest payments, then the bank would eventually get back its face value, and—provided it had the "intent and ability" to keep the paper to maturity—it should be allowed to carry it at face value. The chief SEC accountant spoke scornfully of the "intent" criterion as "psychiatric accounting." The banks and the Fed staved off Breeden long enough to get a new president and a new SEC chairman who didn't have market-value accounting for banks anywhere near the top of his agenda—especially when the banks made such a strong recovery after 1992.

But the fact remains that accounting which ignores present value, not market-value accounting, is the twentieth-century novelty in the old business of banking. Historic cost accounting for financial institutions first poked a nostril into the tent of the insurance industry in 1931, when the predecessor organization to today's National Association of Insurance Commissioners authorized insurance companies to value the bonds and equity securities in their portfolio on December 31 of that year at the prices that had prevailed on June 30. For 1932, the companies were permitted to continue reporting the values they had asserted in their year-end statements the previous year, and in 1933 companies were authorized to report their equity securities holdings "at the lower of cost or book value."[2] Banks began using what is now the standard evaluation procedure only in 1938, after the economic relapse of 1937 caused a drastic decline in the value of investment portfolios and the federal banking regulators reacted with a "Uniform Agreement" to change bank examination standards.

This agreement, Professors Donald G. Simonson and George H. Hempel wrote, "established an historical cost (book) valuation standard that had the effect of protecting the level of the banks' regulatory capital." Permission to hold securities portfolios at book value was a total departure from previous procedures, and a matter of great importance in 1938, when the average bank had 43 percent of its assets in securities. Similar grace was accorded to the loan portfolio. Orders went out to examiners to reduce "the placing of improper emphasis on maturity . . . if ultimate repayment seems reasonably assured." The authors note that "by focusing on loans' ultimate collectibility, this provision ignores the fundamental economic tenet of the time value of money. . . . The historical cost accounting framework . . . conceals the true value of the institutions' net worths."[3]

A quarter of a century later, the Financial Accounting Standards Board validated this neglect of the time value of money by approving FAS 15, a rule permitting financial institutions to carry restructured loans at par on their balance sheets so long as all prospective payments on the loan, principal and interest together, would total more than its face value. It was under the shelter of this rule that banks were permitted by regulators to continue to carry their obviously impaired loans to less developed countries at full book value, though these loans were being traded for less than half that value on an active international market which moved an annual dollar volume considerably greater than the dollar volume of all trading on the American Stock Exchange.

At the end of 1990, however, FASB published an "Exposure Draft" of statement entitled *Disclosure About Market Value of Financial Instruments*, which would require the presentation of the market value of such loans or securities, at least in footnotes. "Quoted prices," said the FASB draft, "even from thin markets, provide useful information because investors and creditors regularly rely on those prices to make their decisions.[4]

Both the historical cost and the market-value accounters see systemic misvaluation by their rivals. "Two banks with the same or similar portfolios," write the Federal Reserve Board researchers, claiming the impossibility of finding the market value of loans, "could honestly arrive at very different market value calculations because of the way in which the market discount rate is chosen or the payment probabilities are determined for their various loans and other unmarketable instruments."[5] But Lawrence J. White, NYU economics professor and former member of the Federal Home Loan Bank Board, attacking the utility of the historic cost information the Fed finds preferable, notes that "identical financial assets, with identical market and maturity value, may be carried on the books of different thrifts at different values, depending on the times of acquisition and market conditions at the times of acquisition. Conversely, different financial assets with very different market values will be carried by thrifts at identical accounting values. Thus, the accounting information creates a murky and misleading picture."[6]

And, of course, history happens. The supporters of historic cost look to the wisdom of Ecclesiastes, that this too shall pass, that the interest-rate spikes are indeed spikes. "[L]ife company investments," former American Council of Life Insurance economist Kenneth M. Wright points out, "were able to come through the depression years with minimum damage, thanks in large part to stabilized values which departed from current market prices. All parties avoided catastrophe to their mutual advantage: policyholders, life companies, debtor corporations, financial markets, and the general public."[7] The supporters of market value by contrast believe that God really does play dice with the universe, that the real world is a series of discrete transactional quanta, each with its own measurable bottom line—after which the game begins again. "The real problem here," says one of the accounting theoreticians at the FASB, "is a primeval resistance to any accounting system that may force you to take a loss on day one." And the obvious truth is that one side is right in some industries at some points in time (insurance in the 1930s, commercial banks in 1990), while the other side is right in other industries at other points in time (the S&Ls in the 1980s).

For market-value advocates, the prototypical problem with historic cost is "gains trading." Assets that go up in price, the banks sell to generate a profit; assets that go down in price, they keep in the portfolio at historic cost. Professor White illustrates how easily and systematically this can be done in the modern world of synthetic and segmented instruments by the simple act of stocking the bank's mortgage security portfolio with interest-only (IO) and principal-only (PO) strips of mortgage-backed securities rather than with the whole loans. The valuation of these separable parts of a single mortgage when they are initially separated out from the mortgage is based on statistical analyses of how quickly and how frequently householders repay their mortgages by selling the house or refinancing.

If interest rates go up, the value of the IO strip increases because people are less likely to pre-pay their mortgages and thus the income stream from interest payments will be larger than originally anticipated. The bank or S&L sells the IO strip at a profit, and buries the PO strip in the portfolio at historic cost, because its market value has declined with the slower than expected rate of redemption of the mortgages. If interest rates go down, the value of the PO strip increases because people *do* prepay their mortgages, and the income stream from repayment of principal is larger than anticipated. The bank or S&L sells the PO strip at a profit, and buries the IO strip in the portfolio at historic cost to hide its loss of market value.

By purchasing *both* strips of mortgage paper, an S&L or bank manager can guarantee the growth of his reported earnings in the short term. The increased profits make him a hero, and he can move on to a better job before anyone is the wiser. The decline in the value of the strip that has been buried in the portfolio will appear only as part of a disclosure of the aggregate value of all investments in a footnote to the financial statements, which will not be widely noticed.

The pernicious effects of these accounting rules were multiplied by the "risk-based" standards for capital adequacy adopted by the banking regulators of the developed world in 1988 under the auspices of the Bank for International Settlements in Basel.

The agreement (not easily won from the Japanese, who later had great reason to be glad they had got on board) required each nation's banking authorities to impose upon their banks a minimum level of capital to back the assets they held, depending on the credit risk connected with the assets. The level was at least 4 percent equity ("Tier I") and another 4 percent of reserves and subordinated debt ("Tier II") against those assets weighted at 100 percent (commercial and industrial loans, loans to less developed countries, commercial mortgages). But no capital had to be kept as backing against default on loans to governments of developed countries, and a weighting of only 20 percent was required for holdings of mortgage-backed securities, including strips of such securities, issued by government-sponsored enterprises like Fannie Mae and Freddie Mac. Combining all the rules, such mortgage-based securities require only 80 cents of equity capital to back every hundred dollars of paper purchased. If you buy both sides, you can't lose (at least in your reports to regulators and stockholders), and the return on equity is likely to be spectacular. In fairness, the Comptroller's Office caught some of that in the early 1990s, and gave the banks involved orders to cut it out, which they did.

At bottom, all these valuation disputes grow out of the failure of the United States government to count the costs the private sector must bear when official action is unwise. Monetary policy was an effective and efficient tool to cool down an overheated economy in the days when the Federal Reserve—through its control of bank liabilities—could impose a true credit crunch. Technology, however, liberated credit extension from the money supply, leaving the central bank with no weapon other than drastic interest-rate manipulation to reduce the demand for credit. Violent interest-rate volatility punishes soundly managed as well as feckless financial intermediaries. Hedging helps—many of the derivatives discussed in Chapters 9 and 10 find their origins and nourishment here—but it doesn't always provide answers. Mean-

422

while, the fine-tuning of tax codes to achieve narrow governmental objectives creates monstrous asset misvaluations.

In 1981, the Congress passed a tax law that through its generosity to real estate investors added perhaps 25 percent to the effective value of commercial property in the United States. In 1986, the Congress took away the candy. Banks and insurance companies that had made loans based on the artificial valuations stimulated by the 1981 tax code found the collateral backing their loans worth less than the outstanding principal. In the S&L business first (because it was the most lightly capitalized) and the banking business next (because regulators had permitted the egregious overstatement of its capitalization), the damage done by an inconsistent and careless government had passed the poor powers of accounting procedure to add or detract.

There is a middle ground (which may well prove to be the bridge of the *Titanic*): greatly increased disclosure of market values for those—and it will be a widening circle—who can make use of this information. Even after the mechanisms for gathering and disclosing such information are in place and functioning, financial institutions could continue to report their results on the more stable basis of historic cost. But they would have to reveal their holdings of, say, IO and PO strips, separately. And straight mortgages. And structured notes. And credit card debt. And currency options. And interest rate swaps.

Disclosure of the damage the computers say was done by a spike in interest rates would not create an audited report of insolvency (or trigger a government takeover of an institution crippled, probably only for a matter of months, by the government's own policies). More public analysis of the differences among what are now compendiously described as "nonperforming loans" would permit banks to adjust and accommodate the embarrassment of a borrower whose present cash flows leave him short although his future remains reasonably promising. The evaluation of these judgments would pass in an orderly fashion (rather than today's disorderly fashion) from government regulators to those who have their own money at risk, as banks provided increasing information to investors and depositors.

Information conduces to security; secrecy conduces to panic. Well-managed banks and insurance companies would command the support of the market in bad times, because those whose support is in the end essential would have reason to give it. Badly managed banks would be reorganized or consolidated with less political or bureaucratic intervention. And accountants, as an FASB task force director put it, "will begin to do the job people have always thought they were doing."

I once quoted Albert Hettinger, now long dead, then the grand old man and human balance wheel of Lazard Freres in the United States: "Most influential teacher I ever had was the fellow who taught me accounting. He used to say, 'Accounting is a way to tell the truth.' " And I commented, "It would be a pity if that idea died off with Hettinger's generation." But it did: the story of the 1980s in the financial markets is in many ways the story of the death of honest accounting.

In June 1996, the FASB made yet another effort to gain general consent for accounting procedures that would make banks reveal the real values of the portfolio. Derivatives, the agency proposed in an "exposure draft" passed by a 5–2 vote, should be put on the balance sheet as assets (if they are in the money) or liabilities (if they show a loss): "The ability to settle a derivative in a gain position by receiving cash is evidence of a right to a future economic benefit and indicates that the instrument is an asset. Similarly, a cash payment that is required to settle a derivative in a loss position is evidence of a duty to sacrifice assets in the future and indicates that the instrument is a liability." Derivatives should be carried on the books at "fair value": "The Board believes that fair values for financial assets and liabilities provide more relevant and understandable information than cost or cost-based measures."[8]

What the banking regulators and the examiners will make of all this, time will tell. It always does. In the case of FASB rules, considerable time is often required. But the SEC *can* force bank holding companies to follow FASB rules.

2

"I hate mark-to-market," said David Berry of Keefe, Bruyette & Wood. "FASB is trying to get the accountants to do my job." And no small part of the regulators' job, too. As Comptroller Ludwig puts it, "When you have complete transparency, you have a helper in the market." What is available to the public and stockholders now is only the "call reports" in which banks tell their regulators every six months how they think they are doing, which can be deliberately or accidentally misleading, and which are in any event available only after a ninety-day lag. William Isaac in his farewell to the FDIC suggested that the time had come to publish the first five-sixths of the examiner's report, which is factual rather than judgmental, and let stockholders and depositors alike decide on the basis of that statement whether they want to have their money in that particular bank.

Jerry Jordan, president of the Federal Reserve Bank of Cleveland and before that the senior economist of the Federal Reserve Bank of St. Louis who kept that bank on the straight and narrow of monetarism, told a Bank Administration Institute conference in Orlando in spring 1996 that the time had come to substitute auditors for regulators in the policing of the banks. Derivatives and the globalization of credit had made centralized supervision impossible. "Investors," he said, "need to know that the risks are being monitored, and periodic examinations can't do that."[9] Unfortunately, Jordan wants these internal auditors to report to the CEO of the bank, who would, he says, ensure that the department is independent and effective. And no doubt, the CEO would do so, until the auditors brought him word of trouble in the department headed by the husband of his wife's best friend.

The truth is that effective regulation of banks in a market-based economy can be accomplished only by the market itself, which means an end to much of the secrecy now surrounding bank portfolios. As more and more of the portfolio of the banks is securitized, there is less and less reason to worry that competitors or enemies will learn about a company's or an individual's borrowings. Large commercial loans are already participated out to a number of banks, and these participations trade just like bonds, on the same desks that handle bonds, at both banks and investment houses. They can be priced, and are, not only by the traders but also on the screens of Bloomberg Financial Services. Just as the law now requires credit card companies (banks and non-banks) to publish the delinquency rate among cardholders, the law can require banks to tell the world what proportion of their other assets are nonperforming, by class, and what the stress tests show in the valuation of derivatives. Some of that already happens, but much more could be done.

Once again, the Federal Reserve Board stands in the way. In this era of mergers and acquisitions, when lawyers and investment bankers are performing their due diligence chores through all the books and records of the firm to be acquired, the one thing they cannot see when the subject is a bank is the examiner's reports on the bank. The Board of Governors in late 1995 specifically warned banks and bank holding companies that they were not permitted to show potential acquirers what it was that the bank examiners had to say about the bank.

In May 1996, the Shadow Financial Regulatory Committee of academic economists and academic-minded lawyers issued a statement of *Disclosure of Examination Reports and Ratings*.

"[T]he arguments for continuing secrecy," they argued, "are outweighed by those in favor of disclosure." The shadowers were willing to go well beyond what Bill Isaac had recommended: they wanted not only the information sections of the examination published, but also the opinion sections: "permitting public disclosure of criticism of an institution's management or policies—information that is routinely included in examination reports—would provide a greater incentive for improvements by management, and supervision by its board of directors, than a confidential report. . . . The argument that full disclosure of a depository institution's true condition could be a threat to stability of the financial system is without demonstrated merit and is not a justification for veiling institutions in secrecy." Disingenuously, the committee recommends that the choice of whether or not to reveal the examination results should be left to the bank itself, which would have "the choice of what to disclose to the public."[10] It is hard to think of anything more likely to start a run on a bank than an announcement that it didn't wish to disclose the contents of its most recent examination report.

Debates about the reform of banking regulation are mostly useless, because they ignore the context of bank secrecy in which government regulation is imposed and carried forward. In the heyday of concern about deposit insurance, after the dimensions of the S&L disaster had been recognized, the General Accounting Office proposed as a shorthand means for determining the solvency of banks a requirement that a bank have some percent of its capitalization, perhaps 10 percent, in the form of subordinated notes. If the market would not buy subordinated notes from the bank, the message would be that purchasers of such paper did not believe there was enough value in the bank to pay them off after payments to depositors and secured creditors (like the counterparties in derivatives, whose claims by law are prior to those of other creditors). The variation in interest rates that different banks would have to pay to sell subordinated notes would be a form of variable deposit insurance premium. The inability of a large publicly held bank to sell subordinated debt would be a prima facie case for closing the place down.

Stock market valuations of bank shares would not be an acceptable substitute, in this analysis, because—as a Federal Reserve research study notes rather breathtakingly—stock prices include a value for the "put option on the bank's loans which is issued by the deposit insurance agency and is held by the bank." The GAO suggestion did not get off the ground, in large part because of the belief among the regulators that in 1991 *most* large banks could not have sold subordinated debt. Instead, to the fury of both the Fed and the FDIC, Congress issued strict orders in the new Federal Deposit Insurance Corporation Improvement Act that when a bank's capital fell below 2 percent of its total assets, regulators should initiate steps to shut it down. The practical effect of this rule in a crisis, of course, will be to make examiners take a generous view of impaired assets, to keep the bank's capital above the trigger.

For years, debate in the Congress about banking regulation has focused on the McFadden Act and the Glass-Steagall Act and the Bank Holding Company Acts and the limits they impose on what banks can do. The McFadden (and 1956 Bank Holding Company) restrictions on interstate banking and branching were eliminated by the Riegle-Neal act of 1994, following on almost a decade of regional compacts by state governments and desperate resolutions of banking crises that had permitted the growth of interstate (but not nationwide) banks. The Glass-Steagall restrictions that separated lending operations from market-related money-raising were breached by the technology that erased most of the differences between participations in term loans by commercial banks and junk bonds issued by investment banks. Meanwhile, the Federal Reserve Board steadily increased the size of the

428

wagons that could be driven through the Section 20 loophole in the act, permitting banks to do certain market-related activities provided their contribution from these activities to the total revenues of a bank was not a major factor in its operations.

Opponents of Glass-Steagall sold the Congress and academia on the idea that the New Deal law had been written by men who wrongly believed that involvement in the stock market and its crash had destroyed a third of the American banking system in the first years of the Depression. When they felt they had to justify expansion of Section 20 powers, the Federal Reserve Board majority soothed worries that banks permitted to securitize assets would sell off the good stuff in a crisis, leaving the Fed and the FDIC with the losses on the bad stuff. The truth, as Paul Volcker pointed out in one of his few dissents as chairman, was that banks always had and always would use their information advantage over the public to sell off the bad stuff, rescuing their own balance sheets from losses.

What was in the minds of the congressmen who passed Glass-Steagall was the fact that well over half the corporate bonds the banks had issued in the 1920s as underwriters for their clients had gone into default by 1933. National City Bank of New York had cleared out of its own Peruvian exposure entirely by these means, leaving its customers holding truly worthless paper. And market activities by banks, using other people's money, had exacerbated the financial boom of the late 1920s and thus dug a deeper hole for the economy in the 1930s.

But by the late 1980s, the evidence was clear that keeping banks out of underwriting securities was permitting a handful of large investment houses and hedge funds to charge monopoly rents for their services without protecting corporate America, investors, or the banks. Indeed, as the system worked in the 1980s, the banks wound up as sources of "mezzanine financing," the "bridge loans" to do the deal before the public actually bought the paper, which was the riskiest part of the game. Resistance to liberalization persisted from the Investment Company Institute, the trade organization of the mutual funds, which was afraid that the established bank trust departments, which ran commingled funds for clients of the bank, would be permitted to sell to the general public in competition with the mutual funds. But as the banks entered the brokerage business, they became sales offices for the mutual funds, which were easy to sell because they were advertised in the magazines their customers read and in the golf tournaments their customers watched on television. By 1996, banks formed almost half the membership of the ICI, and senators and congressmen who had been stalwarts of the mutual fund industry dropped their opposition to repeal of Glass-Steagall.

In 1996, what kept Congress from taking action to break down the barriers between the financial services was the opposition of the insurance agents. There is a strong argument for permitting banks to underwrite life insurance—the New York savings banks have done so for more than a hundred years, with good results for themselves and for the purchasers of the insurance—and there is no safety-and-soundness argument against allowing banks to act as insurance agents, which would not risk their capital or their depositors' money. Insurance is much more expensive than it ought to be, because high commissions for insurance agents come off the customer's first payments, which is the money that would multiply the most under conditions of compound interest.

The original draft of the banking legislation that the newly Republican House Banking Committee was to bring forward in 1995 would have permitted banks to act as insurance agents, but House Speaker Newt Gingrich told the Republican caucus that there are more places with influential insurance agents than there are places with influential bankers, and there was no point getting the agents mad. The first rule of politics, of course, is that people remember only with difficulty what you did *for* them, but they never forget what you did *to* them. "Negotiating a Glass-Steagall reform approach that obtains widespread industry consensus and advances the public interest," Congressman Jim Leach of Iowa, chairman of the House Banking Committee, told the 1966 Conference on Bank Structure at the Federal Reserve Bank of Chicago, "rivals all but the Middle East peace process in sophistication and number of land mines."

Jim Leach is a very smart, soft-spoken, gray-haired man in a sweater, a Rhodes scholar who became a congressman after serving as an administrative assistant to a congressman, and has been so popular in his district that half the time he has no opposition. He had been waiting for years in what seemed a permanent Republican minority to be chairman of the House Banking Committee, and he did not give up easily when the Speaker backed off his reform bill. He and his colleagues had designed a mostly bipartisan bill that empowered bank holding companies to engage in virtually any financial activity, under the overall supervision of the Federal Reserve. When the Supreme Court ruled (9–0, by the way) that Congress had given banks with small-town branches power to broke insurance policies and the states could not interfere, Leach returned to the attack. In his Chicago speech, he claimed that this *Barnett* decision had given his bill new life. What was blocking him, he reported, was the insistence of the Comptroller of the Currency, backed by the Treasury Department, that non-banking activities should be conducted inside the bank, where the Comptroller would regulate them, and not in a holding company which would respond to the Fed.

"The issue," Leach said, "isn't simply, as the Comptroller would have it, a safety and soundness concern, but one of extending the deposit insurance safety net and competitive equity. Congress prefers the holding company model with banks required to deal with certain new powers in separately capitalized affiliates in order not to expand deposit insurance coverage to these activities and in order to ensure that banks are functionally regulated. Competitor companies—such as investment banks and insurance companies and brokers—have a compelling case not to be subject to competition from a rival able to tap low-cost, federally insured deposits for activities which go well beyond traditional lending functions."[11]

Leach idealizes the Fed: "It is universally agreed," he said, "that it has remained above partisan politics"—but in fact there is not universal agreement. Arthur Burns (who consulted with Commerce Secretary Maurice Stans) pumped up the money supply in 1972 to help the Nixon re-election campaign (he had been economics adviser to the 1968 campaign). Many in the Clinton White House felt that Alan Greenspan should not be reappointed in 1996, because so much of what he said and did was political in intent. When the balanced budget question dominated the news, Greenspan testified before Congress that a Fed study had demonstrated that a vote to balance the budget would reduce interest rates, and in fact no such study had been made. Seeking to conceal what had been said at meetings of the Open Market Committee, Greenspan testified to Congress on October 19, 1993, that the tapes of these meetings had been destroyed after summaries were prepared, and no transcripts existed. A week later, after learning that Arthur Burns had left his set of transcripts to the Nixon Library, he sent a letter to Banking Committee chairman Henry Gonzales admitting that he had known for years that transcripts were kept, but he "gave the matter of these procedures no further thought until recently . . . until a staff member jogged my memory in the last few days."[12]

On the issue, however, Leach is right: financial services holding companies, with each subsidiary regulated by a government agency that understands the subject, is the correct template. And the Fed, which will be increasingly marginalized in the next few years by its disjunction from the technologies that control the future of banking, may be a better regulator of holding companies after its attention is no longer absorbed by its efforts to control markets it can no longer control.

Much of the legislation affecting banks since the 1960s has dealt with affirmative obligations rather than limits—an obligation not to discriminate in lending (no "redlining" of parts of town), not to confuse people about the interest rates they would pay on loans ("truth in lending"), not to confuse people about the interest rates they would receive on deposits ("truth in savings"), not to keep someone from using the money in the checks he deposited once his payor's bank has in fact paid off on the check, not to cash checks for more than $10,000 or accept cash deposits of more than $10,000 without knowing who is getting or giving the money and telling the Treasury Department about it. Probably the bumpiest bone in the banks' throat has been the Community Reinvestment Act, which demands that banks lend not too far from the office at least some of the money a branch in a poor neighborhood receives from depositors.

One of the most remarkable debates in economics in the 1990s was a fight over whether or not banks discriminated against blacks and Hispanics when making mortgage loans. After a study by the Federal Reserve Bank of Boston said they did, great statistical artillery was drawn up to prove that the study was deficient, though nobody outside an academic cloister or a government bureaucracy could doubt the truth of the conclusion. The solution found by the Justice Department was to order Chevy Chase, a suburban Washington bank, to open a branch in one of the city's black neighborhoods. Justice then asked the Fed and the Comptroller to block an acquisition by Barnett Banks in Florida on the grounds that its record of mortgages to black applicants was inadequate, but the department would not share its information with the regulators. In the absence of any reason to believe Justice knew what it was talking about, they gave Barnett the approvals. Barnett announced it would fight any Justice Department complaint in court, and apparently Justice walked away.

The Chevy Chase solution is clearly not viable over time, because the banks are all going to close branches by the thousand between now and the new millennium. On the mortgage front, it's Fannie Mae and Freddie Mac that must be pressured—not only to lean on their suppliers to bring mortgages to minority home-owners, but also not to purchase abusive mortgages and fund cheapjack mortgage bankers who exploit the information debility of poor communities. The question of how banking services are to be delivered to people in poor neighborhoods transcends mort-gage loans, and we shall look at it in the Epilogue.

Some state laws are more helpful. New York, for example, requires state-chartered banks to offer very inexpensive consumer accounts with no minimum balance and eight free checks a month. This causes a certain amount of inconvenience all around when the consumer writes nine checks, subjecting himself to charges on the first eight, too, but it points in the direction the banking system must go to serve the American economy and American society. Unfortunately, Eugene Ludwig as Comptroller of the Currency exempted nationally chartered banks from the law.

Indeed, the great question in banking regulation is not how to shuffle the deck chairs among the federal regulators. The provi-sion of more timely information about bank portfolios will greatly relieve the "supervisors" of the need to supervise. Even Commu-nity Reinvestment Act matters may be best handled by publishing enough details of the banks' loan portfolio to let local and neigh-borhood press publicize whether the banks are meeting their com-mercial obligation to their depositors. There will continue to be a need for rules to remedy the informational disadvantages of bank customers, not only in calculation of true interest rates but also, for example, to make sure that banks do not sell overpriced or insufficient home insurance to people taking home mortgages by packaging disparate products into a single unit. The banks' record in selling credit insurance (paying off your car or credit card debts if you die) has been truly dreadful in this regard: New York State has limited their profits on this enterprise to 52 percent of the pre-miums paid.

434

And there will continue to be a need for "dual banking"—for state licensing and state supervision of banks as well as federal licensing and supervision. State regulation, much of which has been preserved in the Riegle-Neal nationwide banking act, ensures at least a degree of geographic diversity. The United States is too big a country, and too varied in its sectional interests and economic conditions, to benefit from a truly national banking system, or from truly national bank regulation.

EPILOGUE
The Future of Banking

Founders Bank in Bryn Mawr, Pennsylvania, is the creation of a square-jawed, tanned, rather military-looking, almost bald, fiftysomething entrepreneur named Robert Whalen. Whalen had come to banking from systems work with IBM, and had been an officer of the Bryn Mawr Trust Company for seventeen years when he started his own bank in 1988. Founders in spring 1996 was a one-office, $85 million bank with only 1,500 depositors. That works out to an average deposit of $57,000, which is skewed high by several very large deposits, like the escrow account for a Chicago travel agency which often has $7 million in the bank as part of its contract with the travelers who have bought but not yet received its packaged tours. Even after deducting the elephants, however, Whalen's average depositor has over $25,000 in this bank.

The single office was a remodelled school gymnasium with room for three tellers behind a chest-high mahogany partition and an old-fashioned pendulum clock on the wall behind the tellers. Not much banking is done in this office. "People have a need to identify with a banker, not with a bank," Whalen says, "and the people I want to have bank with me don't have time to go to a bank. We never see most of them after they open their account." In summer 1996, he was one of the earliest vendors of the EDS PC-based bill-paying system, which in time might save him from any need to issue checkbooks to his customers.

The essence of Whalen's banking is that "we do business only with people we know." To open an account at Founders Bank, a depositor must go through the same credit check to which he would be subjected if he wished to get a loan. Whalen believes that a bank should be "a network of people helping each other. If you're a customer of ours and you need to see somebody for knee surgery, I can get you someone better at knee surgery and I probably can get him faster than your internist could." Whalen refers customers to other customers—law firms, home-builders, plumbers, chiropractors. If they have an international problem, Founders Bank maintains close correspondent relations with Brown Brothers Harriman of New York, the last great private bank (partners, not stockholders), which will represent Whalen's customers abroad.

The Chicago travel agency wires money in from a Chicago bank, but most of the customers work and/or live in Pennsylvania and western New Jersey, and they make their financial contact with Founders Bank through automated teller machines on the MAC network, most of them owned by Mellon Bank, though Founders has similar arrangements with PNC and CoreStates. In early 1996, the owners of the ATMs charged Founders 75 cents for each withdrawal its depositors made (though they were beginning to mutter about larger charges), and $1 for each deposit envelope, with a maximum of twenty checks per envelope. Whalen absorbs the charges. In summer 1996, First Union added a $1 per deposit charge, deducted for its own benefit. Whalen took ads

437

implicitly dissing First Union and assuring *his* depositors that Founders would refund their dollar.

Mellon picks up these deposits at these machines at about two in the afternoon, and puts them through the usual check-collection process, separating out the deposit slips that direct the receipts to Founders Bank. Knowing its depositors, Founders is prepared to certify to Mellon that it will cover any bounced item immediately, and Mellon has agreed to accelerate credit to Founders for all items. In fact, after running the checks through its usual proofing process to imprint the amount on the MICR line under the signatures, Mellon adds up the total and immediately puts an electronic credit item to Founders through the MAC settlement system. Founders has the money tomorrow from MAC, which permits Whalen to offer his customers next-day availability on their deposits. Where a check has to be collected outside the Philadelphia clearinghouse, *Mellon* doesn't have next-day availability on the funds. Why are these banks giving Whalen this service? "I don't know," Whalen says. "I don't think these gentlemen have thought it through."

Whalen has several score partners who among them put up $10 million in capital for the bank, plus two active collaborators in operating it. One is EDS, which does all the data entry and data processing for the deposit accounts. Mellon sends the payments message through MAC to Founders via EDS, and it is EDS that credits the depositor on Founders' books. "Of course," Whalen says, "we have to have a place to store all the information we have about our customers." EDS supplies that system, too. The other collaborator is Bell Atlantic/NYNEX Mobile. Whalen and his four or five most senior associates are available to a depositor any hour of the day or night anywhere in the world, through the cellular phone system. And any information in the bank's computer is available to Whalen and his senior associates through the modem on a DEC notebook, which links to the cellular phone.

Sitting in a bedroom in The Wigwam Resort in Phoenix, at a convention (some hours after East Coast banks had closed for the day), Whalen accessed the details of his own account, his voice mail, any messages his secretary wanted him to look at, and his schedule for the next weeks. He could have done the same for any customer's account and any information the customer has shared with Founders Bank, and he could have responded to a customer's question with as much knowledge of the customer's situation as he would have had sitting in his office in Bryn Mawr. One notes in passing that this has turned out to be not quite enough, and two of Whalen's most senior associates will be opening "branches" of the bank in living rooms in adjacent counties because Whalen has decided that customers like to relate to "*some* physical presence" of their bank.

Founders Bank is a little more than 60 percent loaned up, and four-tenths of 1 percent of that portfolio (one loan) was not current as of spring 1996. Most of the borrowers, of course, are the selected depositors; this is niche banking par excellence. The bank has a state charter and a Fed membership, thus escaping FDIC examination, and expects to use all the powers this combination will allow. Whalen says what he really would like to do is give people a single statement of all their financial positions, à la the Merrill Lynch Cash Management Account. His minimum balance for no-fee checking is $500 for individuals, $5,000 for businesses, but that's not been a significant factor: his fee income tends to lag the industry. If your average deposit is more than $25,000, you have minimal expense for brick and mortar and tellers—and people feel they are getting significant personal service from your bankers—you can make a living by lending.

By contrast, we look at the published plans for Wells Fargo, once it has digested its acquisition of First Interstate. Between the two of them, they had about 1,200 brick-and-mortar branches at the end of 1993. By the end of 1996, the unified bank will have fewer than four hundred brick-and-mortar branches, and about 750 banking offices in supermarkets. Most of the supermarket branches will consist of one or more ATMs in a kiosk and one or two employees to sell bank "products," but about two hundred of them will be larger operations with four hundred square feet of floor space in the store and perhaps six or seven employees. By and large, the people who work in the supermarkets will be interchangeable, trained to help people fill out forms, not authorized to exercise judgment. At best, they will be brokers, referring requests for home mortgages, for example, to a subsidiary of Norwest Corporation in Minneapolis, which pays Wells a fee for every customer it delivers.

The small businessman in the same mall with the Wells branch will not have any sense that there is a banker near him, and will not get any of the help with his problems that historically a banker offered. His loan, like all small- and medium-sized business loans at Wells, will go through a telecommunications process to a central computer which will score it and make a decision untouched by human hands. Indeed, Wells has opened phone lines to all over the country, and established an oft-hit site on the World Wide Web, to permit small businesses to borrow without actually meeting anybody from Wells Fargo. "We will do everything we can over the next four or five years," said executive VP Dudley Nigg, "to make all transactions electronic."

What is interesting about the Wells Fargo model is its explicit rejection of growth as a strategy for banks. Prospectuses issued to analysts in connection with the long fight to acquire First Interstate indicated a hope for a rise in fee income, but basically the increased profits promised from the deal were to come from executing a relatively unchanged amount of business with lower costs of execution. "As our assets shrink," said president William Zuendt, "our labor base shrinks and our costs shrink, we will simply be running at a higher octane."[1]

It is not entirely clear that this strategy works. Speaking of the mini-branches Wells and Bank of America have scattered through Arizona, Phoenix-based bank consultant Carl Faulkner says that "B of A and Wells are very good at selling services, not so good at delivering them." John McGuinn, a San Francisco lawyer who represented a dozen laid-off branch managers in a suit against Wells in 1988, says that "They hire them, burn them out and spit them out. Employees are like disposable commodities. It's a pretty ugly piece of work."[2] To the extent that the strategy involves using ATMs to make loans—Bank of America has an elaborate "Versateller" with a TV screen on which the applicant can see a banker in a central office looking through papers—the ATM service can be degraded while people who want to take out fifty bucks wait for someone who is arranging a loan or checking out his securities portfolio.

But the name of this electronic banking game is reduction of personnel, and reduction of reliance on personnel. Defenders of the trends in banking in the 1990s like to stress that although the number of *banks* is down by one-third since 1980, the number of *banking offices* has continued to rise, to almost sixty thousand in mid-decade. But that is clearly a transition phenomenon. Deloitte, Touche in early 1996 reported a study of the banking industry which said that no fewer than half the present employees of the banks would be working in other industries (or not working at all) in as little as five years. This represents an enormous change from banking at it was. While the success of a bank was a function of the wisdom of its lending, banking almost as much as advertising was a business where the inventory walked in the front door every morning and walked out every afternoon. George Moore when he was president and chairman of Citibank took the first forty minutes of every day having coffee with four or five Citibankers, some from the far reaches of his building and some from the far reaches of the world. After each morning coffee, he sat with his personnel director and entered comments into the permanent folders of the people to whom he had just spoken. George always did most of the talking.

When I worked with Moore on his memoirs, I could not do a satisfactory first draft of the personnel chapter, and he had to write one himself for me to edit before he felt comfortable with my description of his procedures. A bandy-legged, irritable, egotistical self-made man, he spoke interestingly if not always wisely on a surprising variety of subjects. He was chairman of the Metropolitan Opera and the Hispanic Society as well as the largest bank in America; as banker to the Cisneros family of Venezuela he helped build one of the largest international empires; as banker to Aristotle Onassis he helped Maria Callas get what she wanted and helped Christina Onassis keep Jacqueline Kennedy from getting everything *she* wanted. Moore believed that banking was a personal service business and that the quality of the people who did the services would determine the long-term profitability of the bank. He promised the stockholders in what became Citicorp during his tenure that he would deliver annual growth of 15 percent in footings and 15 percent in profits (targets later associated in the public mind with his successor Walter Wriston). To increase the size of the bank pre-computer necessarily involved increasing the number of people who worked for the bank.

When Wells is finished with its restructurings, it will have ten thousand fewer employees than it had in 1996, and the average person manning Wells's interface with customers will have had training that amounts to the equivalent of a few weeks at McDonald's Hamburger U. (Luke Helms at Bank of America actually took the McDonald's course to help him decide what he wanted to do to train the people who would work in his supermarket branches.) On the other hand, it's only fair to say that the average salary at Wells is the highest in the industry—and the fraction of its senior managerial jobs held by women is by far the highest in the industry.

The contrast between Wells and Founders Bank is even more stark. Founders Bank is using technology to reduce the costs of standardized services for the purpose of offering a more tailored service to its patrons, whose deposits will carry the freight and generate a profit. Wells is using technology to standardize the services it offers, with the expectation of selling them for more than they cost. *The payments system, once the cost center at the heart of the bank—because the depositors who wrote the checks provided the banks with the raw material of their manufacture—has come to be regarded as a profit center.* Even where direct revenues from payments work are sacrificed for other purposes, the measurements are on a sophisticated allocation of other earnings to the operations departments. Citibank under John Reed, an engineer before he was a banker, the inventor of modern cost accounting for payments services, is offering electronic services without charge in a carefully planned drive to increase the fraction of its funding that comes from retail accounts and to intensify cross-selling of other financial products.

The new model of banking expressed in all these companies is something quite different from anything we have known before. Banking as it was did not exhibit economics of scale. It was cheaper to make large loans than small loans because certain expenses were common to all loans, but the market took over the lending beyond a certain size even in the old days. Generally speaking, the most profitable banks for generations were those between $500 million and $1 billion in 1996 dollars. These are the banks that are now being absorbed into mergers at the fastest rate, and are the most likely to disappear in the next century. Banking as we defined it earlier, as the agglomeration of transaction balances to lend at interest, has been declared superfluous. Now, instead of looking at banking and saying there are no economies of scale, bankers look at financial processes that do reveal economies of scale—electronic payments services, trading, derivatives, mortgage processing, credit card issuance, syndicated lending—and we define those as banking. "Because this is a sophisticated business," said Gordon Clancy, Citibank's chief derivatives trader, "it requires a large infrastructure." That's what big banks have: a large infrastructure.

On the evidence of 1995 and 1996, this really works as a way to run big banks. For the three decades from 1965 to 1994, big banks considered themselves remarkably well off if they earned as much as three-quarters of 1 percent on total assets. A full percentage point was the impossible dream. (Note that with 5 percent equity, which was the absolute maximum Walter Wriston thought Citicorp should need, a 1 percent return on assets converts to a 20 percent return on equity.) In the first quarter of 1996, virtually all the larger banks reported more than 1.3 percent return on assets, and Wells Fargo reported an ROA of more than 2.2 percent. If you're going to support the basic business on fees, if the mortgage department makes its profits by referring customers to Norwest and never puts a hand in the bank's own pockets, you don't need many assets to generate a large return.

2

Expansion across state boundaries, though clearly implied by the increased use of telecommunications in banking, got its impetus from the bank failures of the 1980s. Bank of America, which had been evicted from its interstate role in the Depression, was called upon to rescue Seafirst, an Arizona bank—and if all had been known that could have been known, it also rescued its fellow Californian Security Pacific, which looked healthy only because the cosmetics had been applied just so. NationsBank got a toehold in Florida by finding a loophole in the law which permitted out-of-state trust companies, but it rose to prominence only when the FDIC gave it First Republic in Texas. Its ex-Marine chairman Hugh McColl, a candidate for the least-liked CEO in banking (I built a file of stuff about NCNB sent to me by hostile North Carolina and Texas bankers), then won bloody takeover battles in Georgia and Virginia (some of them against banks that had previously merged in an effort to defend themselves against

NCNB) to spread NationsBank's net over the entire southeast quadrant.

NationsBank intends to take full advantage of relaxations in the Visa and Master pricing rules to charge as much as $3 per transaction when people who are not NationsBank depositors use NationsBank ATMs. As NCNB, the bank never had a retail tradition in its native North Carolina (except for its employees and an occasional importunate corporate customer, the bank didn't even write home mortgages), and Tom Storrs, its Harvard Ph.D. chairman in the 1970s, specifically eschewed any attempts to increase its market share within the state. NationsBank's interest is still primarily in paper, and its activities in areas that affect real economic behavior tend to be through other subsidiaries of the holding company—though in 1995 the bank made an apparently serious push in lending to medium-sized businesses, especially in the Southeast.

Similarly, Fleet Financial, grown from Industrial Bank of Providence, Rhode Island, took advantage of the fact that it was one of the few New England banks still standing after the late 1980s real estate bust (its borrowing base was in costume jewelry, which did not have a bad recession), and absorbed the deposit bases of Bank of New England, Shawmut and Connecticut Bank and Trust. With that money, Fleet became one of the largest mortgage bankers in the country—compiling in the process, alas!, one of the worst records in the South, especially Georgia, for exploiting people who couldn't afford the cheesy homes they were sold by builders offering mortgages from Fleet.

That these mergers were regional rather than national was in part the result of legislation passed by the states to prevent the New York, California and Illinois holding companies from taking over their banks, and in part the death of foreign lending as a major interest of the government or most of the industry following the bloodbath of loans to less developed countries in the 1980s.

Providing foreign exchange and letters of credit for people and businesses continued to be a money-spinner for banks. Trading in foreign exchange and the derivatives associated with it and in the "Brady bonds," which were the detritus of bad 1980s lending, became a big business indeed. But the relationship of such profit centers to banking was increasingly remote. When Mexico blew, again, in late 1994, it was almost a non-event to the banks which had suffered so in 1982. They had brokered customers' money into Mexican securities at the customers' own risk, but made few direct new loans to Mexican borrowers.

Citibank continued to have an old-fashioned banking relationship with borrowers in Latin America and parts of Asia. Most of the rest, once they had paid the price of entry, went looking to provide fee-remunerated services rather than money to rent. In the 1970s, the party line at the banks was that they lent money into these poor countries only as a service to their U.S. customers, who were expanding in those markets. In the early 1990s, the party line became the truth. A caveat is needed in mid 1996, however. The "success" of the Mexican bailout of early 1995 appears to have convinced a number of lenders that countries, like big banks, had become "too big to fail." Cross-border lending, some of it stimulated by the easy-money policies of the Bank of Japan (which was happy to pour yen to the world to bring down the job-destroying overvaluation of the currency), gained astonishing and dangerous momentum as 1996 proceeded.

With few exceptions, foreign-owned banks have been no more than modest successes in the United States. Like the American banks in Europe in the 1970s, German and Swiss banks exploited the strong currencies and low interest rates of their homelands to expand their commercial and industrial lending base in the United States, much of it to German and Swiss manufacturing companies operating here. Allied Irish Banks did well with a modest purchase in Maryland, the Dutch thrived at LaSalle Bank in Chicago, and Spain's Santander made a very good thing out of First Fidelity in New Jersey and its environs. In the early 1990s, as Americans warily withdrew, more than a quarter of the C&I lending in the United States was by foreign-owned banks.

But the failures are more common—Japanese-owned Bank of California, Union Bank and Manufacturers in California were not moneymakers, Bank of Montreal's investment in Chicago's Harris Trust was only a modest success prior to its mid-1996 expansion, Hong Kong and Shanghai's purchase of New York's Marine Midland didn't do much for either party, Britain's Midland dropped a billion dollars on California's Crocker and went home, Britain's Barclays' and NatWest pretty much abandoned their American operations (NatWest sold out to Fleet in 1996), and the multinational effort to resuscitate New York's Franklin National Bank as European-American sank slowly into the sea. Crédit Lyonnais from France wound up owning MGM Studios, among other turkeys, and had to sell off everything as part of a French government bailout.

Meanwhile, many U.S. banks found profitable foreign niches. Americans continued to dominate the London money market (which operated mostly in dollars). Citibank especially leveraged its expertise abroad, creating a worldwide network of consumer banking operations funded in the local currencies, and using the deposits those operations created to wedge itself into selected industries as a knowledgeable lender. But the idea that banking profits in the future would be worldwide in their origin—and that American banks had to be behemoths to fight back against foreign giants—has pretty much disappeared. The essential reason for size as the century came to a close was that only by merger and acquisition could one painlessly shrink an industry that had incurred liabilities beyond the size of the bankable assets in which those liabilities could profitably be invested. In the end, the fewer larger banks in the American future would have fewer employees and smaller balance sheets than the total work force and balance sheets of the larger number of smaller banks in the American past.

Though commentators criticized, the most encouraging aspect of banking in the 1990s was the way bank holding companies used their temporary high profits to repurchase their own stock and prevent their capital base from growing with retained earnings. At a time when the markets dominate, and the markets pick up every plant by the roots every day to see how the return on equity is coming, banks are more likely to get in trouble because they have too much capital than because they have too little capital. Too much capital demands higher earnings that can be got over time only by taking greater risks—and the leverage inherent in banking means that last year's capital can easily be decimated by this year's losses if the gambles don't pay off. As a practical matter, the lesson of the mid 1990s was that consumers did not demand anything like a market return on their savings if the banks did not seek to expand by bidding for deposits. In the go-go 1980s, banks had found that to draw new money they had to raise the interest they paid on large portions of their existing funding. In the profit-centered 1990s, they learned that by giving up the marginal deposit dollar they could hold down their funding costs on a sizable fraction of their liabilities. It is possible, though not certain, that the industry has truly learned this lesson.

3

There is a vision of banking for the twenty-first century shared by the regulators, the banking trade associations, many banking professors and most of the officers in the big bank holding companies.

It is, to begin with, a vision of nationwide or nearly nationwide institutions, certainly no more than twenty of them, with electronic links to their corporate customers, to the markets and other financial service institutions, to each other and to smaller banks, and to many if not most of their individual customers.

Those who do not have telephone or computer links to the bank will do most of their business with plastic, while an ever-shrinking cadre of older depositors will still write checks. Customers will pay fees for services, including standardized stock brokerage and insurance agency, and the money left on account, a steadily diminishing fraction of the country's financial assets, will be invested in a variety of securities, including packages of loans.

Some of these institutions will be banks, some will be brokerage houses, some will be data processors like the credit card banks and consortia, the ATM networks, Microsoft and Intuit, ADP, First Data, EDS and FiServ, delivering services to consumers who don't have the faintest notion who really supplies them. It is by no means impossible that some of these institutions will be subsidiaries of holding companies in the telecommunications business, for the link between telecommunications and banking tightens daily. It will be noted that this pattern of industrial organization makes no contact whatever with our current system of government regulation.

These nationwide institutions will be what the retail trade calls "category killers." Their central feature is not that they charge less for service (though they do) but that they give less service. As the discount and warehouse stores demonstrate, many people are more than happy to pay less for less service—especially when the service they get where they pay more does not seem worth the premium. Unfortunately, the information imbalance between service providers and consumers in banking is so great that people normally do not know whether they get value for money, or could get much more value for a little more money. Prior to the day of the ATM machine, when people could cash their checks at the supermarket or at their own bank—and could make deposits only at their own bank—it was universally understood that the choice of bank was dictated by personal convenience. The bank with the best locations—Bank of America was the leading example—could pay less for deposits or charge more for checking services.

The first ATMs in workplaces heightened that tendency to seek convenience, but once the ATM networks were up and almost any card could be used in almost any machine (through Visa's Plus or MasterCard's Cirrus, if not agreement among local networks), a remarkable insensitivity to price was noted. In a shopping center where a consumer's own bank had a machine that could be used for nothing, she would often use the machine at the door to the supermarket, paying $1—even $3—for the privilege of withdrawing perhaps $50 to $100. Some of this unrealistic fee structure probably derived from the loss of brand recognition that the credit cards had imposed on all plastic—not knowing the bank that issued their credit card (if it was a bank at all), the consumer didn't realize that only his own bank could issue him a debit card. Presumably, this phenomenon will last only until the owners of the ATMs—many of whom, again, are not banks—find it worth their while to advertise that they charge low fees even to people using "foreign" cards. The ATM networks and switches have to be careful not to violate the anti-trust laws, especially as their number diminishes through mergers and acquisitions, but they can offer volume discounts. Here, too, there are economies of scale.

In addition to the commodity business of payments services, large banks expect to offer their best customers extensive personal services, from financial planning, trust accounts and custodial services to large lines of credit, free credit cards and customized mortgages. "Private banking" is the term of art, and these days it means more than the concoction of tax-avoidance and money laundering strategies the term connoted when it was a Swiss specialty with branches in Belgium and the Caribbean. With varying degrees of standardization, private banking services might in time be available to as much as 10 percent of the population.

4

Two things are wrong with this model of banking, of which the most serious is that it leaves a large part of the country unbanked. The fraction of households in the United States that don't have a bank account passed one-quarter in 1996, and is rising. Next to mutual funds and financial planners, the most rapidly growing sector of the American financial services industry is the store-front check-cashing shop. As of 1995, there were 6,000 such in the United States, up from 2,150 in 1985. They cashed more than 200 million checks worth more than $60 billion. In New York City, there were 550 check-cashing shops, which cashed 30 million checks worth more than $10 billion. They are all licensed by the state, and they are protected from competition: state law says that no new check-cashing store can open within three-tenths of a mile of an existing check-cashing store.

Stephen Wolf, chairman of the National Check Cashers Association in 1996, is treasurer of New York's Pay-O-Matic, which was founded in 1950 and has more than a hundred locations in that city alone. A youthful fifty, he has long, wavy black hair, an Abraham Lincoln beard and a mustache; he has been in the business since 1968. Wolf reports that about half the checks he cashes are payroll checks, a quarter are welfare payments, and the remainder are other government payments. He says that 99 percent of checks written in government benefit payments are cashed at institutions like his, and that he runs the Electronic Benefit Funds Transfer program for New York City. New York State sets a maximum charge of 1.1 percent per check—still almost $10 a month for a man with a $200-a-week paycheck (which is likely to be all that is left from $250 in wages, after deductions).

"We provide a service to the people in these neighborhoods," Wolf says. "There are no ATMs, and local groceries don't have cash on hand in the morning when people are lined up at our locations. The sign on the door says 'Check Cashing,' but we provide a range of services. It's a good bill-paying place. People have cash in their hands, and before they leave they pay their Con Edison [electricity] bill [939,190 payments in 1995], cable TV [865,509 payments], telephone [356,070], Brooklyn Union Gas [314,107]." It should be noted in passing that these companies give Pay-O-Matic deposit slips for their bank accounts, because New York State has not okayed electronic payments by check cashers to public utilities. Security is pretty tight in Wolf's places, but he says he has very few bad experiences, because 90 percent of the people who come into one of his offices have been there before, and everybody—security officers, the people behind the glass, the other patrons—recognizes them. "Our big growth these days is in the suburbs," Wolf adds. "A lot of people have opted out of traditional banking."

What is happening here is that corporate America with the encouragement of the banks is sloughing the cost of paying its workers onto the workers themselves. Once upon a time there were envelopes with cash, delivered by Brinks truck. Then there was the check that could be cashed at some bank with which the company had made an arrangement. (New York City paid more than $2 million a year to a bank that agreed to cash its paychecks, until the financial crunch of the 1970s led to elimination of this cost, too.) George Kaufman, financial economist at Loyola University and adviser to the Chicago Fed, supervised a study of check-cashing places in Illinois, where the maximum charge is 2 percent of the check, and came out with strong views that these people earned their fees. Given Kaufman's political and economic views, it would be surprising for him to find that any successful business does not deserve to be successful, but within that frame, he was, as always, undoubtedly right. The problem is that the external costs of a fractured payments system are very high. And unnecessary, too.

Electronic payment will save money—and a lot of it: ballpark estimate, $35 billion, one-half of 1 percent of GDP—only if the system is essentially universal. Building the telephone system in the early years of the century, Theodore Vail insisted that every telephone added to the network benefited all the existing users of the network, and therefore it was worth stringing wire across the North Dakota plains to bring the telephone to remote farmhouses. This was not even arguably true for extensions of the electricity grid, and government in the form of the Rural Electrification Administration had to subsidize the supply of power to the countryside. By the time we got to cable television, gimlet-eyed Wall Street was measuring the cable companies by the number of non-poor homes passed per mile of wire, which left a lot of the country open for peddlers of satellite dishes a few years later. As the tone of the debate over health service reform indicated in 1994, Americans are not in the habit these days of considering the values of universal access. But in the case of payments, the cost of serving another customer electronically is usually zero or something like it, while the cost of even infrequent paper exception items can sabotage the economies of an electronic system.

Some work has been done to extend the benefits of electronic payments to people who do not have bank accounts. Chase Bank in New York arranged with the Veterans Administration for direct deposit of benefits checks to homeless vets, and issued them ATM cards to withdraw the money as they needed it. Erica L. Coover, a Citibank assistant VP in charge of services to the unbanked, arranges with corporations to set up limited-purpose accounts for employees, who can have their pay deposited directly to these accounts and withdraw it either from ATMs or at supermarkets where the ATM card serves as a debit card for a purchase plus change. (The ATMs pay out in ten-dollar increments, which will not mesh well with the deposits. Part of the Citibank plan is a "Holiday Savings Account" that pays interest, and credits the difference between deposit and withdrawal as savings.) The heaviest users of these Citibank plans are agencies that provide temporary help.

"Banks," Coover reports, "don't want to cash checks today even for corporate clients. They're closing branches." Citibank did a survey of users of its new service, and found that most of them "hated banks. They'd had accounts at banks, they were constantly overdrawing them. Banks were inconvenient, ID'd them, subjected them to long lines on payday. Even if a company provides a bank to cash checks, some people may use storefront check-cashing." The same division of the bank manages Electronic Benefits Transfer programs for the government from the same technology center (manned with operators speaking several languages) in Tampa, Florida; and that's a rapidly growing business.

Other expenses are needlessly unloaded on the unlucky or poorly informed. For many years, Western Union was the only company offering wire transfers of money to consumers, and until 1979 the service was regulated by the Federal Communications Commission. As part of Jimmy Carter's drive to deregulate, the FCC deregulated wire transfer of funds, observing that "We are confident that the public will be served by enabling multiple entry into this market."[3] Western Union promptly raised rates, and continued to do so at a 5 to 8 percent per year clip, and Citicorp decided to offer competition. But it would not build the network of retail stores Western Union had already established, and even before the rest of the bank got in trouble, this operation was canceled. American Express then got in the game, putting its MoneyGram operation into its First Data subsidiary, which handled credit cards. When First Data was spun off, MoneyGram went with it.

Western Union was charging $13 to $29 per domestic transfer; First Data set a price of $9; Western Union sued on antitrust grounds, accusing First Data of "predatory pricing." (Western Union lost.) A telegraph company, Western Union came out of the bankruptcy court with all its creditors whole because of the profits on its money transfer business. At a time when rich folks can send money through the ATM network to their kids in college for a price of one dollar (or nothing), poor people have to pay ten to twenty times as much. Mexicans, Guatemalans, Salvadorans and immigrants from the Caribbean pay even more to send money home. For no reason. In fairness, the banks rip off middle-class people, too, both for wire transfers and when they want to make payments abroad in currencies other than dollars.[4]

What is required here is a vision of the payments system as a public utility, and this vision is totally lacking at the Board of Governors of the Federal Reserve. The simple fact of the matter is that more than a third of the employees of the Federal Reserve System work in activities related to processing checks, and like any bureaucratic organization the Fed exists first of all to protect its own full-time employees. The authors of the Depository Institutions Deregulation and Monetary Control Act of 1980, which required the Fed to charge for its payments services, assumed that private-sector competition would either take over the business or force the Fed to improve its performance. Instead, the Fed enforced old rules or wrote new ones to make effective competition very difficult.

The ability of banks to truncate correspondents' checks and cut out some steps required for clearance through the Fed has made it possible for the private sector to grow its share of check-processing work in the 1990s. Competitors of the Fed have also benefited by agreement among the banks to stop charging each other fees for immediate credit on checks directly presented at the bank on which they are drawn. Because the law prohibited banks from charging such fees to the Fed when the Fed did the presenting, it had been cheaper for banks to push high-value checks through the Fed rather than through correspondents and clearinghouses. The Fed had to okay this deal among the banks, by the way. The approval required three years, and in the end the banks got permission not to charge fees only on checks presented before eight in the morning, while the Fed could get same-day credit free for presentment up to noon.

The Fed's enormous investment in imaging plants—while denying its assistance to the industry in developing standards for electronic check presentment—represents what may or may not be a successful effort to claw back some of the business the banks have gained. Despite the requirements of the Monetary Control Act that the Fed cover its expenses when offering services in which it has private-sector competition, the costs of this investment are being "deferred." In 1996, the General Accounting Office reported that "Some Reserve Bank officials told us that the growth in scope of [automated services], particularly to include check processing, had made it difficult for them to comply with the requirements in the Monetary Control Act."[5] A month later, the Fed announced a reduction in fees. . . .

In establishing the rules for electronic payments, the Fed has been more successful in frustrating efforts by competitors and potential competitors. When General Electric wanted to start an automated clearinghouse in California, for example, the Fed established new "presentment schedules," which meant that banks wishing next-day credit for payments would have to get their paperwork into GE an hour earlier than the closing time at the Fed for similar credit—though GE was delivering completed tapes while the banks delivering to the Fed were submitting raw material from which tapes would be made. The question of which transactions do and which do not require paper rather than electronic confirmations has been left deliberately murky by Fed lawyers. When cost-conscious corporations began making large payments overnight through the ACH at 85 cents each rather than by FedWire instructions at $17, the Fed caused to be raised in the specialized media a huge fuss about whether ACH was *really* safe enough—despite a long history of "cash concentration" through the ACH by retail chains that deposit cash and checks into local

456

banks every night but wish to centralize their financing at just a few of them.

The solution, as the General Accounting Office suggested in its 1996 report on the efficiency of the Federal Reserve, is to spin off the retail payments system to a private corporation. This will have to be done by legislation. The Fed would then learn to regulate as an outside authority, not combining regulation and operation. The details of the process would require considerable and careful exploration. At the end of the day the Fed would probably continue to operate FedWire for high-value payments and to provide final settlement on its books for members of private clearinghouses, credit card settlement consortia and ATM switches, after they have balanced their accounts with each other. But the work should start with everyone chanting the same three mantras: EDI (for electronic data interchange), EFT (for electronic funds transfer) and RTGS (for real-time gross settlement).

Electronic data interchange involves the intrusion of the banking system into bookkeeping procedures used by companies that make and receive payments. They would have to be able to format their invoices and keep their accounts receivable in forms susceptible to standardized reporting—in itself, incidentally, quite a Good Thing. Bills could then flow from the supplier to the purchaser in machine-readable form, to be paid directly to the supplier's account, with multiple "fields" of information identifying the payor and the reason for the payment. This is not very sophisticated, by the way: the scanners at the checkout counters, which control the supermarket's inventory and supply the buyer with an itemized list of purchasers, are a version of the process already in widespread use. But it is essential.

Standards could be somewhat flexible: the Kleindienst machinery that processes German payments orders for Deutsche Bank already permits the use of as many as eleven data fields to identify different elements in the payment. Individual participation in the system could be by pre-authorized payment of repetitive bills, by entry through personal computers, by telephone, or by ATM-like devices for public use. For business use, the most important block right now is the combination of Fed mumbo-jumbo and lawyer overkill: the average contract arranging payments through EDI runs nineteen pages of small print.

The potential savings from full-scale EDI are at least in the high tens of billions of dollars. People now doing very dull work would doubtless lose their jobs, but it should not be beyond the wit of a society where public service and health standards are deteriorating to find employment for them. It is not clear whether the banks will be able to gear up to be part of this system. Donald K. Charney, a young man with white hair, CFO for U.S. AID in the Clinton State Department, reorganized the expenditure of $1.9 billion a year on an electronic chassis (but also got the U.S. Treasury to keep its Birmingham, Alabama, disbursing office open twenty-one hours a day so Charney's agents around the world could access it). "We are accountants," he says, "we are not in the program business. On February 19th, 1993, Clinton signed a memo saying everyone in the government should move to electronic commerce. We took him seriously. The hardest thing to do for us is to find the person in the organization who handles EDI. We approached Chemical Bank, and we got back a query, 'What is EDI?' We knew we had the wrong person." In twenty-nine out of forty-four AID offices in 1994, bills submitted by local contractors were paid within four days.

Electronic fund transfer is of course a system by which payment orders are given by a payor to a payments agency to be delivered by electronic means to a payee. Direct deposit costs recipients nothing today, and it will cost them nothing in the future—costs are eliminated, not incurred, when the money flows directly to the recipient's bank account rather than circulating about through paper handlers. The means can be direct wire transfer in real time, entry to an ATM switch or credit card clearing center, or an automated clearinghouse for delayed netting.

Real-time gross settlement is trickier, and would require banks or other payments agencies to equip themselves not only for electronic payment and receipt, but for continuous posting of both credits and debits to customer accounts. This too is less of a problem than might be thought. Brazilian banks at the height of the inflation did something of the sort internally, enabling them to offer their customers payment out in Puerto Allegre in the afternoon on deposits made that morning in Salvador, three thousand miles to the north. On-line debit card verification involves some degree of instantaneous posting. But the existence theorem is in Switzerland, where the Swiss Interbank Clearing System, launched in 1987, operates 22 hours and 45 minutes a day. Payments are made through the Swiss National Bank, and must be covered by the payments agency's deposits at the bank before they will be processed. "This type of system," Akinari Horii and Bruce J. Summers write, "implies real-time computer processing and operational controls that permit the central bank to prevent use of intraday credit."[6] So does the point-of-sale system already in private use in the United States.

In spring 1996, Britain's privately operated CHAPS (Clearing House Automated Payments System) adopted a real-time gross settlements procedure with credit (if any) to be extended privately, not by the Bank of England. The Germans, we are authoritatively told, are coming, and bringing the new European Central Bank with them. "Payments are executed," Wendellin Hartman of the Bundesbank told a Goldman Sachs meeting on settlement systems in January 1996, "only if they are covered by account balances or by intra-day credit lines. . . . Owing to the cover principle, the central banks are kept from free risks. . . . There are no systemic risks arising from deferred finality and the possibility of an unwinding, which do exist in the case of net settlement systems."[7]

Real-time gross settlement in the United States would not mean that the paying institutions could not pay with credit, for most of the participants in the ultimate clearance would be external switches paying each other, and the switch could have arrangements with its members to extend intraday credit to each other, probably on some secured basis. The Fed would operate the ultimate real-time switch, but in an atmosphere of absolute rules, with no discretion, and no extension of daylight overdrafts.

Among the rules would be a requirement that interbank payments must be made in public through the Fed switch, even if their effect was merely to move money from one correspondent account to another at the same bank. Private bilateral netting, which the Fed has been touting as a solution to derivatives market risks, can create the most unstable system of all, because no participant knows the extent of its customer's borrowings from other participants. The Fed would retain lender of last resort functions in a real-time settlement system, but to the intermediary switches rather than to individual institutions. Intensive and timely open market operations, permitting banks to sell and repurchase quantities of paper to meet their payments obligations without depressing markets, would presumably be the means of choice.

Gerald Corrigan, out of the Fed and into Goldman Sachs but still in his attitudes very much a creature of the Federal Reserve, argues that "The role of Central Banks in *both* the oversight and operation of payments systems must be preserved, if not expanded, even as technological and other forces tend to work in the other direction."[8] But that is a recipe for stalemate and eventual disaster. The important thing is to get started now, before the insularity, arrogance and—let's face it—ignorance of the Federal Reserve Board subjects the country to the loss of international competitiveness implied by an inefficient and expensive payments system, and the social costs of a payments system that excludes large fractions of the community. This is one area where the markets will not help us, for they are in thrall to an economic philosophy that makes decisions by reducing to the same abstract numbers the work of a prison guard and the work of a dairy farmer.

5

The other great danger of the new banking system projected and welcomed by the industry is its failure to find room for the information-intensive lending that has been historically the central economic and social role of the banks. The problem is less easily remedied, for technology has changed forever the relationship between information and risk. Loans are going to be scored in a mechanical way. Like the scoring and packaging of home mortgages and car loans, the scoring process for small-business loans will result in lower interest rates for the borrower and fewer losses to the lender. The net benefit in this process, in other words, exceeds the cost from the failure of the standardized information form to pick up borrowers whose potential for success can be found only by judgment. A higher fraction of the smaller loans available after the computer has creamed the high scorers will produce heavy, maybe total loss, and thus the rates charged to the borrower who doesn't fit the mold will be higher. Reward structures for lenders giving the banks greater profits from successful loans will be necessary to keep the money flowing to those whose efforts could enrich us with new products and processes.

But this is an area where the magic of the market should be deemed trustworthy. Finance companies are growing as the banks shrink. S&Ls can lend more than a quarter of their footings to small businesses without losing their eligibility for low-priced credit from the Federal Home Loan Banks, which are eager to put their wards into this business (as is Congress: one of the finance industry bills introduced in 1996 would have renamed the Home Loan Banks as Enterprise Banks and concentrated their efforts on small-business loans). Merrill Lynch has a billion-dollar fund for lending to smaller businesses, hoping no doubt to secure Initial Public Offering work from the successful borrowers. American Express "would like to be the money center for small business," said George L. Farr, vice-chairman of Amex.[9] Amex has a new wrinkle on bundling: it has formed subsidiary firms of accountants, which will offer services to borrowers at reduced rates. The certified public accountant firms are laboring in the state legislatures to make sure that such commercial ventures are not permitted to certify statements for their clients. . . .

Large banks may limit their lending essentially to high scorers, but small banks will need borrowers who don't meet computerized criteria. With luck, the most talented will survive in the shrunken cadre of lending officers. The history of Silicon Valley and its imitators argues that investors are susceptible to initial public offerings that don't meet the usual prudential criteria. Small businesses could benefit if Glass-Steagall can be amended to permit small banks to bring small issues to market from local enterprises—but even without Glass-Steagall amendments one could imagine systems not unlike mortgage-origination systems by which small banks would be encouraged to seek standardized loans for small businessmen in their catchment area.

The Levy Institute has suggested the potential importance of factors for financing small manufacturers. Moreover, there are ways by which government could put a thumb on the scales of judgment to invoke market forces. Credit unions, which already enjoy tax breaks, could be encouraged to be neighborhood business lenders. Community-development banks can be given a basis for leveraging their funding to serve a clientele of small borrowers. One must be careful: the Small Business Administration and its lending offices have been a mixed blessing. But it takes only a normal reasoned faith in capitalism to believe that good loans will somehow get made.

It's an interesting question where the lenders will get the money to lend. In the 1980s, following on work done by Henry W. Simon and John Williams in the 1930s, the Brookings Institution economist Robert Litan advocated what he called a "narrow bank," which would offer payments services and invest only in short-term government securities, obviating the need for what then seemed threatened deposit insurance funds. This proposal died away as the banking system resumed profitability in the 1990s, but payments systems based on real time gross settlement will require a much more liquid portfolio than a bank can get from lending. This increased need for liquidity will push the larger banks toward purchases of short-term government paper as their basic source of interest income. Smaller banks that continue to make smaller commercial loans will be willing to pay a premium for their money—certainly more than banks can hope to earn on a securitized package of loans—and may be an appealing source of extra interest income for the larger banks. In Japan, this tendency of large general-purpose banks to finance riskier lending by smaller specialized banks turned out to be a source of financial instability when asset inflation stopped, but more information about what banks are doing would presumably punish the bank stocks in the market and force a change of course before disaster.

6

Increasing the information available to stockholders, depositors and lenders to banks will be key to effective regulation of financial service institutions in the years ahead.

Direct government regulation of banks and other financial service institutions will be a function of what these institutions do. Under any circumstances, we will continue to need rules to prevent concentrations of market power. Mergers and acquisitions will have to be investigated to determine their effect on competition among suppliers of banking services. Government agencies will have to enforce rights of access to ATMs for the customers of banks other than those that own the machines, and limits on the ways banks can induce customers of one service to buy others. (One argument against letting banks broker insurance is that they may bundle insurance and mortgage services in ways that freeze out other mortgage lenders or insurance brokers.) We will also need rules to keep banks on the straight and narrow with regard to equal opportunity for potential borrowers regardless of color, creed, gender, age, ethnicity or zip code. Though monetary policy will be much more difficult to execute in the age of market interest rates and electronic payments than it was in the age of controlled interest rates and debit transfers, there will certainly be a need for open market operations to influence the size of the money supply and the height of short-term rates, not to mention the control of crises.

If the banks' and regulators' preferred scenario comes true, and we get a small number of large banks seeking activities that yield economies of scale and processing checks through the Fed, a regulatory structure not far from today's will probably persist and suffice. After a few more Orange County disasters with greater bank involvement, functional regulation will move control over banks' securities and derivatives operations to the SEC, making banks subject to the "suitability" rules that now govern what well-informed agents can do to uninformed principals. Once SEC regulation is in place, relaxation of Glass-Steagall to permit the underwriting of debt securities should not be a serious problem.

Bank and thrift insurance funds will be merged, restrictions on operating interstate banks as a single entity will be removed, and there will be much contention over the extent to which states can regulate banks chartered by the Comptroller or by another state.

As securities holdings increase as a proportion of bank portfolios, pressure will grow on the Federal Reserve to adopt market value accounting, and the accounting theoreticians will find acceptable ways to value bank liabilities like five-year CDs and the low-interest passbook accounts that seem to have unlimited duration. With market value accounting, much control of bank behavior that is now allocated to examiners and rule-makers can safely be left to the better-informed investors and large depositors who, after all, have their own money at risk.

Decisions to privatize the payments system, establish continuous gross settlement and encourage small-business lending would imply quite different patterns of regulation. The separation of payments and lending would reduce the need for Federal Reserve supervision of banking powers, increase the role of state supervisors as charterers of niche banks, enhance the status of the FDIC as a rule-maker for insured banks while enabling uninsured institutions to participate in payments services. In general, the financial services institutions rigorously divided by the New Deal at a time of post office technology will increasingly come together in the age of data processing and telecommunications, and the government will permit it for the same reason Margaret Fuller accepted the universe: by God, Carlyle said, she'd better.

For readers of books, the new world of electronic banking will be cheaper, more convenient, and eventually less intimidating than the old world of paper and bricks. Whether people with less education and money will benefit to anything like the same extent is a decision to be made politically, and soon, and probably wrong.

The bankers displaced by the changes in banking will, I suspect, do just fine. Banking has never been a licensed occupation, let alone a profession. It requires, George Moore liked to say, a mixture of the salesman and the analyst. The man who was *both* a salesman and an analyst, Moore said, was worth ten times as much as the man who was merely one or the other. "You know," said Herbert Rutland of St. Petersburg Bank and Trust, "banking is the highest profession in the world—doctors come second."

It was always a mistake to idealize the bankers of yesteryear, as Arthur Burns as chairman of the Fed did in a memorable speech: "a man who was concerned with his community, who put service to customers above other considerations, who did not bother about comparing his earnings with some other banker down the street, and who never gave a thought to the price/earnings ratio at which his stock is selling." Tom Storrs of what was still NCNB made reply: He was reminded, he said, "of a gentleman who operated the one bank in a small town in the Carolinas several decades ago. He had many of the attributes which Dr. Burns enumerated: he *was* concerned with the growth of his community, for he owned a substantial part of it and managed his holdings through the information which he acquired at his bank. He did *not* worry greatly about bank earnings, but while he owned enough of the shares of the bank to protect his position, he did not look to them for any substantial income. He did *not* concern himself with the price/earnings ratio set by the market; he *was* the market for the stock. Sellers came to him and he placed their shares in the hands of new owners whom he considered friendly to himself—the transaction taking place at book value. He did *not* worry a great deal about internal efficiencies since the help did not get paid overtime and he played golf several afternoons a week regardless of the workload."[10]

There will be good jobs for good bankers at insurance companies and brokerage firms and finance companies—Sanford Weill, who runs all three under the Traveler's umbrella, has hired scads of bankers. Mike Milken when he kept his nose clean was one of the great bankers of the century, and the people with whom he surrounded himself at Drexel Burnham were expert at valuing the assets that underlay his junk bonds. As the nationwide giant banks take over most of the business and standardize it, bankers like Bob Whalen will uncover niches in which they can flourish and give service. Banks as we know them, from the Medici and the Fuggers to First National This and First National That, have seen their day. But the bankers we will have with us always.

EPILOGUE TO THE
1998 PLUME EDITION

Much to the surprise of everyone, this book, on publication in early 1997, became a techie's delight: www.Amazon.com featured it, ran an interview with the author, made place on its website for reviews and discussions of the book. The early adopter sector of the banking community saw the web pages, picked up the book, and contacted the author's lecture bureau. The electronic payments chapters and the derivatives chapters—between them, about one third of the book—were assigned reading not only in business schools but in a surprising number of banks. Writing those chapters, I had felt myself floundering in swamps—swamps, moreover, from which there could be no escape, because fast-moving rivers bordered them. But it remains true that in the kingdom of the blind the one-eyed man is king, and the fact of the matter is that even in early 1998, those introductions remain a reasonable guide to safe footing, still ahead of the curve.

But 1997 was a year of accelerating change, and in 1998 the banking industry will have to adapt to a major alteration in its relations with the federal government. For, starting on January 1, 1999, the U.S. Treasury will be required by law to make *all* its payments (except income tax refunds) by electronic funds transfer. The cause of this change was presented in the book (see p. 124), but the time horizon quoted there was ten years. What pushed it to immediate consideration is an interesting example of how the government of the United States *really* operates.

Through the dismal winter of 1995–96, the President and the Congress remained at loggerheads over the federal budget, with the President refusing to sign on to the cuts and program eliminations the newly elected, feisty Republicans thought they had a mandate to achieve and the Republicans refusing to approve interim appropriations that would keep the government going as the arguments raged. Workers were furloughed, and the work they did went undone. By March 1996, the country, the Congress, and the President were all sick of this nonsense, but it remained necessary to make the numbers work. Deputy Secretary of the Treasury Lawrence Summers had said, as reported *supra*, that it cost the Treasury 43 cents to make a paper payment and only 2 cents to make an electronic payment. The staffers of the congressional budget conference did some arithmetic: the Treasury made 700 million paper payments a year. Times 40 cents is better than a quarter of a billion dollars. Times six years, which was the supposed time horizon, and by mandating that the Treasury pay by direct deposit, Congress could save $1.5 billion. So the Omnibus Consolidated Rescission and Appropriations Act of 1996 contains a Chapter 10 amending 31 U.S.C. 3332, requiring all federal agencies to convert to electronic funds transfer.

No banking regulator recommended this change. No banking committee in the House or Senate held hearings on it or reported a bill. The budgeteers needed the money. Both the Office of Management and Budget in the White House and the Congressional

Budget Office accepted Deputy Secretary Summers' numbers. It no longer matters whether those numbers were right or not. The shift to EFT has been "scored" by the appropriate authorities at more than $1 billion. Anybody who wants to change the law must find that $1 billion-plus elsewhere before the change can be made. It is fair to say that the appetite for such an amendment is very weak in the Congress. *Mea culpa*, by the way—this book was still in proof when the first suggestions for regulations to execute the law were published, and I could have written something about it. But nobody in the banking industry *knew* it had passed, so nobody told me.

What little publicity this change in the law has received has dealt with the Treasury's problem in finding ways to make direct deposits for the benefit of the unbanked. The check cashers, of course, want in. So does First Data, which made an elaborate presentation to the Treasury about how it would go about processing accounts for recipients who don't have other accounts. But the Undersecretary for Domestic Affairs John (always "Jerry") Hawke, a Washington banking lawyer, told them, not unreasonably, that Treasury wants insured accounts for these very vulnerable people, and as of early 1998, the matter was still unresolved. Citibank has pioneered the use of mag-stripe cards for electronic *benefits* transfers—welfare payments and food stamps, which don't go well together because the government puts the money into accounts before the welfare recipients get it but doesn't fund food stamps until they have been used and presented by the grocer to his bank. And Citibank also (p. 453) has a program for employers to establish limited-purpose paperless accounts (no checks, but bills can be paid by phone, and cash can be taken at ATM machines).

But the glamor and human interest of paying the poor conceal the true importance of the new rules. The Treasury makes an enormous number of payments to *vendors*, who sell the government everything from paper clips and wheelbarrows to mainframe computers and F-16s. In 1995, four fifths of those payments were by paper check. Starting January 1, 1999, all of them must be by electronic funds transfer. Direct deposit of payroll, which has been by far the most important use of the Automated Clearing House, does not require the movement of any significant information other than the payment itself. The employer separately gives the employee a piece of paper detailing what has been deducted from the "paycheck" that was electronically deposited in his bank account. All the bank has to do is accept a file from the employer (or more likely, from ADP or its lesser rival Paychex) listing the money to be credited to the employee and the employee's bank account. But the payment to the vendor will have to have a memo item telling the payee which invoice has just been paid. As of spring 1997, a professional closely involved with electronic data interchange work estimated that only thirty-five banks in the United States could really handle the problem of receiving and processing that memo and passing it on to their customers. I wrote 750 in this book; she said I was wildly optimistic.

The most ambitious mixture of data and payments has been the EDI/BANX project at the Chicago Clearing House. Three corporate clients of the big Chicago banks—Motorola, Walgreen's, and Minnesota Mining—provided the incentive for the development of a system that would permit them to take care of their accounts payable at the touch of a key. Walgreen's gives EDI/BANX a monthly file of 83,000 payments to be made to the suppliers of the drugstore chain, who are required to have accounts at a member bank of the Chicago Clearing House. The remittances go to the suppliers, and Walgreen's receives electronic confirmation that the payments have been made. EDI/BANX has tried to get the Clearing House members to offer this service to their correspondent banks, but it would take a significant capital investment, which the members are simply not willing to make. So the Clearing House has been permitted to offer associate membership to EDS, which will handle the relations between EDI/BANX and smaller banks that might wish the service.

In late 1996, the National Automated Clearing House Association joined with the telephone company MCI to offer banks with

486 PCs or better a software package enabling them to handle NACHA's corporate trade payments format and communicate the information companies will need when the government (and others) begin paying by EFT. The cost was $500; the demand was very small. The New York Clearing House in early 1997 began offering *its* 900 members and associate members a *free* software package for Pentium PCs. Out of the 900 members, 60 took the offer. In fall 1997, NACHA passed a rule requiring all its members to be prepared to receive and pass on to their customers whatever extra "fields" of data were required in the acceptance of electronic payments. But NACHA has no disciplinary powers to back its rules. And the Fed, which runs most of the automated clearing houses and could enforce such rules, hates the whole idea.

Thirty-five years ago, when the newly formed Xerox company sought help from IBM in manufacturing its strange new copying machine, the computer giant asked Arthur D. Little to estimate the size of the market for such devices. Little reported back that it was too small for IBM to bother about. Sol Linowitz, the lawyer who was then nonexecutive chairman of Xerox, said later that the growth of that company's business was a case of invention becoming the mother of necessity. The Federal Reserve's certainty that there is no demand for electronic payments (based, like the Little opinion, on a survey) will founder on the existence theorem of Treasury payments. For, once companies have been forced to gear up to receive their federal payments electronically, they will want to use the system for private-sector payments, too. Between 1999 and 2002, when the banking industry and its customers will have dug out from the debris of the Year 2000 computer crisis, there will be a dramatic shift in the United States from paper checks to EFT for business enterprise. The question is the extent to which the new payments system will in fact involve the banks—or whether the "content providers" will simply take over.

The most common device for electronic payments will undoubtedly be the purchasing card. Indeed, the General Services

Administration, which handles most federal payments, has already moved to institute a system that permits office managers and purchasing agents in the government to make purchases up to $2,500 with a mag-stripe credit card. The file of payments made with the card was communicated back to the GSA electronically, giving the agencies that used the card an updated record of their purchases without any need to punch keys. GSA hopes that by 1999 90 percent of the 90 percent of government payments that involve less than $2,500 will be handled on this chassis.

First Bank in Minneapolis had the contract for purchases other than travel in 1997 (American Express had the travel contract), and treated it much as any other Visa or Master card, giving the merchants credit the day after the purchase and billing the government at the end of the month. (Some agencies paid every week: GSA gave them the option.) At year's end, an RFP (request for proposal) was on the street for three separate functions—purchasing, travel, and "fleet," covering the government's cars—and the government was looking for some innovative suggestions. American Express put an ad in the *Wall Street Journal*, offering "complete 'audit-ability,' " and going on: "Streamlined recordkeeping. Inventory control. Fraud prevention. American Express smart card technology and proprietary systems help you manage and apply information in the simplest, most time- and cost-effective ways possible, with a higher level of security." The American Express smart card for government agencies even offered "refunds for amounts in your electronic purse in case of lost or stolen cards." Ideally, the system of government purchases on a card should be paid for by the prompt-payment discounts offered by the vendors, who are, indeed, overjoyed at getting away from government payments delays.

The purchasing card movement grows from private-sector initiatives, especially at the American Petroleum Institute and the Automotive Industry Action Group, and in these organizations derives from a movement to standardize bookkeeping entries throughout the industry. Both in the government and in these groups there will be a migration from the mag-stripe card to the chip card, which will keep its own records, enabling the purchaser to download purchase and payment information into the computer whenever convenient.

One of the (few) technical challenges associated with this system is the blending of information from the larger payments, which will be made by EFT, with the smaller payments on the purchasing card. As noted earlier in the book, for a payment to flow electronically from payor to payee the system must know everybody's bank account number and customer; the company that owns the file will rule the world. One does not get the file by paying the bill for the payor; one gets the file by collecting the bill for the payee. Microsoft and First Data have set up a joint venture to collect bills for corporate customers. (Microsoft's deal with EDS, noted on p. 182, fell through because Microsoft insisted on taking *all* the payments banks would make for the service since EDS could make money on all its other services to these banks once the Microsoft payments system was there.) CheckFree has also offered to corporations that it can set up collection procedures and in fall 1997 entered into an agreement with Integrion, an IBM-led consortium of very big banks. But Integrion doesn't have anything like the money Microsoft and First Data have to develop the system and the data base. Stay tuned.

Some of the smart-card discussion in the book has been over-taken by events, though the future remains very uncertain. Congress put a hold on the adoption of the revisions the Fed had proposed to Regulation E, and while the hold expired in fall 1997, the Fed postponed movement in that area to 1998. As noted, American Express, which has acquired the American rights for the Belgian proton system that dominates in Europe, has based much of its pitch for the new government contracts on its smart-card expertise. It has also entered into an arrangement with Mercantec, a Chicago technology company, to use cards for Internet purchases with security for the buyer and quick payment to the seller. This is something of a preemptive strike, it should be noted, for the Fed probably cannot grandfather Amex into the chip card business if it tries to enforce a rule against nonbanks issuing cards (as the Florida banking commissioner has tried to put Florida State University out of the smart-card business). MasterCard has acquired Mondex, and will push it.

The smart-card test on New York's Upper West Side, which got started nine months later than expected, has been something less than a great success. I tried it out in December, well into its second month, seeking to make a purchase at Zabar's, the bargain hunter's gourmet palace. I was told at a checkout counter that the only one of the ten counters where the card could be used was the one labeled "Cash Only," and unfortunately, that one was closed. By making something of a fuss, I got an assistant manager to take my card over to the smart-card register at the unused counter and let me buy my Swedish fish roe and lingonberry jam, but with a hundred or so customers in the store and stickers on the windows advertising that both the Visa and Master chip cards could be used here, the pilot project looked a little lost.

What the experiment has proved, I think, is the inherent superiority of Mondex. Citibank with its Visa card staffed the pilot more intensively than Chase did for Mondex, but the success ratio with Mondex was higher. Mondex offers the customer a card reader on a keychain that allows him to check at any time on how much he has on the card without going to an ATM machine or a store kiosk, and—most important—a locking device that guarantees that the card cannot be used by anyone else if stolen. Indeed, the serial number and code systems built into Mondex provide much greater security for the user than any of the other systems. The Visa card offered by Citibank is merely an unsigned traveler's check that anybody can use, and the Citibank salespeople were indeed careful to tell prospective purchasers that a lost card was like lost cash. Because Citi was pushing a chip card that would also be the customer's ATM card, the warning about loss was devastating to the selling effort (I stood around at 72nd Street and Broadway and watched a personable salesman fail with a good proportion of those who asked for a demonstration). In the end, the security issue will be primary in determining which smart card wins public support. Meanwhile, the range of uses—the "consumer value," as one of the Chase people put it artlessly—was very limited in the New York test. Not until January 1998 did the banks succeed in installing smart-card capability at the area's laundromats, the most obvious of uses.

On the wholesale payments front, Europe moved steadily toward the establishment of the TARGET system that will provide continuous settlement of large Euro payments, and the European central bankers prepared the ground for the fight they will have with the Fed on the linkage of FedWire and TARGET. The Europeans want the Fed to make banks collateralize their daylight overdrafts before TARGET establishes its FedWire liaison. The Fed is conscious that cheap, uncollateralized overdrafts are its greatest weapon now in its competition with the private CHIPS system, which will be providing a rolling settlement rather than a one-time netting at the close. Late in 1997, the Fed added another weapon, opening FedWire at 12:30 A.M. for the convenience of customers in Europe and Asia. But as the Asian nightmare moves commerical banks toward collateralization of interbank loans, the Fed will probably accept the European demand.

2

In the derivatives area, the collapse of the Asian markets demonstrated once again, to quote the spiritual, that "all the people talkin' 'bout heaven ain't gettin' there." The warning on page 436 about cross-border lending turned out to be more prophetic than I had imagined. In theory, the banks should have been hedged against their exposure to declines in the value of the Korean won and the Thai baht, the Malaysian ringgit and the Indonesian rupiah; in fact, they were not. Hedging costs money the banks would rather pocket.

They will run matched books of long and short positions when executing client orders, pocketing the brokerage commission, but when it's their own business that's in danger from foreign exchange or interest-rate risk they have a tendency to maximize returns.

My favorite victim of the Asian currency crisis was a Philadelphia bank that had found its own way to reduce its dependence on the exchange value of the baht. This bank loaned dollars to Thai property developers on a contract which not only provided that the developer would repay his debt in dollars but also that he would rent the space only to tenants who would pay *him* in dollars. When the crunch came the tenants couldn't get the dollars to pay the developer, who couldn't get the dollars to pay the bank, and the bank found that while it had not suffered any losses in the exchange market, it was the proud owner of a mortgage on an office building that had no tenants.

Interbank lending was the great villain of the Asian piece, some of it stimulated by the Bank for International Settlements rule that loans to Korean banks would bear only a 20 percent risk-weighting because, as a developed country, Korea was a member of the Paris-based OECD. Bankers think interbank loans are safe because the government that chartered the bank will not let it default, and regulators think interbank loans are safe because they believe the banks police each other. This is still a business of low time horizons—and also, still a business subject to Minsky's instability "hypothesis": that periods of stable growth and low default rates lead banks to drastically reduce their risk premiums and run much bigger risks.

The major change in the derivatives world was already in process when I wrote this book, but it had fallen below my screen. It was the growth of "credit derivatives," which in theory permitted banks or other lenders to lay off default risks on packages of loans. This instrument obviously grows out of the boom in asset-based lending, where the seller of the loans overcollateralizes the package to gain a better credit rating and lower interest rate from the buyers. This was not expensive historically because it made possible the creation and sale of the "toxic waste" tranche of the instrument, which retained its value if the total losses on the auto loans or credit card loans or mortgages over the life of the package were less than the value of the collateral. Bank, insurance, and pension-fund regulators all became concerned about the value of this "Z-tranche" and shooed their wards away from purchasing such stuff.

The replacement for overcollateralization, pioneered years ago in the mortgage area (first, of course, by the government with the Federal Housing Authority program), was insurance against default, which became routine not only for credit card receivables but also for municipal bonds. Insurance, however, still left the lender responsible for everything beyond the first 10 percent or so of loss, to avoid "moral hazard" (a term from the insurance industry: if a man has insured a property for more than it's worth, it pays him to burn it down). In the case of the credit derivative, the lender pays someone—another bank, an insurance company, a hedge fund—to bear the risk on a package of loans. The lender remains responsible for some fraction off the top, like an insurance deductible, and if that fraction does not go sour, the seller of the derivative simply keeps the purchase price as an insurance company keeps the premium. If the losses exceed that fraction, the seller of the derivative is on the hook to the full limit of the face value of the package, or perhaps (terms differ), for losses down to a limit which sets a further deductible.

A credit derivative is of course a put on the loan and is one of the many "trigger" instruments that our inventive financial engineers have designed to make people think they are getting money for old rope. Its obvious value is to the geographically limited bank that has too concentrated an exposure to a single industry because it can spread that exposure around through a derivative instrument without sacrificing its informational advantages as the bank on the spot. Banks can trade such exposures, making the banker in the garment district less dependent on the fortunes of the rag trade and the banker in the heartland less at the mercy of the weather. The device can be structured in various ways, the most popular being a "total return swap," in which one party receives the safe return on a Treasury note *plus* an agreed-upon fee, expressed as an interest payment on the notional value of a loan, so long as the loan stays good. If it defaults, the purchaser of the credit risk pays an agreed-upon penalty.

Two kinds of investigation are obviously necessary: by the lender, to make sure he is dealing with a counterparty who can really deliver if the losses trigger the put, and by the seller of the derivative, to make sure that the package of loans is reasonably representative of the credits in the market and not the dregs of the portfolio. Credit derivatives have been the most rapidly growing area of derivative creation in the second half of the 1990s. How they will play out in a less benign atmosphere, nobody knows.

Regulators assured everybody in 1997 that cowboy behavior had all but disappeared from derivatives territory, and that the overwhelming bulk of the business was in simple swaps, where the banks and the investment banks acted as market makers, bringing sellers and buyers together, rather than as principals. Fed Chairman Alan Greenspan publicly denounced the efforts by the Financial Accounting Standards Board to compel "fair value" accounting for derivatives in bank holding company annual reports, and former S.E.C. chief accountant Walter Schuetze said the reason was that banks had serious losses in their derivatives port-folios and wished to conceal them. As 1998 began, it was unclear whether the combination of the Fed and the political contributions of the derivatives dealers could hold off the FASB standards this time around, but eventually market-value accounting will win the day. I am persuaded that the solution I suggested here (p. 423), which was essentially the same as the solution offered by Green-span, does not work: disclosure in footnotes is much less signifi-cant than recognition on the balance sheet, because the punishments for inadequate or inaccurate public disclosure are nil in the con-text of bank secrecy and bank regulatory examinations.

3

Some things have come to pass. The bank and S&L insurance funds have been merged, giving everybody the same luxurious deposit insurance, mostly at the expense of the banks, though the S&L survivors made a large one-shot contribution. I have revised the text *supra* to account for major merger activity among American banks through the end of 1997. Merger mania still grips the industry and has spread abroad. The British banks have been absorbing their "building societies" (S&Ls), and the German banks have been acquiring their *Landesbanken*. In late 1997, two of the three Swiss giants—Union Bank of Switzerland and Swiss Bank Corporation—were joined in matrimony (partly because UBS had suffered major losses in Japanese equity derivatives). My comments on the Euro (pp. 46–47) were too cautious: in spring 1998, the nations participating in the new pan-European currency will have been selected, and the conversion rates of their currency to the new currency will be known—and there will be a lot of them, perhaps as many as eleven of the fifteen members of the European Union. Whether this will turn out to have been a good idea is veiled in the mists of time. I am old-fashioned enough to believe that different countries in Europe will need different monetary policies from time to time. But the disappearance of regional credit-supply differences in the United States, which were common as late as the 1960s, has not impeded the prosperity of this country.

In the United States, displeasure with the services given by the new giant banks has stimulated a rash of new bank charters issued to businessmen and displaced bankers who see geographic or functional niches that the big banks do not fill. The cost savings from mergers are often visible to the customers as threadbare services. Wells Fargo, especially, has lost some of its optimism about replacing branches with machines and a few attendants in supermarkets. But the basic statements of the final chapter remain true: the superhighway to economics of scale produces a certain amount of roadkill. In the future, standard customers will get better service for less money, and nonstandard customers will find everything associated with banking more expensive—except, perhaps, for payments matters in the bottom quintile of the income distribution, where the new programs mandating electronic payments will compel the government to control the costs of deposit accounts for the poor.

In general, the discussion of the condition of the banks in the final chapter now looks a touch optimistic. Although banks have not lost their balance reaching for business to anything like the extent that they toppled in the 1980s, it is universally agreed (by the cadre of bank lending officers who form the Robert Morris Associates as well as by the Comptroller's examiners) that lending standards declined seriously in 1997. The apparent prosperity of the industry in that year was on its face suspicious, because a fair amount of normal profitability in banking grows from the slope of the yield curve—the extent to which longer loans, which are bank assets, command higher interest rates than shorter loans, which are bank liabilities. In 1997 the yield curve flattened to an extraordinary degree: at the end of the year, there was only about 60 basis points (three fifths of one percentage point) between the cost of overnight money in the Fed Funds market and the rate for thirty-year Treasury bonds. To earn anything at all on the loan portfolio, banks had to go after less plausible borrowers, who have to match the extra risk to lenders with extra reward. Large institutions got involved with "sub-prime" lending to people with poor credit ratings and began offering foolish loans secured by "125 percent of the equity in your home." Involvement in "emerging markets" has already proved much less profitable than what has already been credited on the books (and, given the regulators' permissive standards, may be some time working its way out of the books). And in the general prosperity, companies with earnings that did not cover their debt service were allowed to continue borrowing from the bank, storing up loan losses for later years. There is no disaster scenario out there, but in the years 1992–97 the bank stocks have had one hell of a ride (Citibank from $9 a share to $140 a share), and it's by no means certain that there's that much gas in the balloon.

The legal framework of banking in the United States looks to be relatively unchanged in the near future, despite universal agreement that the divisions of authority don't make any sense. The disabilities that the banks felt were destroying the value of the banking charter have been largely eliminated through stretchings of the existing law by the Federal Reserve (for securities operations) and the Comptroller (for insurance agenting—and most state laws now permit state-chartered banks to exercise whatever powers the Comptroller gives federally chartered banks). Securities firms have long been able to offer checking accounts and credit cards through the Merrill Lynch Cash Management Account subterfuge, and in the 1991 amendments to the deposit insurance law they gained, in effect, access to the Federal Reserve's discount windows in case of systemic emergency. Nonfinancial corporations that wish to get involved in the payments system can acquire a thrift charter, which gives them an end-point in FedWire and membership in an Automated Clearing House. And corporations that want to be in the lending business can acquire or start finance companies without permission from anybody—indeed, GE, Travelers Insurance, Ford, GM, and Household International are all major lenders without so much as a by-your-leave from banking regulators. The insurance companies want to roll back the tide of liberalization and get the banks out of the competition for insurance products, and there are insurance agents in almost every county in the United States. It takes only a little cynicism to observe that all these businesses have reason to contribute to congressional campaigns so long as the legal framework for financial services is still in process of construction.

The hang-up in 1997 was on the question of the mixture of banking and commerce—can banks own nonfinancial companies, and can nonfinancial companies own banks? Both securities firms and insurance companies have nonfinancial subsidiaries and would not wish to give them up for the right to own a bank, and the

481

banks argue that the playing field is not level if their competitors and putative competitors can operate a holding company with greater operating powers than a bank holding company. There are echoes in the argument of the 1980s fallacy that universal banks with major commerical interests (the German banks, the French banks, the Swedish and Finnish banks, the Spanish banks, and in effect, the Japanese and Korean banks) were inherently stronger than the limited American banks. Taxpayers in all those countries except Germany later had to shoulder huge burdens (in the Scandinavian case, greater than the burdens American taxpayers picked up after the S&L fiasco), and these disasters were caused mostly by the deregulated banks' wrongheaded direct investments in their borrowers' businesses. One would have expected the demand for the mixture of banking and commerce to fade away, but it hasn't.

One change in banking law remains reasonably likely. Assuming that the Community Reinvestment Act requirements can be resolved—and they probably can—one would expect Congress to authorize "Woofies" (wholesale financial institutions), which would fund themselves exclusively in the money markets and would not be able to offer deposit insurance. Otherwise the battles in the last years of this millennium look likely to be mostly over regulator turf. The issue will be enterprise regulation versus functional regulation: Should a banking regulator or the Securities and Exchange Commission supervise the securities activities of a bank, and should the state insurance commissioners have power over its insurance activities? The answer to the latter is that the Comptroller can by law preempt state rules but, as Deputy Comptroller Julie Williams put it, any bank subsidiary that fails to get an agents' license from a state insurance commissioner will find that no insurance company will take business from it. The answer to the former is clearly that the regulation must be functional, banking regulators being fundamentally out of sympathy with securities regulation's requirements for full disclosure and transparency, and securities regulators being dubious about the secrecy of bank portfolios.

482

But Alan Greenspan is not wrong when he insists that there must be an umbrella regulator for the panoply of activities that will eventually be exercised by a single bank or holding company. His problem is that the natural regulator in a market-dominated financial world will be not the banking supervisor but the securities commission. Perhaps the most important event in banking in 1997 was the decision of the new British Labor government to take banking supervision away from the Bank of England and vest it in a new and improved Securities and Investments Board. When the U.S. Congress begins considering changes like that, a great deal of fur will fly.

Acknowledgments

Almost a quarter of a century has passed since Mac Talley first came to me with the idea of a book about banks and bankers—and at least ten years have elapsed since he returned to say, "Let's do it again." More than half my working hours in the last twenty-five years have been spent with banks and bankers and banking, and a great number of men and women have contributed to my education in the subject. I have noted six of them in my dedication, and many of the others are quoted.

Academics have been more important in my preparation for this book than they were the last time around, and I owe thanks to Ed Kane, Allen Berger, George Kaufman, Paul Horvitz and Jan Kriegel. Walker Todd has repeatedly enlightened me, sometimes by shining torches obliquely into strange corners. Bill Ford and the late Maury Mann raised my spirits as well as enlightening me. Cathy Allen brought me back to smart cards at just the right time.

485

ACKNOWLEDGMENTS

Paul Volcker and Ernest Patrikis have been ready with assistance when needed but should not be blamed for anything here. The Levy Institute's annual banking conference has given me a chance to meet a number of researchers I would not otherwise have seen; George White's conferences on payments system matters have introduced me to the people in the trenches whom the P.R. departments at the banks, helpful as they are, would not know about.

Bill Zimmerman as editor of *American Banker* commissioned the twice-monthly front-page columns that kept me involved in this business through the late 1980s, and manfully withstood a lot of criticism for them.

For much of the time of my work on this book, I have been a Guest Scholar at the Brookings Institute in Washington, where I enjoyed and profited by the companionship of George Martin of the University of Massachusetts, who instructed me on derivatives—which does not mean he agreed with what is said on the subject in these pages. I am grateful to Brookings—especially then-president Bruce MacLaury and director of economic studies Henry Aaron and current director of economic studies Robert E. Litan—for hospitality of various kinds, stimulating company, and library services.

Washington, D.C.
September 1996

Notes

Introduction

1. *Banks Are Special*, 1982 Annual Report of the Federal Reserve Bank of Minneapolis, p. 13.

2. Ron Chernow, *The House of Morgan* (New York: Atlantic Monthly Press, 1990), p. 122.

3. *The Collected Works of Walter Bagehot*, vol. 9, ed. N. St. John-Stevas (London: The Economist, 1978), p. 156.

4. Walter Bagehot, *Lombard Street* (Homewood, Ill.: Richard D. Irwin, 1962), p. 119.

5. George Moore, *The Banker's Life* (New York: W.W. Norton, 1987), p. 136.

6. Franklin R. Edwards and Frederic S. Mishkin, "The Decline of Traditional Banking: Implications for Financial Stability and Regulatory Policy," *Economic Policy Review* 1, no. 2 (July 1995), p. 27.

7. Marshall E. Surratt, *What's Happening to U.S. Banking? . . . How You Can Be Protected* (Dallas: Commercial Publishers, 1993), pp. 106–107.

8. Marquis and Besse James, *Biography of a Bank* (New York: Harper & Bros., 1954), p. 156.

9. Hyman Minsky, *Stabilizing an Unstable Economy* (New Haven, Conn.: Yale University Press, 1986), p. 233.

10. Bagehot, op. cit., pp. 43–44.

11. Lowell Bryan, *Bankrupt* (New York: HarperBusiness, 1991), p. 41.

12. John Schulz, *The Financial Crisis of Abolition, 1875–1901* (São Paulo, Brazil: Fernand Braudel Institute of World Economics, 1993), p. 47.

13. Constance R. Dunham, "New Banks in New England," *New England Economic Review*, 1989, pp. 30, 33.

14. Cyril B. Upham and Edwin Lamke, *Closed and Distressed Banks: A Study in Public Administration* (Washington, D.C.: Brookings Institution, 1934), p. 39.

15. Office of the Comptroller of the Currency, *Duties and Liabilities of Directors of National Banks* (Washington, D.C.: Office of the Comptroller of the Currency, 1972), p. 2.

16. *Federal Reserve Bulletin*, March 1933, p. 115.

17. Martin Mayer, *The Bankers* (New York: Weybright & Talley, 1974), p. 16.

18. *Wall Street Journal*, March 29, 1994, p. A10. The information is from tables "based on a study by Edward P. Foldessy, *Wall Street Journal* news systems editor, of computer tapes obtained from the U.S. Government."

19. *Are Banks Special?*, Annual Report for 1982 of the Federal Reserve Bank of Minneapolis, p. 7.

20. George S. Moore, *The Banker's Life* (New York: W.W. Norton, 1987), pp. 159–60. The reader should be aware that I helped Moore write this book.

21. "Why Banks Keep Bulking Up," *Business Week*, July 31, 1995, p. 66.

22. I suspect it is worth noting that the members of the Housing Commission, several of whom were distinguished, experienced and smart, had not the faintest notion that we were deepening the crisis of the S&Ls. Indeed, one of the members of the commission's finance committee went on to become chairman and CEO of Imperial Savings of San Diego, which became a member of the club of billion-dollar losers. He used his access to insured deposits and Garn–St. Germain asset powers to fund, among other things, the introduction of the Yugo automobile to the American market.

23. Surratt, op. cit., p. 184.

24. A. A. Sommer, Jr., letter to the accounting profession, Jan. 2, 1991. Public Oversight Board, American Institute of Chartered Public Accountants, 540 Madison Avenue, New York, N.Y., pp. 1–3.

1. The Nature of Money

1. Augustin Cournot, *Researches into the Mathematical Principles of the Theory of Wealth, 1838*, translated by Nathaniel T. Bacon (New York: Macmillan, 1929), p. 10.

2. W. S. Jevons, *Money and the Mechanism of Exchange*, 23rd edition (London: Kegan Paul, 1910), pp. 1–2.

3. Robert Skidelsky, *John Maynard Keynes*, vol. II, *The Economist as Savior* (New York: Penguin, 1994), p. 312.

4. Hyman P. Minsky, *Stabilizing an Unstable Economy* (New Haven, Conn.: Yale University Press, 1986), p. 228.

5. Wright Patman, *A Primer on Money* (Washington, D.C.: Subcommittee on Domestic Finance, Committee on Banking and Currency, House of Representatives, 88th Congress 2nd Session, 1964), p. 16.

6. Paine, in Bray Hammond, *Banks and Politics in America*, (Princeton, N.J.: Princeton University Press, 1967), p. 61.

7. R. A. Lehfeldt, *Money* (London: Oxford University Press, 1926), p. 25.

8. Sarah Ferguson, "Star Trek: The Next Currency," *Worldbusiness*, spring 1995, p. 14.

9. R. S. Sayers, *Central Banking After Bagehot* (London: Oxford University Press, 1957), p. 4.

10. Andrew Dickson White, *Fiat Money Inflation in France*, 1980 edition (New York: The Bank of New York, 1980), pp. 62–63.

11. Lester V. Chandler, *America's Greatest Depression* (New York: Harper & Row, 1970), pp. 164–65.

12. Charles P. Kindleberger, *A Financial History of Western Europe* (London: George Allen & Unwin, 1984), p. 21.

13. Lionel D. Edie, *Easy Money* (New Haven, Conn.: Yale University Press, 1937), p. 83.

14. Augustin Cournot, *Researches into the Mathematical Principles of the Theory of Wealth*, translated by Nathaniel T. Bacon (New York: Macmillan, 1929), p. 25 fn.

15. Robert Triffin, *Gold and the Dollar Crisis*, revised ed. (New Haven, Conn.: Yale University Press, 1961), p. 21.

16. Ernest N. Paolino, *William Howard Seward and American Foreign Policy* (Ithaca, N.Y.: Cornell University Press, 1973), pp. 76 et seq.

17. Milton Friedman and Anna Jacobson Schwartz, *A Monetary History of the United States* (Princeton, N.J.: Princeton University Press, 1971), pp. 696–97.

18. I have an odd example of the power of exchange rate changes in my own life and work. The centennial history of the Metropolitan Opera, which I wrote on commission from the Metropolitan Opera Guild, was packaged as a very handsome coffee-table book with striking illustrations both color and black-and-white, chosen by the late Gerry Fitzgerald. The book was packaged in England by Thames and Hudson, and put out to the world's luxury printers for bids in 1982. The winner was Dai Nippon in Japan, which with the yen at 280 was able to produce a gorgeous book that could be sold in the United States for $35

in 1983. The initial printing of 35,000 sold out within a year or so, but by that time the yen was about 160 and rising, and to print a second edition Dai Nippon (which owned the plates) would have to charge so much that the price in the United States would go to $75. Thus it has not been possible to reprint the book.

19. Karl Marx, *Capital*, vol. I (Chicago: Charles H. Kerry, 1906), p. 101.

20. Kindleberger, op. cit., p. 57.

21. Robert E. Litan, *What Should Banks Do?* (Washington, D.C.: Brookings Institution, 1987), p. 20.

22. Roy Harrod, *The Dollar*, 2nd ed. (New York: Norton, 1963), p. 22.

23. Skidelsky, op. cit., p. 39.

24. Alan Greenspan, "Gold and Economic Freedom," *The Objectivist*, July 1966, pp. 96, 101.

25. In Martin Mayer, *The Fate of the Dollar* (New York: Times Books, 1980), p. 329.

26. John Maynard Keynes, *General Theory of Employment, Interest and Money* (New York: Harcourt Brace, 1936), pp. 215–16.

27. Skidelsky, vol. II, p. 543.

28. John Maynard Keynes, op. cit., p. 293.

29. Committee on the Working of the Monetary System, *Report* (London: Her Majesty's Stationery Office, 1959), para. 345, p. 117.

30. Hume quote in J. R. Hicks, "Monetary Theory and Keynesian Economics," in R. H. Clower, ed., *Monetary Theory* (Harmondsworth, Middlesex, England: Penguin, 1969), pp. 258–60.

31. Ibid., p. 260.

32. Laurie Morse, "Negative Interest Rates Set Swaps Dealers Wrangling," *The Financial Times*, October 31, 1995, p. 24.

33. Warren D. McClam, *U.S. Monetary Aggregates, Income Velocity and the Euro-Dollar Market* (Basel, Switzerland: Bank for International Settlements, 1980), p. 1.

34. Cited in Gerald P. Dwyer, Jr., "Rules and Discretion in Monetary Policy," *Federal Reserve Bank of St. Louis Review*, vol. 75, no. 3 (May/June 1993), p. 5.

2. What Money Does

1. Bray Hammond, *Banks and Politics in America from the Revolution to the Civil War* (Princeton, N.J.: Princeton University Press, 1957), pp. 182–83.

2. Donald R. Adams, Jr., *Finance and Enterprise in Early America: A Study of Stephen Girard's Bank, 1812–1831* (Philadelphia: University of Pennsylvania Press, 1978), pp. 75 et seq.

3. D. R. Whitney, *The Suffolk System* (Cambridge, Mass.: Riverside Press, 1878), p. 35.

4. Charles W. Calomiris and Charles M. Kahn, "The Efficiency of Self-

Regulated Payments Systems: Learning from the Suffolk System," a paper presented at the Conference on Payments Systems Research and Public Policy at the Federal Reserve System, Dec. 5, 1995, pp. 11 et seq.

5. Harold van B. Cleveland and Thomas F. Huertas, *The Bank for All: A History of Citibank 1812–1970* (New York: Citibank, 1984), chap. 13, p. 2.

6. *Report of the Committee on the Working of the Monetary System* (August 1959; Reprint, London: Her Majesty's Stationery Office, 1969), p. 43 (#128).

7. Milton Friedman, *The Counter-Revolution in Monetary Theory*, Wincott Memorial Lecture, Occasional Paper 33 (London: Institute of Economic Affairs, 1970), pp. 22–23.

8. Irwin Ross, "The Race Is to the Slow Payer," *Fortune*, April 18, 1983, pp. 76, 79.

9. Robert I. Friedman, "The Money Plane," *New York*, Jan. 22, 1996, p. 24.

10. Galen Burghardt, "How Long Can This Keep Going On?" *Futures Industry*, February 1995, pp. 9, 10.

11. Statement by Henry C. Wallich before the Subcommittee on Domestic Monetary Policy and the Subcommittee on International Trade of the Committee on Banking, U.S. House of Representatives, July 12, 1979.

12. Hurd Baruch, *Wall Street: Security Risk* (Washington, D.C.: Acropolis Books, 1971), pp. 22, 23, 30, 31. "Wall Street runs on Main Street's money": p. 31.

13. Martin Mayer, "Merrill Lynch Quacks Like a Duck," *Fortune*, October 20, 1980, pp. 132 et seq.

3. Paying Bills

1. *Waste and Abuse in the Federal Reserve's Payment System*, prepared by the Democratic staff of the Committee on Banking and Financial Services, 104th Congress, Second Session, January 5, 1996.

2. Jürgen C. Pingitzer and Bruce J. Summers, "Small Value Transfer Systems," in Summers, ed., *The Payment System: Design, Management and Supervision* (Washington, D.C.: International Monetary Fund, 1994), p. 109.

3. UCC Section 4A-103(a)(1)(ii), official comment 4.

4. Jim McTague, "Checks Turn Into Orphans of the Storm," *Barron's*, January 15, 1966, p. 56.

5. Statement by Alan S. Blinder, Vice-Chairman, Board of Governors, before the Subcommittee on Domestic and International Monetary Policy of the Committee on Banking and Financial Services, U.S. House of Representatives, October 11, 1995, p. 9.

6. Remarks by Alan Greenspan at the Conference on Payment Systems Research and Public Policy: Risk, Efficiency and Innovation, Washington, D.C., December 7, 1995, pp. 5, 8, 9.

7. Alison Smith, "Change in Law Could Save Banks Millions," *The Financial Times*, January 5, 1966, p. 5.

8. Donald R. Hollis, "Commentary," in David B. Humphrey, ed., *The U.S. Payment System: Efficiency, Risk and the Role of the Federal Reserve* (Boston: Kluwer Academic Publishers, 1990), p. 91.

9. *Federal Reserve System Summary of ECP Discussions* (Washington, D.C.: n.d.), pp. 1, 2, 3.

10. Manuel H. Johnson, "Conference Summary: An Overview of Payment System Issues: Where Do We Go From Here?" in David B. Humphrey, ed., *The U.S. Payment System: Efficiency, Risk and the Role of the Federal Reserve* (Boston: Kluwer Academic Publishers, Boston, 1990), p. 286.

11. Ibid., p. 288.

4. The Computer Age, Part I

1. Cited from an unpublished manuscript by Dee Hock entitled "Institutions in the Age of Mindcrafting," 1994, in a manuscript of Gordon R. Sullivan and Michael V. Harper, *Hope Is Not a Method*, to be published by Times Books in 1996.

2. Joseph Nocera, *A Piece of the Action* (New York: Simon & Schuster, 1994), p. 63.

3. Ibid., p. 158.

4. Peter Z. Grossman, *American Express: The Unofficial History* (New York: Crown Publishers, 1987), pp. 238 et seq.

5. *Bank Credit-Card and Check-Credit Plans*, a Federal Reserve System Report (Washington, D.C.: 1968), p. 75.

6. David B. Humphrey and Allen N. Berger, "Market Failure and Resource Use," in Humphrey, ed., *The Payment System*, (Boston: Kluwer Academic Publishers, 1990), pp. 45 et seq.

7. David A. Balto, "Payment Systems and Antitrust: Can the Opportunities for Network Competition Be Recognized?", *Federal Reserve Bank of St. Louis Review*, vol. 77, no. 6 (Dec. 1995), pp. 19, 34.

8. Ibid., p. 24.

9. Ibid., p. 23.

10. Balto, op. cit., p. 22.

5. The Computer Age, Part II

1. *Applications in Action*, Conference Proceedings, Car Tech-SecurTech, Volume II, "Applications," May 13–16, 1996, p. 696.

2. Richard Perez-Pena, "Now, from the M.T.A., the Card That Can Also Pay for Sandwiches," *New York Times*, Jan. 22, 1996, p. B-1.

3. David B. Humphrey, Lawrence B. Pulley and Jukka Vesala, "Cash, Paper

and Electronic Payments: A Cross Country Analysis," a paper prepared for the Federal Reserve Board Conference on Payment Systems Research and Public Policy: Risk, Efficiency and Innovation, December 7–8, 1995. Table III.

4. Martin Mayer, "Here Comes the Smart Card," *Fortune*, August 8, 1983, pp. 74 et seq.

5. Saul Hansell, "It's Coming: Your Pocket Cash on a Plastic Card," *New York Times*, April 10, 1996, p. D-1.

6. Giles Keating, "Electronic Money in a Race with Emu," *The Financial Times*, November 2, 1995, p. 15.

7. John Wenninger and David Laster, "The Electronic Purse," *Current Issues in Economics and Finance*, April 1995, p. 5.

8. Steven A. Bercu, *Smart Card Privacy Issues Overview*, (Washington, D.C.: Foley, Hoag & Eliot, 1995), p. 5.

9. Wenninger and Laster, op. cit., p. 4.

10. Testimony of David Boyles Before the Subcommittee on Domestic and International Monetary Policy, House Banking Committee, June 11, 1996, p. 8

11. *The Future of Money*, Part 2; Hearing before the Subcommittee on Domestic and International Monetary Policy, House Banking Committee, October 11, 1995, Serial No. 104-27, GPO, Washington, 1996, pp. 5, 6.

12. Simson Garfinkel, *Pretty Good Privacy* (Sebastopol, Calif.: O'Reilly & Associates, 1995). Not every page of this book is easy reading, but the reader who penetrates the first fifty pages will find it a fascinating story as well as a manual in the search for privacy. It is, I fear, a hopeless search: what the computer does for a living, really, is store and retrieve. Improvements in storage and retrieval are the enemy of privacy. Law professor Harry Kalven of the University of Chicago thirty years ago feared a future when through computers "Mankind will lose its benign capacity to forget."

13. Michelle Singletary, "Banks Branch Out over the Phone," The *Washington Post*, June 21, 1996, p. D-1.

14. Martin Mayer, *The Money Bazaars* (New York: Dutton, 1984), p. 308.

15. George Graham, "Rise of Internet Threatens Traditional Banks' Market," *Financial Times*, London, August 12, 1996, p. 1.

16. Steven Marjanovic, "Purchases over the Internet Are a Step Closer," *American Banker*, September 26, 1995, p. 17.

17. Wesley R. Iversen, "The Maverick of Internet Commerce," *Online*, May–June 1996, p. 15.

18. *The Future of Money*, Part I: Hearing before the Subcommittee on Domestic and International Monetary Policy, House Banking Committee, July 25, 1995, p. 26.

19. Jim McTague, "Bank Regulator Pledges to Help Industry Thrive on Internet and Shed Its Glass-Steagall Obsession," *Barron's*, February 12, 1996, p. 29.

20. National Automated Clearing House Association, "NACHA and MCI Deliver RAPID*EDI," in *Automated Payments Update* (Reston, Va.: National Automated Clearing House Association, 1995), p. 1.

21. Jared Sandberg, "VeriFone Expected to Announce System for Purchasing Goods on the Internet," *Wall Street Journal*, September 11, 1995.

6. The Way We Were

1. Hyman P. Minsky, *Stabilizing an Unstable Economy* (New Haven, Conn.: Yale University Press, 1986), p. 229. Emphasis added.

2. Lauchlin Currie, *The Supply and Control of Money in the United States* (Cambridge, Mass.: Harvard University Press, 1934); cited in J. A. Kregel, "Monetary Policy, Central Bank Operating Procedure and the Evolution of Financial Institutions," a paper prepared for a Levy Institute conference, April 15, 1994.

3. *Banks Are Special*, 1982 Annual Report of the Federal Reserve Bank of Minneapolis, p. 13.

4. *Jim Grant's Interest Rate Observer*, May 10, 1996, p. 10.

5. Cited in Ronnie J. Phillips, *The Chicago Plan and New Deal Banking Reform* (Armonk, N.Y.: M. E. Sharpe, 1945), p. 3.

6. J. T. W. Hubbard, *For Each, The Strength of All: A History of Banking in the State of New York* (New York: New York University Press, 1995), p. 43.

7. Walter L. Buenger and Joseph A. Pratt, *But Also Good Business: Texas Commerce Banks and the Financing of Houston and Texas, 1886–1986* (College Station, Tex.: Texas A & M Press, 1986), pp. 26–27.

8. In Laurence S. Johnson, *A Century of Service: The Concise History of the Victoria Bank & Trust Co.* (Victoria, Tex.: Victoria Bank & Trust Co., 1979).

9. "The Benefits of Firm-Creditor Relationships: Evidence from small business data," by Mitchell A. Petersen and Raghuram G. Rajan, paper presented at a Levy Institute conference, April 1994.

10. Allen N. Berger and Gregory F. Udall, "Lines of Credit and Relationship Lending in Small Firm Finance," Federal Reserve Board, Washington, D.C., mimeo, March 1994, p. 2.

11. George Moore, *The Banker's Life* (New York: W.W. Norton, 1987), pp. 140–41.

12. Ibid., p. 157.

13. Lowell Bryan, *Bankrupt* (New York: HarperBusiness, 1991), p. 127.

14. Jerry Adler, *High Rise* (New York: HarperCollins, 1993), p. 347.

15. Robert A. Mamis, "Can Your Bank Do This," *Inc.*, March 1996, p. 29.

16. Michael Selz, "Big Banks Fall Short of Their Claims," *Wall Street Journal*, April 17, 1995, p. B-1. The figures are taken from the accompanying table rather than from the article.

17. "Red, White and Blue," *Jim Grant's Interest Rate Observer*, September 29, 1995, p. 9.

7. The Money Lenders

1. Lowell Bryan, *Bankrupt* (New York: HarperCollins, 1991), p. 161.

2. "Banks Are Obsolete—And Who Cares?" Remarks by Edward Furash for a panel, On the (Declining?) Role of Banking, at the 30th Annual Conference on Bank Structure and Competition sponsored by the Federal Reserve Bank of Chicago. Furash and Co., Washington, D.C. (Furash & Co., May 1994), pp. 4–5.

3. Bryan, *Bankrupt*, p. 134.

4. Ellen Leander, "Bank Loans: Why Investors Relish Leveraged Loans as Securities," *Global Finance*, October 1995, p. 13.

5. *Mutual Funds: Impact on Bank Deposits and Credit Availability*, GAO-GGD-95-230, September 1995, General Accounting Office, order from U.S. General Accounting Office, P.O. Box 6015, Gaithersburg, MD 20884-6015; pp. 9, 13. It has been argued that the drop in deposits as a share of total bank liabilities is an accounting artifact, the result of a change in the rules of the Financial Accounting Standards Board, which required banks to stop netting their winning and losing derivatives positions and required all winners to be listed on the balance sheet as assets and all losers as liabilities. But the drop in deposits as a share of liabilities precedes the adoption of the accounting rule.

6. Allen N. Berger, Anil K. Kashyap and Joseph M. Scalise, "The Transformation of the U.S. Banking Industry: What a Long, Strange Trip It's Been," Washington, D.C.: Brookings Papers, Fall 1995.

7. Philip E. Strahan and James Weston, "Small Business Lending and Bank Consolidation: Is There Cause for Concern?" *Current Issues*, Federal Reserve Bank of New York, March 1996, p. 3.

8. Michael Selz, "Big Banks Lend More to Small Business, But Some Fear Gains May Be Short-Lived," *Wall Street Journal*, December 28, 1995, p. B-1.

9. Cited in Daniel E. Nolle, *Banking Industry Consolidation: Past Changes and Implications for the Future* (Washington, D.C.: Bank Research Division, Office of the Comptroller of the Currency, 1994), citing data from the Federal Financial Institutions Examination Council.

10. David P. Apgar, *Business Loan Underwriting Evaluation Proposal*, presented to The Levy Institute of Bard College, April 1995.

11. See Written Testimony of Donald B. Susswein, Counsel, The Coalition for Asset Backed Securities, in support of H.R. 1967, before the Committee on Ways and Means, House of Representatives, July 27, 1995, p. 8.

12. Tim Smart, "GE's Money Machine," *Business Week*, March 8, 1993, p. 62.

13. Saul Hansell, "Loans Granted by the Megabyte," *New York Times*, April 18, 1995, pp. D-1, D-4.

14. Udayan Gupta, "Where the Money Is," *Wall Street Journal*, May 22, 1995, p. R-6.

15. Stephanie N. Mehta, "Banks Set Loans for Small Firms in New York City," *Wall Street Journal*, October 27, 1995, p. B-7A.

16. David Bornstein, "The Barefoot Bank with Cheek," *The Atlantic Monthly*, December 1995, pp. 40, 44.

17. Dimitri B. Papadimitriou, Ronnie J. Phillips and L. Randall Wray, *Community-Based Factoring Companies and Small Business Lending* (Annandale-on-Hudson, N.Y.: Jerome Levy Institute of Bard College, 1994), p. 19.

18. Thomas Mattesen, "Factoring: The Service Challenge for the Nineties," *The Secured Lender*, March-April 1992, p. 54.

8. The New Mergers

1. Kathleen Abruzzo, "Hubris at Chase," letters column, *New York Times*, March 8, 1996, p. A-30.

2. Saul Hansell, "First Union to Buy First Fidelity to Form Big Eastern Bank," *New York Times*, June 20, 1995, pp. D-1, D-4.

3. Stephen Davis, "Marooned in Paradise," *Institutional Investor*, April 1995, p. 64.

4. I am indebted for much of this information to Irwin Perry of Gruntal International.

5. Saul Hansell, "Loans Granted by the Megabyte," *New York Times*, April 18, 1995, p. D-1.

6. Gary Whalen, "Wealth Effects of Intra-Holding Company Bank Mergers: Evidence from Shareholder Returns," OCC Economic & Policy Analysis Working Paper, 1994.

7. Task Force on Urgent Fiscal Issues, *Report on FDIC Bailouts of First Republic and MCorp Banks*, Office of Representative Charles E. Schumer, 2412 Rayburn Office Building, Washington, D.C., January 1991, p. 23.

8. A. J. Michaels, "Nothing Comes to Those Who Wait," *Fortune*, December 28, 1992, p. 126.

9. Nikhil Doghum, "A Tough Bank Boss Takes on Competition with Real Trepidation," *Wall Street Journal*, July 25, 1996, p. 1.

10. Stephen A. Rhoades, *Bank Mergers and Industrywide Structure, 1980–1994* (Washington, D.C.: Board of Governors, January 1996).

11. Susan McLaughlin, "The Impact of Interstate Banking and Branching Reform: Evidence from the States," *Current Issues*, Federal Reserve Bank of New York, May 1995, p. 3.

12. Edward E. Furash, "What Do You Do for an Encore?" *The Stonier Forum*, Stonier Graduate School of Banking (Washington, D.C.: American Bankers Association, 1995), p. 2.

13. Rhoades, op. cit., pp. 26, 28.

14. George Benston, Gerald Hanweck and David Humphrey, "Scale Economies in Banking: A Restructuring and Reassessment," *Journal of Money, Credit and Banking*, November 1982, p. 435.

15. Robert DeYoung and Gary Whalen, *Banking Industry Consolidation: Efficiency Issues* (Washington, D.C.: Office of the Comptroller of the Currency, 1994), p. 20.

16. Martin Mayer, "Too Big Not to Fail," *Forbes*, April 15, 1991, pp. 68, 71.

17. Furash, "What Do You Do for an Encore?" p. 3.

18. Paul Nadler, "Fee Strategies Often Penny-Wise, Pound-Foolish," *American Banker*, December 20, 1994, p. 7.

19. "Money-Center Banks' Trading Activities," Testimony provided to the House Committee on Banking by David S. Berry, Director of Research, Keefe, Bruyette & Wood, New York, 1993.

9. Trading: The Zero-Sum Game

1. Financial Economists Roundtable, "Statement on Derivatives Markets and Financial Risk," *The Financier*, November 1994, pp. 11, 13.

2. Raj Bhala, "Risk Trade-Offs in the Foreign Exchange Spot, Forward and Derivative Markets," *The Financier*, August 1994, pp. 34, 50.

3. George Garvy and Martin R. Blyn, *The Velocity of Money* (New York: Federal Reserve Bank of New York, 1969), pp. 86, 88.

4. Carter H. Golembe, "Our Remarkable Banking System," *Virginia Law Review*, vol. 53, no. 5 (June 1967), pp. 1091, 1106.

5. Adam Smith [George J. W. Goodman], *Supermoney* (New York: Random House, 1972), p. 43.

6. Jesse H. Jones with Edward Angly, *Fifty Billion Dollars* (New York: Macmillan, 1951), p. 47.

7. Irvine H. Sprague, *Bailout: An Insider's Account of Bank Failures and Rescues* (New York: Basic Books, 1986), p. 155.

8. Martin Mayer, *The Money Bazaars*, pp. 222–32.

9. Roger M. Kubarych, *Foreign Exchange Markets in the United States* (New York: Federal Reserve Bank of New York, 1978), p. 5.

10. Henry C. Wallich, "Capital Movements—The Tail That Wags the Dog," in *The International Monetary System: Forty Years After Bretton Woods*, Proceedings of a Conference Held in May 1984 Sponsored by the Federal Reserve Bank of Boston, pp. 179, 183.

11. Anthony Ramirez, "Global Trade in Currency Shows Surge," *New York Times*, September 20, 1995, p. D-3. Singapore figure from Kieran Cooke, "Rising Hub of Global Trading," *The Financial Times*, Foreign Exchange Supplement, June 4, 1995, p. 4.

12. John Lipsky and Sahar Elhabashi, *Swap-Driven Primary Issuance in the International Bond Market* (New York: Salomon Brothers, 1986), pp. 1, 2.

13. Ernest T. Patrikis et al., *Derivatives, Foreign Exchange and Commodities Activities Approved by the Board of Governors* (New York: Federal Reserve Bank of New York, February 1, 1995), Appendix A, p. 2.

14. Karen Spinner, "Decoding the Codes of Conduct," *Derivatives Strategy*, August 21, 1995, pp. 1, 5.

15. "Fannie Mae Minestrone," *Grant's Interest Rate Observer*, January 20, 1995, p. 2.

16. K. Michael Fraser, "The Pot Calling the Kettle Black," *Global Finance*, January 17, 1995, p. 39.

17. CFTC Docket No. 95-a, *In the Matter of BT Securities Corporation*, Complaint Pursuant to Sections 69(c) and 6(d) of the Commodity Exchange Act and Opinion and Order Accepting Offer of Settlement, December 22, 1994, p. 8.

18. Steven Lipin, "Bankers Trust Sued on Derivatives," *Wall Street Journal*, September 13, 1994, p. C-1.

19. George J. Benston and George G. Kaufman, *Staff Memoranda: Risk and Solvency Regulation of Depository Institutions: Past Policies and Current Options*, by Federal Reserve Bank of Chicago, 1988, p. 37. It should also be noted that among their central recommendations was that banks should be audited annually by CPA firms "acceptable to the authorities. The CPAs would be charged with attesting to the numbers reported as being no greater than current market values of the statement date. . . . Thus a bank would have to put up additional capital if it wanted to invest in assets of undeterminable value. . . . Because their reputations and fortunes are at stake, the CPAs have a strong incentive to be conservative." As the authors wrote, Big Six accounting firms were attesting to all sorts of nonsense on the books of the savings and loans, where the rules required annual auditing. Professor Benston, indeed, had been the great advocate of allowing Charles Keating to invest the assets of Lincoln Savings and Loan wherever he pleased, and to hold them with the backing of insured deposits essentially at whatever valuation he could get somebody to put on them.

20. Robert Merton, "Financial Innovation and Economic Performance," *Journal of Applied Corporate Finance*, 4 (Winter) 1992, p. 12.

21. This paragraph is taken from my article "Hiding Places" in the June 20, 1994, *Barron's*, p. 33.

22. "Derivatives: The Ultimate Freudian Slipup," in *The U.S. Financial Structure in the Years Ahead: Domestic and International Issues*, Conference Proceedings, The Jerome Levy Economics Institute of Bard College, 1995, pp. 20, 23.

23. Robert Triffin, *Gold and the Dollar Crisis*, 2nd ed. (New Haven, Conn.: Yale University Press, 1961).

24. *The United States Balance of Payments*, Hearings before the Joint Economic Committee of the Congress, 1963, p. 138.

25. Michael R. Sesit, "Treasurers of Multinationals Plan Ways to Handle Currency Swings," *Wall Street Journal*, Jan. 24, 1984, p. 35.

26. Galen Burghardt, "How Long Can This Keep Going On," *Futures Industry*, February 1995, p. 9.

27. Rotberg, loc. cit.

28. *Leo Melamed on the Markets* (New York: John Wiley, 1993), p. 129.

10. Derivatives

1. Carol Loomis, "The Risk That Won't Go Away," *Fortune*, March 7, 1994, p. 40.

2. Andre F. Perold, *The Global Financial System: A Functional Perspective* (Cambridge, Mass.: Harvard Business School Press, 1995).

3. John Plender, Long View, "Fiendish Booby Traps," *The Financial Times*, May 19, 1994.

4. *Grant's IRO* (date not available).

5. *Safety and Soundness Issues Related to Bank Derivatives Activities—Part 3*, Hearings before the Committee on Banking, 103rd Congress, First Session, Oct. 28, 1993, Serial No. 103-88, Government Printing Office, 1994, p. 574.

6. *Technology, Regulation and Competition in U.S. Financial Services*, remarks by Scott E. Pardee, chairman, Yamaichi International (America), at an "Industry Summit" sponsored by MIT and the World Economic Forum, Cambridge, Mass., Sept. 9, 1993, mimeo, p. 8.

7. *Safety and Soundness*, p. 339.

8. *Proposed Statement of Financial Accounting Standards: Accounting for Derivative and Similar Financial Instruments and for Hedging Activities,* No. 162-B, Financial Accounting Standards Board, Norwalk, Connecticut, 1996.

9. Lisa Polsky, "The Second Wave," *Derivatives Strategies*, August 21, 1995, p. 9.

10. John Thackray, "The Two Faces of Kevin Hudson," *Derivatives Tactics*, Nov. 6, 1995, pp. 3, 5, 7.

11. William C. Rupert and Walter W. Oakes, "Interest Rate Swaps Accounting—What's Market Value?" by *Bank Accounting and Finance*, Summer 1990, pp. 3–14.

12. *Before the Board of Governors of the Federal Reserve System*, Docket No. 94-082-WA/RB-RC, December 4, 1994, p. 1.

13. Janine Schulz, "Latin Bonds Without the Bromo Seltzer," *Institutional Investor*, December 1994, pp. 105, 111.

14. *Wholesale Transactions Code of Conduct*, Draft—January 17, 1995, Federal Reserve Bank of New York, pp. 3, 4, 6. Italics added.

15. *In the Matter of Askin Capital Management, L.P. and David J. Askin, Respondents*, Investment Advisers Act of 1940 Release No. 1492, Securities Act of 1933 Release No. 7171, Securities and Exchange Commission, May 23, 1995, Section F subsection 3.

16. Susan Arterian, "Does Anybody Understand Index-Amortizing Swaps?" *Derivatives Strategy & Tactics*, November 29, 1993, p. 1.

17. Ibid.

18. *Financial Derivatives: Actions Needed to Protect the Financial System* (Washington, D.C.: General Accounting Office, May 1994), p. 92.

19. David Folkerts-Landau and Alfred Steinherr, "The Wild Beast of Derivatives: To Be Chained Up, Fenced In or Tamed?" *Journal of Finance*, November 1994, pp. 1, 17; italics in the original.

20. The Group of Thirty, *Derivatives: Practices and Principles* (Washington, D.C.: July 1993), p. 19. Italics added.

21. Cheryl Beth Strauss, "The Shadow War at AIG," by *Investment Dealers Digest*, September 6, 1993, pp. 14, 18.

22. *Randall I. Rackson* v. *Howard B. Sosin*, U.S. District Court Southern District of New York, original complaint, February 16, 1995, p. 12.

23. Dean Tomasula, "Study Showing Derivatives Profits at Banks Criticized as One-Sided," *American Banker*, Oct. 19, 1994, p. 30.

24. Keith Bradsher, "Derivative Holdings of U.S. Banks Rose in First Quarter," by *New York Times*, June 15, 1995, p. D-4.

25. Both the Beder and the Dembo quotes are from "Measuring Value at Risk," *Derivatives Strategy*, Nov. 21, 1994, pp. 1, 4.

26. David Shirreff, "Danger—Kids at Play," *Euromoney*, March 1995, p. 43.

27. Suzanne McGee, "Derivatives Could Hedge Career Growth," *Wall Street Journal*, August 24, 1995, p. C-1.

28. Keith Bradsher, "Derivatives Holdings of U.S. Banks Rose in First Quarter," *New York Times*, June 15, 1995, p. D-4.

29. Samer Iskandar, "OTC Financial Transaction at Record Levels," *Financial Times*, July 11, 1996, p. 18.

30. Philip Gawith, "Forex Market Growth Startles Exchanges," *Financial Times*, Sept. 20, 1995, p. 4.

31. Richard Evans, "Coveting the Business in Long-Dated Swaps," *Global Finance*, Nov. 23, 1994, p. 54.

32. "The Odd Couple," *The Banker*, October 1993, p. 17.

33. *Economic and Financial Prospects Special: Understanding Derivatives* (Swiss Bank Corporation, 1994), p. 31.

34. Pardee, op. cit., p. 11.

35. Robert H. Litzenberger, "Swaps: Plain and Fanciful," *The Journal of Finance*, July 1992, pp. 831, 836.

36. *Macroeconomic and Monetary Policy Issues Raised by the Growth of Derivatives Markets*, Report prepared by a working group established by the Euro-currency Standing Committee of the central banks of the Group of Ten countries, Basel, November 1994, p. 18.

37. "Soros Sizes Up the Markets," *Fortune*, Sept. 4, 1995, pp. 90, 94.

38. Testimony of Martin Mayer to the House Banking Committee, October 28, 1993.

39. David Folkerts-Landau and Alfred Steinherr, "Derivatives: Taming the Beast," *The Amex Bank Review*, Nov. 16, 1994, pp. 2, 3.

40. "CP Dealer Scam Exposed," *Derivative Tactics*, New York, Nov. 27, 1995, pp. 1, 2.

41. Scott Pardee, op. cit., p. 15.

42. 184 U.S. 425.

43. *Otis* v. *Parker*, 187 U.S. 606 (1903).

44. *New York General Business Law*, Article 23—Bucket Shops, Section 351. Acts prohibited.

45. Timothy L. O'Brien, "Bankers Trust Pays $67 Million to Settle Derivatives Dispute with Chemical Firm," *Wall Street Journal*, Jan. 25, 1996, p. A-5.

46. *International Recovery Systems v. Gabler*, 210 Mich. App. 422, 1994.

47. Remarks by William J. McDonough, President, Federal Reserve Bank of New York, at The International Center for Monetary and Banking Studies, Geneva, Switzerland, March 14, 1995, mimeo, The Federal Reserve Bank of New York, 1995, p. 18.

11. The Bad Example: Barings

1. John Gapper and Nicholas Denton, "Danger Signals Ignored," *Financial Times*, September 20, 1996, p. 10; excerpted from their book *All That Glitters* (London: Hamish Hamilton, 1996).

2. Philip Ziegler, *The Sixth Great Power* (New York: Alfred A. Knopf, 1988), p. 270.

3. Judith H. Rawnsley, *Total Risk: Nick Leeson and the Fall of Barings Bank* (New York: HarperBusiness, 1995), p. 25.

4. *Report of the Board of Banking Supervision Inquiry into the Circumstances of the Collapse of Barings*, Her Majesty's Stationery Office, London, 1995, Chapter 13, #1. Hereafter, *Report*, with chapter followed by a period, followed by paragraph number.

5. See Martin Mayer, *Stealing the Market* (New York: Basic Books, 1991), for an extended discussion of this subject.

6. Rawnsley, op. cit., p. 60.

7. Bob Tamarkin, *The Merc* (New York: HarperBusiness, 1993), p. 292.

8. *Report*, 2.58.

9. Ibid., 2.60.

10. Stephen Fay, *The Collapse of Barings* (London: Richard Cohen Books, 1996), p. 211.

11. Martin Mayer, *Markets* (New York: W.W. Norton, 1988), p. 89.

12. *Report*, 6.20.

13. Ibid., 3.38.

14. Ibid., 6.49.

15. I argued this case in an op-ed piece in the *Wall Street Journal* the week the story broke.

16. *Report*, 6.47.

17. *Report of the Inspectors of Barings Futures (Singapore) PTE LTD*, 19 October 1995, available on Singapore Government Home Page, www:mof 2.html, Executive Summary, #10.

18. Ibid., #17 iv, #18.

19. *Report*, 7.94.

20. Ibid., 12.33

21. *Inspectors*, #11.

22. Ibid., #13.

23. *Report*, 11.46.

24. Ibid., 11.47

25. Ibid., 11.48

26. Ibid., 11.49

27. Ethan B. Kapstein, "Shockproof: The End of the Financial Crisis," *Foreign Affairs*, January–February 1996, pp. 2, 7.

28. E. Gerald Corrigan, "Luncheon Address," in David B. Humphrey, ed., *The U.S. Payments System*, pp. 129–30.

29. "The Barings Crisis and the CFTC's Response," remarks of Mary L. Schapiro, Chairman, Commodity Futures Trading Commission, 20th Annual National Futures Industry Conference, Boca Raton, Fla., March 16, 1995, CFTC, Washington, pp. 4–5.

30. Fay, *Collapse*, p. 211.

31. Ibid., p. 228.

32. *Inspectors*, #24.

12. Government Gone Mad

1. Jonathan E. Gray, *Financial Deregulation and the Savings and Loan Crisis*, prepared for the Federal Deposit Insurance Corporation, Office of Research and Strategic Planning, 1989, p. 3.

2. See Martin Mayer, *The Greatest Ever Bank Robbery* (New York: Scribners, 1991).

3. Christi Harlan, "Ruling Favoring Ex-Thrift Head Cheers Accused S&L Executives," *Wall Street Journal*, Feb. 27, 1980, p. B-5.

4. Friedman and Schwartz, *A Monetary History of the United States* (Princeton, N.J.: Princeton University Press, 1963), 1971 ed., p. 669, fn. 24.

5. Martin Mayer, *The Fate of the Dollar* (New York: Times Books, 1980), p. 141.

6. Andrew S. Carron, *The Plight of the Thrift Institutions* (Washington, D.C.: Brookings Institution, 1981), p. 13.

7. *The Report of the President's Commission on Housing* (Washington, D.C.: Government Printing Office, 1982), p. xxx. I was a member of the Commission, and in fact wrote the Executive Summary from which these words are quoted.

8. See Michael A. Robinson, *Overdrawn: The Bailout of American Savings* (New York: Dutton, 1990), p. 10.

9. *Wellenkamp* v. *Bank of America*, 21 Cal.3rd 943, 582 Pac2nd 970; *Fidelity Federal* v. *De La Cuesta*, 458 US 141, 102 SCt 3014. See discussion in Norman Strunk and Fred Case, *Where Deregulation Went Wrong* (Chicago: United States League of Savings and Loans, 1988), p. 47.

10. Ned Eichler, *The Thrift Debacle* (Berkeley: University of California Press, 1988), pp. 62–63.

11. Ibid., p. 65

12. The figures are from R. Dan Brumbaugh, Jr., *Thrifts Under Siege* (Cambridge, Mass.: Ballinger, 1988), p. 50.

13. *New York Assembly Journal*, 1829, p. 439.

14. *Noble State Bank* v. *Haskell* (1911), 219 U.S. 111.

15. *Federal Reserve Bulletin*, February 1950, pp. 153–54.

16. Housing Commission *Report*, p. xxxi.

17. Martin Mayer, "Earn 100% at Mountebanks," *New York Times*, Dec. 17, 1982.

18. *Agenda for Reform*, Federal Home Loan Bank Board, Washington, D.C., 1983, p. 16.

19. L. William Seidman, *Full Faith and Credit: The Great S&L Debacle and Other Washington Sagas* (New York: Times Books, 1993), p. 52.

20. *Combating Fraud, Abuse and Misconduct in the Nation's Financial Institutions: Current Federal Efforts Are Inadequate.* Seventy-second Report by the Committee on Government Operations, House of Representatives, Oct. 13, 1988, p. 83.

21. Friedman & Schwartz, op. cit., p. 434.

22. J. K. Galbraith, *The Great Crash* (Boston: Houghton Mifflin, 1973), pp. 184–85.

23. *Memorandum* to Members and Staff of the Senate Banking Committee from Gill Garcia, Richard Carnell, Darina McKelvie and Konrad Alt, on the subject of Deposit Insurance Reform, May 10, 1990, p. 7.

24. *Deposit Insurance for the Nineties*, FDIC Staff Study (draft), Jan. 4, 1989, p. 10.

25. *Modernizing the Financial System* (Washington, D.C.: U.S. Treasury, 1991), p. 8.

NOTES

13. The Fed and Other Regulators

1. Richard J. Herring and Robert E. Litan, *Financial Regulation in the Global Economy* (Washington, D.C.: Brookings, 1995), pp. 49–50.

2. Benjamin Hoggart Beckhart, *The Federal Reserve System* (American Institute of Banking, 1972), p. 7.

3. See *Modernizing the Financial System: Recommendations for Safe, More Competitive Banks*, Department of the Treasury, Washington, D.C., 1991, chapter 17.

4. Gary Maggs and David S. Pate, "The New Federal Stance on Bank Expansion," *Durell Journal of Money and Banking*, Fall 1995, pp. 17, 19–20.

5. Alan Greenspan, "Gold and Economic Freedom," *The Objectivist*, July 1966, p. 96.

6. *Examining Circular* #234, pp. 4 and 5. Emphasis added. Copies of this circular were sent to the chief executive officers of all national banks.

7. *Examining Circular Supplement* #1, July 19, 1987, p. 1. Emphasis added.

8. L. William Seidman, *Full Faith and Credit: The Great S&L Debacle and Other Washington Sagas* (New York: Times Books, 1993), p. 64.

9. Steven Solomon, *The Confidence Game* (New York: Simon & Schuster, 1995), p. 230.

14. Examining the Banks

1. *Reforming Federal Deposit Insurance*, Congressional Budget Office, Washington, D.C., September 1990, Appendix D.

2. Kenneth M. Wright, *Managing Financial Crises: A Short History of Life Insurance Industry Experience*, Investment Topics, American Council of Life Assurance, 1001 Pennsylvania Avenue NW, Washington, D.C. 20004-2559, December 1990, p. 2.

3. Donald G. Simonson and George H. Hempel, "Running on Empty: Accounting Strategies to Clarify Capital Values," *Stanford Law and Policy Review* (Palo Alto, Calif.) , Spring 1990, pp. 92, 93, 94, 96.

4. Exposure Draft, Proposed Statement of Financial Accounting Standards, *Disclosures about Market Value of Financial Instruments*, Financial Accounting Standards Board, Norwalk, Conn., File Reference 098-E, para. 44, p. 26.

5. Berger, Kuester & O'Brien, op. cit.; ibid.

6. Lawrence J. White, "Mark to Market Accounting: A (Not So) Modest Proposal," *Financial Managers' Statement*, January/February 1990, pp. 27, 29.

7. Wright, op. cit., p. 3.

8. *Proposed Statement of Financial Accounting Standards: Accounting for Derivative and Similar Financial Instruments and for Hedging Activities.* File 162–B, Financial Accounting Standards Board, Norwalk, Conn., paragraph 54, p. 22; paragraph 56, p. 23.

9. Jaret Seiberg, "Auditors, Not Regulators, Said Key to Supervision of Banks," *American Banker*, March 20, 1996, p. 2.

10. Statement of Shadow Financial Regulatory Committee on Disclosure of Examination Reports and Ratings, Statement No. 132, Loyola University of Chicago, 1996, pp. 1, 2.

11. Excerpts of remarks of Rep. James A. Leach before the Chicago Federal Reserve Conference on Bank Structure and Competition, May 3, 1996, pp. 2–3.

12. *The Federal Reserve's 17-Year Secret*, prepared by the staff of the Committee on Banking, Finance and Urban Affairs, House of Representatives, Jan. 27, 1994, p. 3.

Epilogue

1. Nigg and Zuendt quotes from Saul Hansell, "Seeking the Next Gold Rush," *New York Times*, Nov. 22, 1995, pp. D-1, D-3.

2. Ralph T. King, Jr., "Two Tough Bankers Take on a New Mission," *Wall Street Journal*, Jan. 25, 1996, pp. 1, 12.

3. *Graphnet Systems, Inc.*, 71 FCC 2nd 47, 515.

4. E. S. Browning, "Sending Money Overseas Can Be a Numbing, and Costly, Experience," *Wall Street Journal*, Nov. 2, 1994, p. C-1.

5. *GAO Briefing for Senators Dorgan and Reid: GAO's Review of Federal Reserve Operations*, March 14, 1996, p. 151.

6. Akinari Horii and Bruce J. Summers, "Large Value Transfer Systems," in Summers, ed., *The Payment System: Design, Management and Supervision* (Washington, D.C.: International Monetary Fund, 1994), pp. 73, 75.

7. Wendelin Hartmann, "Future Directions for Real-Time Gross Settlement Systems—the European Perspective," a paper for the symposium on Risk Reduction in Payments, Clearance and Settlement Systems organized by Goldman Sachs, New York, Jan. 25–26, 1996.

8. "Remarks" by E. Gerald Corrigan, at symposium cited *supra*, p. 15.

9. "AmEx Ambition: One-Stop Mart for Small Firms," *Crain's New York Business*, April 22–28, 1996, p. 1.

10. Martin Mayer, *The Bankers* (New York: Weybright & Talley, 1974), p. 21.

Index